fushigi yûgi™

The Mysterious Play
VOL. 14: PROPHET

Story & Art By
YÛ WATASE

FUSHIGI YÛGI
THE MYSTERIOUS PLAY
VOL. 14: PROPHET
SHÔJO EDITION

This volume contains the FUSHIGI YÛGI installments from Animerica Extra
Vol. 7, No. 11 through Vol. 7, No. 12 in their entirety.

STORY AND ART BY YÛ WATASE

English Adaptation/William Flanagan
Touch-up & Lettering/Bill Spicer
Touch-up Assistance/Walden Wong
Design/Hidemi Sahara
Editor/Frances E. Wall

Managing Editor/Annette Roman
Director of Production/Noboru Watanabe
Editorial Director/Alvin Lu
Sr. Director of Acquisitions/Rika Inouye
Vice President of Sales & Marketing/Liza Coppola
Executive Vice President/Hyoe Narita
Publisher/Seiji Horibuchi

Printed in Canada

Published by VIZ, LLC
P.O. Box 77010
San Francisco, CA 94107

Shôjo Edition
10 9 8 7 6 5 4 3 2 1
First printing, March 2005

store.viz.com

www.viz.com

CONTENTS

STORY THUS FAR

In the winter of her third year of middle school, Miaka was whisked away into the pages of a mysterious old book called *THE UNIVERSE OF THE FOUR GODS* and began a dual existence, divided between her life as an ordinary schoolgirl in modern Japan and her role as priestess of the god Suzaku in a fictional version of ancient China. Miaka fell in love with Tamahome, one of the Celestial Warriors of Suzaku responsible for the protection of the priestess. Miaka's best friend Yui was also sucked into the world of the book and became the priestess of Seiryu, the bitter enemy of Suzaku and Miaka. After clashing repeatedly with the corrupt and vengeful Seiryu Celestial Warriors, Miaka summoned Suzaku and vanquished her enemies, reconciled with Yui, and saved the earth from destruction. In the end, Suzaku granted Miaka one impossible wish: for Tamahome to be reborn as a human in the real world so that the two lovers would never again be separated.

THE UNIVERSE OF THE FOUR GODS is based on ancient Chinese legend, but Japanese pronunciation of Chinese names differs slightly from their Chinese equivalents. Here is a short glossary of the Japanese pronunciation of the Chinese names in this graphic novel:

CHINESE	JAPANESE	PERSON OR PLACE	MEANING
Shi-Hang Lian	Shigyo Ren	Transfer student	Worship-Journey Collect
Shun-Yu	Jun'u	Tasuki's name	Handsome home
Tai Yi-Jun	Taiitsukun	An Oracle	Preeminent Person
Daichi-san	Daikyokuzan	A Mountain	Greatest Mountain
Yang	Yô	A Monster	Illness
Lai Lai	Nyan Nyan	Helper(s)	Daughter (x2)
Ai-Tong	Aidô	Tasuki's sister	Love eyes
Ligé-san	Reikakuzan	A Mountain	Strength Tower

fushigi yûgi™

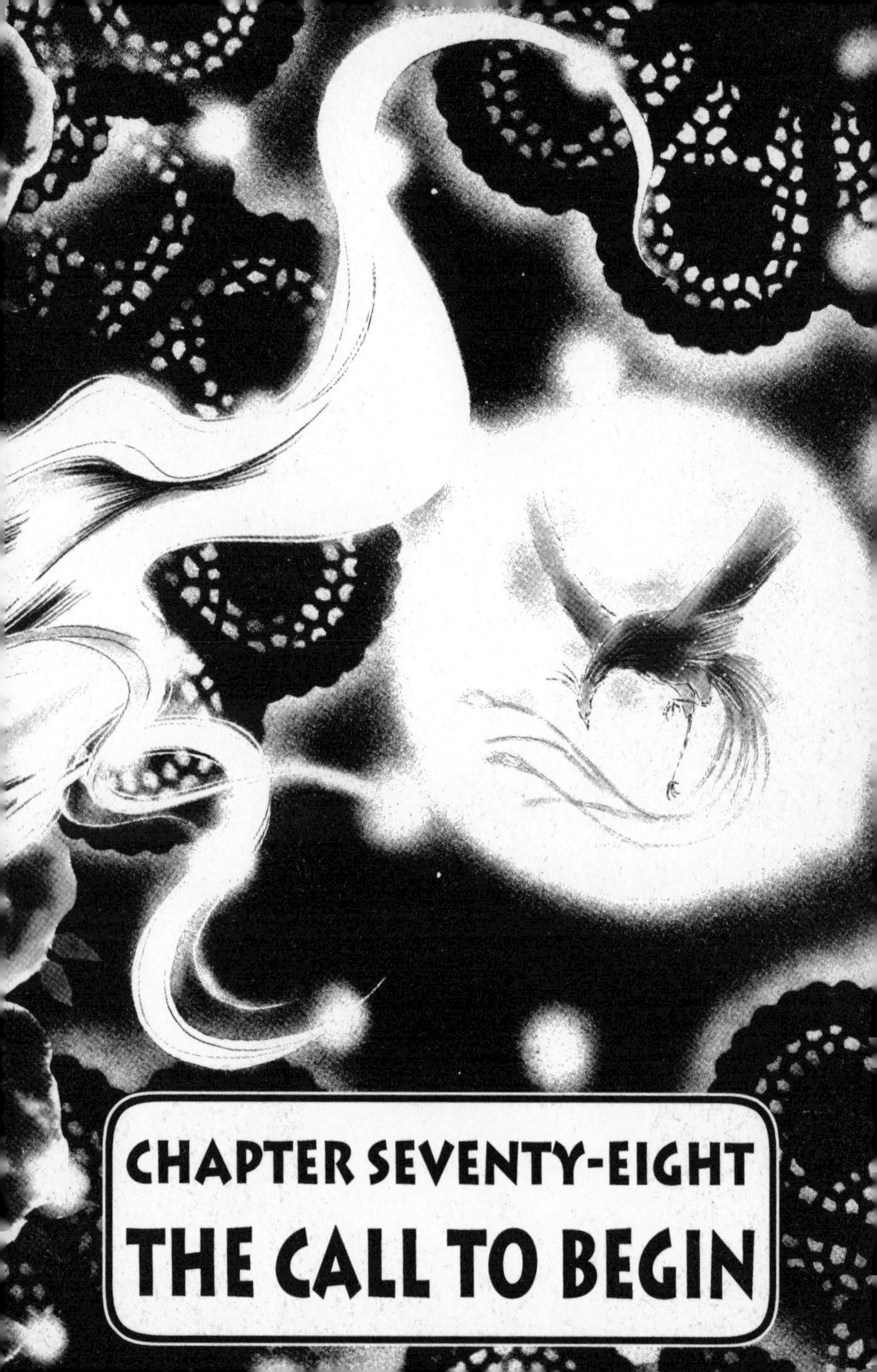
CHAPTER SEVENTY-EIGHT
THE CALL TO BEGIN

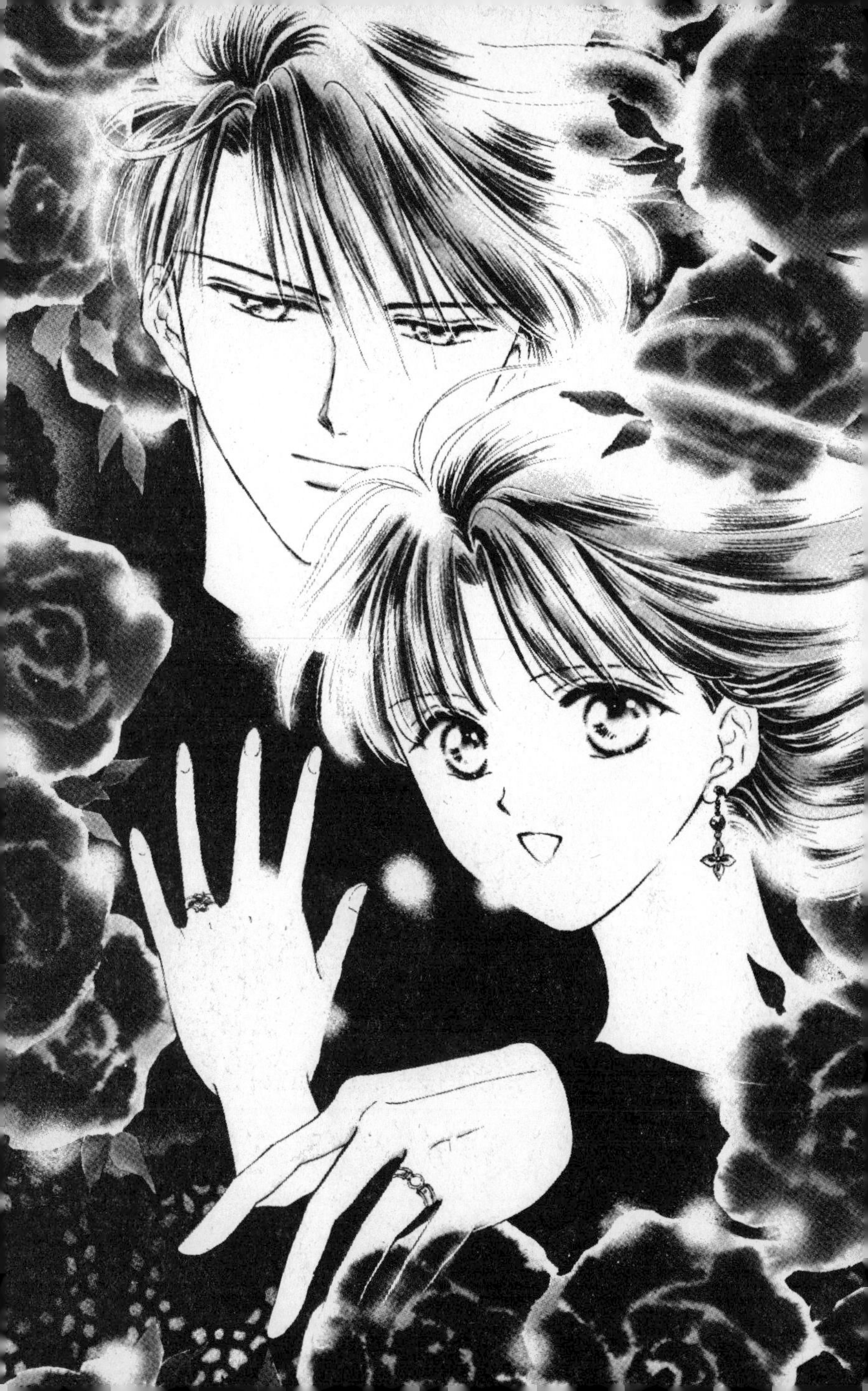

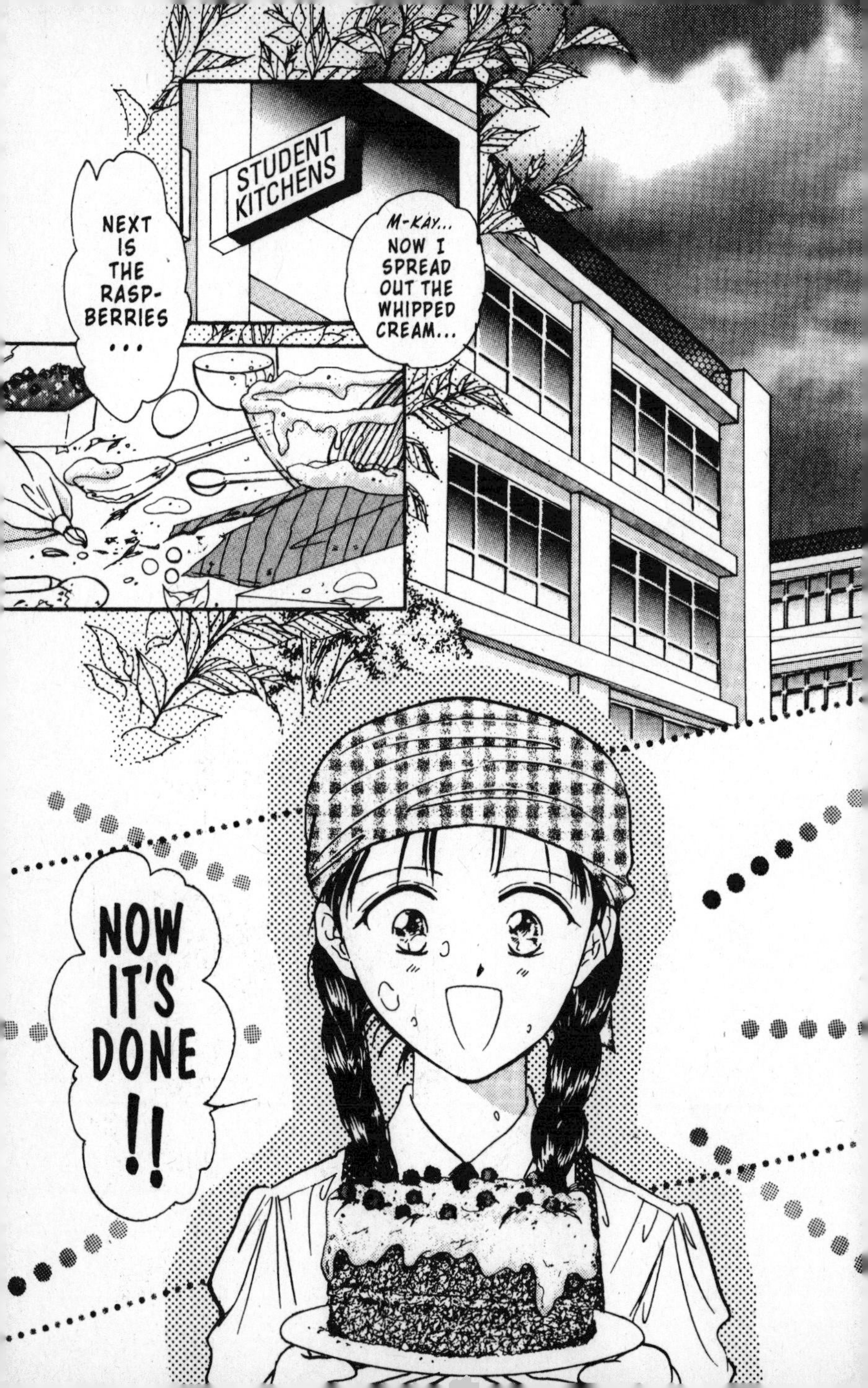
STUDENT KITCHENS
M-KAY... NOW I SPREAD OUT THE WHIPPED CREAM...
NEXT IS THE RASP-BERRIES...
NOW IT'S DONE!!

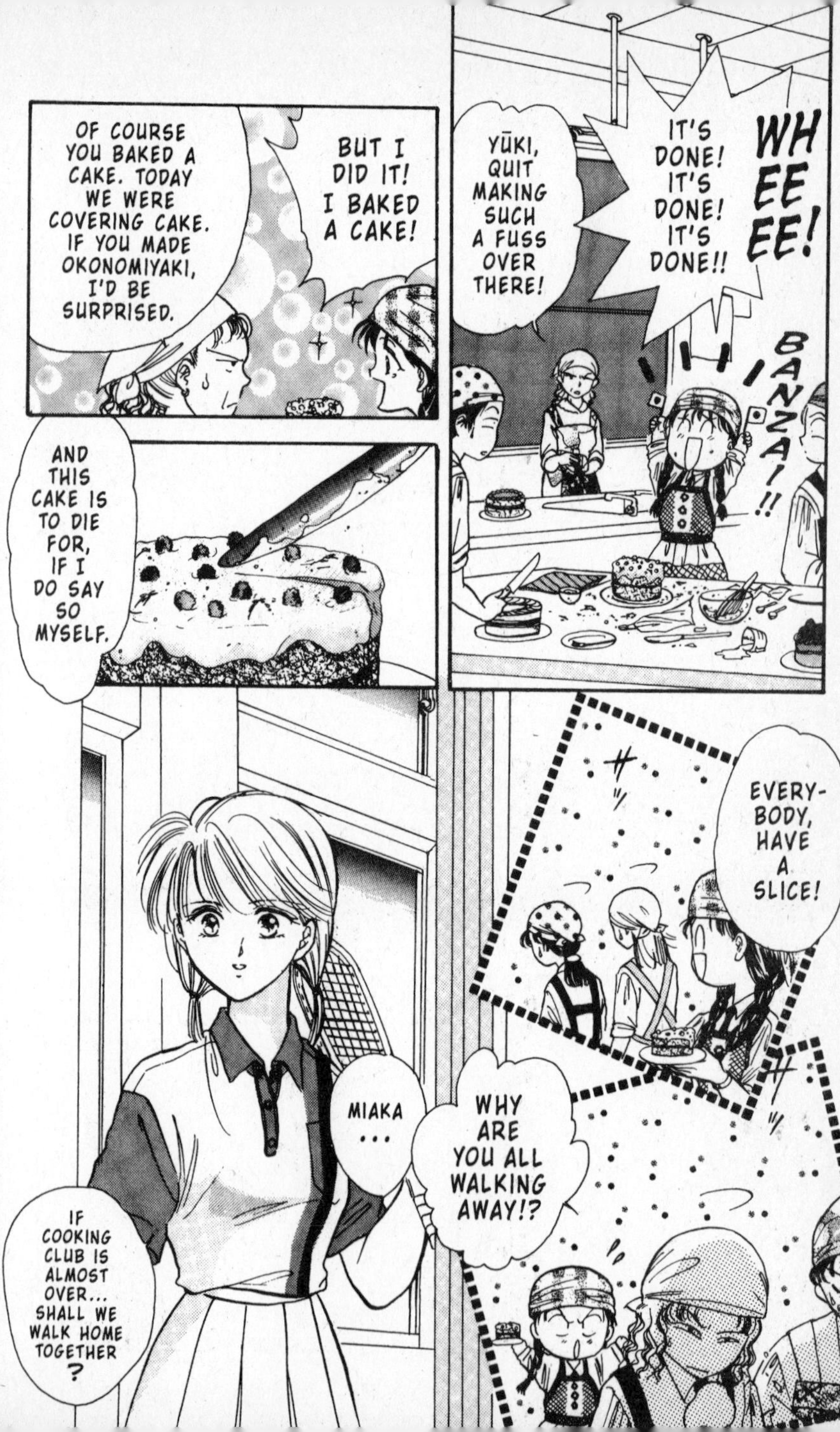
WHEEEEE!
IT'S DONE! IT'S DONE! IT'S DONE!!
YŪKI, QUIT MAKING SUCH A FUSS OVER THERE!
BANZAI!!
BUT I DID IT! I BAKED A CAKE!
OF COURSE YOU BAKED A CAKE. TODAY WE WERE COVERING CAKE. IF YOU MADE OKONOMIYAKI, I'D BE SURPRISED.
AND THIS CAKE IS TO DIE FOR, IF I DO SAY SO MYSELF.
EVERYBODY, HAVE A SLICE!
WHY ARE YOU ALL WALKING AWAY!?
MIAKA...
IF COOKING CLUB IS ALMOST OVER... SHALL WE WALK HOME TOGETHER?

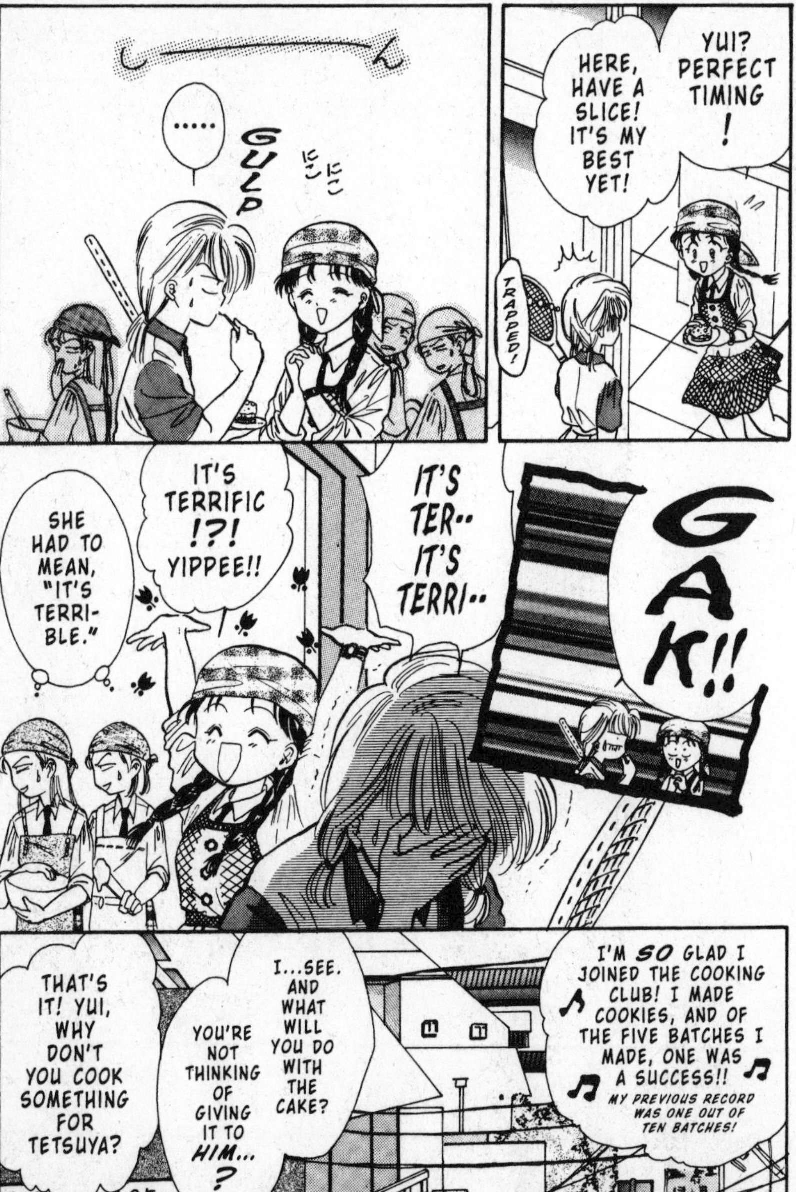
YUI? PERFECT TIMING!
HERE, HAVE A SLICE! IT'S MY BEST YET!
TRAPPED!
......
GULP
にこにこ
GAK!!
IT'S TER.. IT'S TERRI..
IT'S TERRIFIC !?! YIPPEE!!
SHE HAD TO MEAN, "IT'S TERRIBLE."
I'M SO GLAD I JOINED THE COOKING CLUB! I MADE COOKIES, AND OF THE FIVE BATCHES I MADE, ONE WAS A SUCCESS!!
MY PREVIOUS RECORD WAS ONE OUT OF TEN BATCHES!
I...SEE. AND WHAT WILL YOU DO WITH THE CAKE?
YOU'RE NOT THINKING OF GIVING IT TO HIM...?
THAT'S IT! YUI, WHY DON'T YOU COOK SOMETHING FOR TETSUYA?

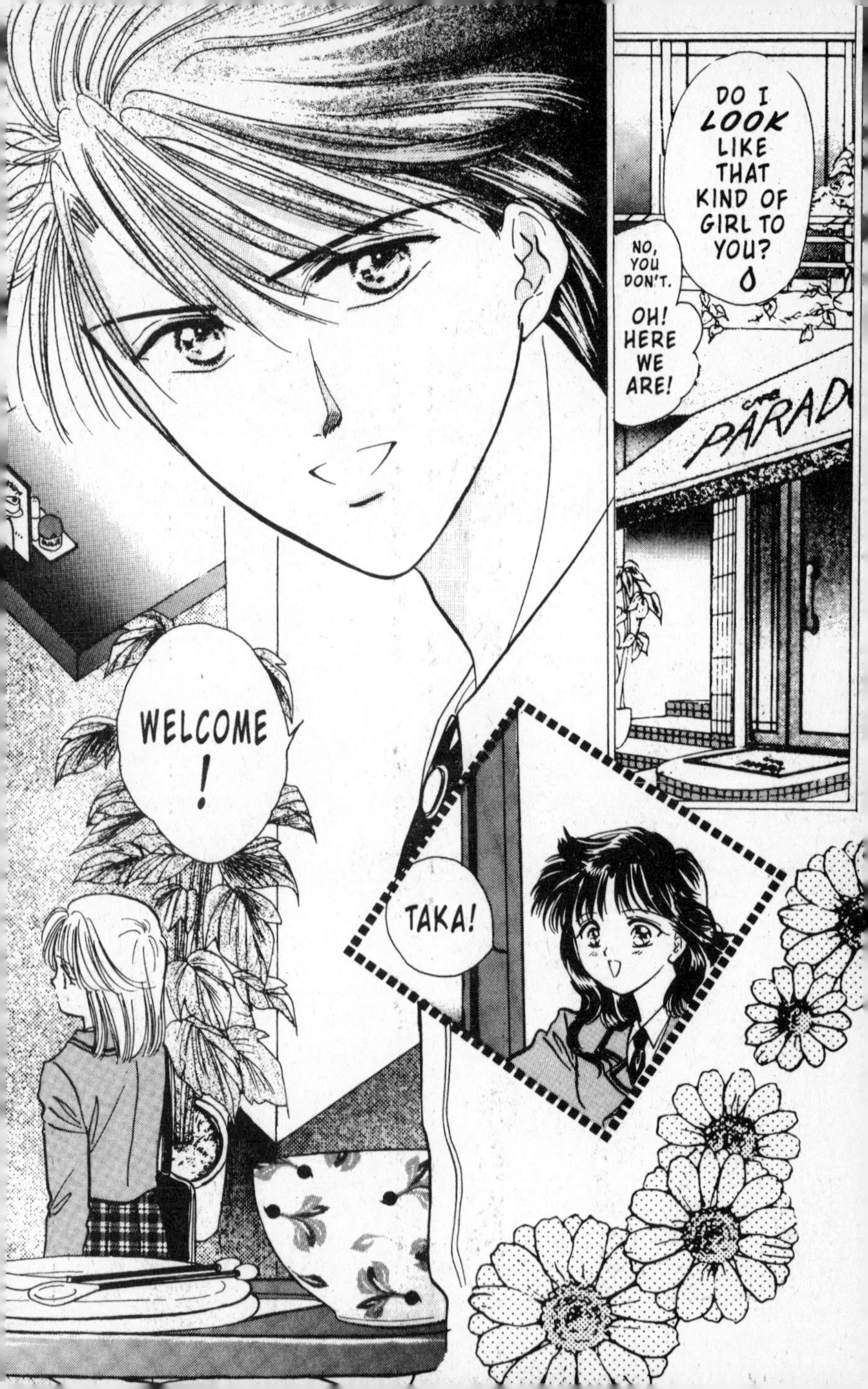
DO I LOOK LIKE THAT KIND OF GIRL TO YOU?
NO, YOU DON'T.
OH! HERE WE ARE!
WELCOME!
TAKA!

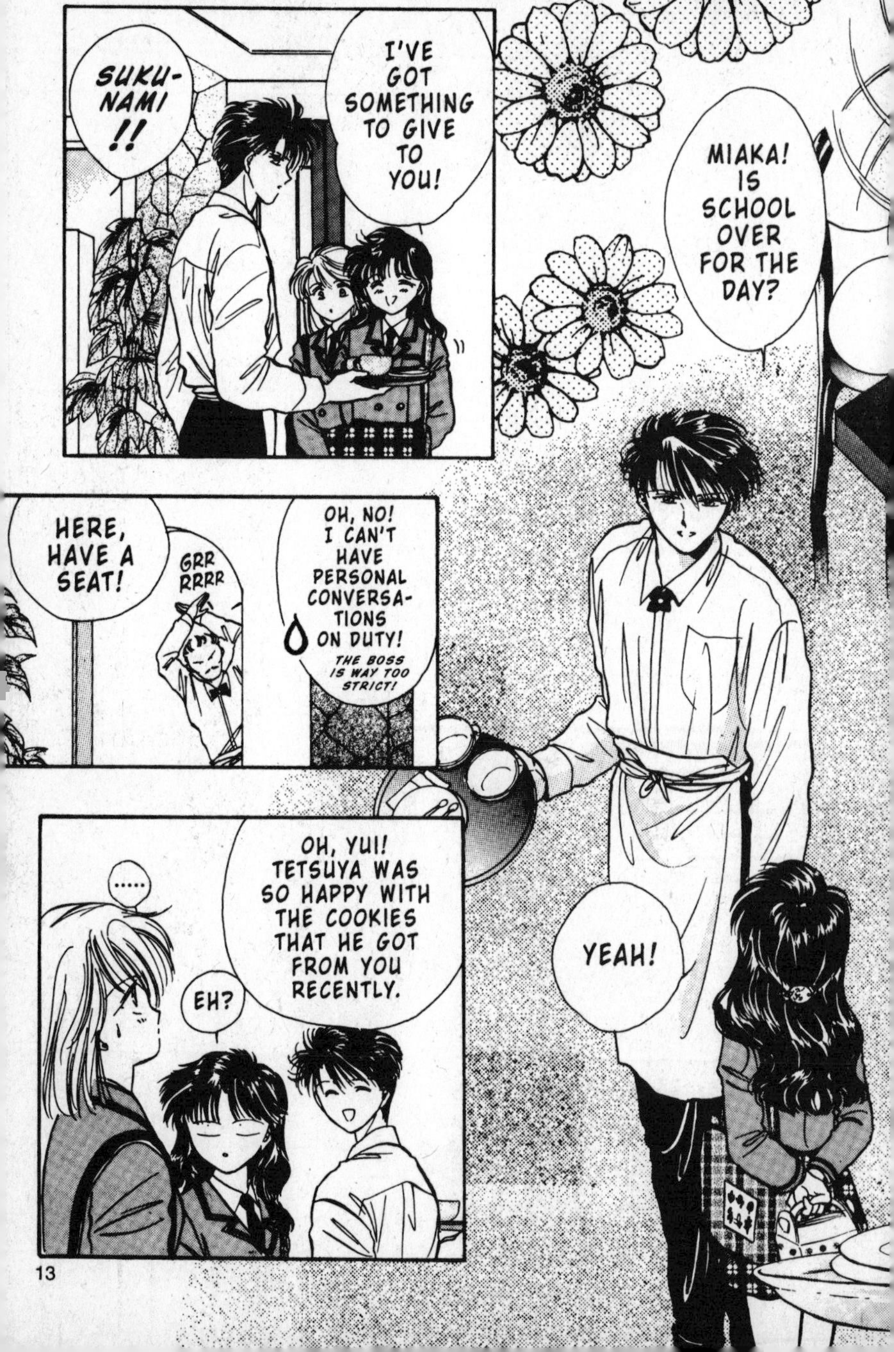
MIAKA! IS SCHOOL OVER FOR THE DAY?
YEAH!
I'VE GOT SOMETHING TO GIVE TO YOU!
SUKU-NAMI !!
OH, NO! I CAN'T HAVE PERSONAL CONVERSA-TIONS ON DUTY!
THE BOSS IS WAY TOO STRICT!
GRR RRRR
HERE, HAVE A SEAT!
OH, YUI! TETSUYA WAS SO HAPPY WITH THE COOKIES THAT HE GOT FROM YOU RECENTLY.
......
EH?

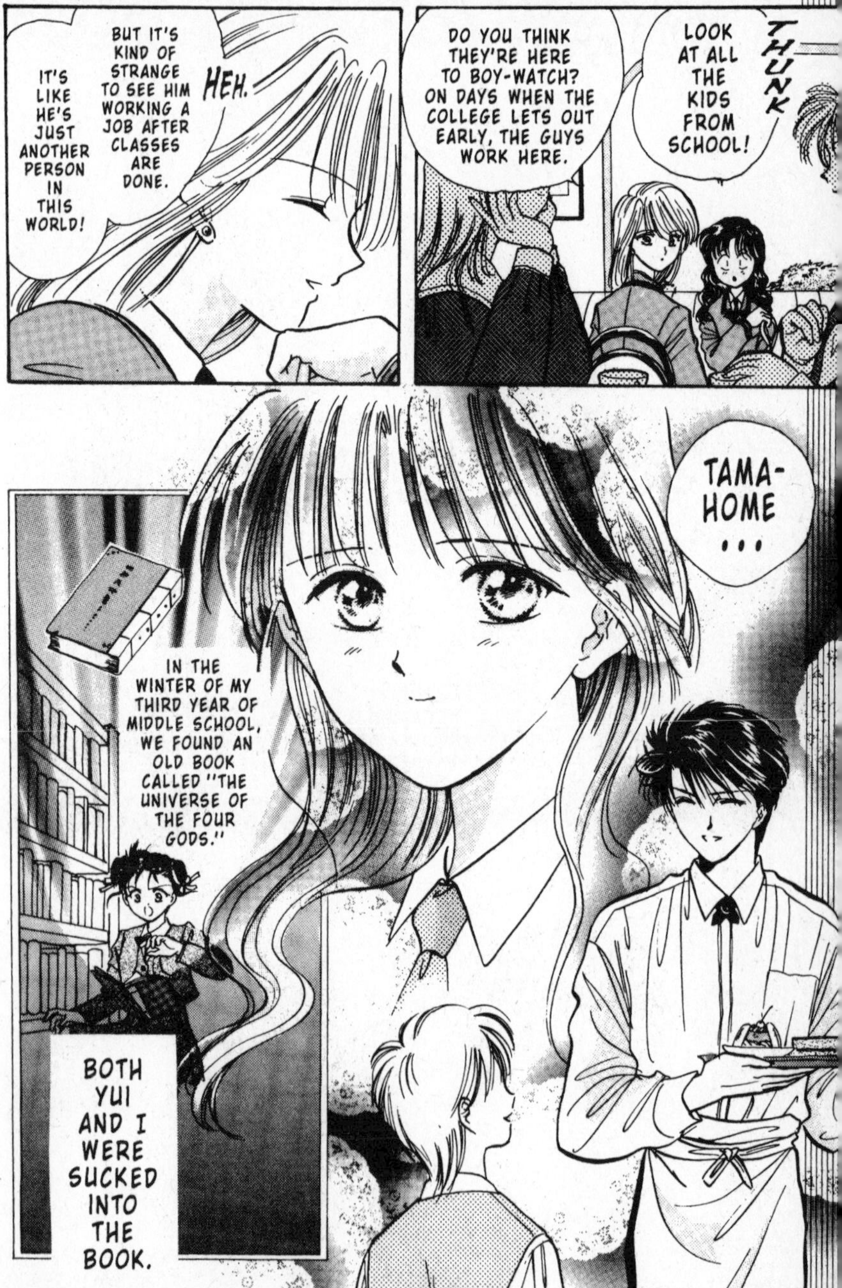
THUNK
LOOK AT ALL THE KIDS FROM SCHOOL!
DO YOU THINK THEY'RE HERE TO BOY-WATCH? ON DAYS WHEN THE COLLEGE LETS OUT EARLY, THE GUYS WORK HERE.
BUT IT'S KIND OF STRANGE TO SEE HIM WORKING A JOB AFTER CLASSES ARE DONE.
HEH.
IT'S LIKE HE'S JUST ANOTHER PERSON IN THIS WORLD!
TAMA-HOME...
IN THE WINTER OF MY THIRD YEAR OF MIDDLE SCHOOL, WE FOUND AN OLD BOOK CALLED "THE UNIVERSE OF THE FOUR GODS."
BOTH YUI AND I WERE SUCKED INTO THE BOOK.

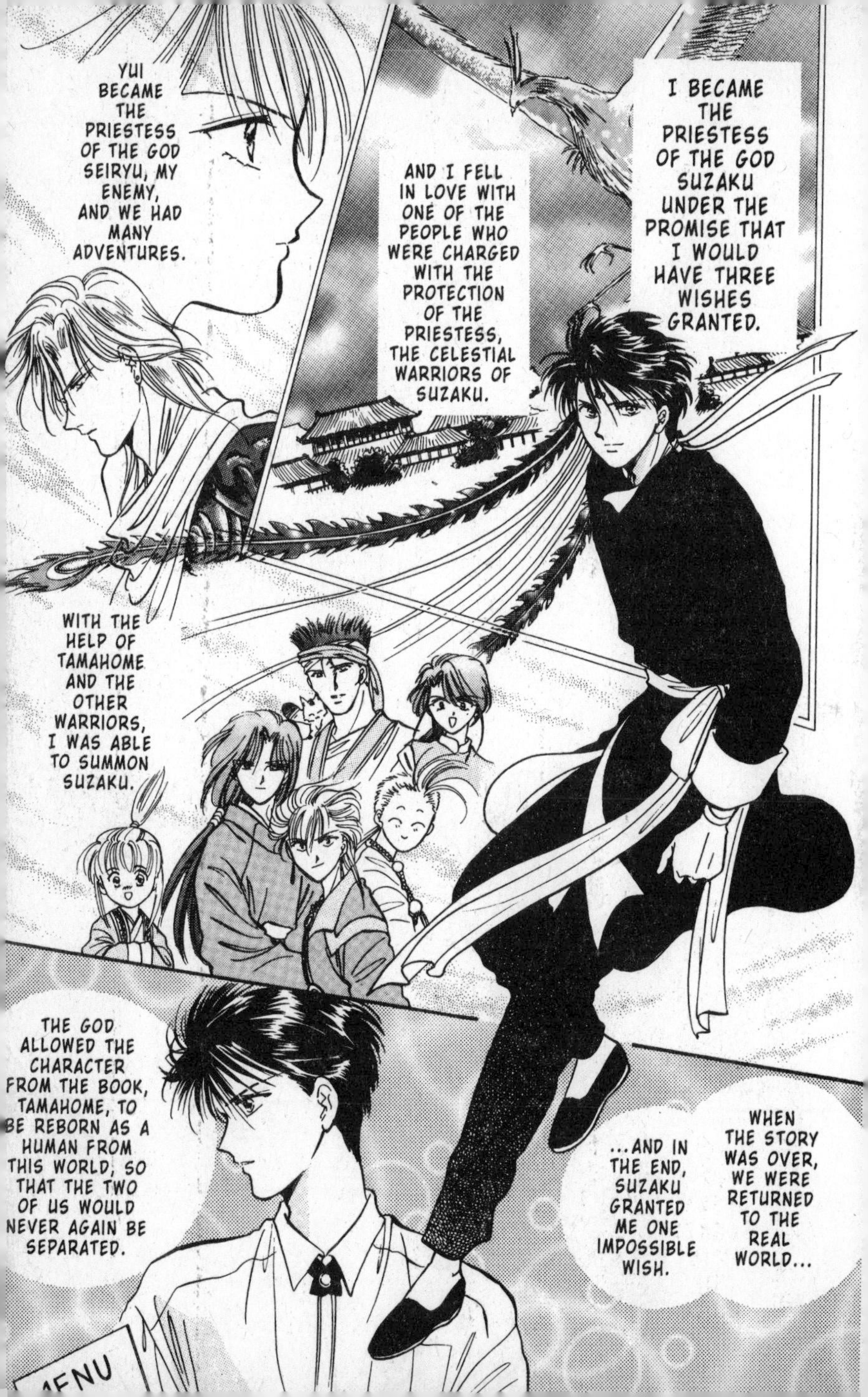
I BECAME THE PRIESTESS OF THE GOD SUZAKU UNDER THE PROMISE THAT I WOULD HAVE THREE WISHES GRANTED.
AND I FELL IN LOVE WITH ONE OF THE PEOPLE WHO WERE CHARGED WITH THE PROTECTION OF THE PRIESTESS, THE CELESTIAL WARRIORS OF SUZAKU.
YUI BECAME THE PRIESTESS OF THE GOD SEIRYU, MY ENEMY, AND WE HAD MANY ADVENTURES.
WITH THE HELP OF TAMAHOME AND THE OTHER WARRIORS, I WAS ABLE TO SUMMON SUZAKU.
WHEN THE STORY WAS OVER, WE WERE RETURNED TO THE REAL WORLD...
...AND IN THE END, SUZAKU GRANTED ME ONE IMPOSSIBLE WISH.
THE GOD ALLOWED THE CHARACTER FROM THE BOOK, TAMAHOME, TO BE REBORN AS A HUMAN FROM THIS WORLD, SO THAT THE TWO OF US WOULD NEVER AGAIN BE SEPARATED.

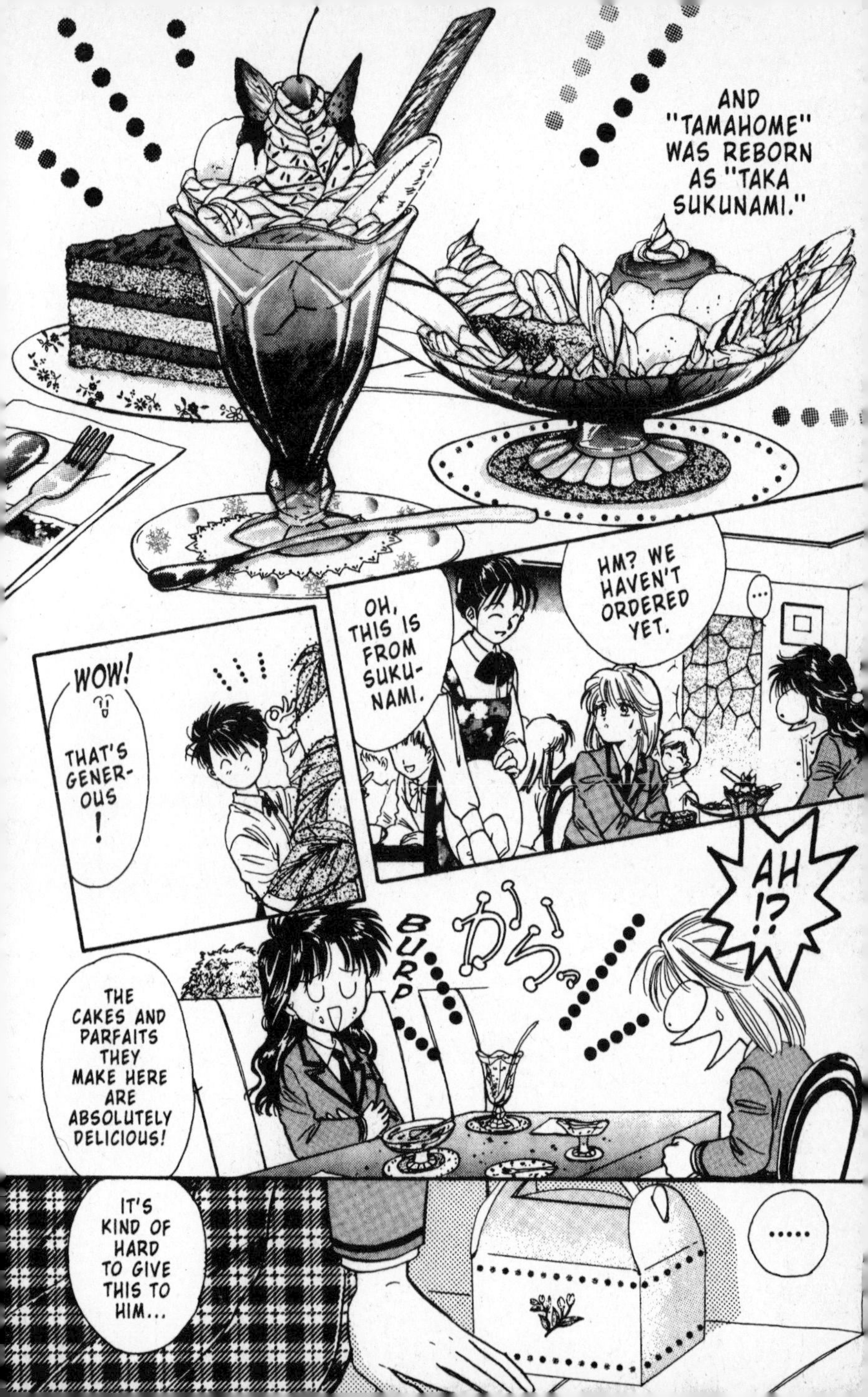
AND "TAMAHOME" WAS REBORN AS "TAKA SUKUNAMI."
...
HM? WE HAVEN'T ORDERED YET.
OH, THIS IS FROM SUKUNAMI.
WOW!
THAT'S GENEROUS!
AH !?
BURP
THE CAKES AND PARFAITS THEY MAKE HERE ARE ABSOLUTELY DELICIOUS!
.....
IT'S KIND OF HARD TO GIVE THIS TO HIM...

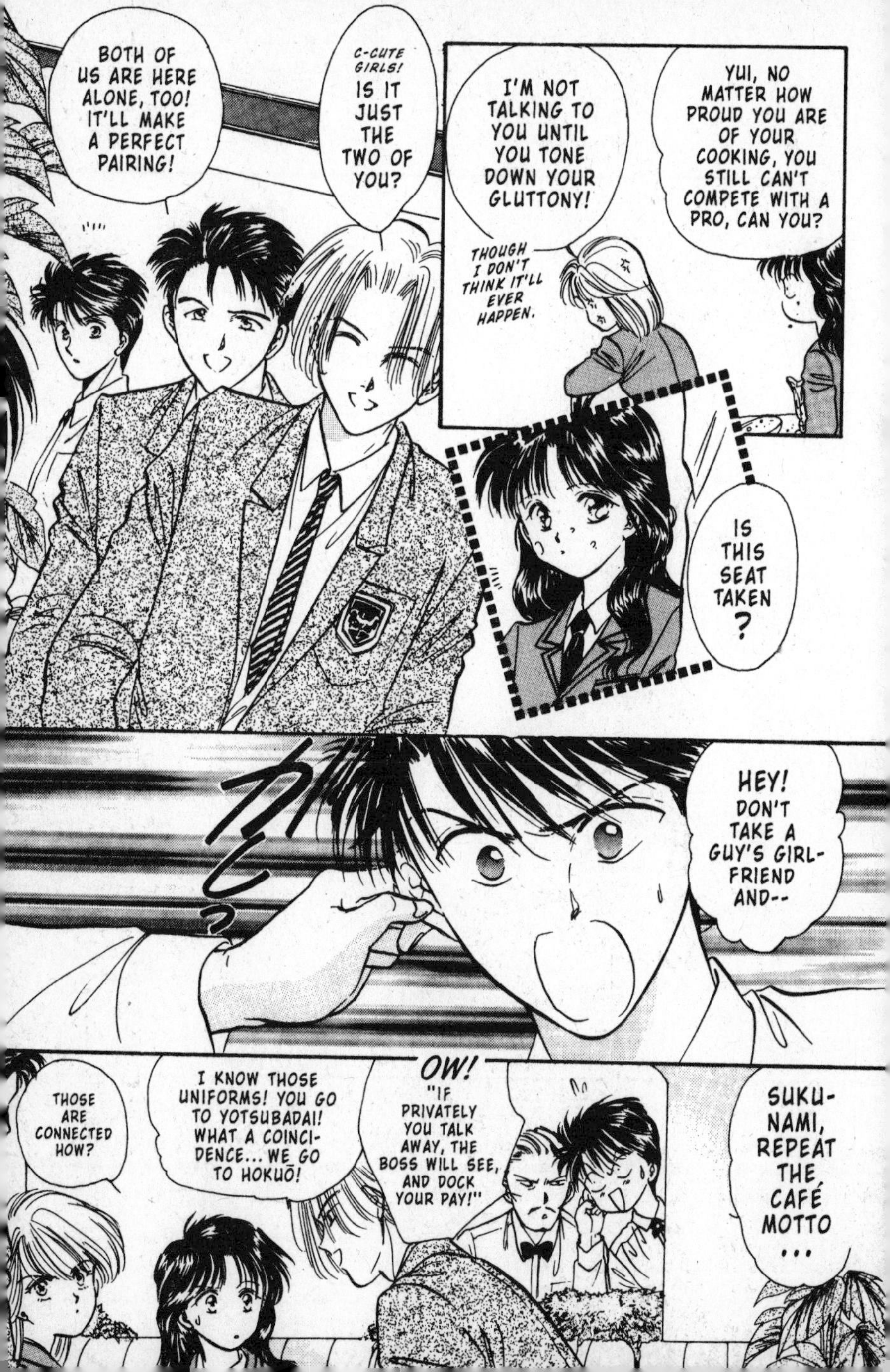
YUI, NO MATTER HOW PROUD YOU ARE OF YOUR COOKING, YOU STILL CAN'T COMPETE WITH A PRO, CAN YOU?
I'M NOT TALKING TO YOU UNTIL YOU TONE DOWN YOUR GLUTTONY!
THOUGH I DON'T THINK IT'LL EVER HAPPEN.
IS THIS SEAT TAKEN?
C-CUTE GIRLS! IS IT JUST THE TWO OF YOU?
BOTH OF US ARE HERE ALONE, TOO! IT'LL MAKE A PERFECT PAIRING!
HEY! DON'T TAKE A GUY'S GIRL-FRIEND AND--
SUKU-NAMI, REPEAT THE CAFÉ MOTTO...
OW!
"IF PRIVATELY YOU TALK AWAY, THE BOSS WILL SEE, AND DOCK YOUR PAY!"
I KNOW THOSE UNIFORMS! YOU GO TO YOTSUBADAI! WHAT A COINCI-DENCE... WE GO TO HOKUŌ!
THOSE ARE CONNECTED HOW?

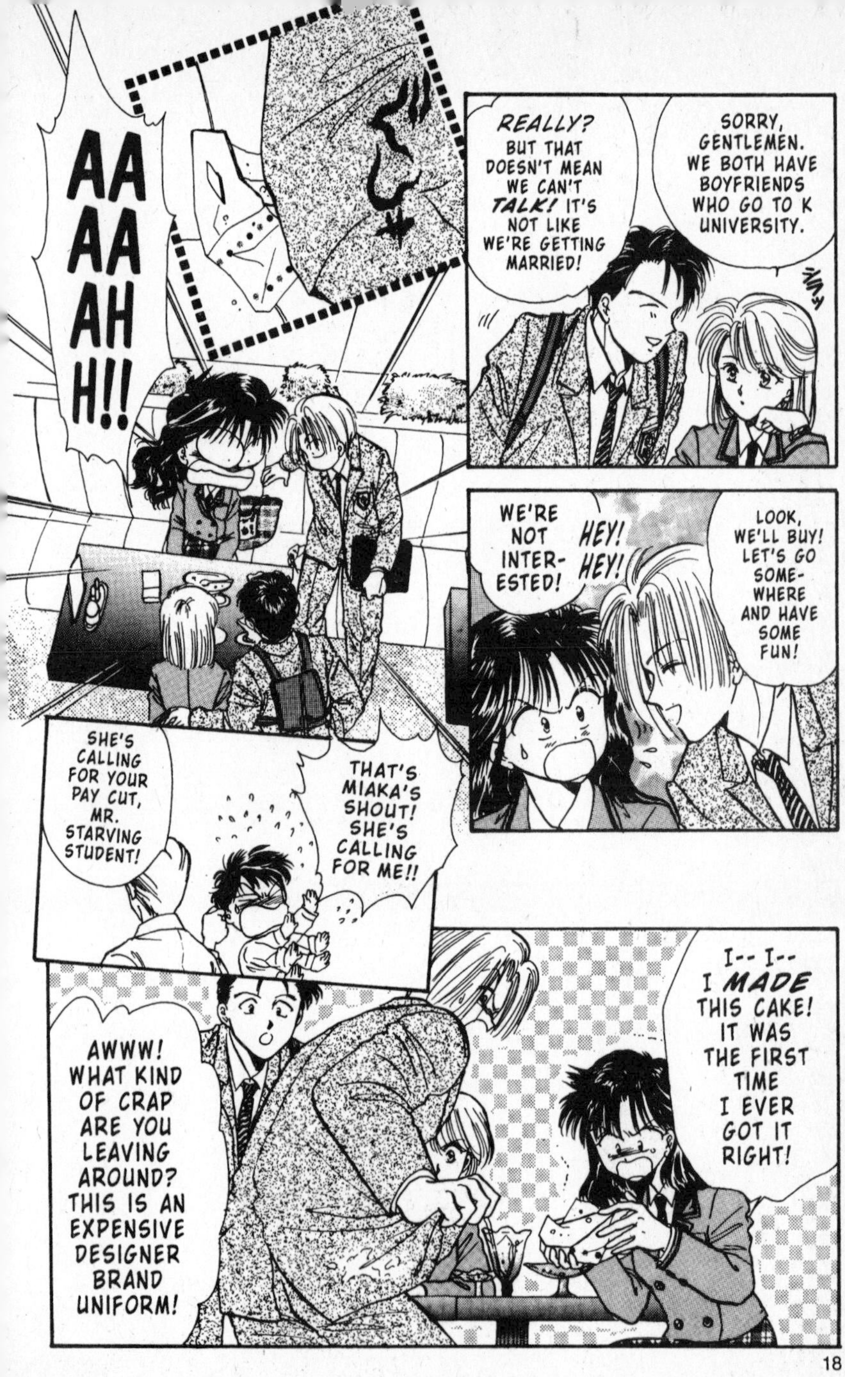
SORRY, GENTLEMEN. WE BOTH HAVE BOYFRIENDS WHO GO TO K UNIVERSITY.
REALLY? BUT THAT DOESN'T MEAN WE CAN'T TALK! IT'S NOT LIKE WE'RE GETTING MARRIED!
LOOK, WE'LL BUY! LET'S GO SOME-WHERE AND HAVE SOME FUN!
HEY! HEY!
WE'RE NOT INTER-ESTED!
AAAAAAH!!
THAT'S MIAKA'S SHOUT! SHE'S CALLING FOR ME!!
SHE'S CALLING FOR YOUR PAY CUT, MR. STARVING STUDENT!
I-- I-- I MADE THIS CAKE! IT WAS THE FIRST TIME I EVER GOT IT RIGHT!
AWWW! WHAT KIND OF CRAP ARE YOU LEAVING AROUND? THIS IS AN EXPENSIVE DESIGNER BRAND UNIFORM!

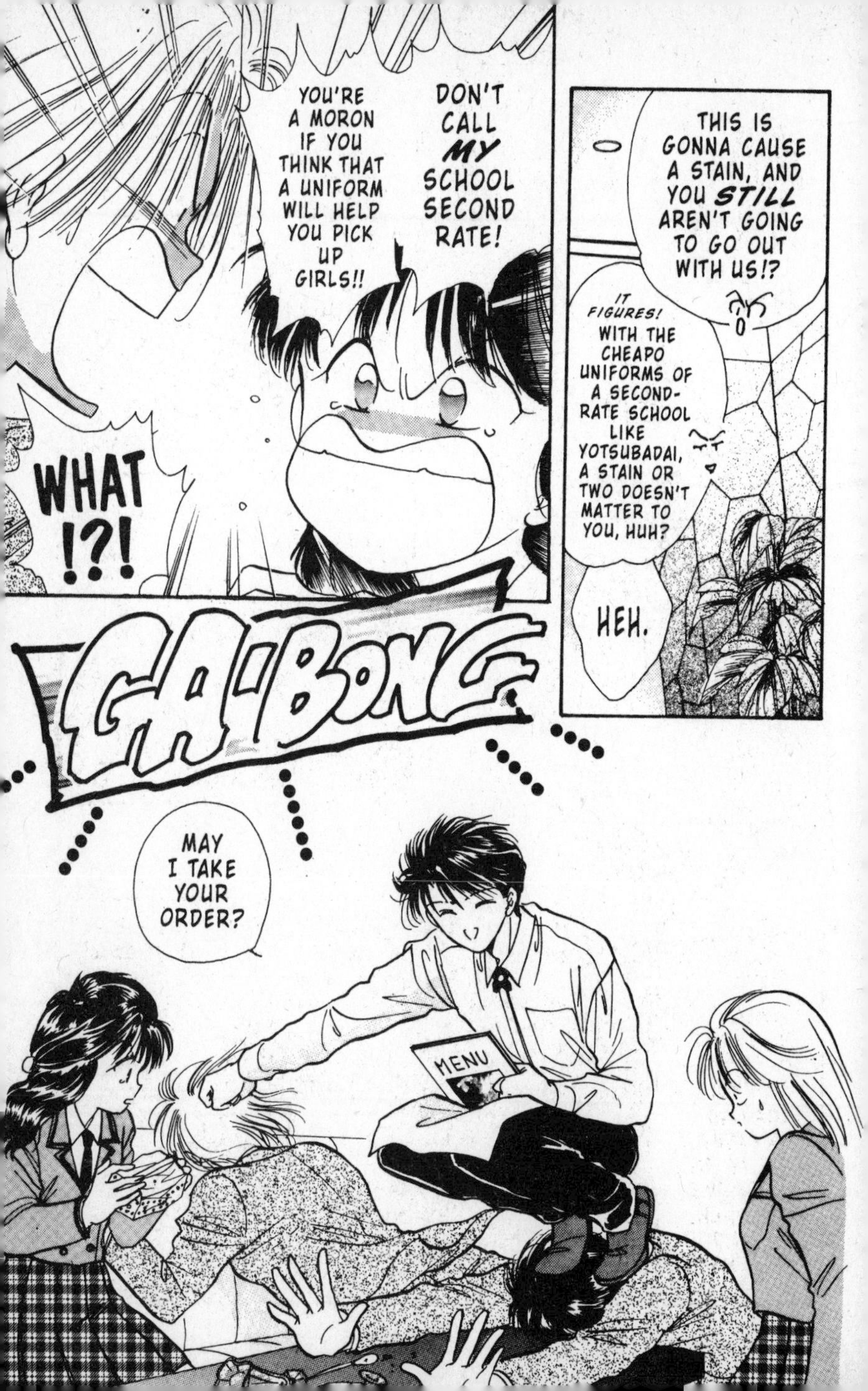

THIS IS GONNA CAUSE A STAIN, AND YOU STILL AREN'T GOING TO GO OUT WITH US!?
IT FIGURES!
WITH THE CHEAPO UNIFORMS OF A SECOND-RATE SCHOOL LIKE YOTSUBADAI, A STAIN OR TWO DOESN'T MATTER TO YOU, HUH?
HEH.
DON'T CALL MY SCHOOL SECOND RATE!
YOU'RE A MORON IF YOU THINK THAT A UNIFORM WILL HELP YOU PICK UP GIRLS!!
WHAT !?!
GA-BONG
MAY I TAKE YOUR ORDER?
MENU

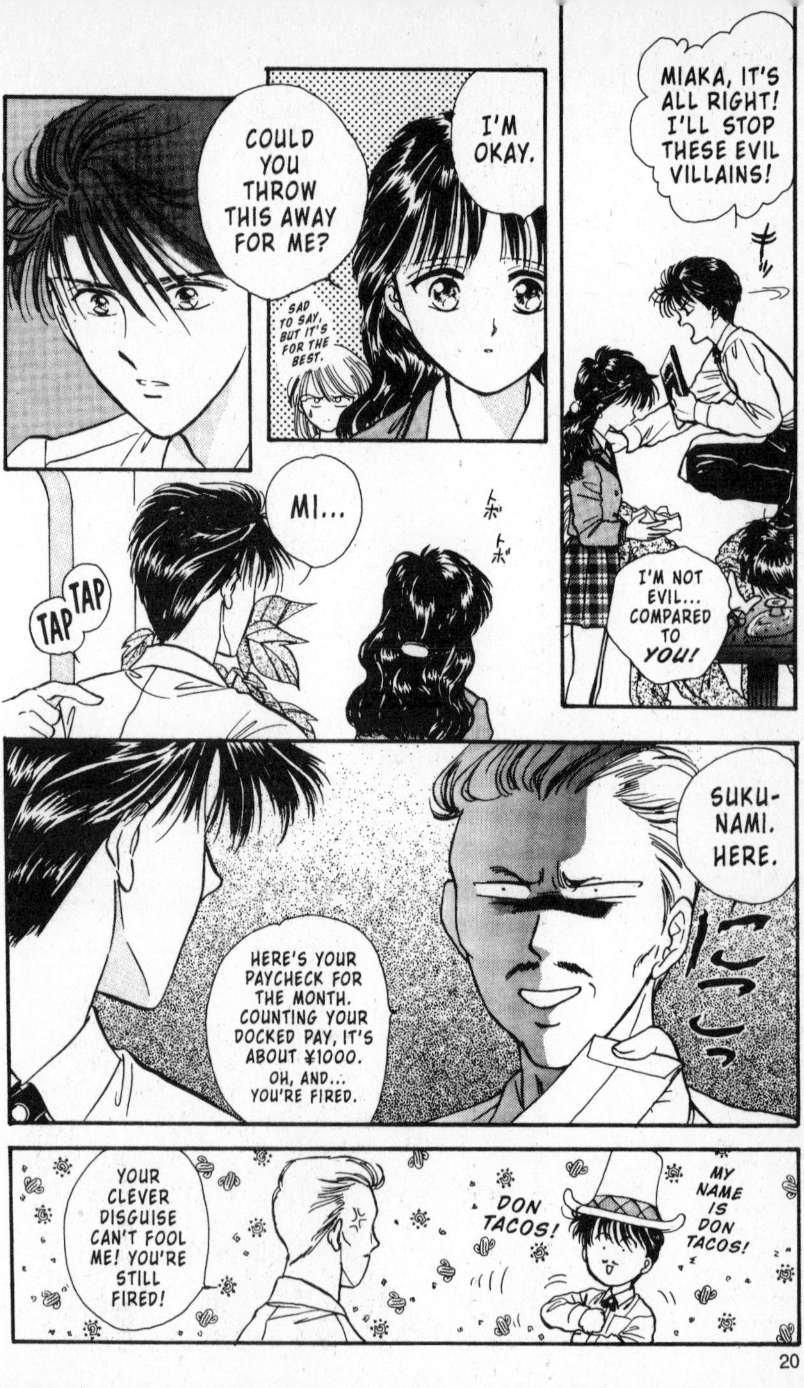
MIAKA, IT'S ALL RIGHT! I'LL STOP THESE EVIL VILLAINS!
I'M NOT EVIL... COMPARED TO *YOU!*
I'M OKAY.
SAD TO SAY, BUT IT'S FOR THE BEST.
COULD YOU THROW THIS AWAY FOR ME?
MI...
TAP TAP
SUKU-NAMI. HERE.
HERE'S YOUR PAYCHECK FOR THE MONTH. COUNTING YOUR DOCKED PAY, IT'S ABOUT ¥1000.
OH, AND... YOU'RE FIRED.
MY NAME IS DON TACOS!
DON TACOS!
YOUR CLEVER DISGUISE CAN'T FOOL ME! YOU'RE STILL FIRED!

Hi everybody! It's Watase!! Welcome to Fushigi Yûgi Part 2! "Give me a break! Where can FY go from here!?" you say, at which the author can only laugh.
HA HA HA HA HA HA HA HA HA HA
Aww, laughing won't make for a good story! This is hard! On the other hand, there were so many letters that said something like, "I'm so relieved that it isn't over," that my only option is to bear down and write it! ☺
When the first request for "Part 2" came in from the editors, my first thought was, "All right! I'll write the story of some other heroine than Miaka!" (At the time, I thought I was going to use the Takamatsu-Zuka Old Mound.) There were all sorts of ideas floating around my head, but in the end, I couldn't avoid the idea that Fushigi Yûgi is pretty much a work that centers on Miaka and the Suzaku Celestial Warriors. And to tell the truth, I was a little worried about how Miaka and Tamahome (Taka) would get on after the story was over, so the main character remained Miaka. *Aren't you happy, Miaka?* And how can I even try to write FY without the Celestial Warriors? (This thought was the strongest!)
I had Tamahome transfer in and become "Taka Sukunami," but it seems a lot of people view him as a different person. They really are one and the same person! This is modern Japan, so we really can't help those differences that creep in because he didn't grow up in ancient China. I didn't want his name to be too different from that of his Celestial Warrior life, so the kanji for "Taka" still has the "demon" part that made up the kanji for "Tamahome." It's also a name that was common in China, and it's a good name, so I settled on it. And the sounds "Taka" and "Tama" are nicely close. I wasn't comfortable with the name at first, but now I'm happy with it.

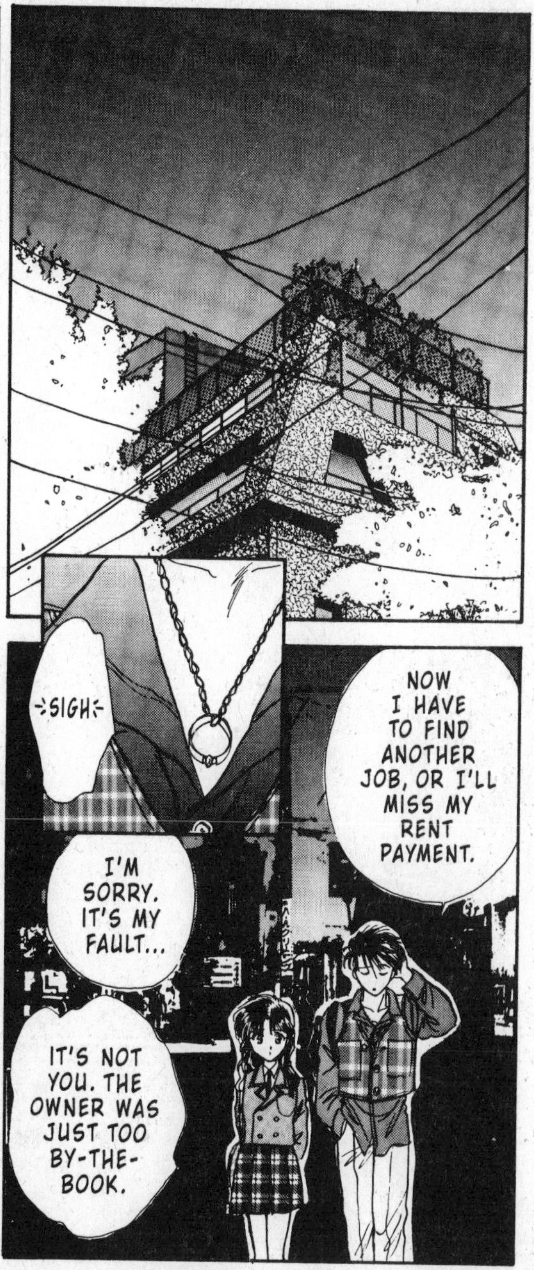
SIGH
NOW I HAVE TO FIND ANOTHER JOB, OR I'LL MISS MY RENT PAYMENT.
I'M SORRY. IT'S MY FAULT...
IT'S NOT YOU. THE OWNER WAS JUST TOO BY-THE-BOOK.

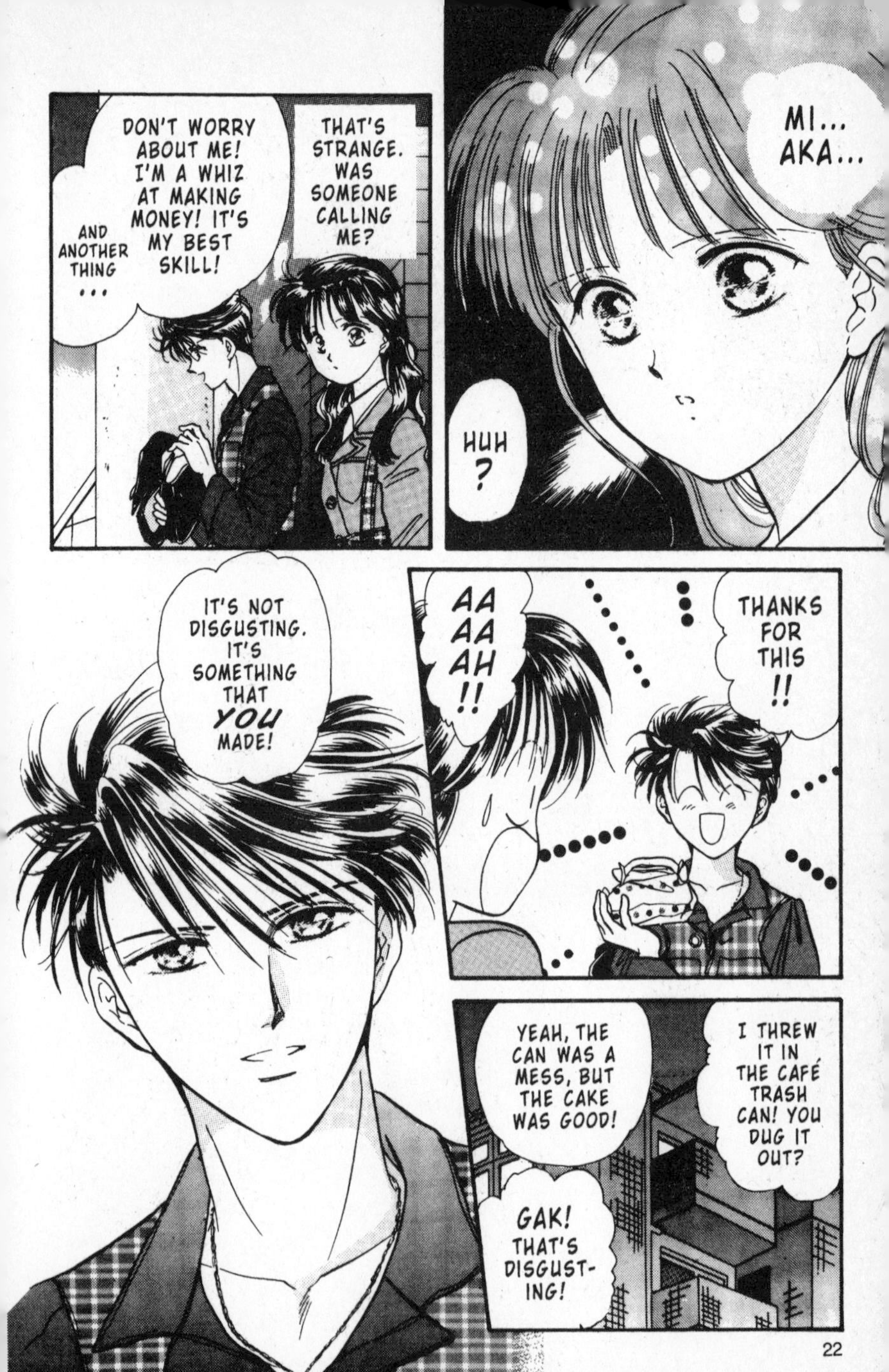
MI... AKA...
HUH?
THAT'S STRANGE. WAS SOMEONE CALLING ME?
DON'T WORRY ABOUT ME! I'M A WHIZ AT MAKING MONEY! IT'S MY BEST SKILL!
AND ANOTHER THING ...
THANKS FOR THIS!!
AAAAAH!!
I THREW IT IN THE CAFÉ TRASH CAN! YOU DUG IT OUT?
YEAH, THE CAN WAS A MESS, BUT THE CAKE WAS GOOD!
GAK! THAT'S DISGUST-ING!
IT'S NOT DISGUSTING. IT'S SOMETHING THAT *YOU* MADE!

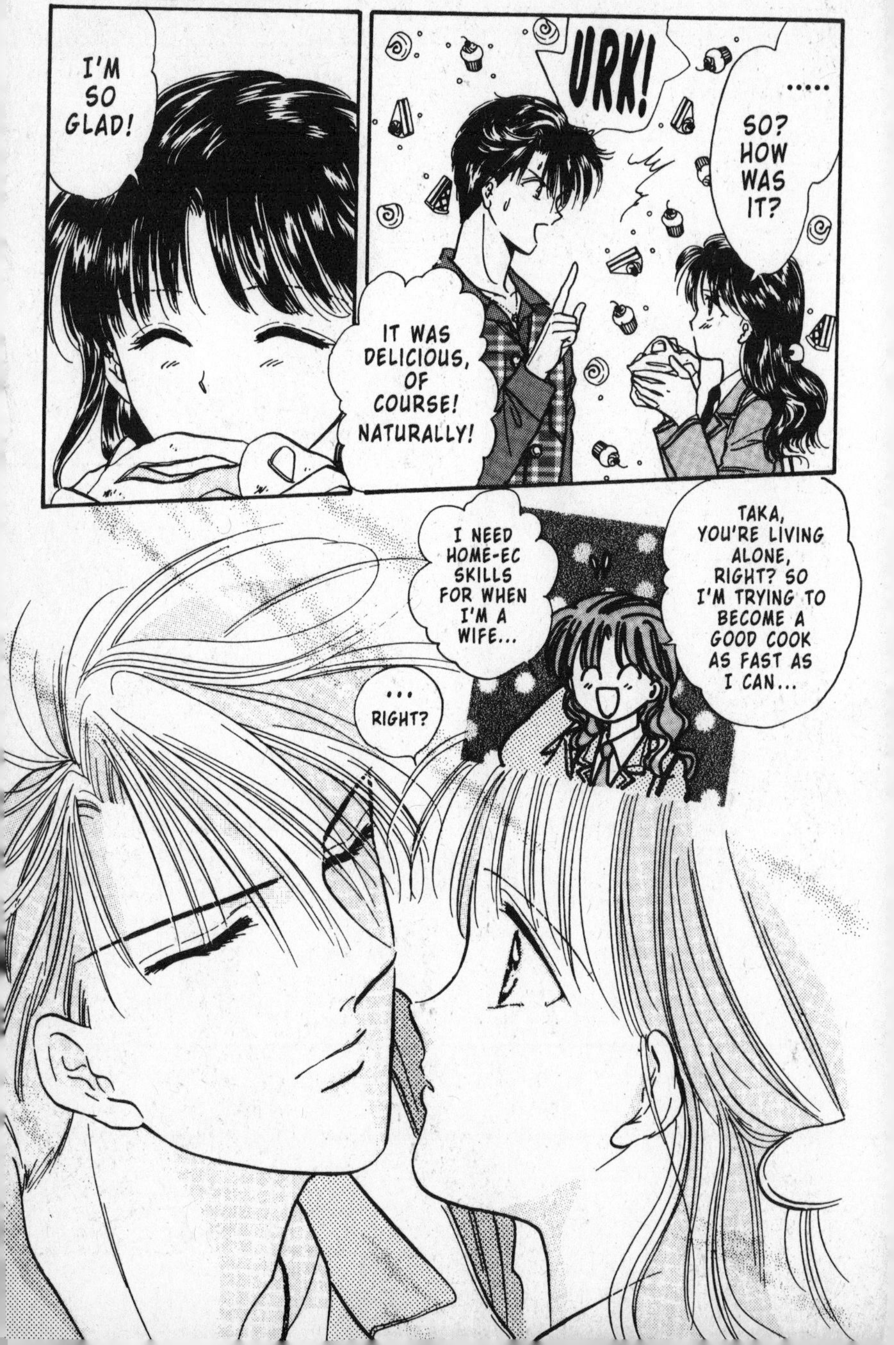
.....
SO? HOW WAS IT?
URK!
IT WAS DELICIOUS, OF COURSE! NATURALLY!
I'M SO GLAD!
TAKA, YOU'RE LIVING ALONE, RIGHT? SO I'M TRYING TO BECOME A GOOD COOK AS FAST AS I CAN...
I NEED HOME-EC SKILLS FOR WHEN I'M A WIFE...
... RIGHT?

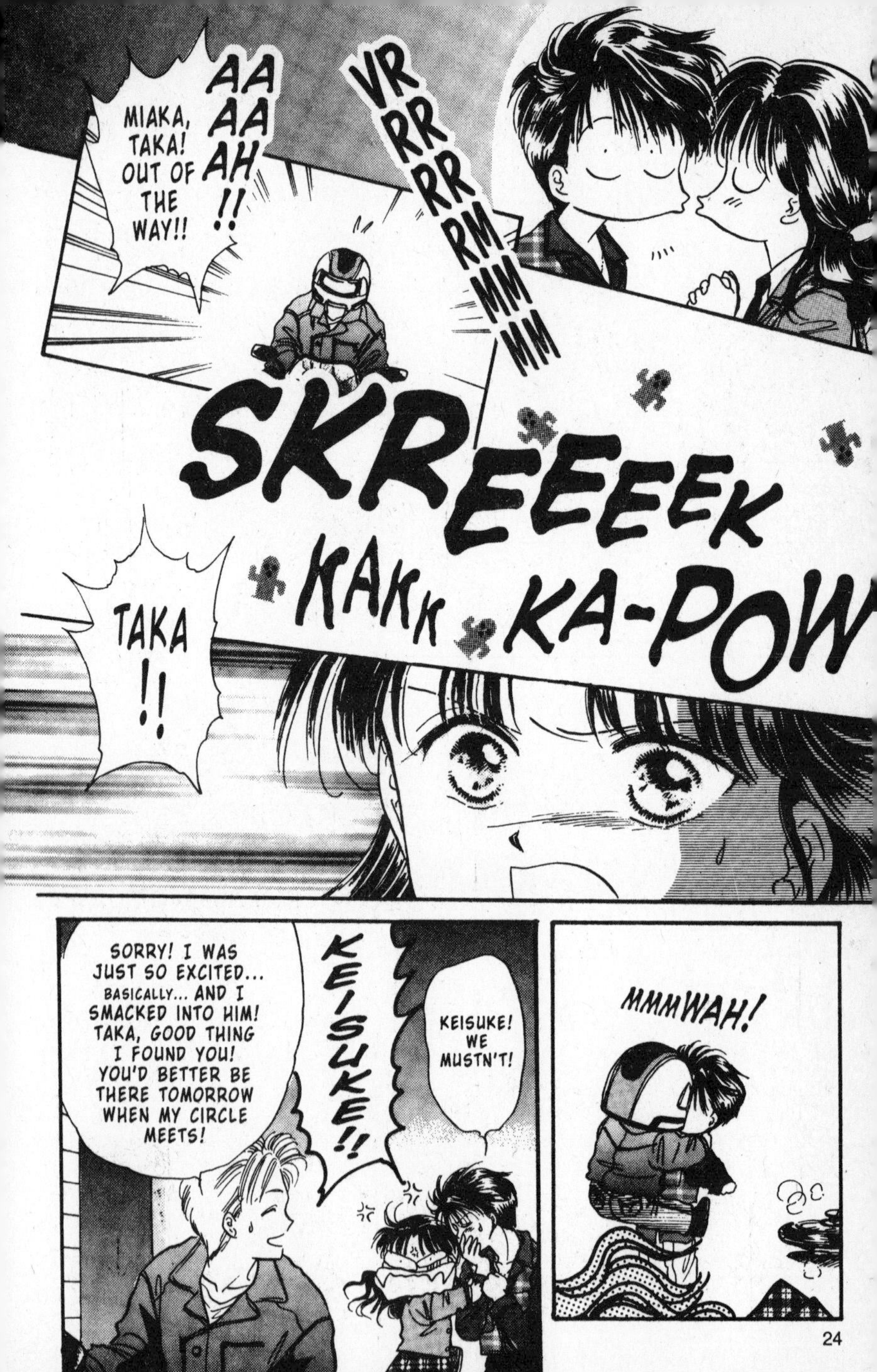
VRRRRRRMMMMM
AAAAAH!!
MIAKA, TAKA! OUT OF THE WAY!!
SKREEEEK
KAKK KA-POW
TAKA!!
MMMWAH!
KEISUKE! WE MUSTN'T!
KEISUKE!!
SORRY! I WAS JUST SO EXCITED... BASICALLY... AND I SMACKED INTO HIM! TAKA, GOOD THING I FOUND YOU! YOU'D BETTER BE THERE TOMORROW WHEN MY CIRCLE MEETS!

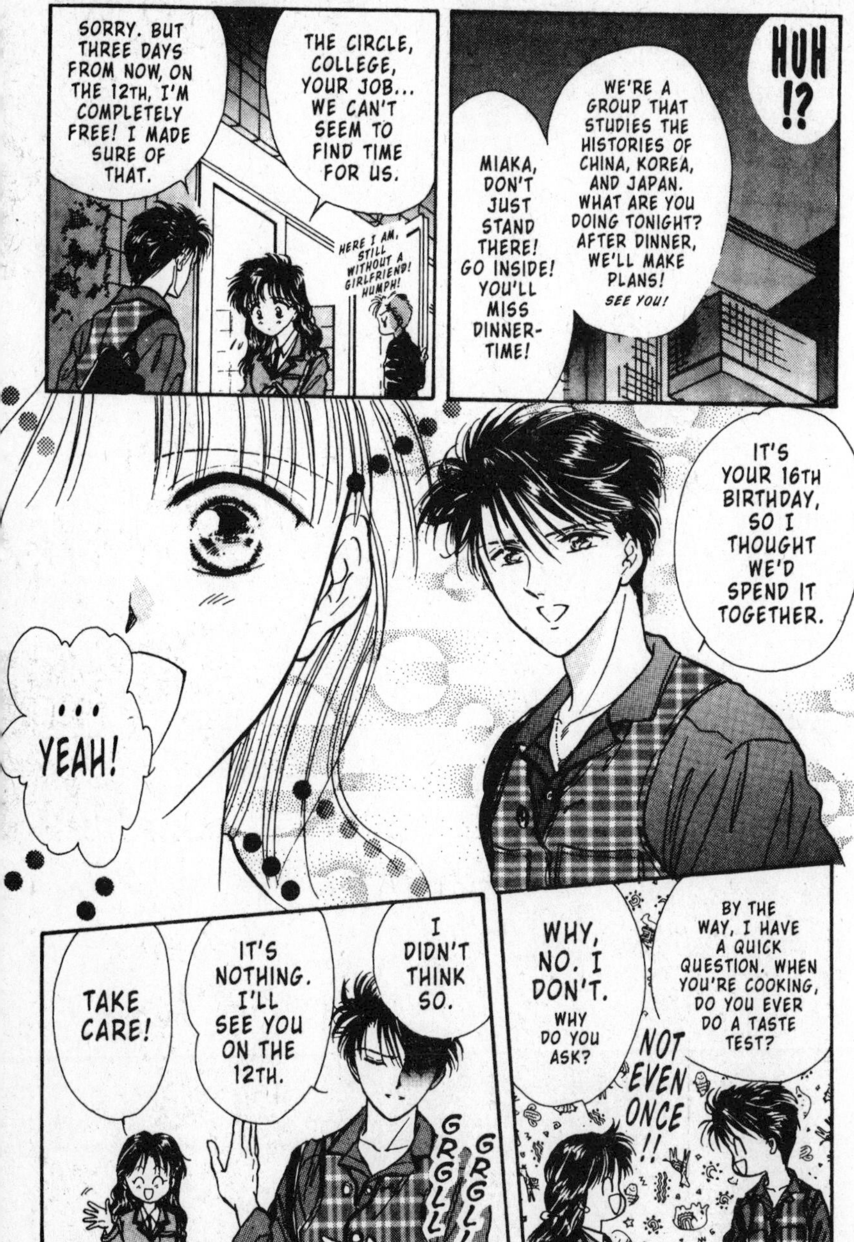
HUH!?
WE'RE A GROUP THAT STUDIES THE HISTORIES OF CHINA, KOREA, AND JAPAN. WHAT ARE YOU DOING TONIGHT? AFTER DINNER, WE'LL MAKE PLANS! SEE YOU!
MIAKA, DON'T JUST STAND THERE! GO INSIDE! YOU'LL MISS DINNER-TIME!
THE CIRCLE, COLLEGE, YOUR JOB... WE CAN'T SEEM TO FIND TIME FOR US.
SORRY. BUT THREE DAYS FROM NOW, ON THE 12TH, I'M COMPLETELY FREE! I MADE SURE OF THAT.
HERE I AM, STILL WITHOUT A GIRLFRIEND! HUMPH!
IT'S YOUR 16TH BIRTHDAY, SO I THOUGHT WE'D SPEND IT TOGETHER.
...YEAH!
BY THE WAY, I HAVE A QUICK QUESTION. WHEN YOU'RE COOKING, DO YOU EVER DO A TASTE TEST?
WHY, NO. I DON'T. WHY DO YOU ASK?
NOT EVEN ONCE!!
I DIDN'T THINK SO.
IT'S NOTHING. I'LL SEE YOU ON THE 12TH.
TAKE CARE!
GRGLL GRGLL

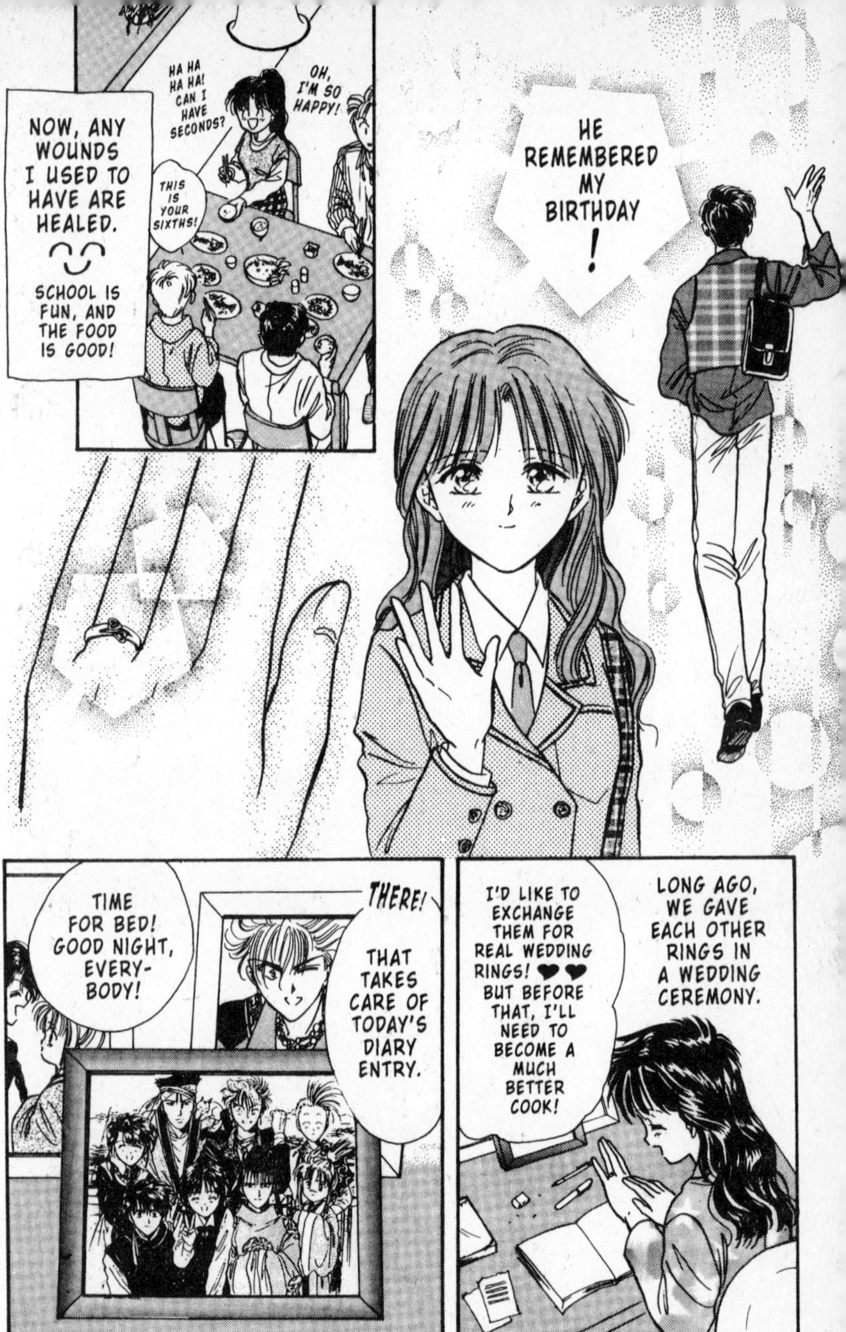
HE REMEMBERED MY BIRTHDAY!
OH, I'M SO HAPPY!
HA HA HA HA! CAN I HAVE SECONDS?
NOW, ANY WOUNDS I USED TO HAVE ARE HEALED.
SCHOOL IS FUN, AND THE FOOD IS GOOD!
THIS IS YOUR SIXTHS!
LONG AGO, WE GAVE EACH OTHER RINGS IN A WEDDING CEREMONY.
I'D LIKE TO EXCHANGE THEM FOR REAL WEDDING RINGS! ❤❤ BUT BEFORE THAT, I'LL NEED TO BECOME A MUCH BETTER COOK!
THERE!
THAT TAKES CARE OF TODAY'S DIARY ENTRY.
TIME FOR BED! GOOD NIGHT, EVERY-BODY!

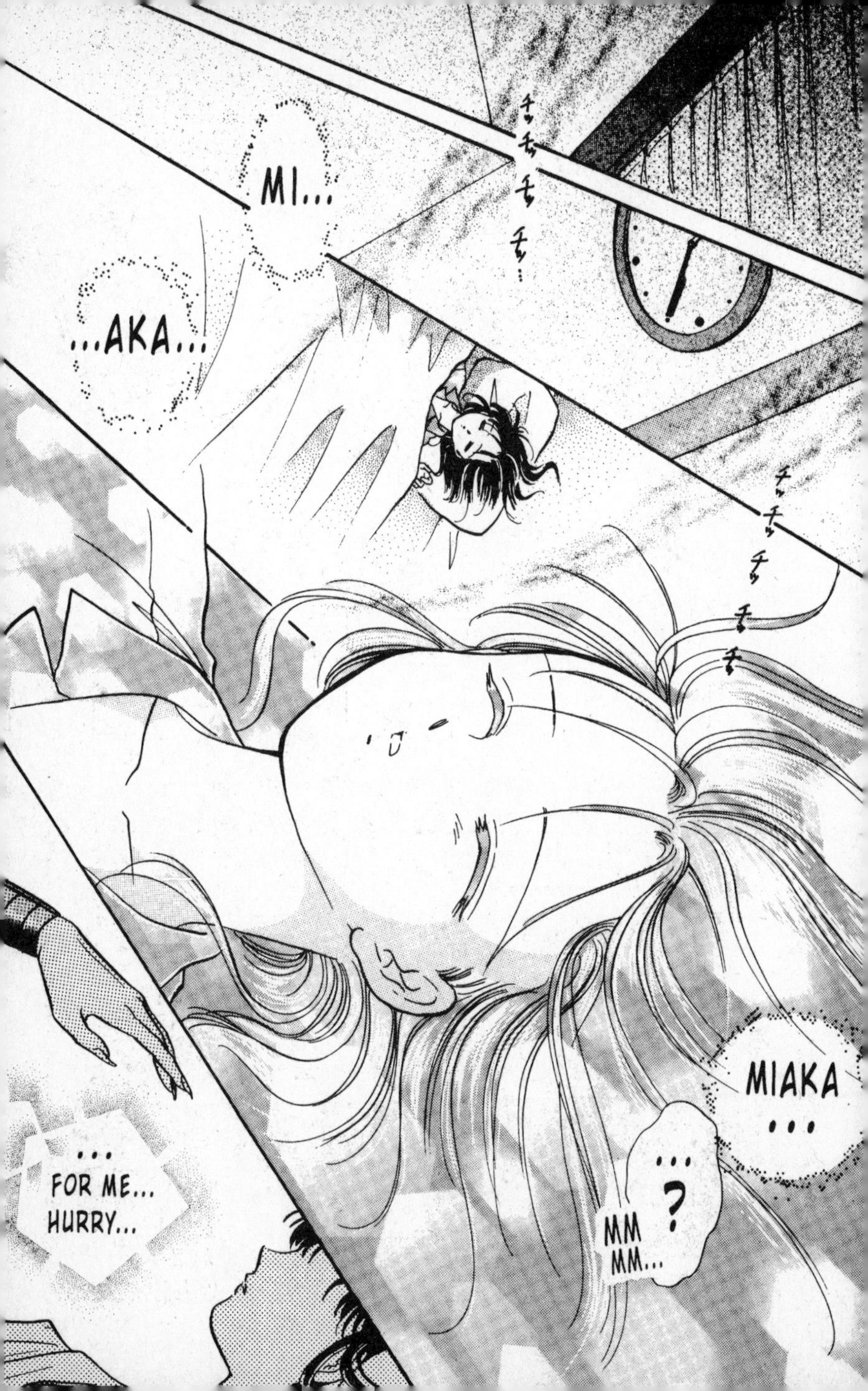
MI...
...AKA...
MIAKA...
...?
MM MM...
... FOR ME... HURRY...

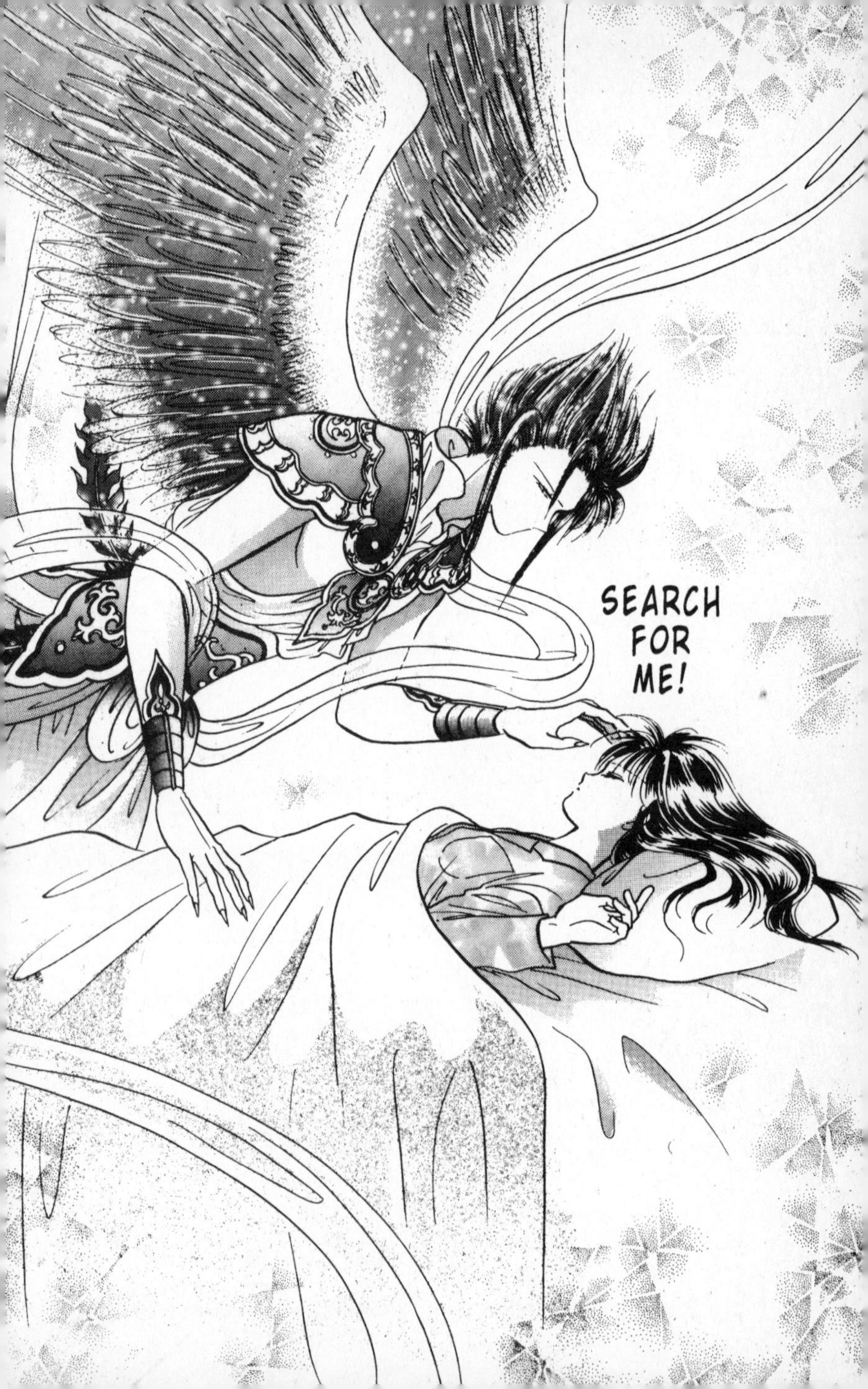
SEARCH FOR ME!

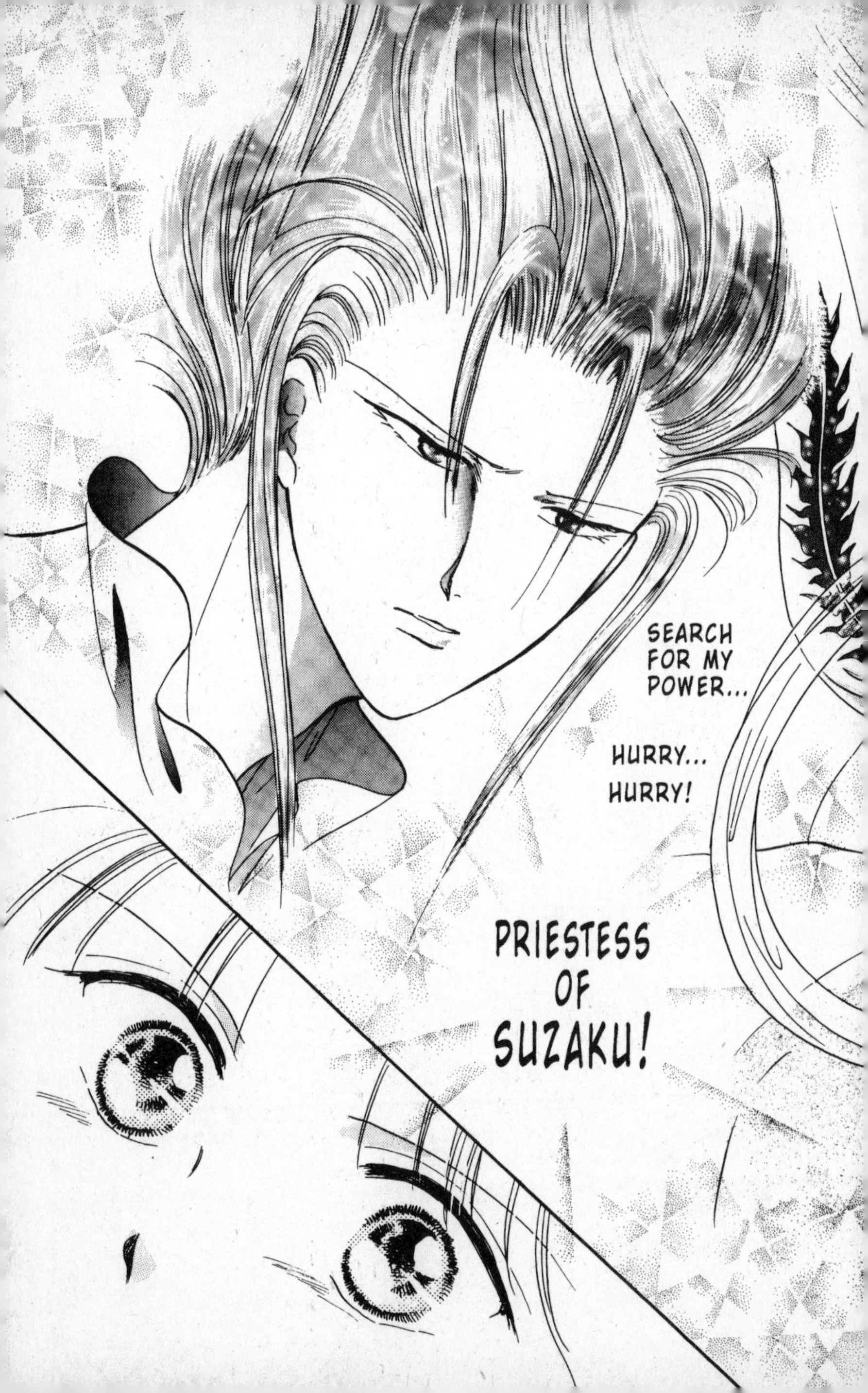
SEARCH FOR MY POWER...
HURRY... HURRY!
PRIESTESS OF SUZAKU!

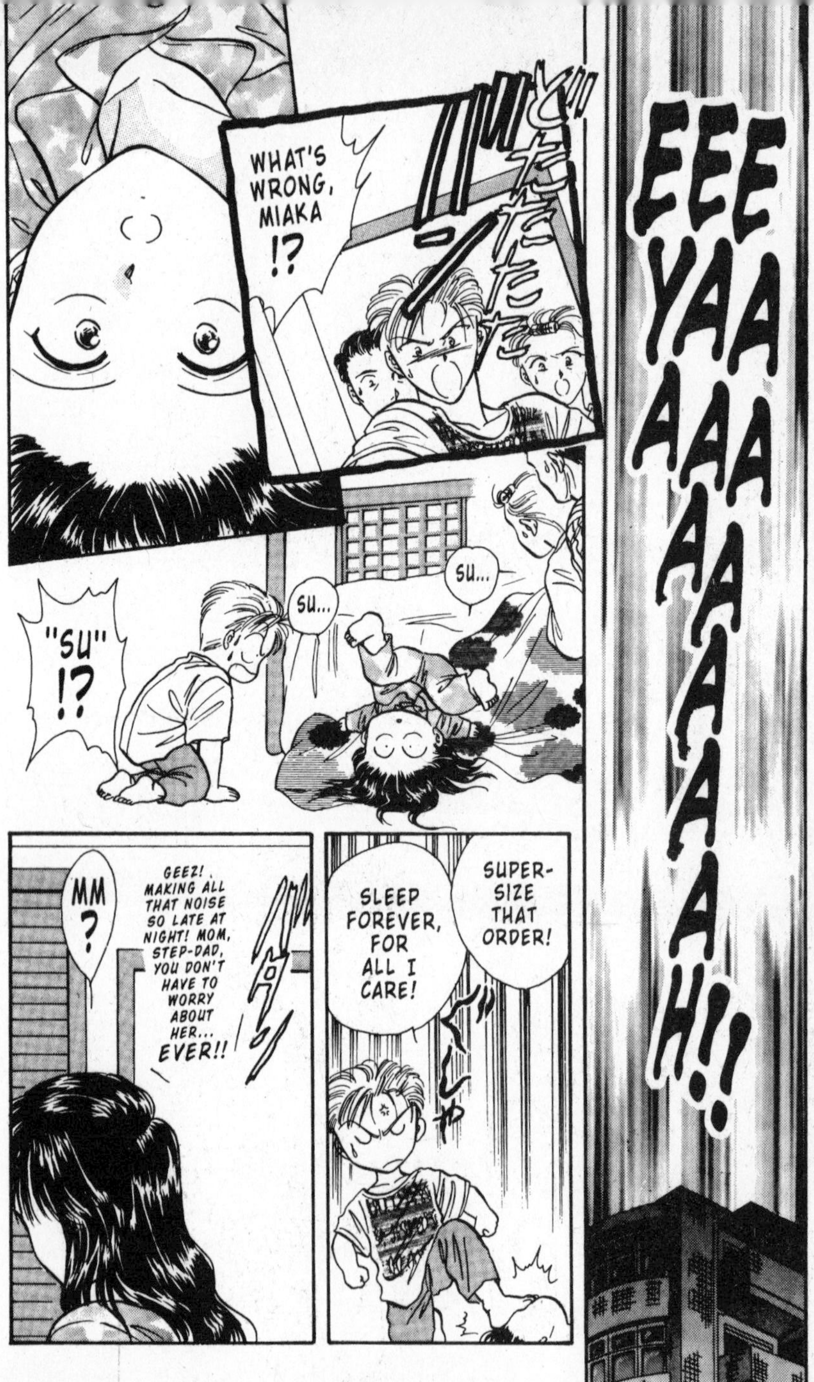
EEEYAAAAAAAAAAH!!
WHAT'S WRONG, MIAKA!?
SU...
SU...
"SU"!?
SUPER-SIZE THAT ORDER!
SLEEP FOREVER, FOR ALL I CARE!
MM?
GEEZ! MAKING ALL THAT NOISE SO LATE AT NIGHT! MOM, STEP-DAD, YOU DON'T HAVE TO WORRY ABOUT HER... EVER!!

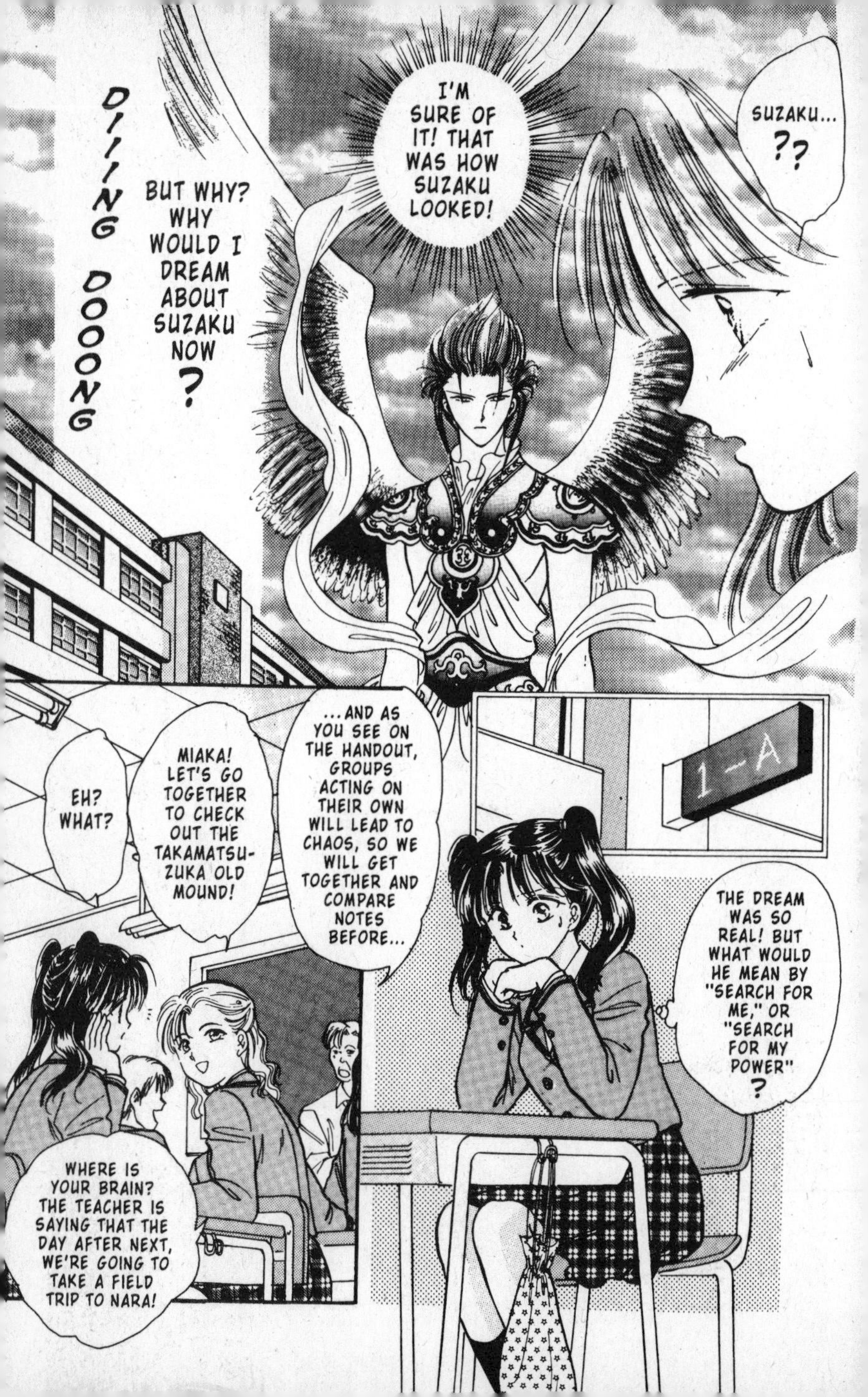
SUZAKU... ??
I'M SURE OF IT! THAT WAS HOW SUZAKU LOOKED!
BUT WHY? WHY WOULD I DREAM ABOUT SUZAKU NOW?
DIIING DOOOONG
THE DREAM WAS SO REAL! BUT WHAT WOULD HE MEAN BY "SEARCH FOR ME," OR "SEARCH FOR MY POWER"?
1-A
...AND AS YOU SEE ON THE HANDOUT, GROUPS ACTING ON THEIR OWN WILL LEAD TO CHAOS, SO WE WILL GET TOGETHER AND COMPARE NOTES BEFORE...
MIAKA! LET'S GO TOGETHER TO CHECK OUT THE TAKAMATSU-ZUKA OLD MOUND!
EH? WHAT?
WHERE IS YOUR BRAIN? THE TEACHER IS SAYING THAT THE DAY AFTER NEXT, WE'RE GOING TO TAKE A FIELD TRIP TO NARA!

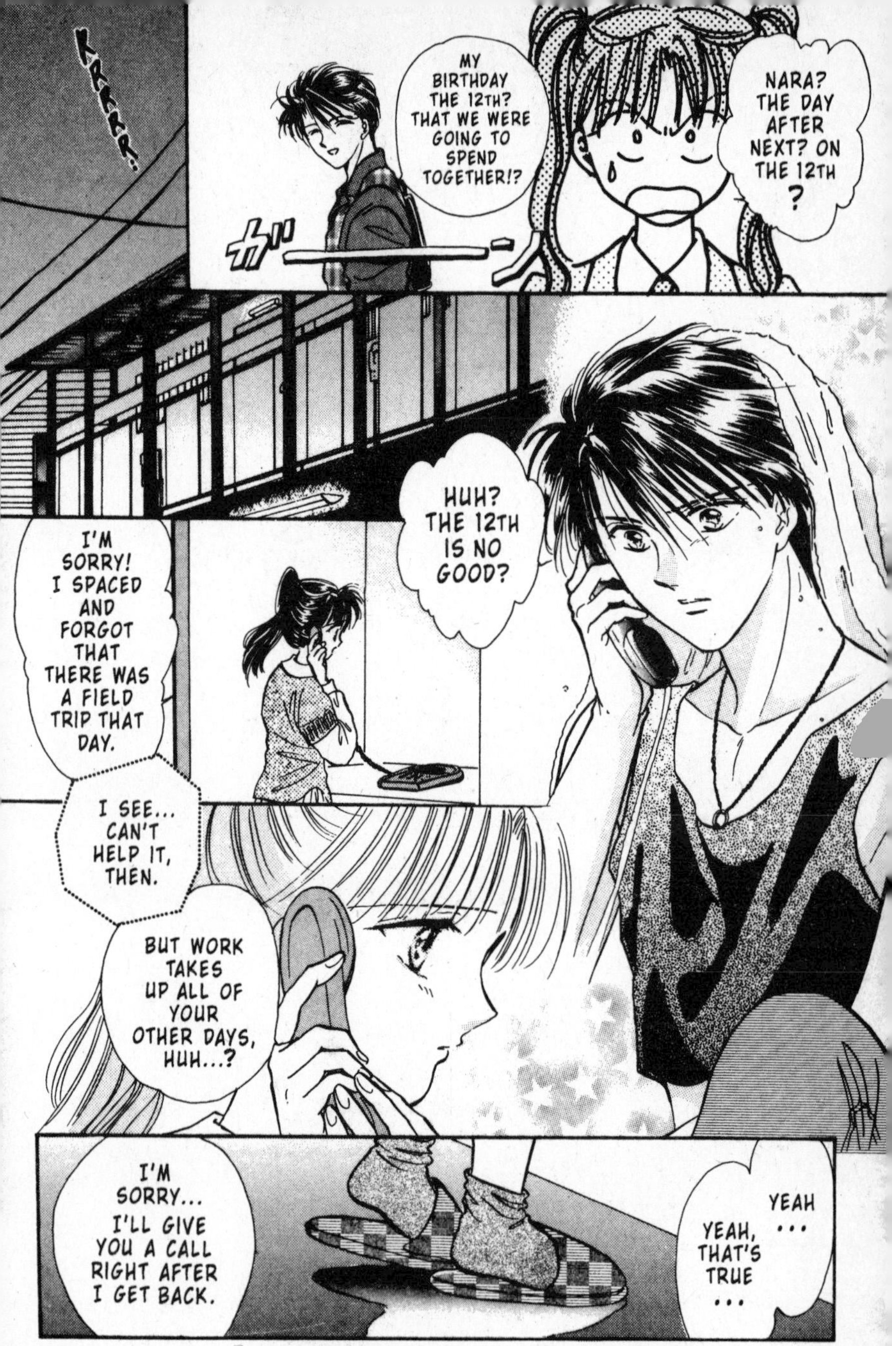
NARA? THE DAY AFTER NEXT? ON THE 12TH ?
MY BIRTHDAY THE 12TH? THAT WE WERE GOING TO SPEND TOGETHER!?
ガ
KRRRR..
HUH? THE 12TH IS NO GOOD?
I'M SORRY! I SPACED AND FORGOT THAT THERE WAS A FIELD TRIP THAT DAY.
I SEE... CAN'T HELP IT, THEN.
BUT WORK TAKES UP ALL OF YOUR OTHER DAYS, HUH...?
YEAH ...
YEAH, THAT'S TRUE ...
I'M SORRY... I'LL GIVE YOU A CALL RIGHT AFTER I GET BACK.

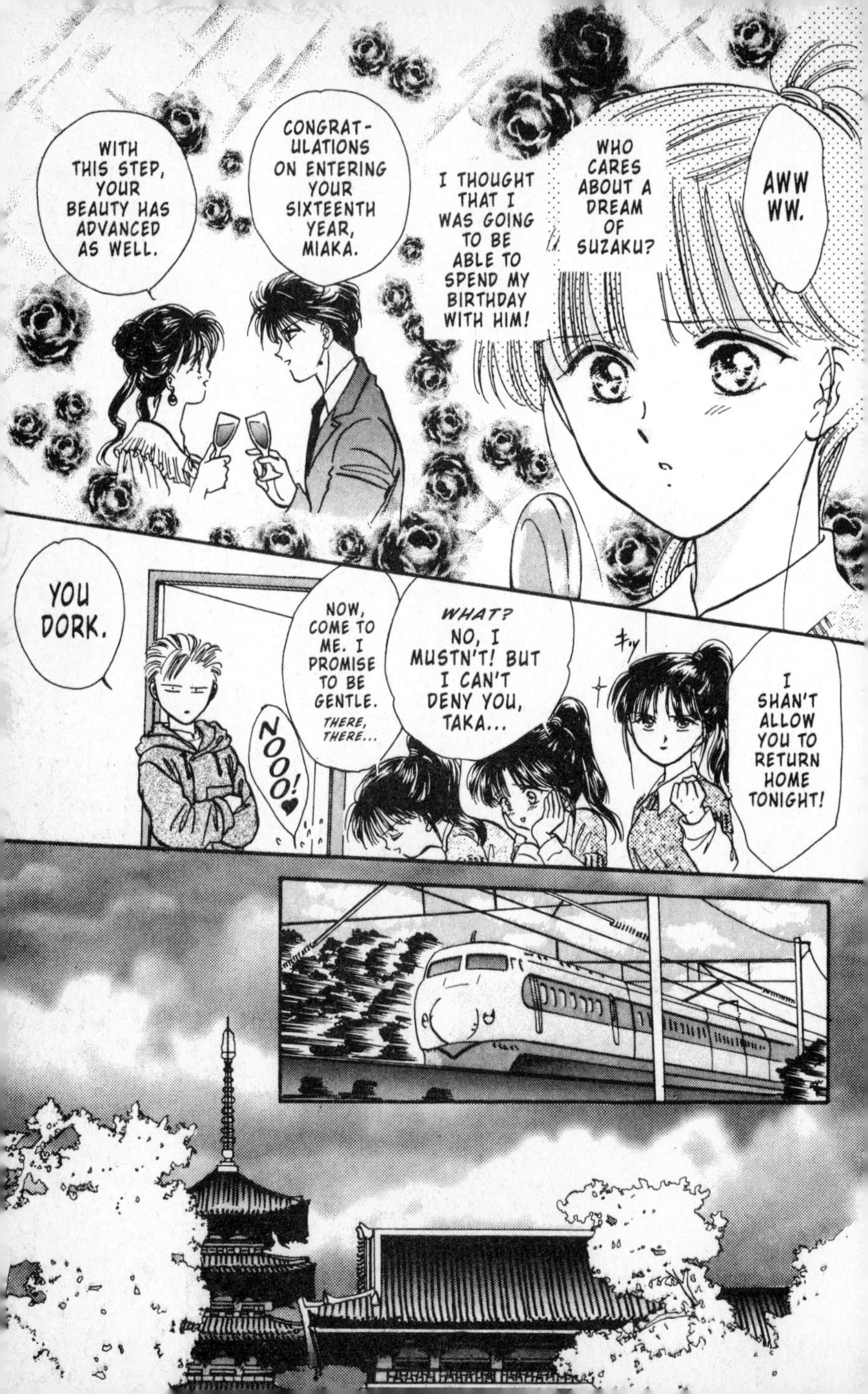
AWW WW.
WHO CARES ABOUT A DREAM OF SUZAKU?
I THOUGHT THAT I WAS GOING TO BE ABLE TO SPEND MY BIRTHDAY WITH HIM!
CONGRATULATIONS ON ENTERING YOUR SIXTEENTH YEAR, MIAKA.
WITH THIS STEP, YOUR BEAUTY HAS ADVANCED AS WELL.
I SHAN'T ALLOW YOU TO RETURN HOME TONIGHT!
WHAT? NO, I MUSTN'T! BUT I CAN'T DENY YOU, TAKA...
NOW, COME TO ME. I PROMISE TO BE GENTLE. THERE, THERE...
NOOO!♥
YOU DORK.

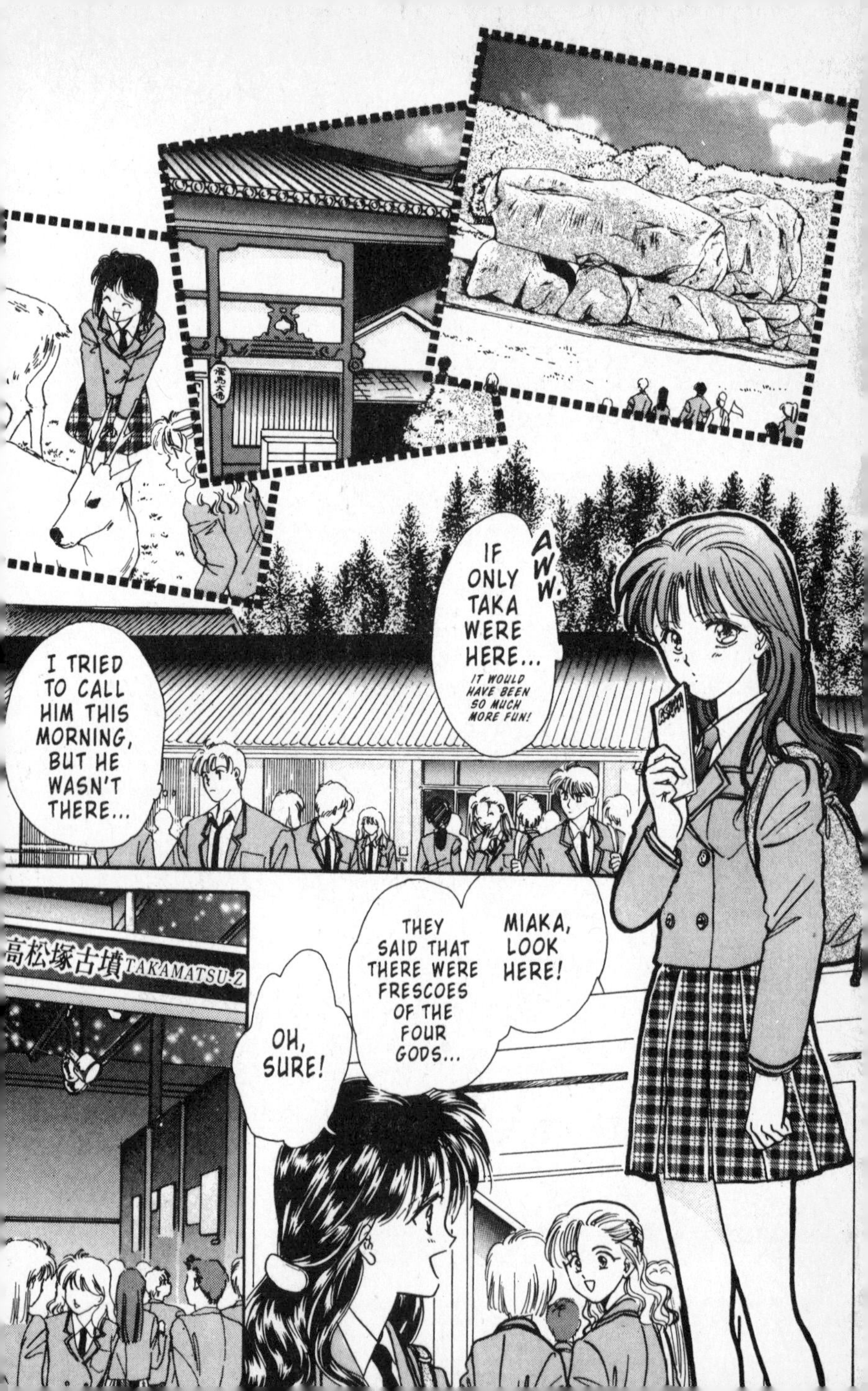
AWW.
IF ONLY TAKA WERE HERE...
IT WOULD HAVE BEEN SO MUCH MORE FUN!
I TRIED TO CALL HIM THIS MORNING, BUT HE WASN'T THERE...
MIAKA, LOOK HERE!
THEY SAID THAT THERE WERE FRESCOES OF THE FOUR GODS...
OH, SURE!
高松塚古墳 TAKAMATSU-Z

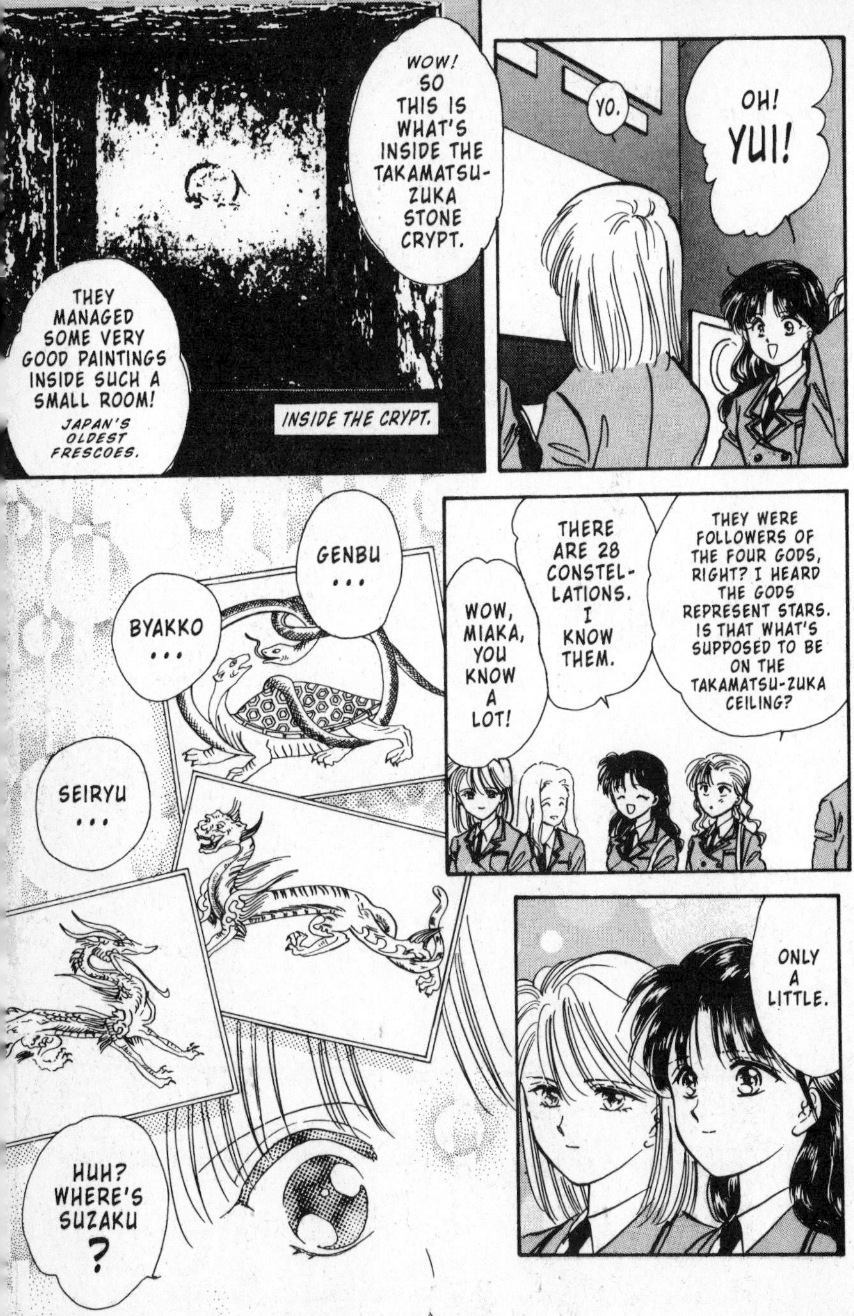
OH! YUI!
YO.
WOW! SO THIS IS WHAT'S INSIDE THE TAKAMATSU-ZUKA STONE CRYPT.
THEY MANAGED SOME VERY GOOD PAINTINGS INSIDE SUCH A SMALL ROOM!
JAPAN'S OLDEST FRESCOES.
INSIDE THE CRYPT.
THEY WERE FOLLOWERS OF THE FOUR GODS, RIGHT? I HEARD THE GODS REPRESENT STARS. IS THAT WHAT'S SUPPOSED TO BE ON THE TAKAMATSU-ZUKA CEILING?
THERE ARE 28 CONSTEL-LATIONS. I KNOW THEM.
WOW, MIAKA, YOU KNOW A LOT!
ONLY A LITTLE.
GENBU ...
BYAKKO ...
SEIRYU ...
HUH? WHERE'S SUZAKU ?

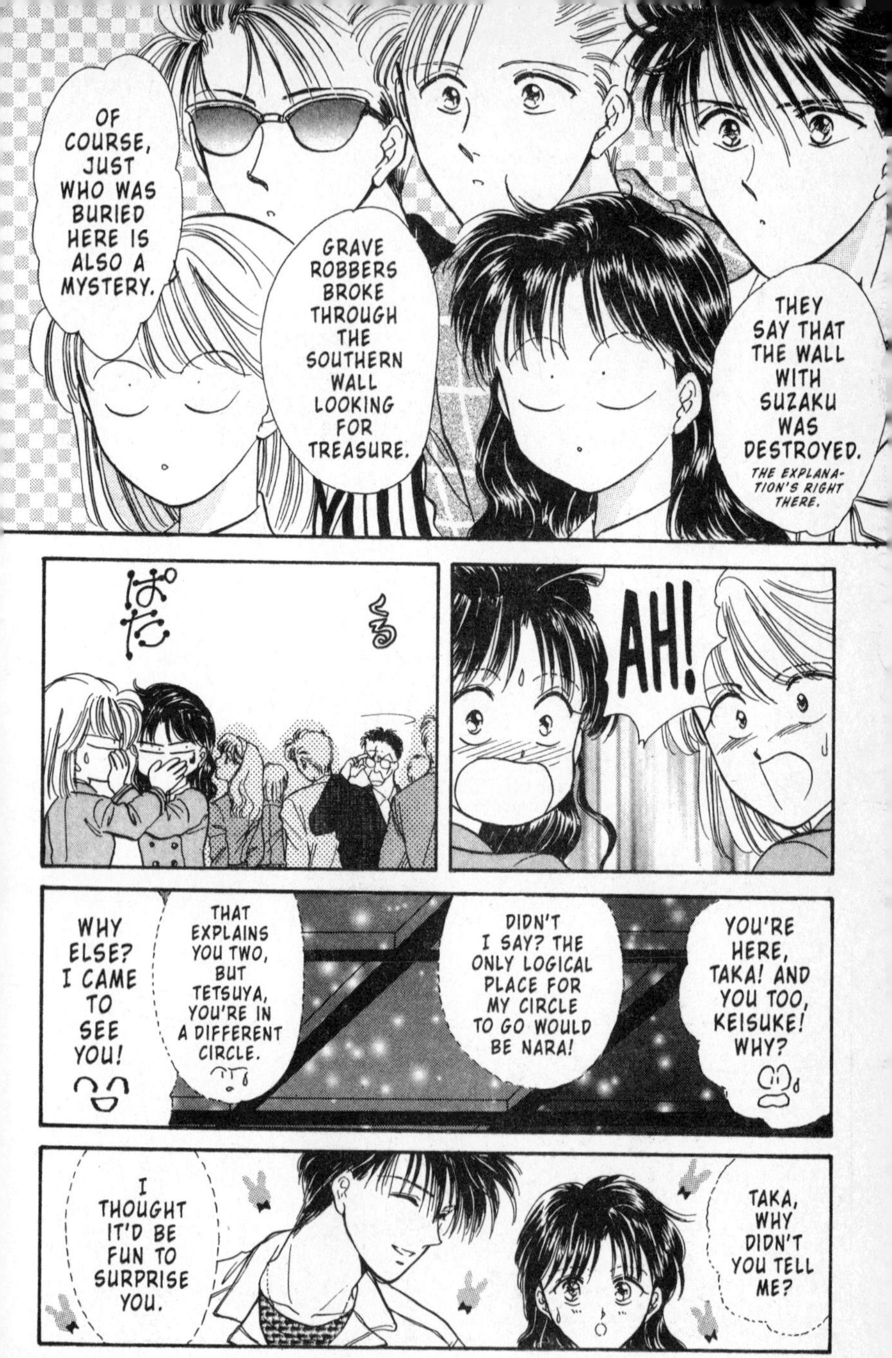
THEY SAY THAT THE WALL WITH SUZAKU WAS DESTROYED.
THE EXPLANATION'S RIGHT THERE.
GRAVE ROBBERS BROKE THROUGH THE SOUTHERN WALL LOOKING FOR TREASURE.
OF COURSE, JUST WHO WAS BURIED HERE IS ALSO A MYSTERY.
AH!
ぱた
くる
YOU'RE HERE, TAKA! AND YOU TOO, KEISUKE! WHY?
DIDN'T I SAY? THE ONLY LOGICAL PLACE FOR MY CIRCLE TO GO WOULD BE NARA!
THAT EXPLAINS YOU TWO, BUT TETSUYA, YOU'RE IN A DIFFERENT CIRCLE.
WHY ELSE? I CAME TO SEE YOU!
TAKA, WHY DIDN'T YOU TELL ME?
I THOUGHT IT'D BE FUN TO SURPRISE YOU.

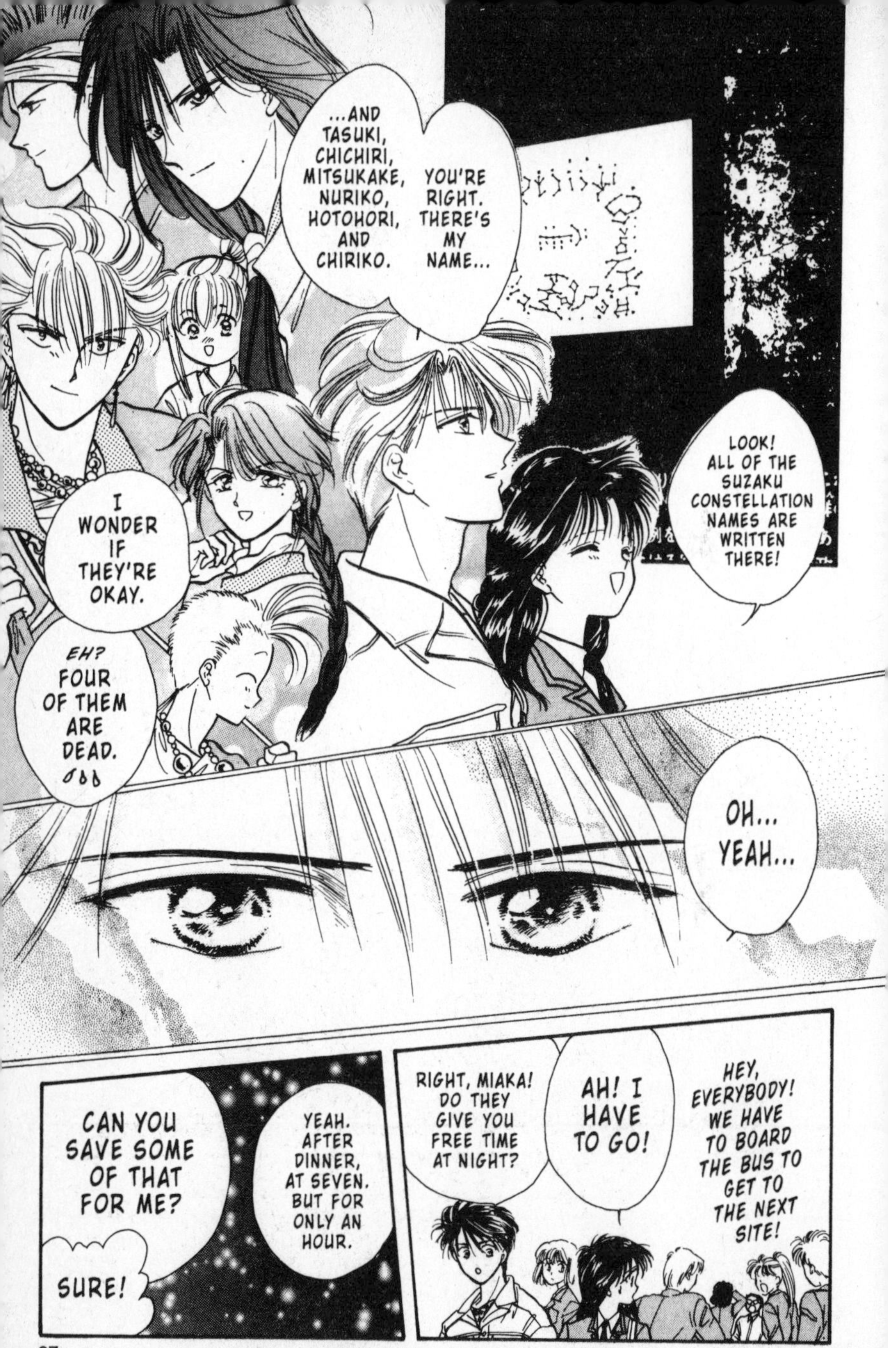
LOOK! ALL OF THE SUZAKU CONSTELLATION NAMES ARE WRITTEN THERE!
YOU'RE RIGHT. THERE'S MY NAME...
...AND TASUKI, CHICHIRI, MITSUKAKE, NURIKO, HOTOHORI, AND CHIRIKO.
I WONDER IF THEY'RE OKAY.
EH? FOUR OF THEM ARE DEAD.
OH... YEAH...
HEY, EVERYBODY! WE HAVE TO BOARD THE BUS TO GET TO THE NEXT SITE!
AH! I HAVE TO GO!
RIGHT, MIAKA! DO THEY GIVE YOU FREE TIME AT NIGHT?
YEAH. AFTER DINNER, AT SEVEN. BUT FOR ONLY AN HOUR.
CAN YOU SAVE SOME OF THAT FOR ME?
SURE!

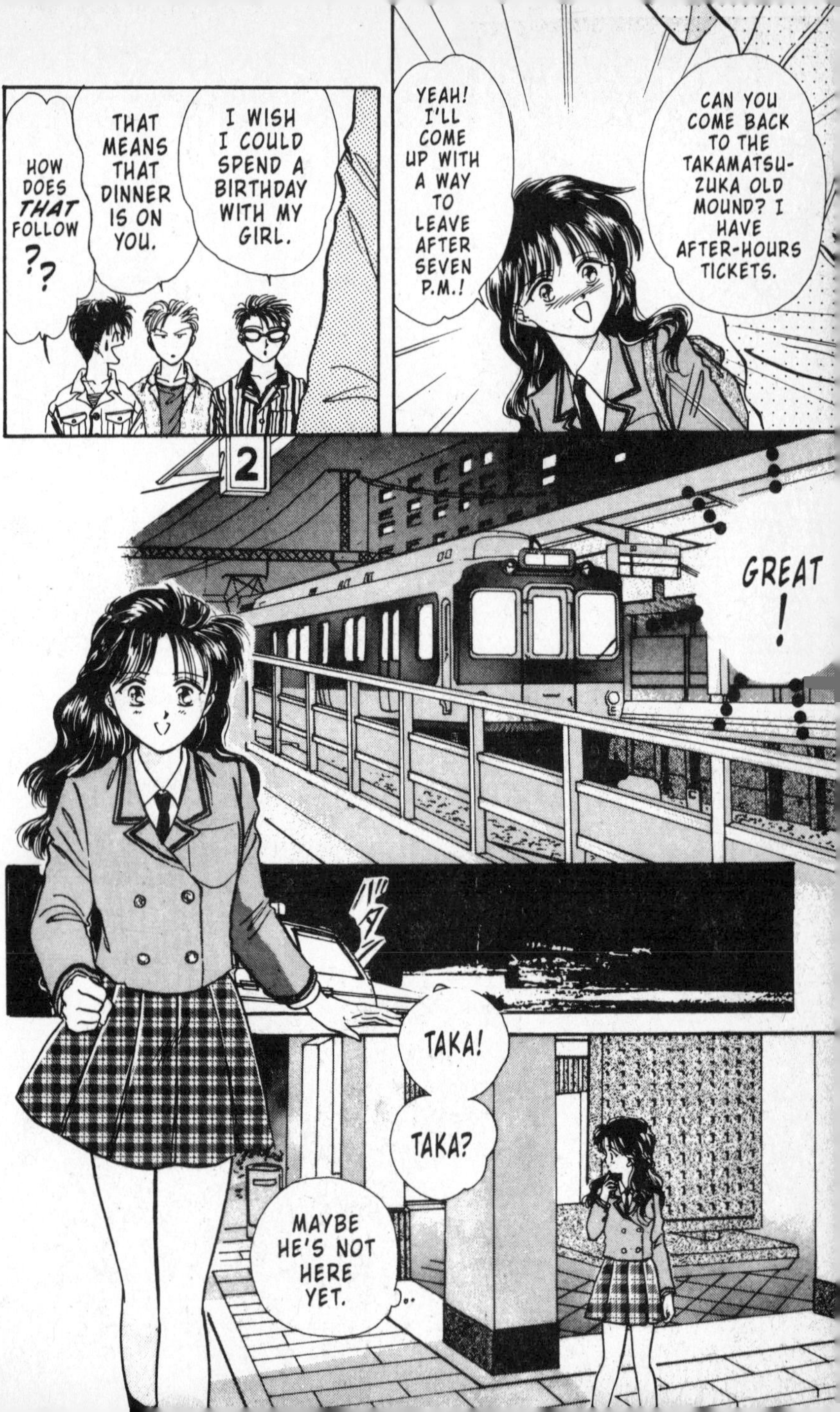
CAN YOU COME BACK TO THE TAKAMATSU-ZUKA OLD MOUND? I HAVE AFTER-HOURS TICKETS.
YEAH! I'LL COME UP WITH A WAY TO LEAVE AFTER SEVEN P.M.!
I WISH I COULD SPEND A BIRTHDAY WITH MY GIRL.
THAT MEANS THAT DINNER IS ON YOU.
HOW DOES *THAT* FOLLOW ??
2
GREAT!
TAKA!
TAKA?
MAYBE HE'S NOT HERE YET.

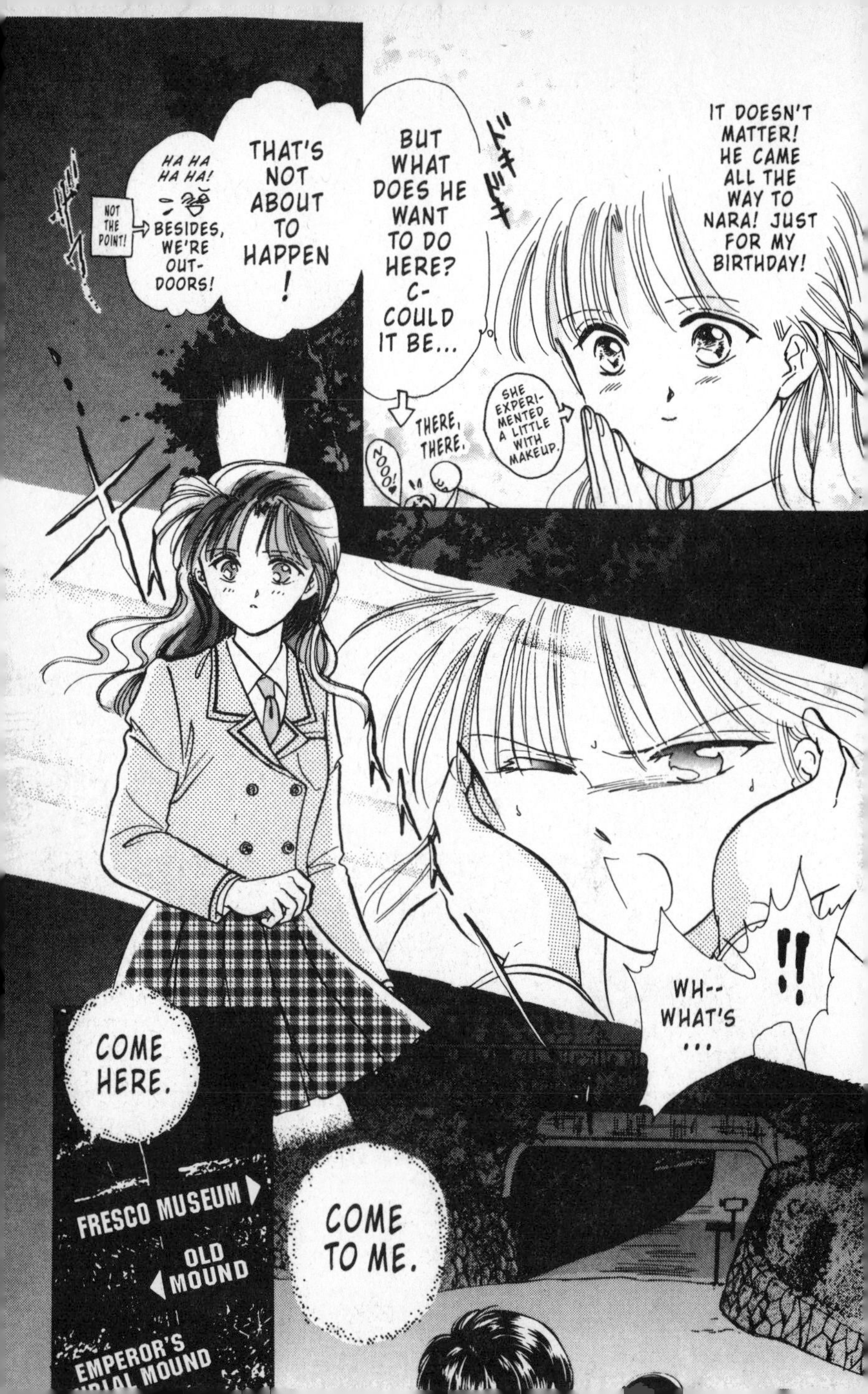
IT DOESN'T MATTER! HE CAME ALL THE WAY TO NARA! JUST FOR MY BIRTHDAY!
SHE EXPERIMENTED A LITTLE WITH MAKEUP.
ドキドキ
BUT WHAT DOES HE WANT TO DO HERE? C-COULD IT BE...
THERE, THERE.
NOOO!
THAT'S NOT ABOUT TO HAPPEN!
HA HA HA HA!
BESIDES, WE'RE OUT-DOORS!
NOT THE POINT!
!!
WH-- WHAT'S...
COME HERE.
COME TO ME.
FRESCO MUSEUM
OLD MOUND
EMPEROR'S
URIAL MOUND

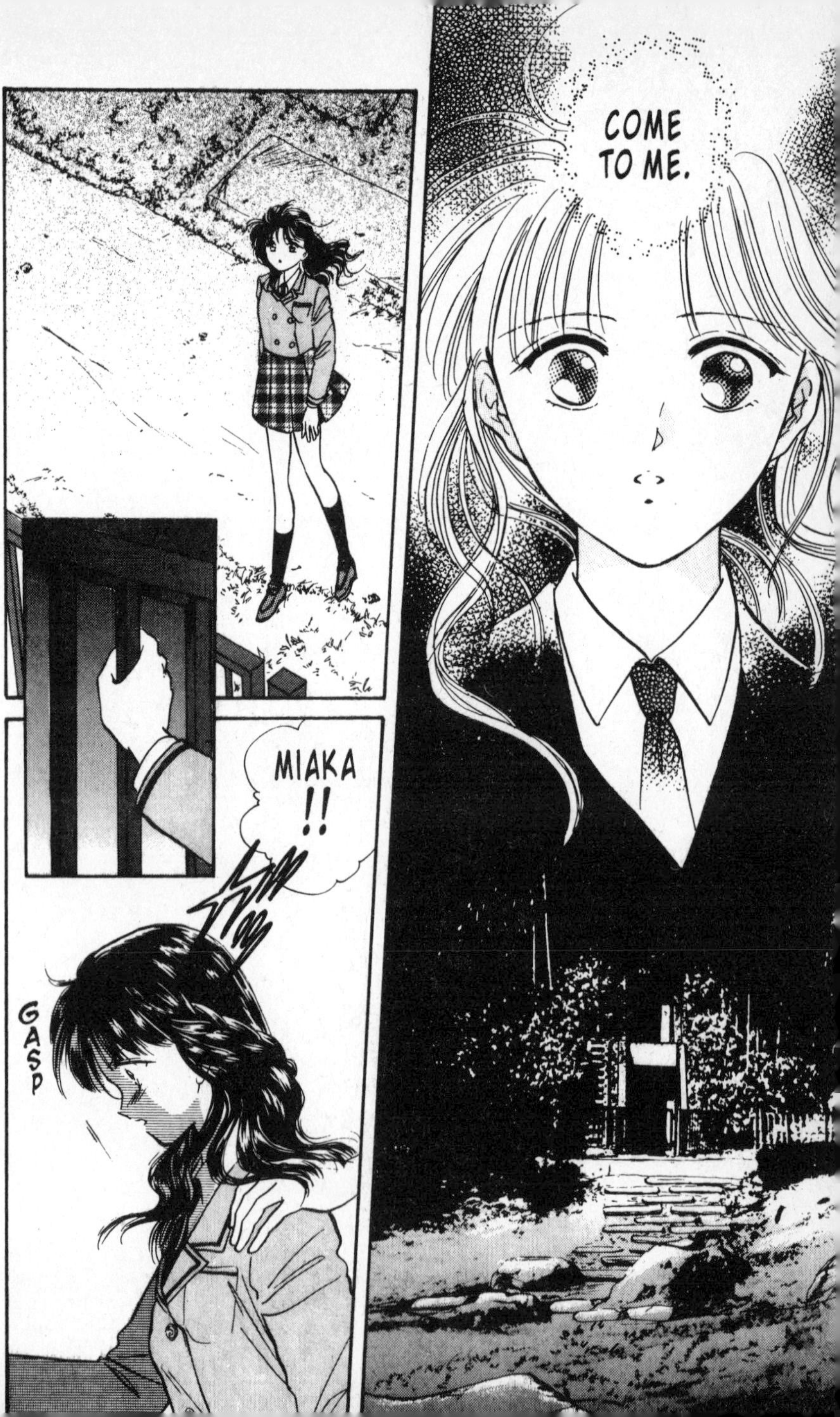
COME TO ME.
MIAKA !!
GASP

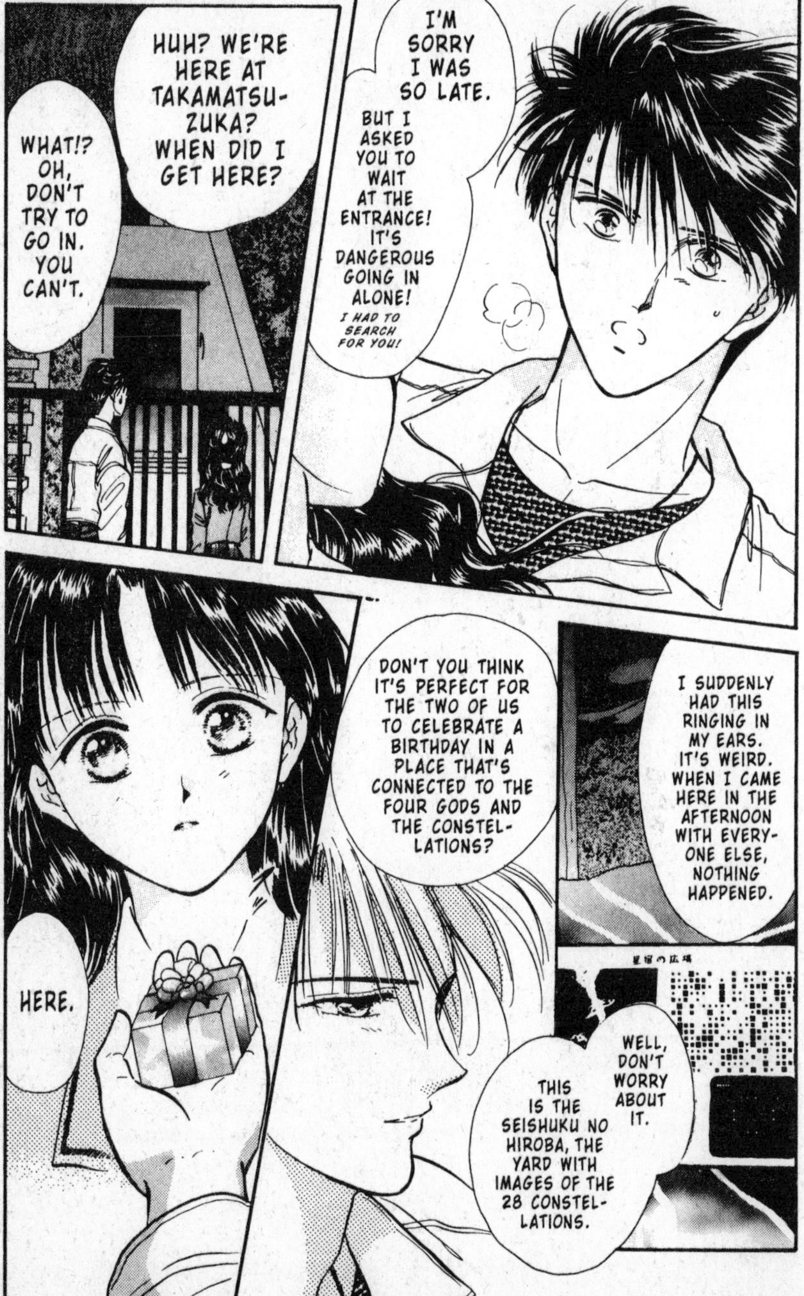
I'M SORRY I WAS SO LATE.
BUT I ASKED YOU TO WAIT AT THE ENTRANCE! IT'S DANGEROUS GOING IN ALONE!
I HAD TO SEARCH FOR YOU!
HUH? WE'RE HERE AT TAKAMATSU-ZUKA? WHEN DID I GET HERE?
WHAT!? OH, DON'T TRY TO GO IN. YOU CAN'T.
I SUDDENLY HAD THIS RINGING IN MY EARS. IT'S WEIRD. WHEN I CAME HERE IN THE AFTERNOON WITH EVERY-ONE ELSE, NOTHING HAPPENED.
星宿の広場
WELL, DON'T WORRY ABOUT IT.
THIS IS THE SEISHUKU NO HIROBA, THE YARD WITH IMAGES OF THE 28 CONSTEL-LATIONS.
DON'T YOU THINK IT'S PERFECT FOR THE TWO OF US TO CELEBRATE A BIRTHDAY IN A PLACE THAT'S CONNECTED TO THE FOUR GODS AND THE CONSTEL-LATIONS?
HERE.

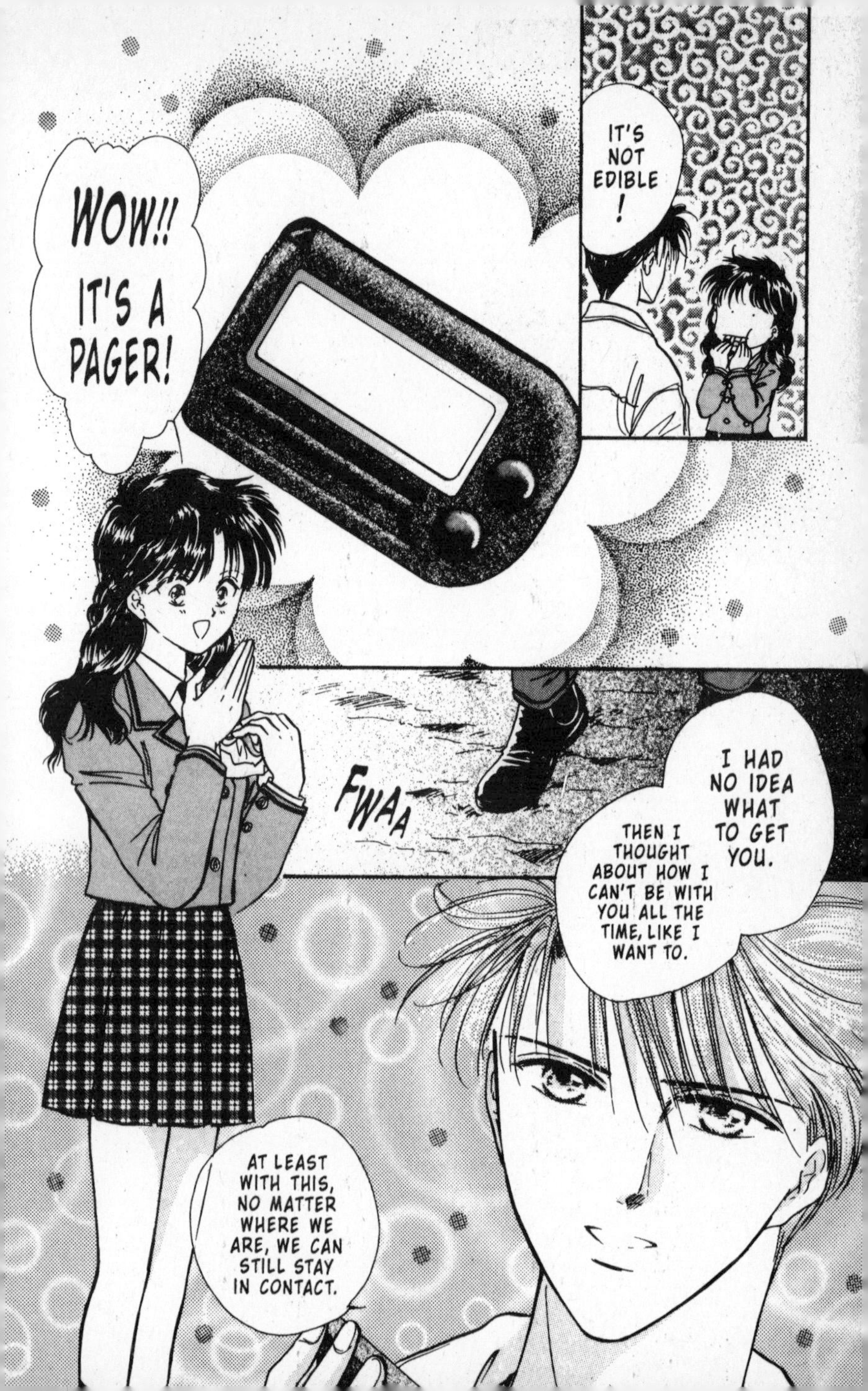
IT'S NOT EDIBLE!
WOW!! IT'S A PAGER!
FWAAA
I HAD NO IDEA WHAT TO GET YOU.
THEN I THOUGHT ABOUT HOW I CAN'T BE WITH YOU ALL THE TIME, LIKE I WANT TO.
AT LEAST WITH THIS, NO MATTER WHERE WE ARE, WE CAN STILL STAY IN CONTACT.

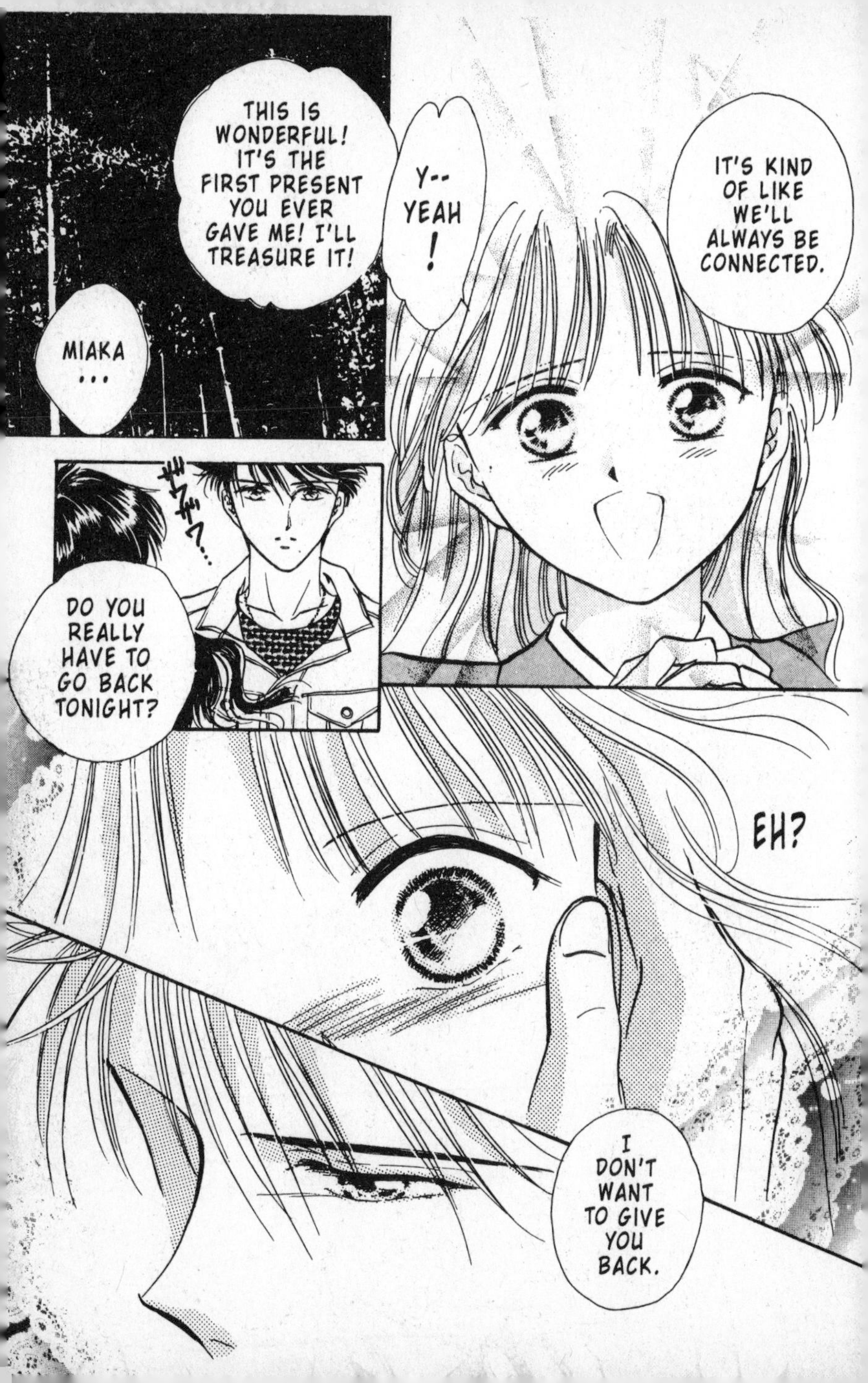
IT'S KIND OF LIKE WE'LL ALWAYS BE CONNECTED.
Y-- YEAH !
THIS IS WONDERFUL! IT'S THE FIRST PRESENT YOU EVER GAVE ME! I'LL TREASURE IT!
MIAKA ...
DO YOU REALLY HAVE TO GO BACK TONIGHT?
EH?
I DON'T WANT TO GIVE YOU BACK.

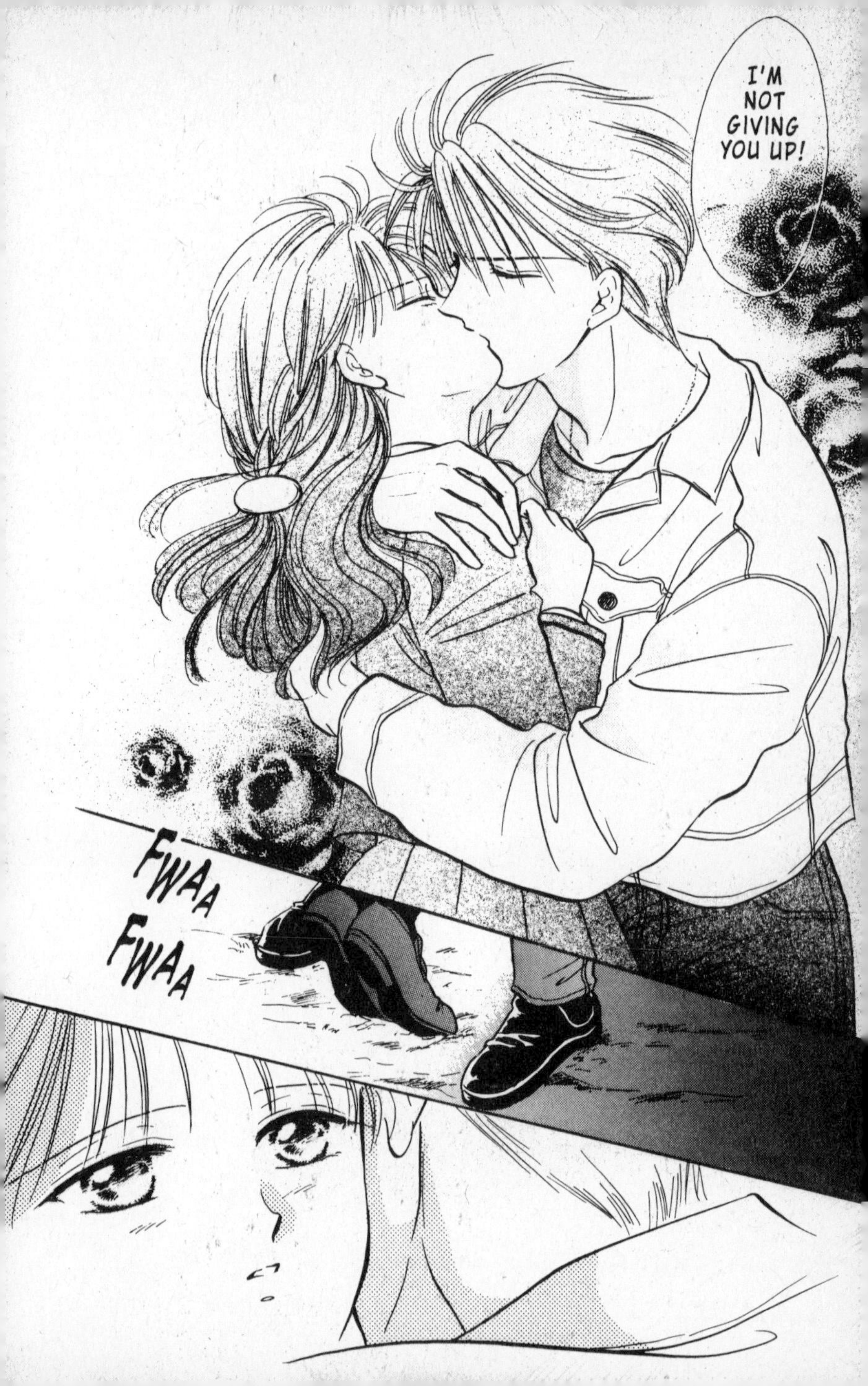
I'M NOT GIVING YOU UP!
FWAA FWAA

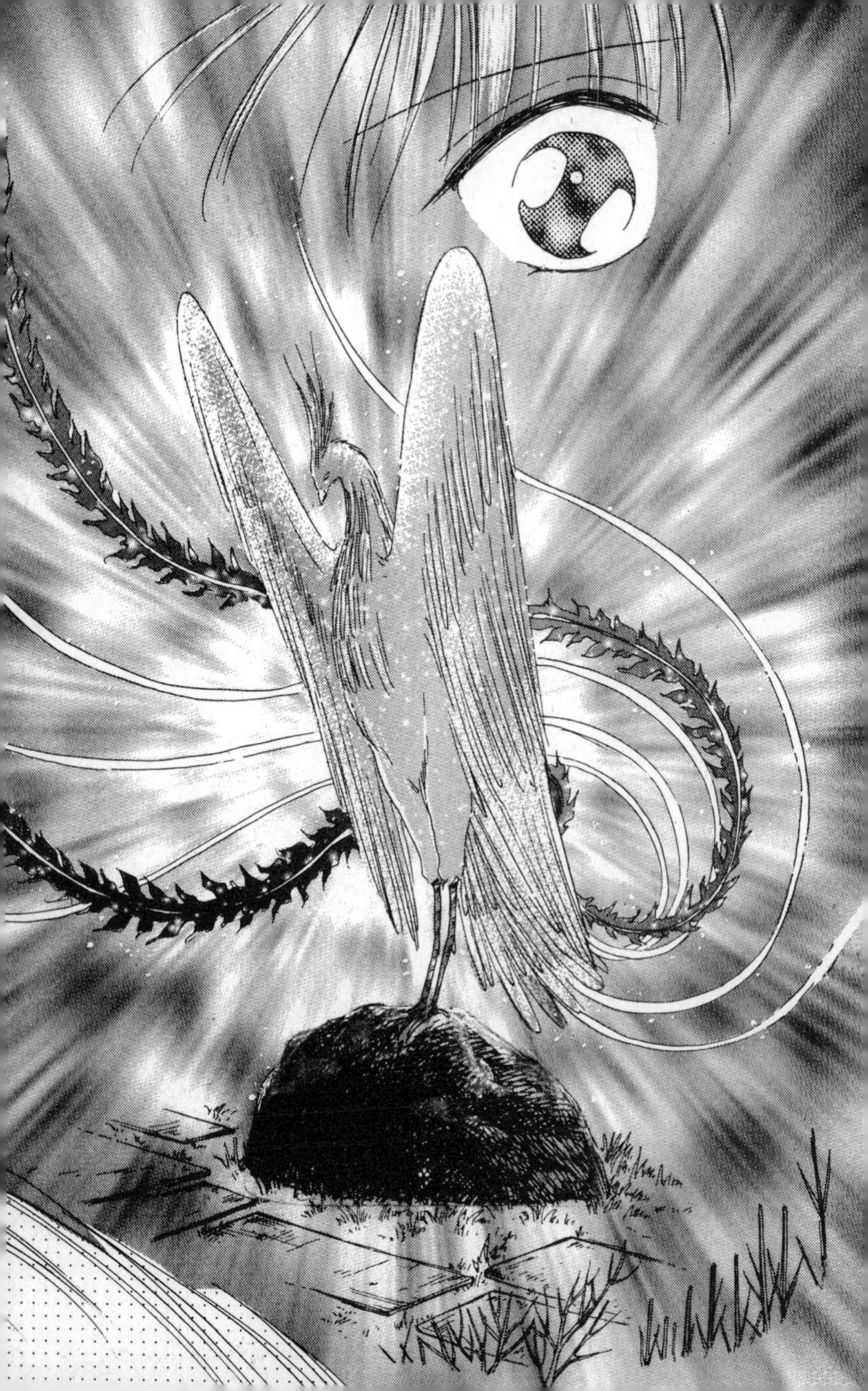

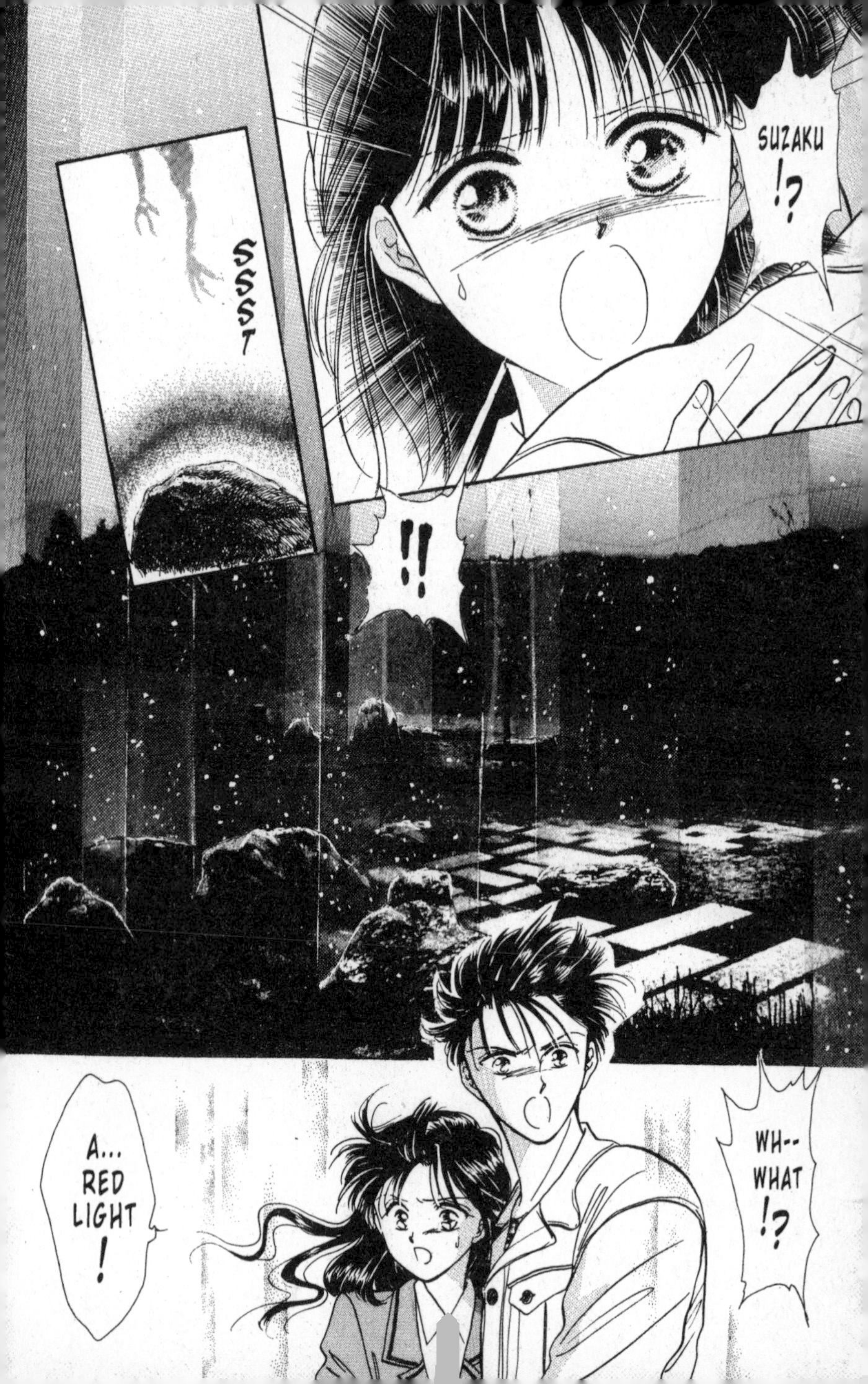
SUZAKU !?
SSST
!!
WH-- WHAT !?
A... RED LIGHT !

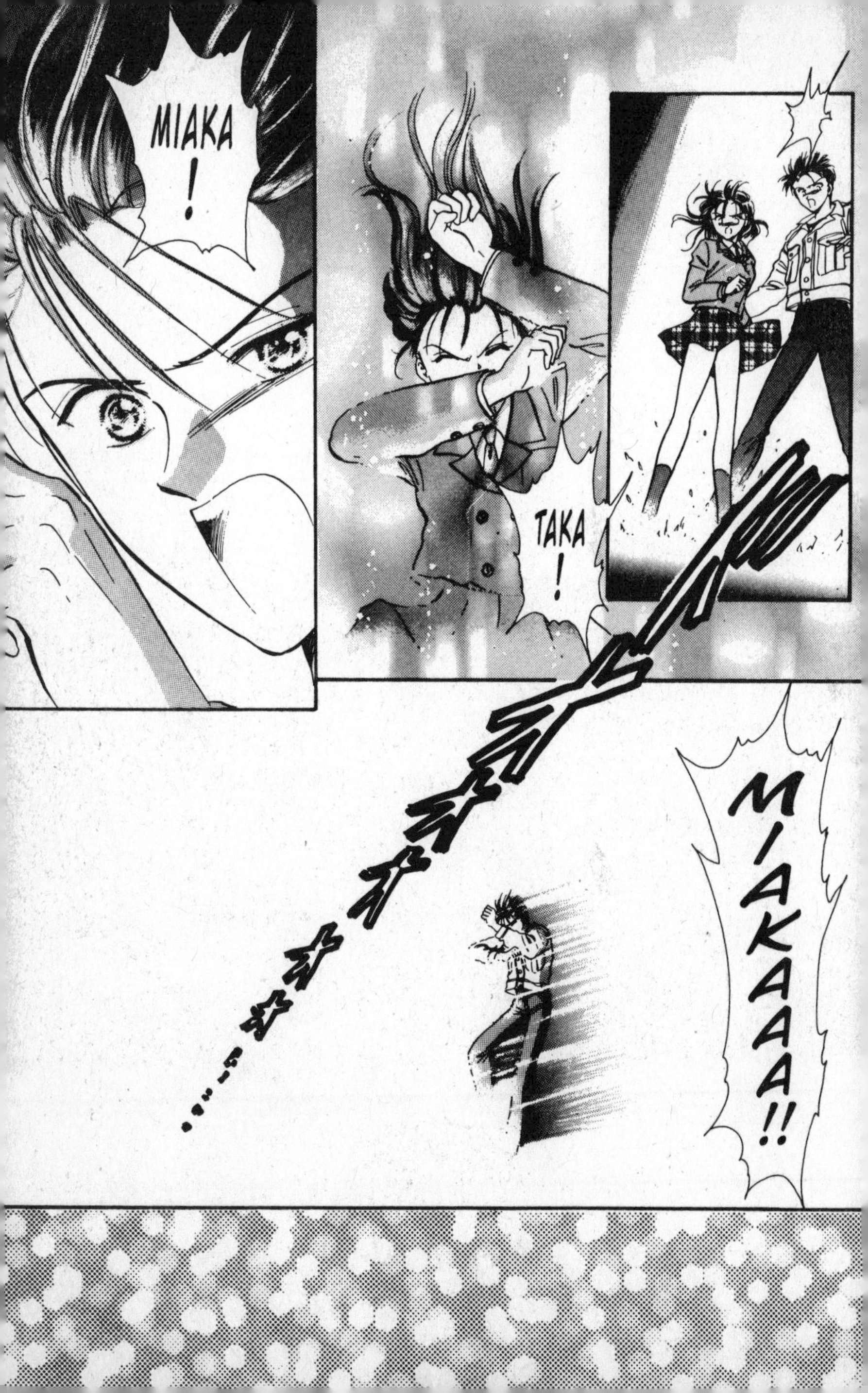
TAKA!
MIAKA!
MIAKAAA!!

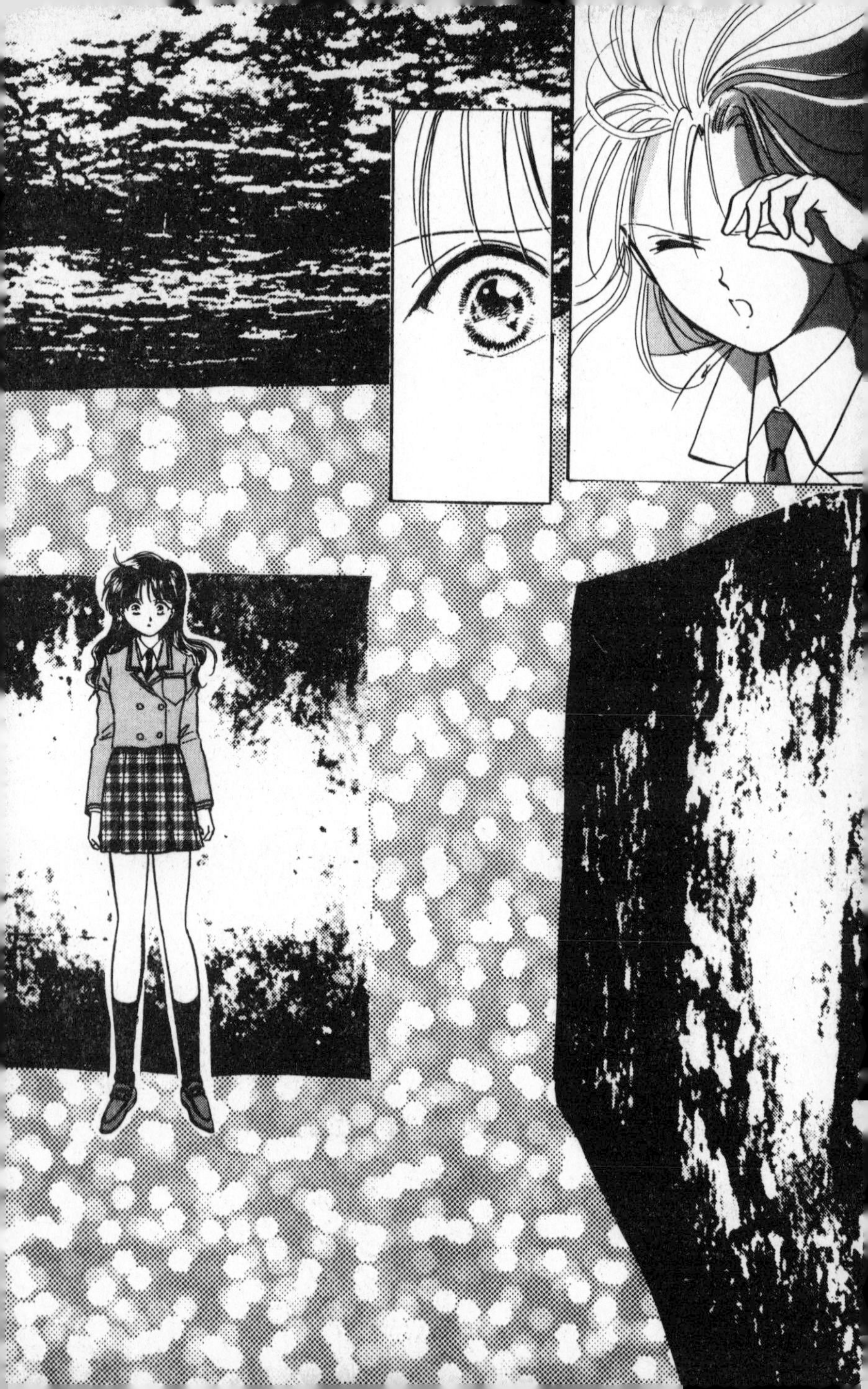

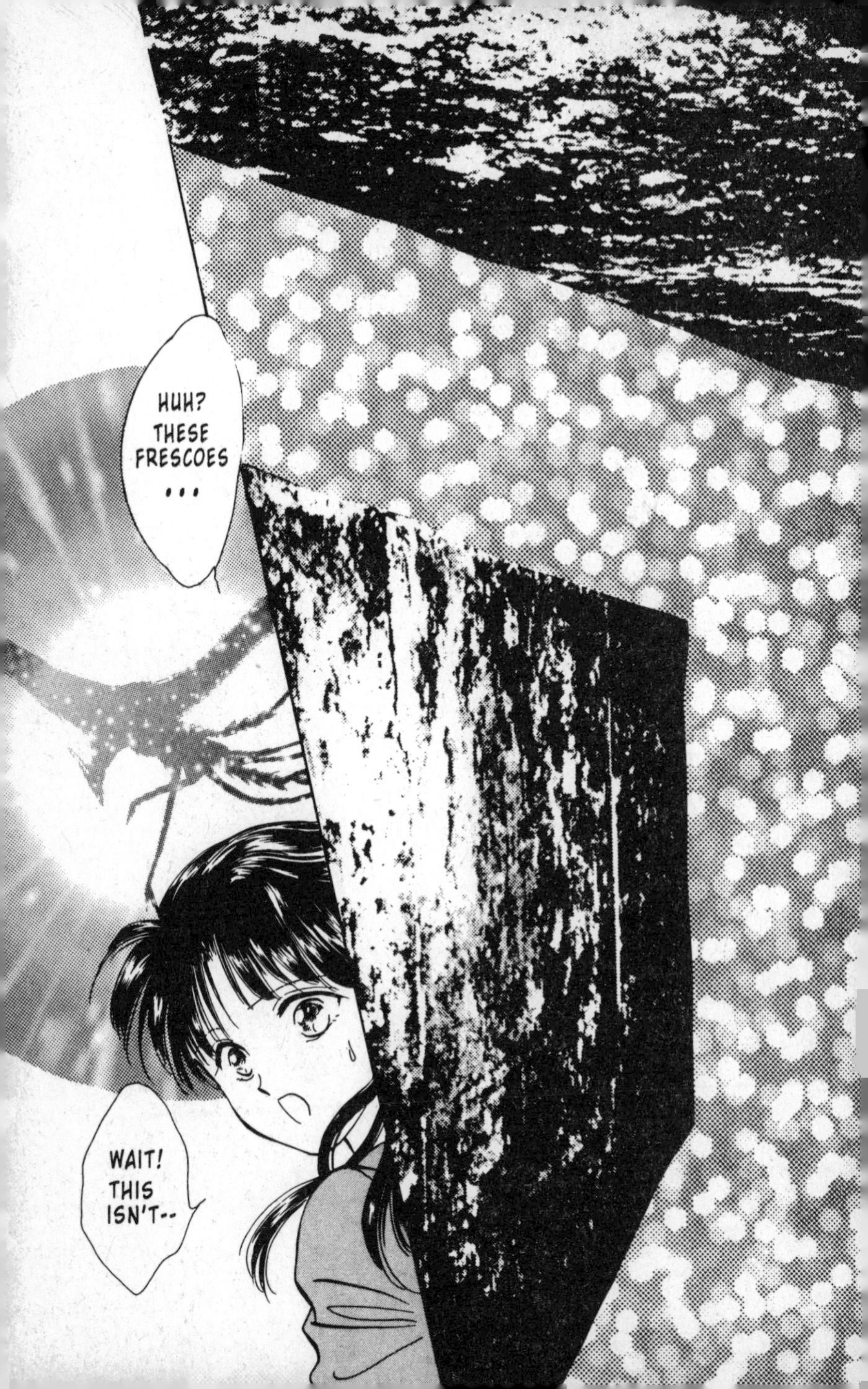
HUH? THESE FRESCOES ...
WAIT! THIS ISN'T--

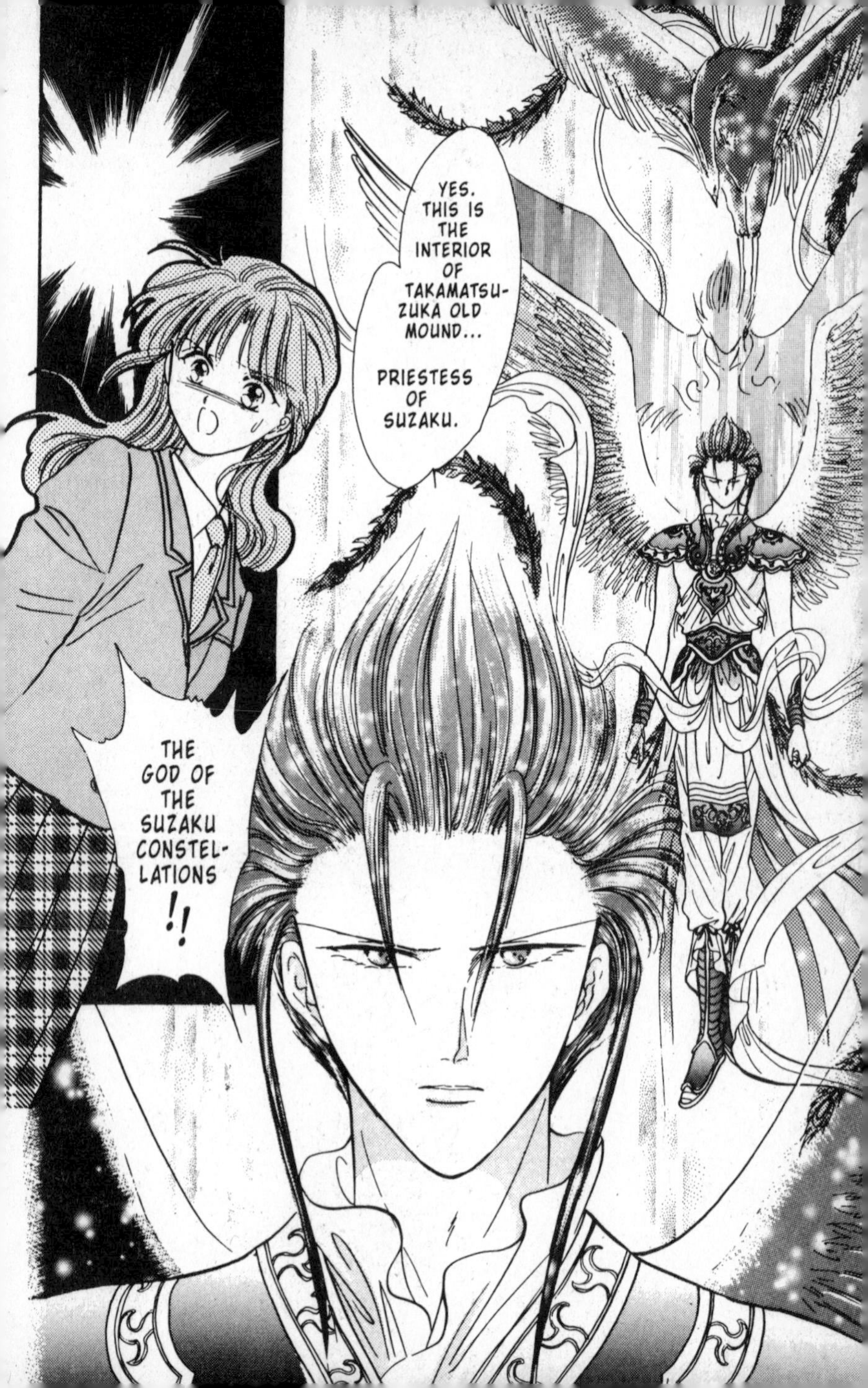
YES. THIS IS THE INTERIOR OF TAKAMATSU-ZUKA OLD MOUND...
PRIESTESS OF SUZAKU.
THE GOD OF THE SUZAKU CONSTEL-LATIONS !!

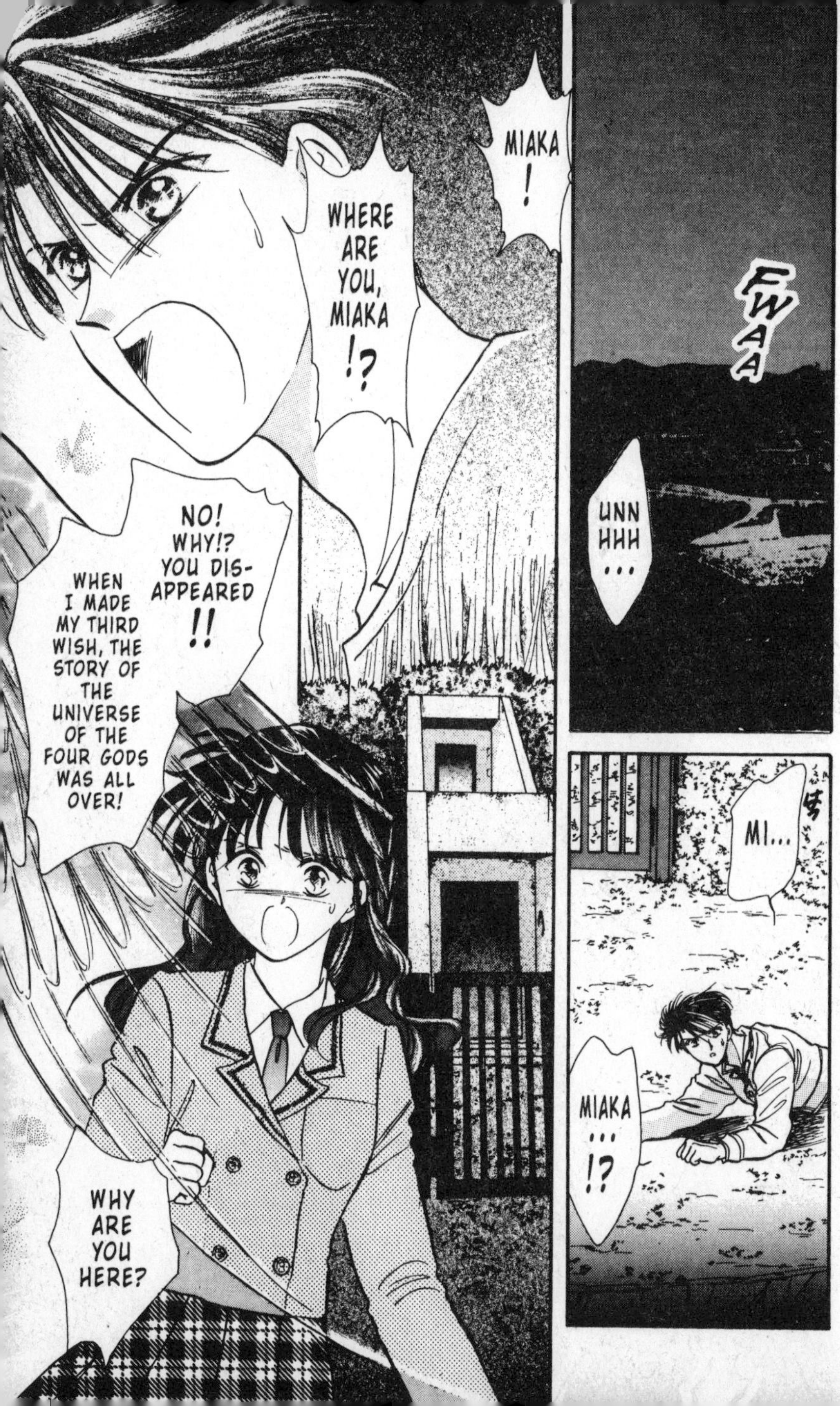
FWAA
UNNHHH...
MI...
MIAKA...!?
MIAKA!
WHERE ARE YOU, MIAKA!?
NO! WHY!? YOU DISAPPEARED!!
WHEN I MADE MY THIRD WISH, THE STORY OF THE UNIVERSE OF THE FOUR GODS WAS ALL OVER!
WHY ARE YOU HERE?

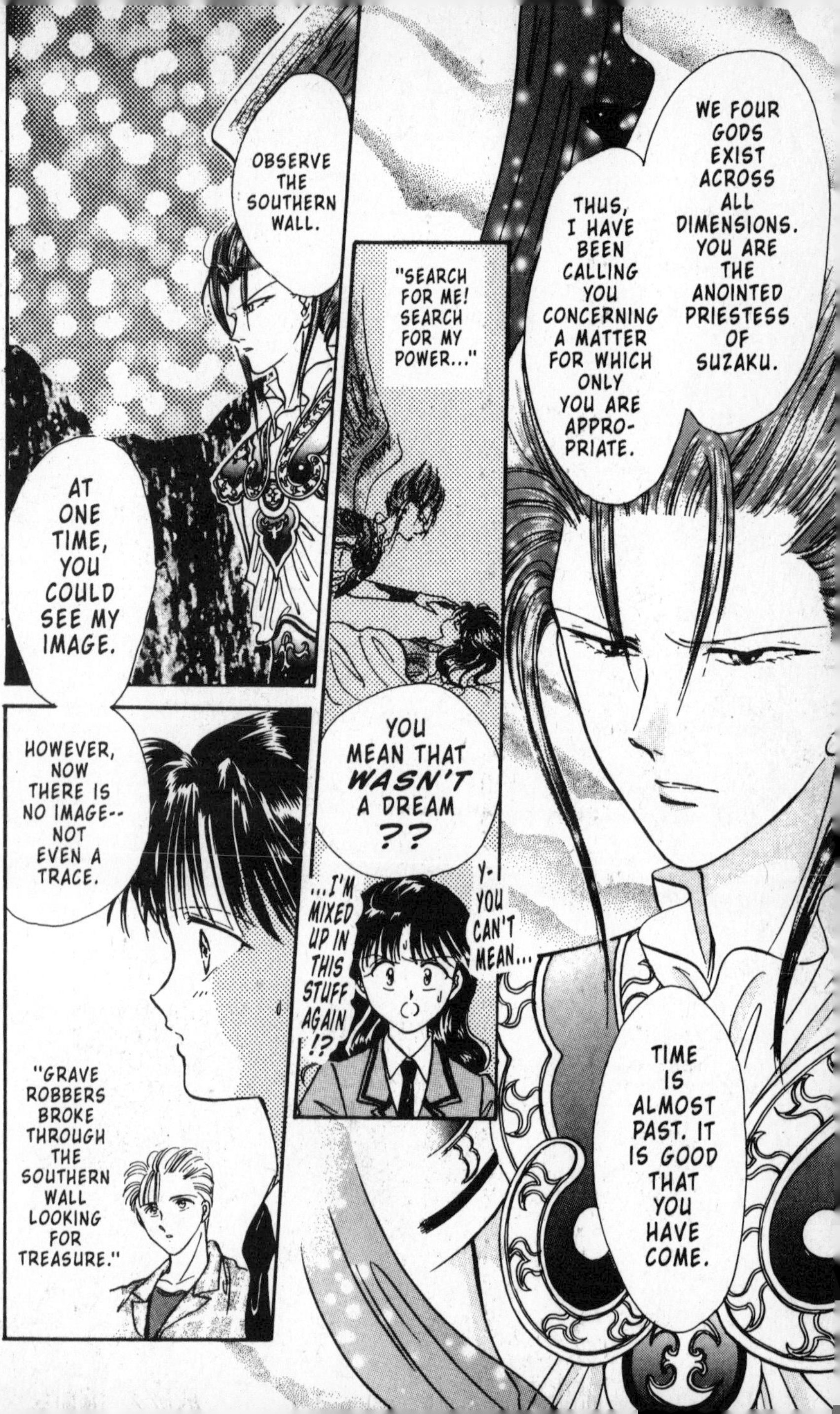
WE FOUR GODS EXIST ACROSS ALL DIMENSIONS. YOU ARE THE ANOINTED PRIESTESS OF SUZAKU.
THUS, I HAVE BEEN CALLING YOU CONCERNING A MATTER FOR WHICH ONLY YOU ARE APPRO-PRIATE.
TIME IS ALMOST PAST. IT IS GOOD THAT YOU HAVE COME.
"SEARCH FOR ME! SEARCH FOR MY POWER..."
OBSERVE THE SOUTHERN WALL.
AT ONE TIME, YOU COULD SEE MY IMAGE.
YOU MEAN THAT ***WASN'T*** A DREAM ??
Y-YOU CAN'T MEAN...
...I'M MIXED UP IN THIS STUFF AGAIN !?
HOWEVER, NOW THERE IS NO IMAGE-- NOT EVEN A TRACE.
"GRAVE ROBBERS BROKE THROUGH THE SOUTHERN WALL LOOKING FOR TREASURE."

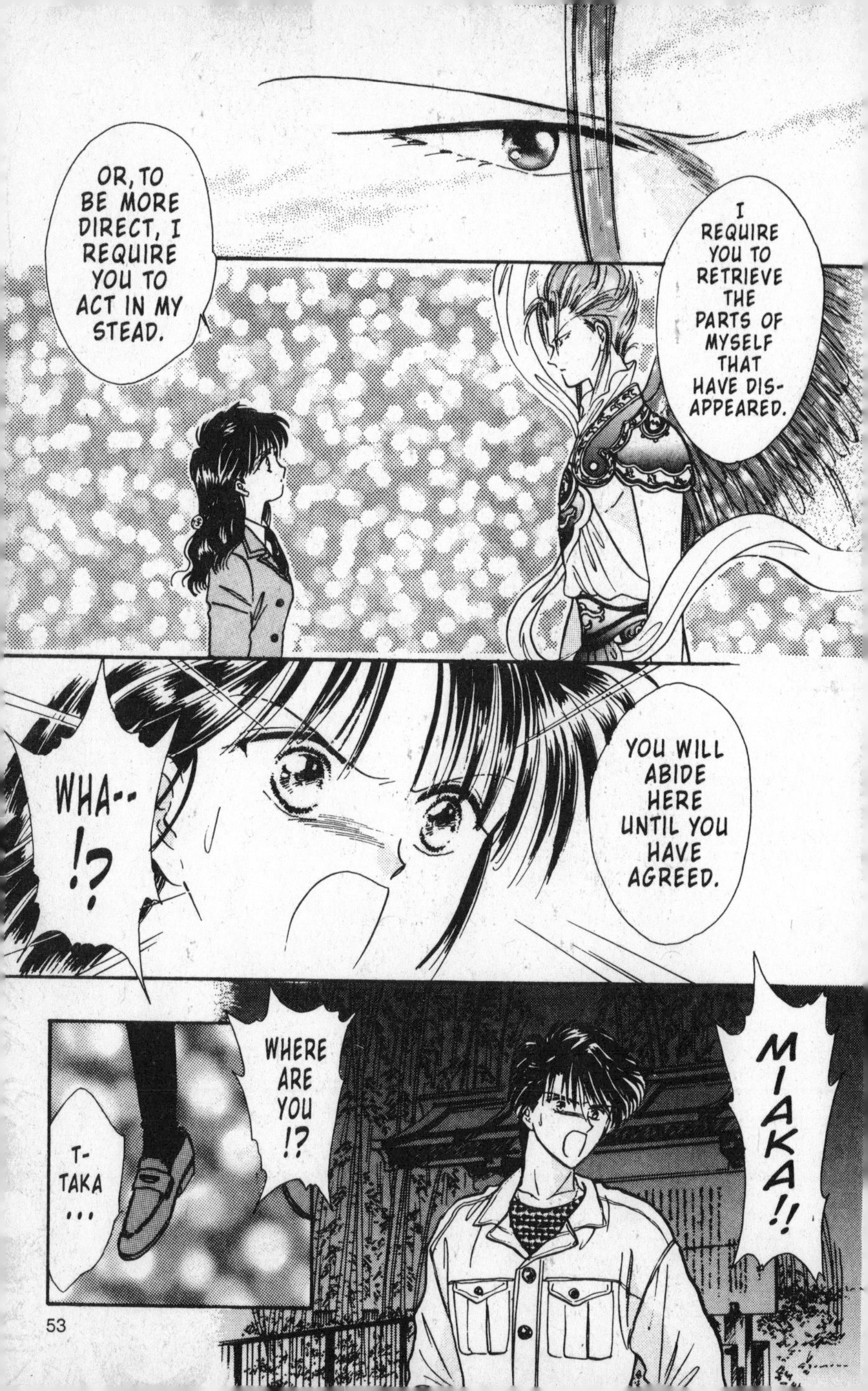
I REQUIRE YOU TO RETRIEVE THE PARTS OF MYSELF THAT HAVE DIS-APPEARED.
OR, TO BE MORE DIRECT, I REQUIRE YOU TO ACT IN MY STEAD.
YOU WILL ABIDE HERE UNTIL YOU HAVE AGREED.
WHA-- !?
MIAKA!!
WHERE ARE YOU !?
T-TAKA...

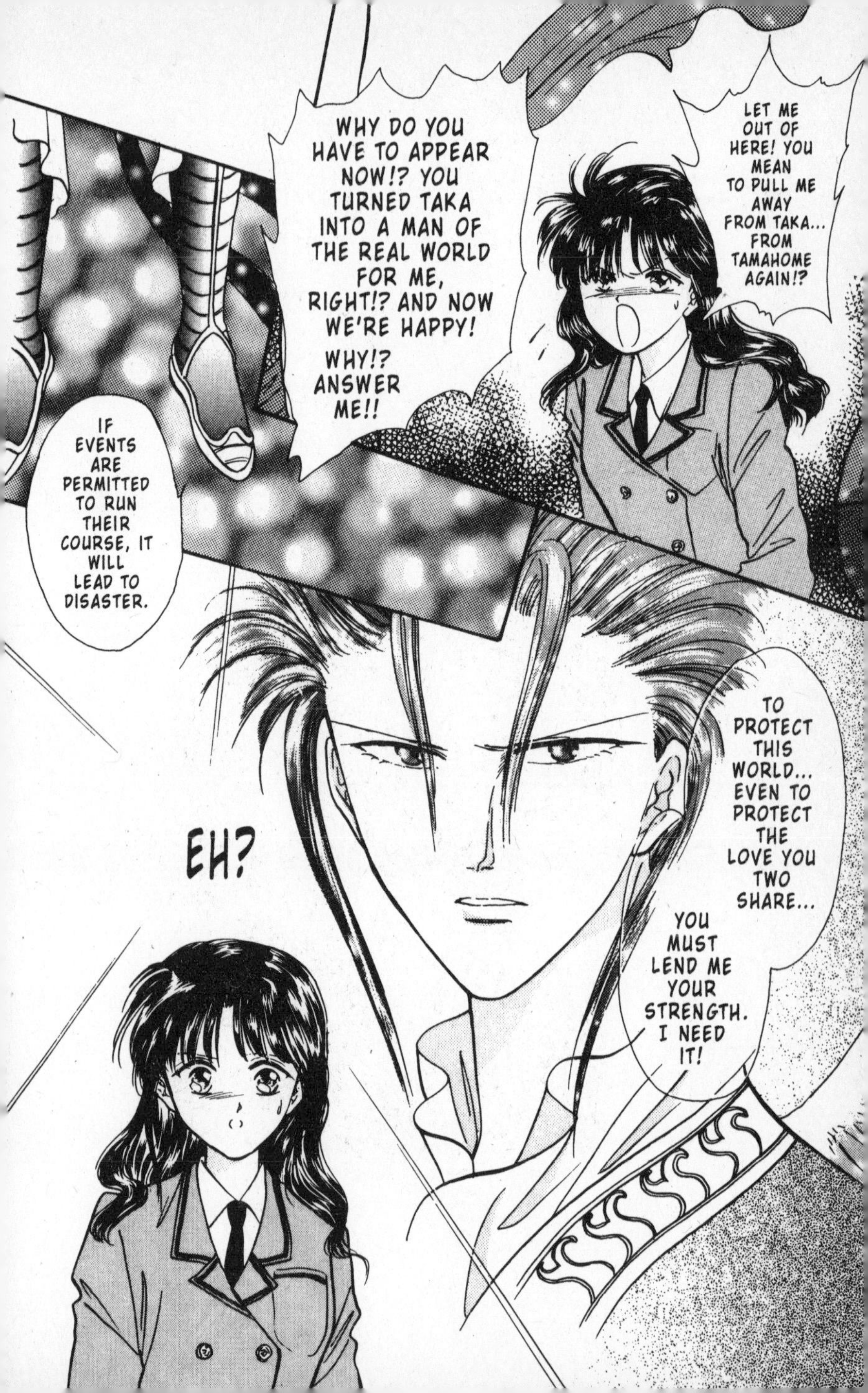
LET ME OUT OF HERE! YOU MEAN TO PULL ME AWAY FROM TAKA... FROM TAMAHOME AGAIN!?
WHY DO YOU HAVE TO APPEAR NOW!? YOU TURNED TAKA INTO A MAN OF THE REAL WORLD FOR ME, RIGHT!? AND NOW WE'RE HAPPY!
WHY!? ANSWER ME!!
IF EVENTS ARE PERMITTED TO RUN THEIR COURSE, IT WILL LEAD TO DISASTER.
TO PROTECT THIS WORLD... EVEN TO PROTECT THE LOVE YOU TWO SHARE...
YOU MUST LEND ME YOUR STRENGTH. I NEED IT!
EH?

ふしぎ悪戯

FUSHIGI AKUGI

THE MALICIOUS PLAY (11)

TITLED: YOU FOOL!

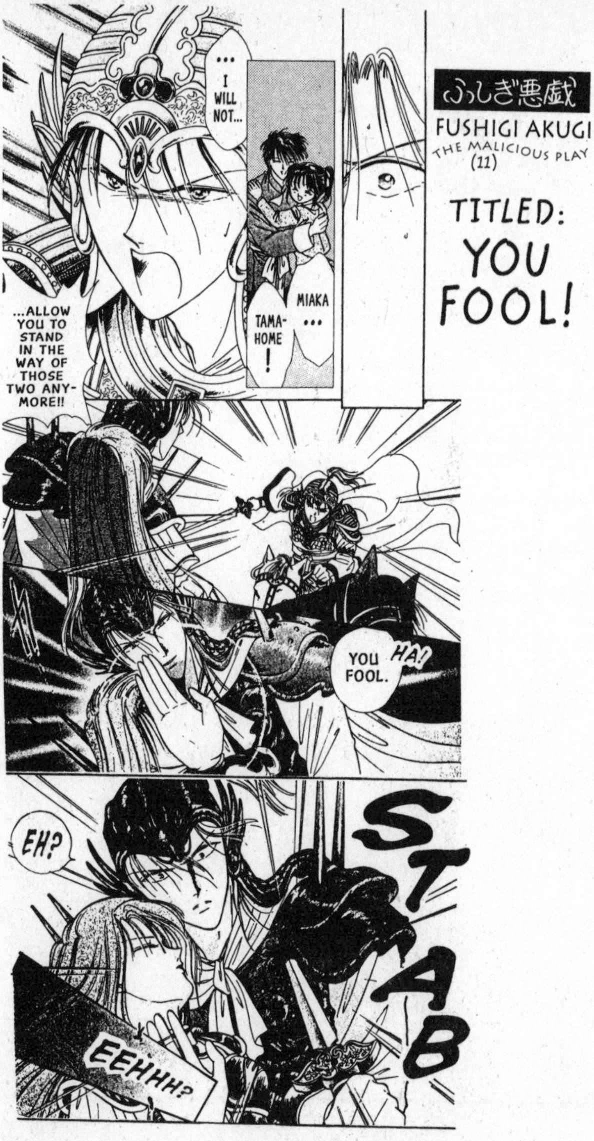
MIAKA...
TAMA-HOME!
...I WILL NOT...
...ALLOW YOU TO STAND IN THE WAY OF THOSE TWO ANY-MORE!!
HA!
YOU FOOL.
STAB
EH?
EEHHH?

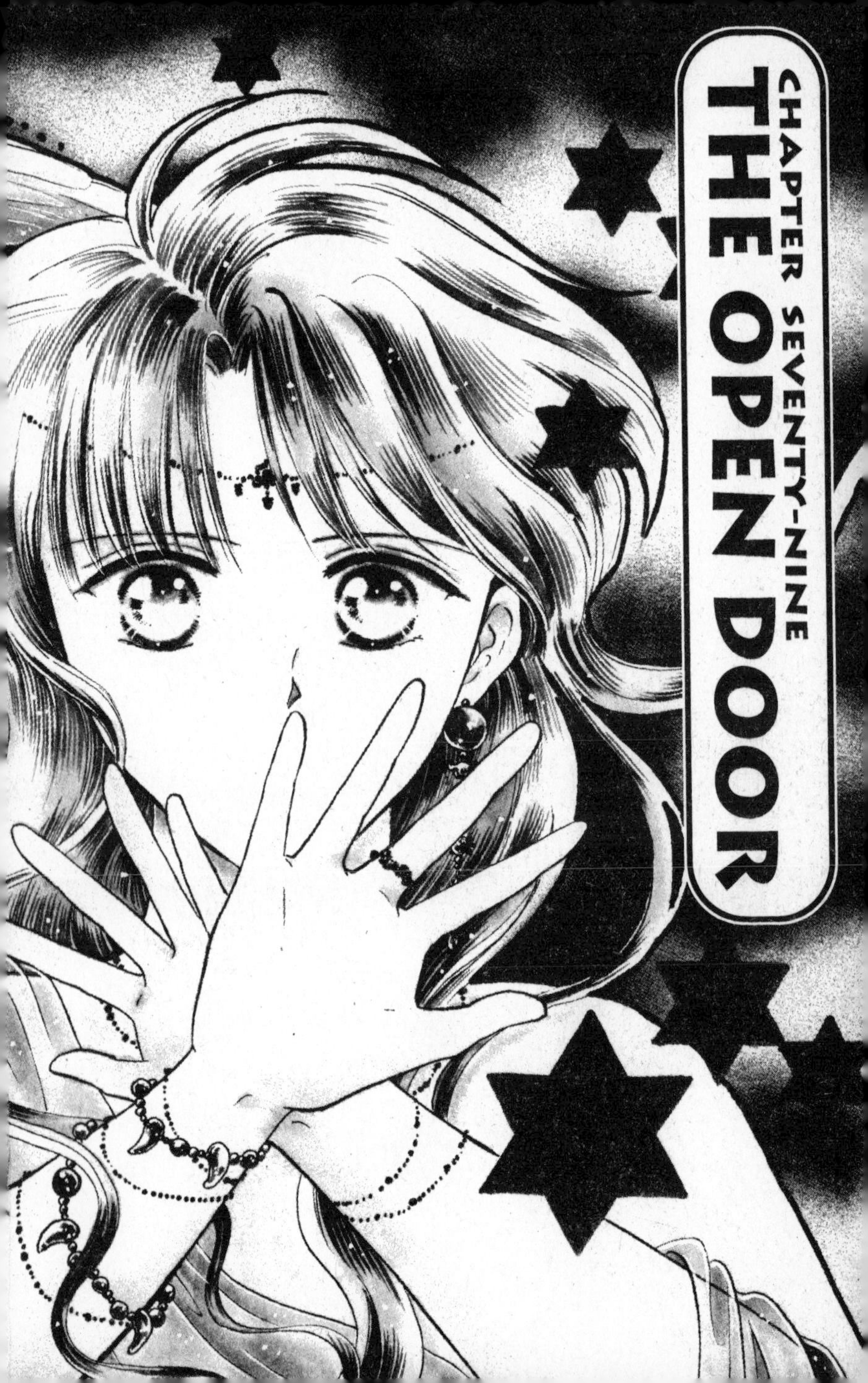
CHAPTER SEVENTY-NINE
THE OPEN DOOR

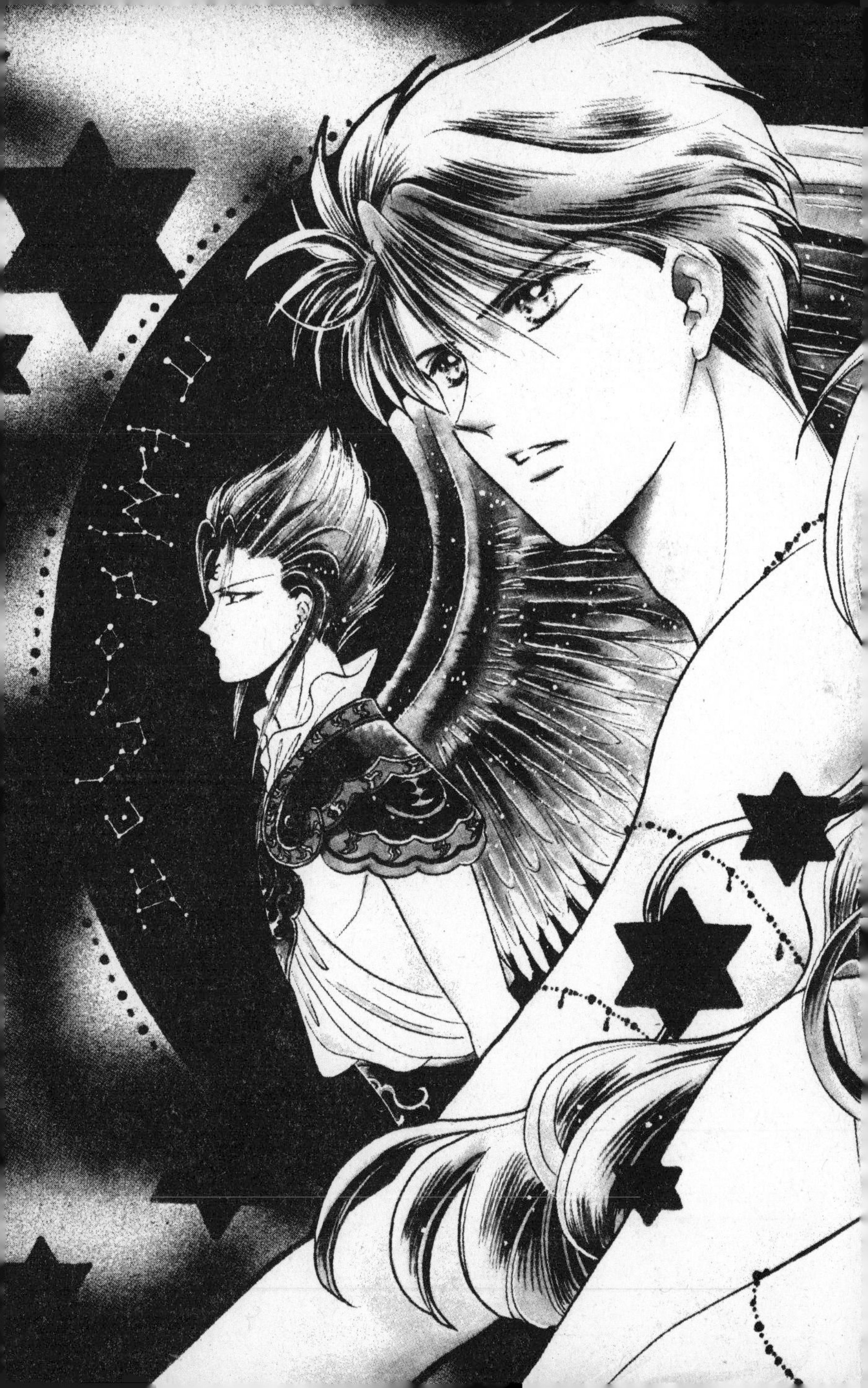

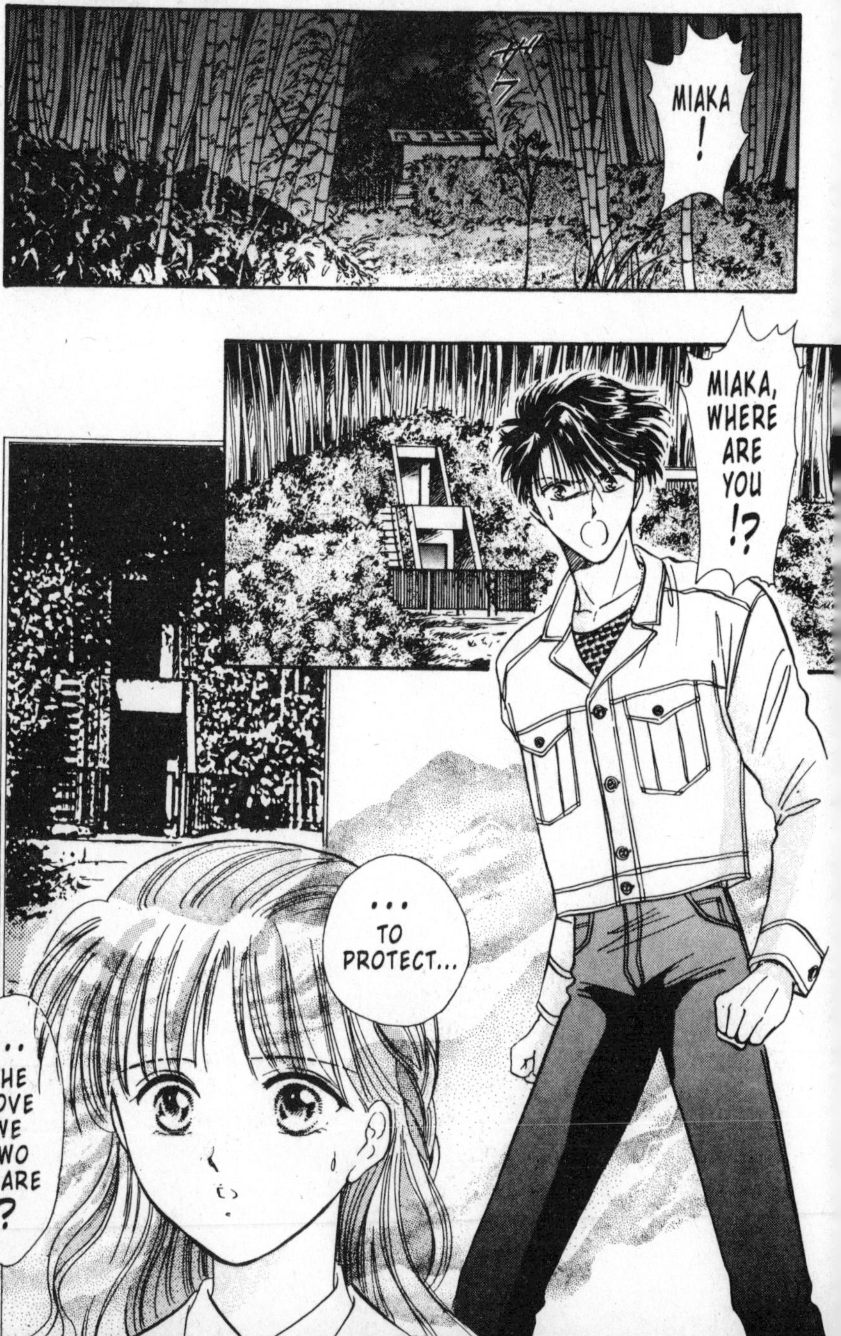
MIAKA!
MIAKA, WHERE ARE YOU!?
...TO PROTECT...
...THE LOVE WE TWO SHARE?

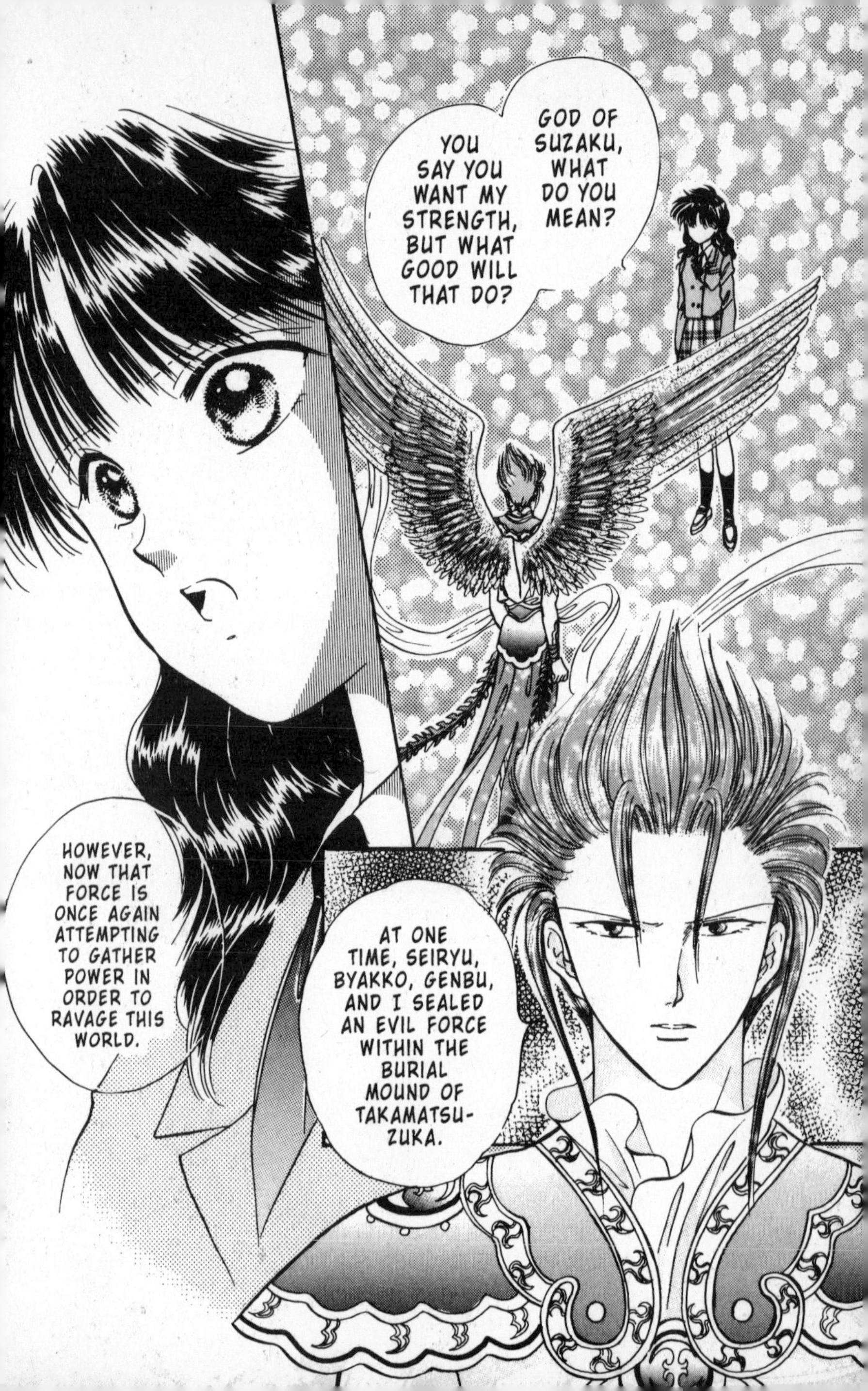
GOD OF SUZAKU, WHAT DO YOU MEAN?
YOU SAY YOU WANT MY STRENGTH, BUT WHAT GOOD WILL THAT DO?
AT ONE TIME, SEIRYU, BYAKKO, GENBU, AND I SEALED AN EVIL FORCE WITHIN THE BURIAL MOUND OF TAKAMATSU-ZUKA.
HOWEVER, NOW THAT FORCE IS ONCE AGAIN ATTEMPTING TO GATHER POWER IN ORDER TO RAVAGE THIS WORLD.

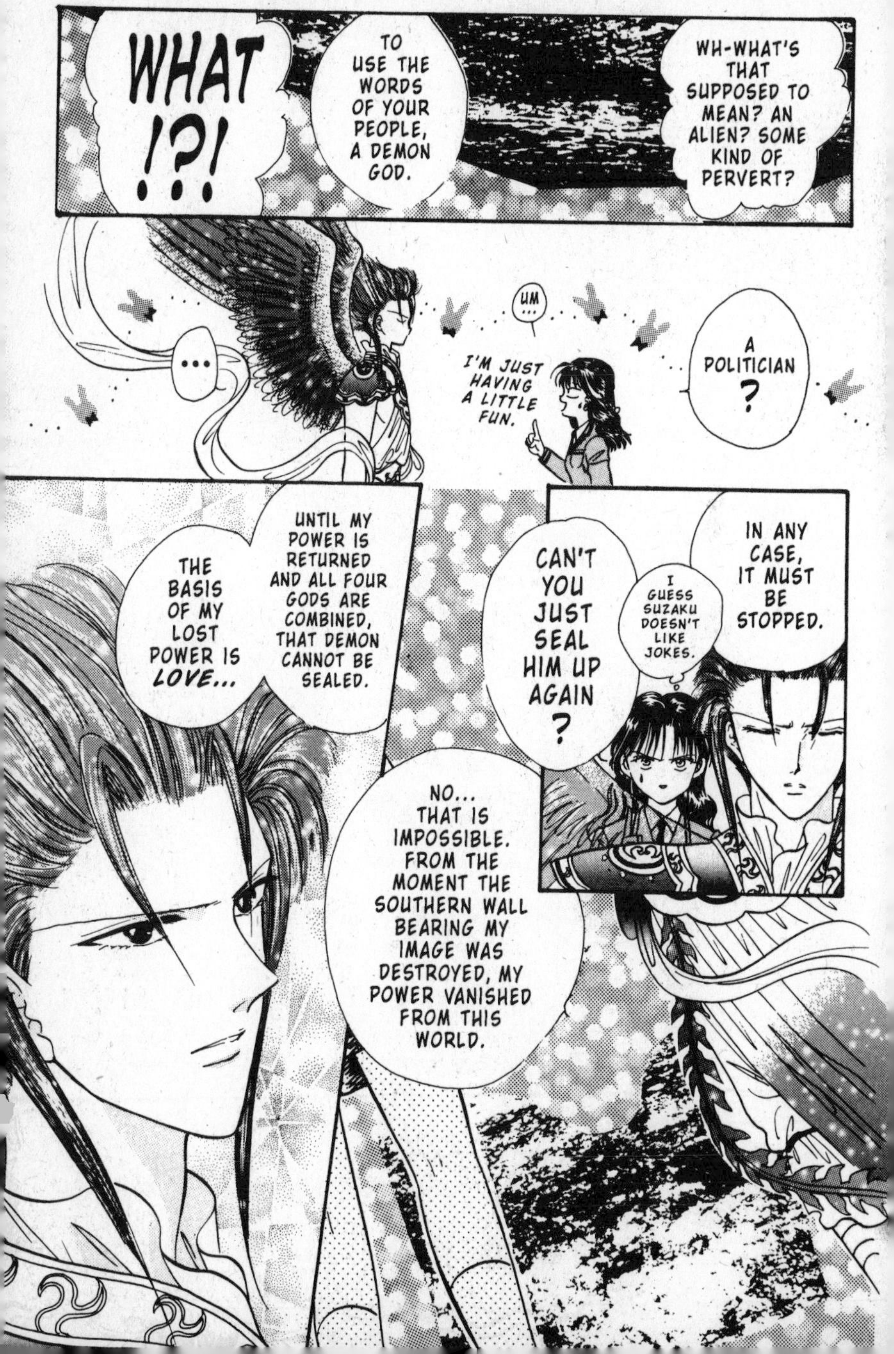
WH-WHAT'S THAT SUPPOSED TO MEAN? AN ALIEN? SOME KIND OF PERVERT?
TO USE THE WORDS OF YOUR PEOPLE, A DEMON GOD.
WHAT !?!
A POLITICIAN ?
UM ...
I'M JUST HAVING A LITTLE FUN.
...
IN ANY CASE, IT MUST BE STOPPED.
I GUESS SUZAKU DOESN'T LIKE JOKES.
CAN'T YOU JUST SEAL HIM UP AGAIN ?
NO... THAT IS IMPOSSIBLE. FROM THE MOMENT THE SOUTHERN WALL BEARING MY IMAGE WAS DESTROYED, MY POWER VANISHED FROM THIS WORLD.
UNTIL MY POWER IS RETURNED AND ALL FOUR GODS ARE COMBINED, THAT DEMON CANNOT BE SEALED.
THE BASIS OF MY LOST POWER IS *LOVE*...

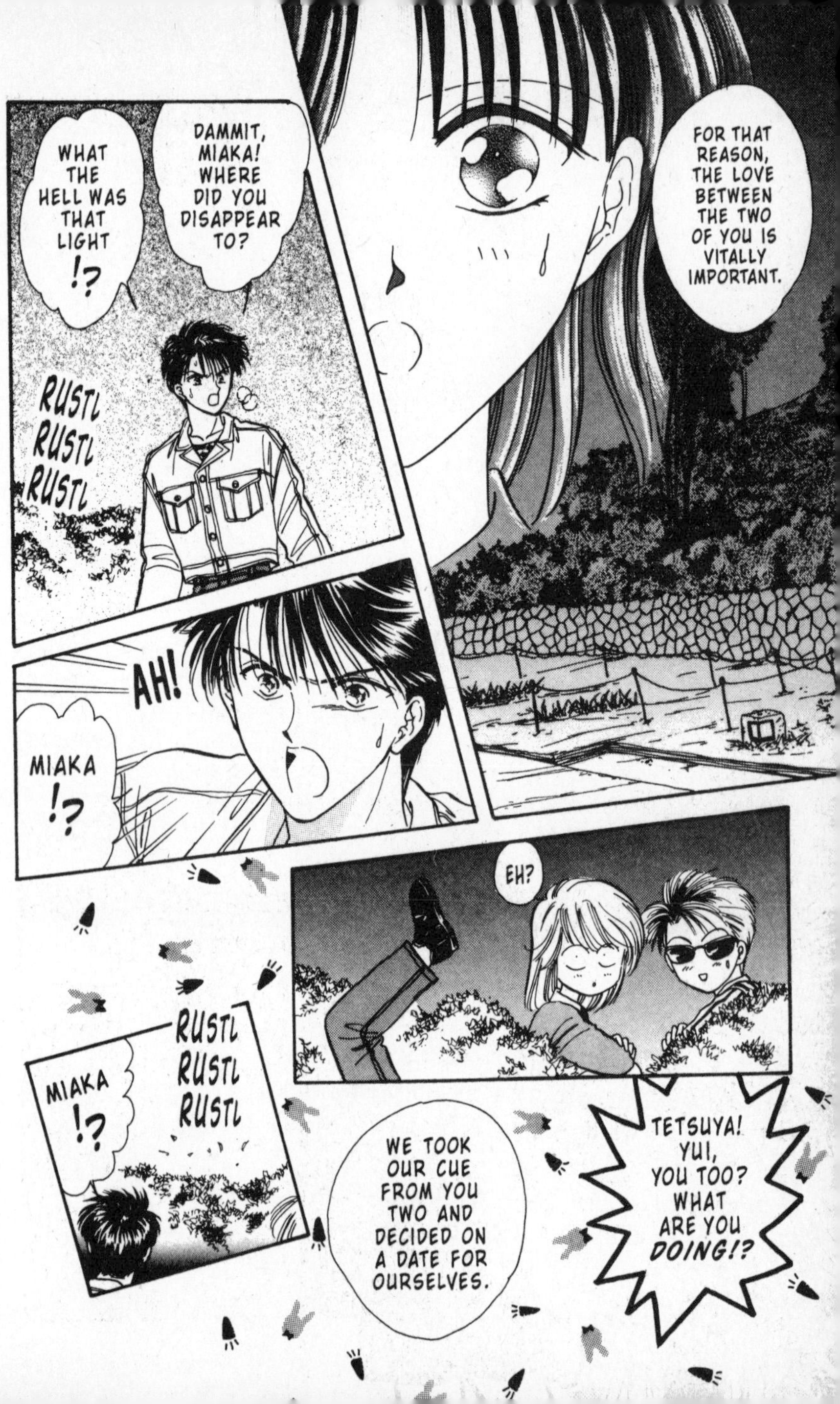
FOR THAT REASON, THE LOVE BETWEEN THE TWO OF YOU IS VITALLY IMPORTANT.
DAMMIT, MIAKA! WHERE DID YOU DISAPPEAR TO?
WHAT THE HELL WAS THAT LIGHT !?
RUSTL RUSTL RUSTL
AH!
MIAKA !?
EH?
RUSTL RUSTL RUSTL
MIAKA !?
TETSUYA! YUI, YOU TOO? WHAT ARE YOU *DOING!?*
WE TOOK OUR CUE FROM YOU TWO AND DECIDED ON A DATE FOR OURSELVES.

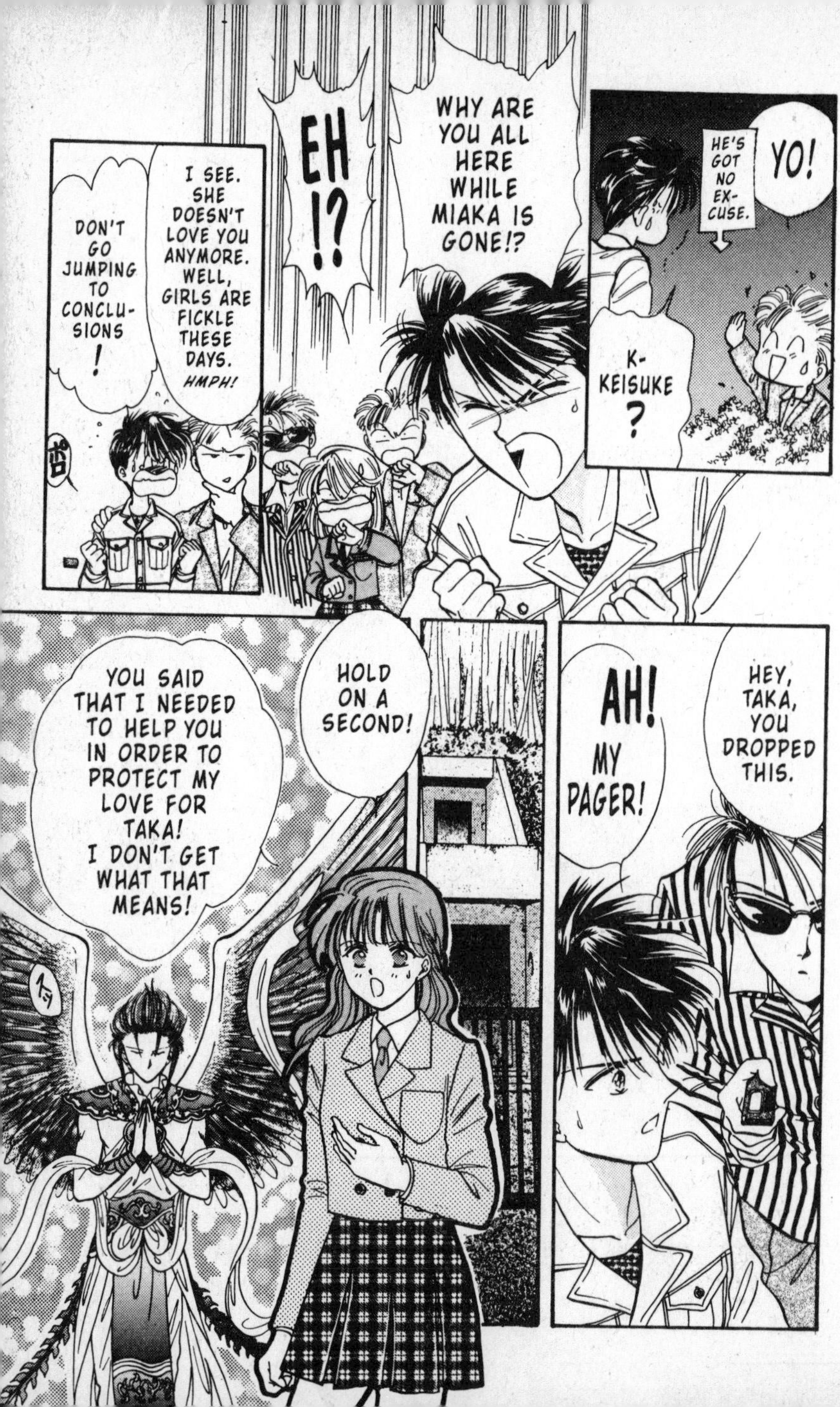
YO!
HE'S GOT NO EXCUSE.
K-KEISUKE?
WHY ARE YOU ALL HERE WHILE MIAKA IS GONE!?
EH!?
I SEE. SHE DOESN'T LOVE YOU ANYMORE. WELL, GIRLS ARE FICKLE THESE DAYS. HMPH!
DON'T GO JUMPING TO CONCLUSIONS!
HEY, TAKA, YOU DROPPED THIS.
AH! MY PAGER!
HOLD ON A SECOND!
YOU SAID THAT I NEEDED TO HELP YOU IN ORDER TO PROTECT MY LOVE FOR TAKA! I DON'T GET WHAT THAT MEANS!

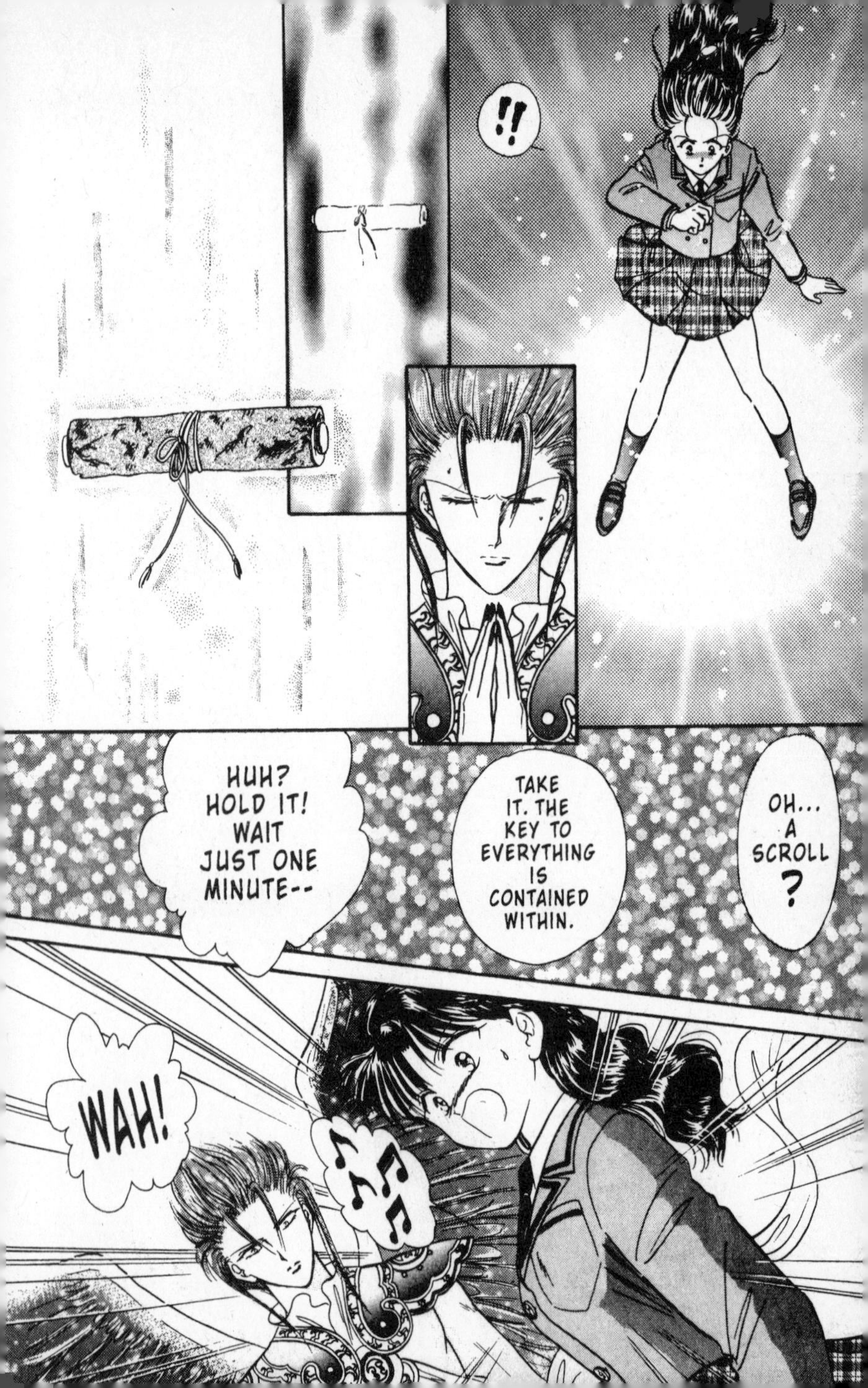
!!
OH... A SCROLL?
TAKE IT. THE KEY TO EVERYTHING IS CONTAINED WITHIN.
HUH? HOLD IT! WAIT JUST ONE MINUTE--
WAH!

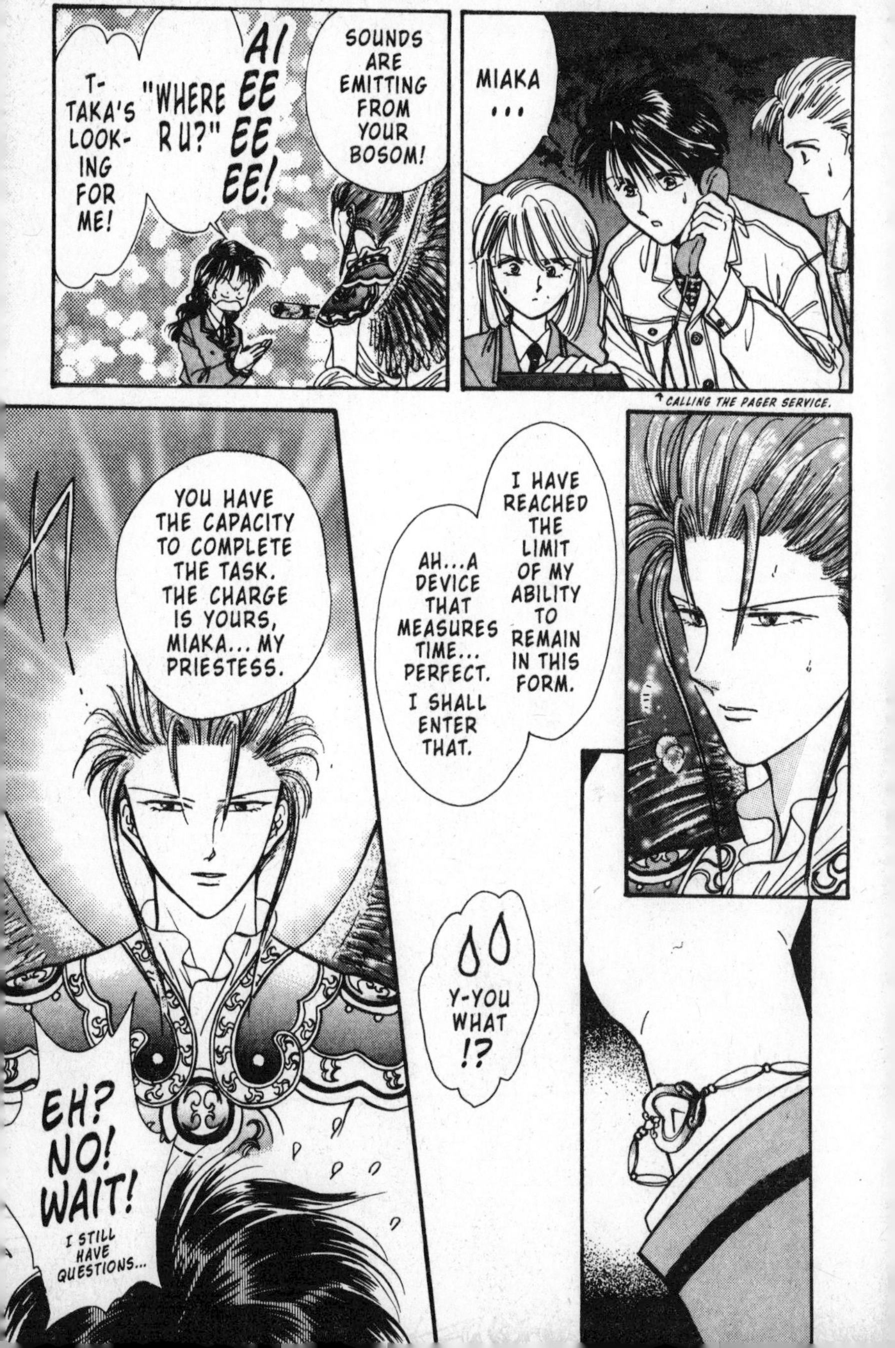
MIAKA ...
CALLING THE PAGER SERVICE.
SOUNDS ARE EMITTING FROM YOUR BOSOM!
AIEEEEEE!
"WHERE R U?"
T-TAKA'S LOOKING FOR ME!
I HAVE REACHED THE LIMIT OF MY ABILITY TO REMAIN IN THIS FORM.
AH...A DEVICE THAT MEASURES TIME... PERFECT. I SHALL ENTER THAT.
Y-YOU WHAT!?
YOU HAVE THE CAPACITY TO COMPLETE THE TASK. THE CHARGE IS YOURS, MIAKA... MY PRIESTESS.
EH? NO! WAIT!
I STILL HAVE QUESTIONS...

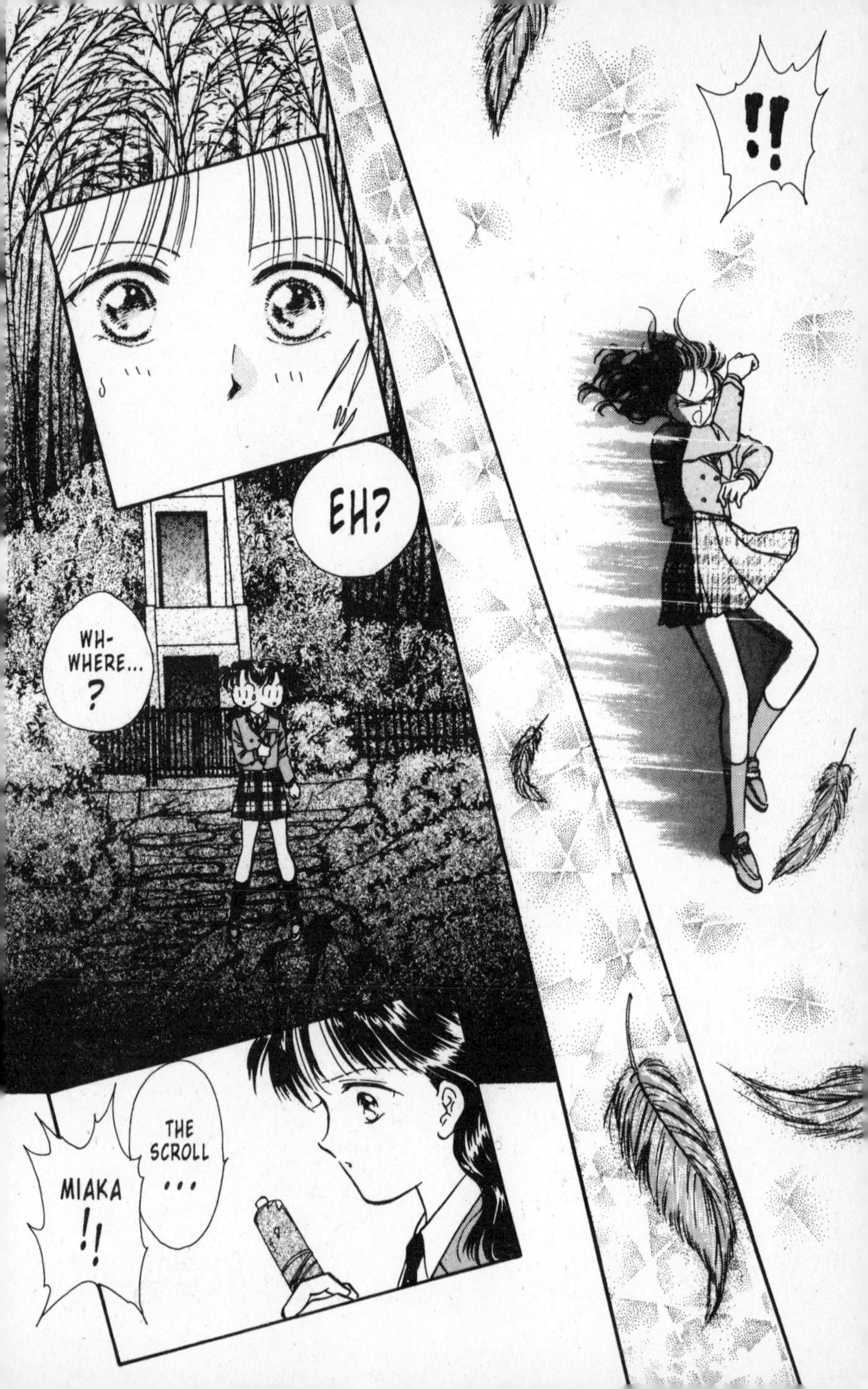
!!
EH?
WH- WHERE... ?
THE SCROLL ...
MIAKA !!

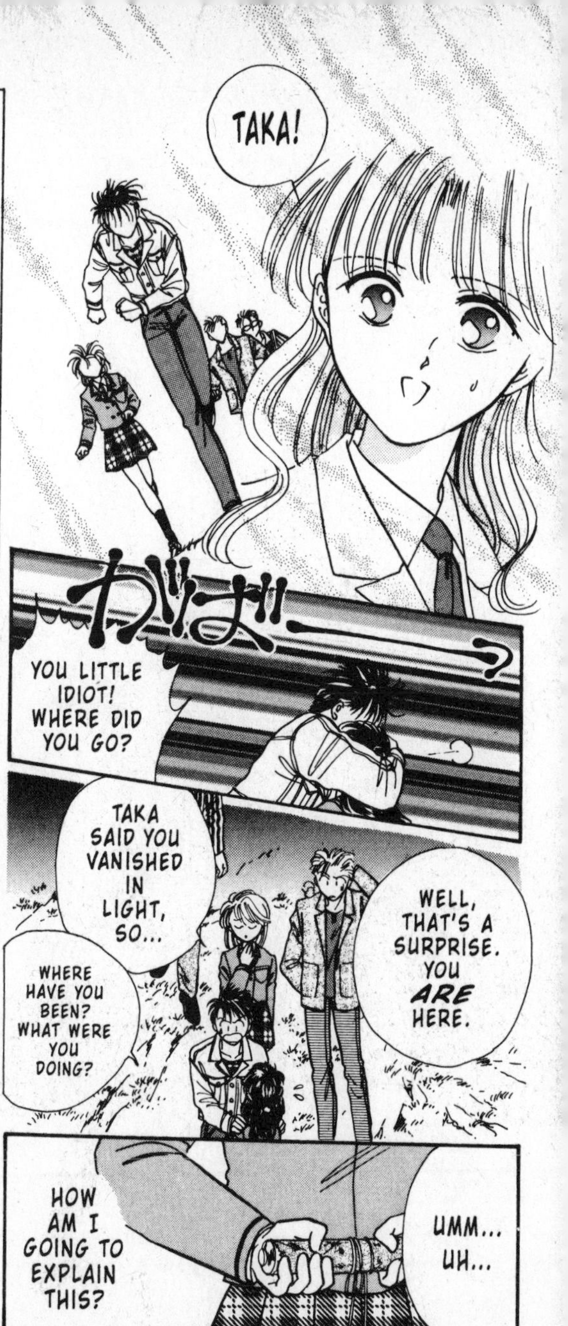
TAKA!
YOU LITTLE IDIOT! WHERE DID YOU GO?
WELL, THAT'S A SURPRISE. YOU *ARE* HERE.
TAKA SAID YOU VANISHED IN LIGHT, SO...
WHERE HAVE YOU BEEN? WHAT WERE YOU DOING?
UMM... UH...
HOW AM I GOING TO EXPLAIN THIS?

Prophet

ABOUT THE FUSHIGI YŪGI ANIMATION

As I anticipated, I've gotten a lot of letters regarding this. There are those that say they're happy about it, and those that plead for me not to do it. The latter are less concerned about the anime ruining their image of the story, and more upset that so many new people will find out about it! I'm surprised at how amazingly quickly the fan community has taken Fushigi to heart, but...well... I understand how you feel, but it's not nice to refuse to recognize fans just because they became fans through the anime! ☺ *I don't mind it at all!*

Also, I thought this question would come, and it did: "***Why are the voices different from the CD Book actors!?***" I'm not in charge of that. The production company makes the decisions about the voice-acting cast. But one member of the company put it this way: "Now the fans have two different ways to enjoy the story!" I suddenly thought, "Lucky!"♫♫ The anime voice-actors were asked not to consider the CD Book when they did their acting. That way, you'll get two different versions that are both good! *Yup. Yup. HMMMM.*

By the way, the anime people did a great job matching my image of what most of the characters' hair color is. Tasuki has a fiery image, so the orange color they gave him is perfect! With Nuriko, when I was at a signing in Kyoto, I mentioned that I thought Nuriko's hair color was purple. The first time I saw Chichiri's design, I thought it was weird. ☺ But on the second or third look, I began to realize how perfect it was. ☺ Loved the color decisions on his body designs! I'm anticipating some great designs for the Seiryu warriors. I expect that Amiboshi's and Suboshi's hair will be green. ☺ But I think it's good to assign colors that will make the characters easy to tell apart. Ah, but the pictures they sent me are so pretty! The Tamahome from the first episode made me positively giddy!

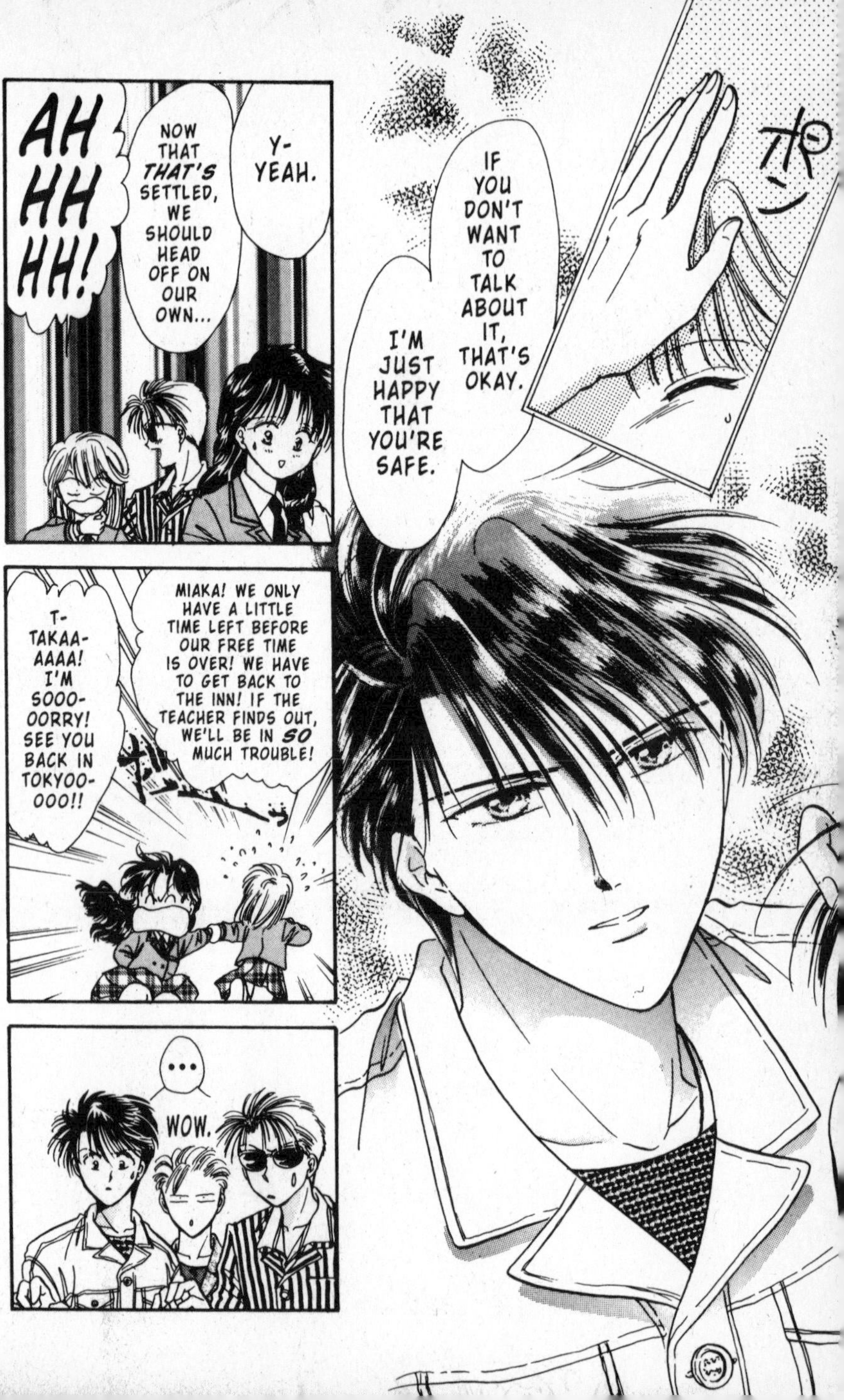
ポン
IF YOU DON'T WANT TO TALK ABOUT IT, THAT'S OKAY.
I'M JUST HAPPY THAT YOU'RE SAFE.
Y-YEAH.
NOW THAT *THAT'S* SETTLED, WE SHOULD HEAD OFF ON OUR OWN...
AHHHHHH!
MIAKA! WE ONLY HAVE A LITTLE TIME LEFT BEFORE OUR FREE TIME IS OVER! WE HAVE TO GET BACK TO THE INN! IF THE TEACHER FINDS OUT, WE'LL BE IN *SO* MUCH TROUBLE!
T-TAKAA-AAAA! I'M SOOO-OORRY! SEE YOU BACK IN TOKYOO-OOO!!
...
WOW.

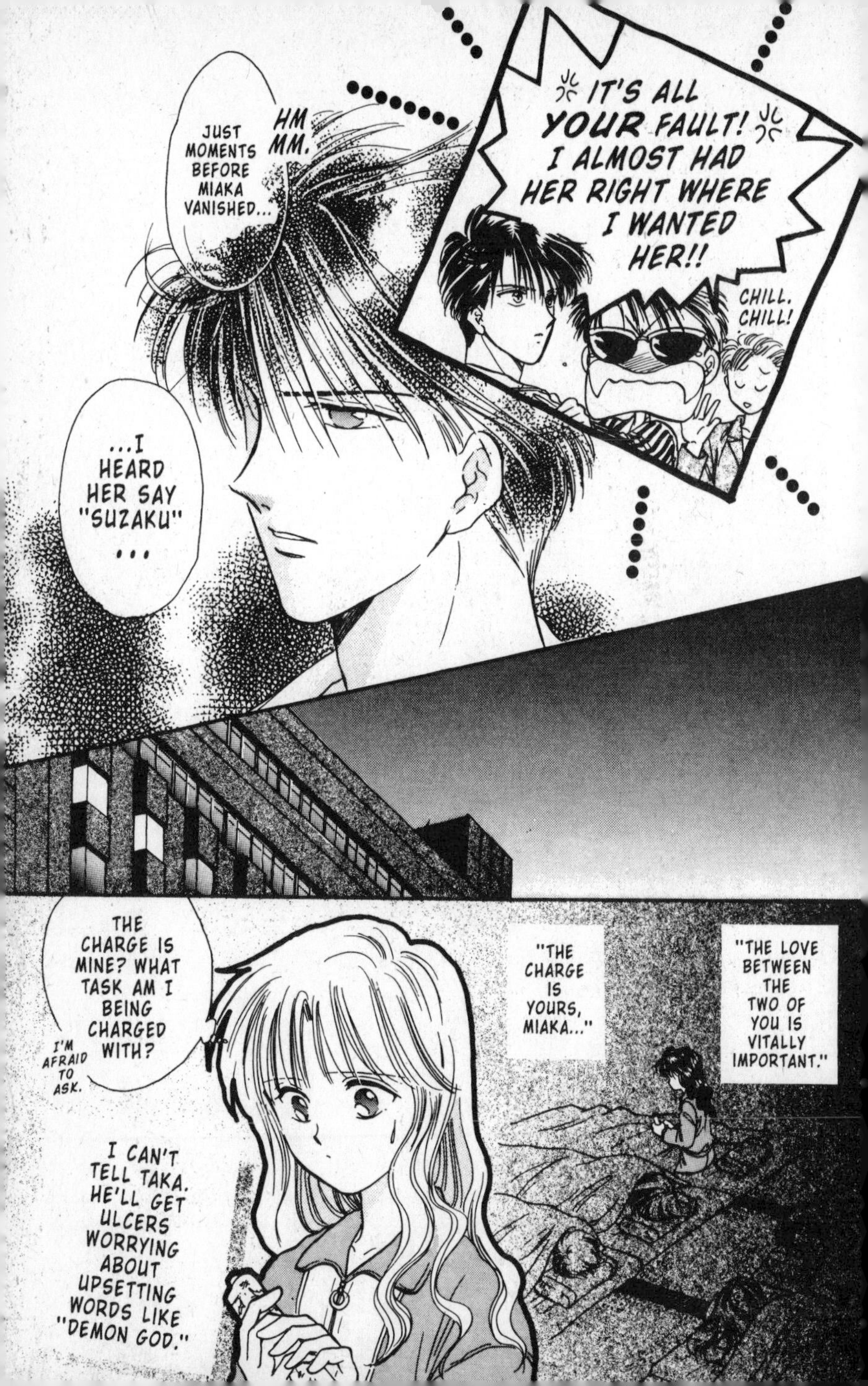
IT'S ALL YOUR FAULT! I ALMOST HAD HER RIGHT WHERE I WANTED HER!!
CHILL, CHILL!
HM MM.
JUST MOMENTS BEFORE MIAKA VANISHED...
...I HEARD HER SAY "SUZAKU" ...
"THE LOVE BETWEEN THE TWO OF YOU IS VITALLY IMPORTANT."
"THE CHARGE IS YOURS, MIAKA..."
THE CHARGE IS MINE? WHAT TASK AM I BEING CHARGED WITH?
I'M AFRAID TO ASK.
I CAN'T TELL TAKA. HE'LL GET ULCERS WORRYING ABOUT UPSETTING WORDS LIKE "DEMON GOD."

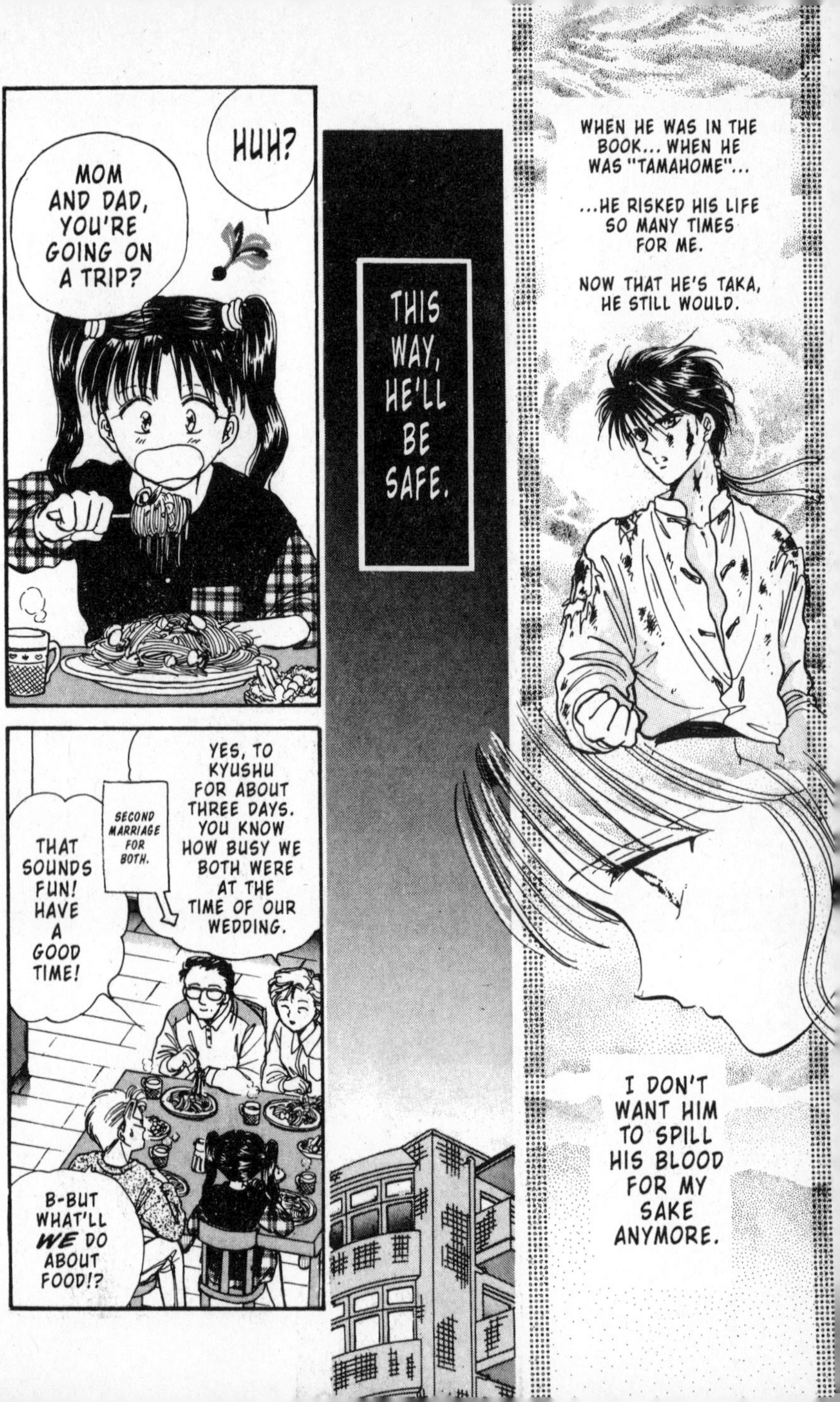
WHEN HE WAS IN THE BOOK... WHEN HE WAS "TAMAHOME"...
...HE RISKED HIS LIFE SO MANY TIMES FOR ME.
NOW THAT HE'S TAKA, HE STILL WOULD.
I DON'T WANT HIM TO SPILL HIS BLOOD FOR MY SAKE ANYMORE.
THIS WAY, HE'LL BE SAFE.
HUH?
MOM AND DAD, YOU'RE GOING ON A TRIP?
YES, TO KYUSHU FOR ABOUT THREE DAYS. YOU KNOW HOW BUSY WE BOTH WERE AT THE TIME OF OUR WEDDING.
SECOND MARRIAGE FOR BOTH.
THAT SOUNDS FUN! HAVE A GOOD TIME!
B-BUT WHAT'LL *WE* DO ABOUT FOOD!?

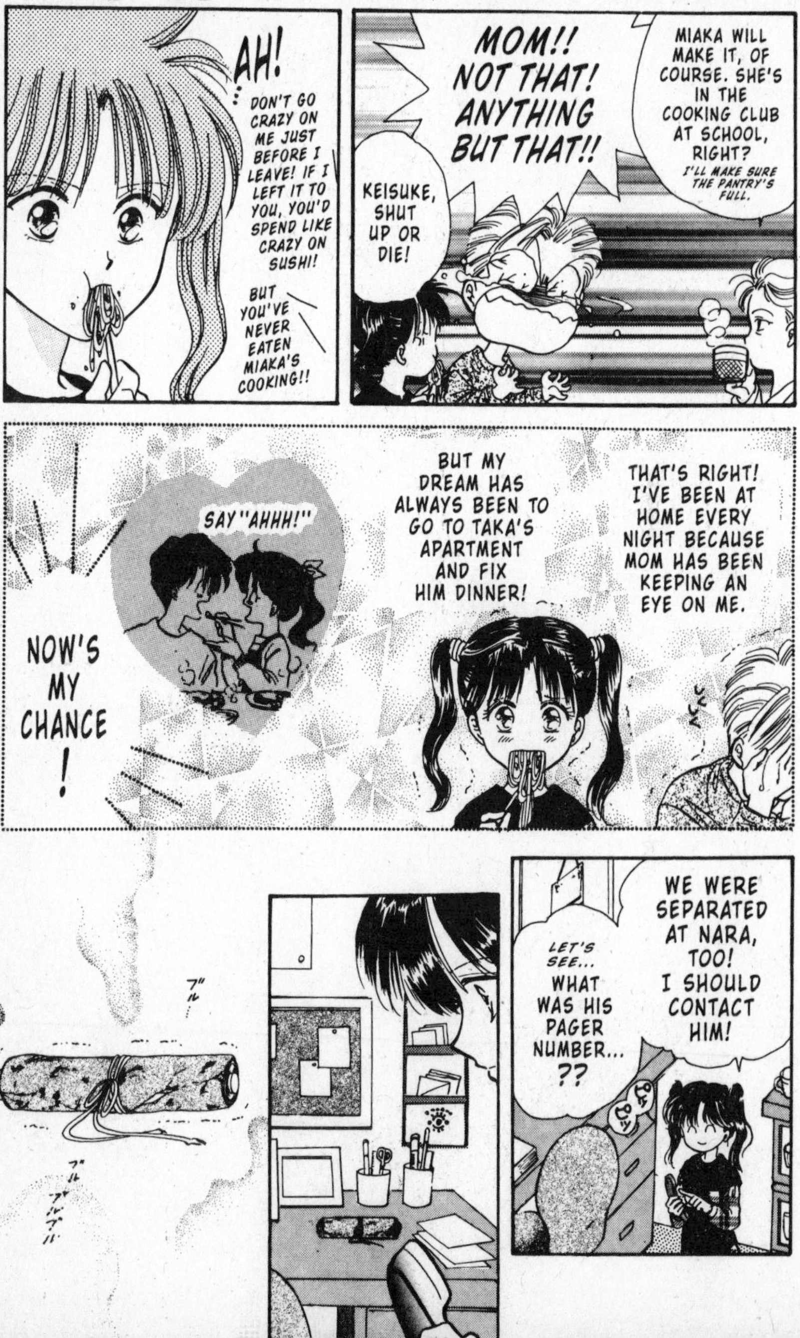
MIAKA WILL MAKE IT, OF COURSE. SHE'S IN THE COOKING CLUB AT SCHOOL, RIGHT?
I'LL MAKE SURE THE PANTRY'S FULL.
MOM!! NOT THAT! ANYTHING BUT THAT!!
KEISUKE, SHUT UP OR DIE!
AH!
DON'T GO CRAZY ON ME JUST BEFORE I LEAVE! IF I LEFT IT TO YOU, YOU'D SPEND LIKE CRAZY ON SUSHI!
BUT YOU'VE NEVER EATEN MIAKA'S COOKING!!
THAT'S RIGHT! I'VE BEEN AT HOME EVERY NIGHT BECAUSE MOM HAS BEEN KEEPING AN EYE ON ME.
BUT MY DREAM HAS ALWAYS BEEN TO GO TO TAKA'S APARTMENT AND FIX HIM DINNER!
SAY "AHHH!"
NOW'S MY CHANCE!
WE WERE SEPARATED AT NARA, TOO! I SHOULD CONTACT HIM!
LET'S SEE...
WHAT WAS HIS PAGER NUMBER...??

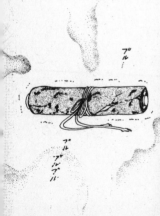

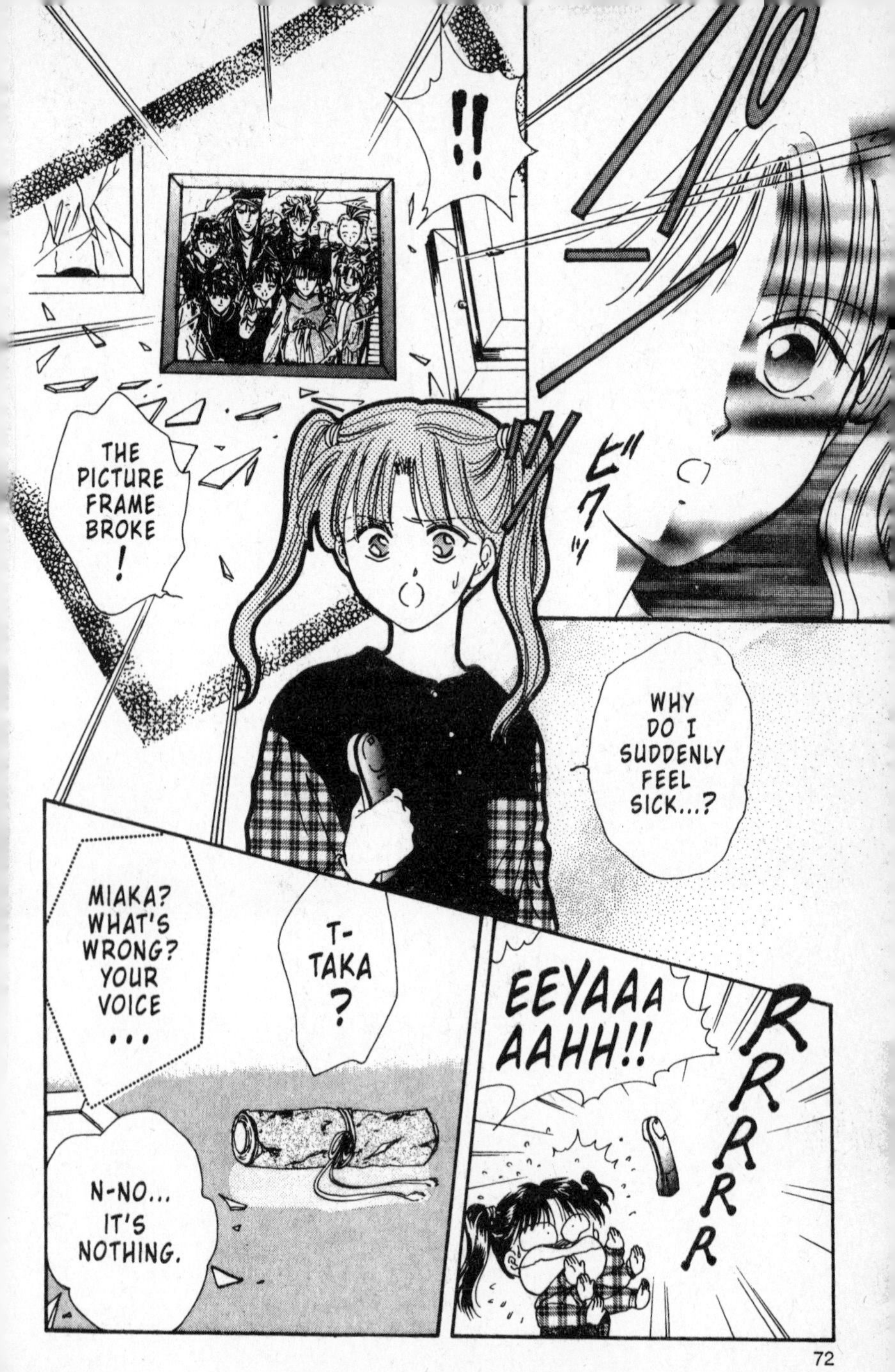

ビクッ
!!
THE PICTURE FRAME BROKE!
WHY DO I SUDDENLY FEEL SICK...?
EEYAAAAAHH!!
RRRRR
T-TAKA?
MIAKA? WHAT'S WRONG? YOUR VOICE...
N-NO... IT'S NOTHING.

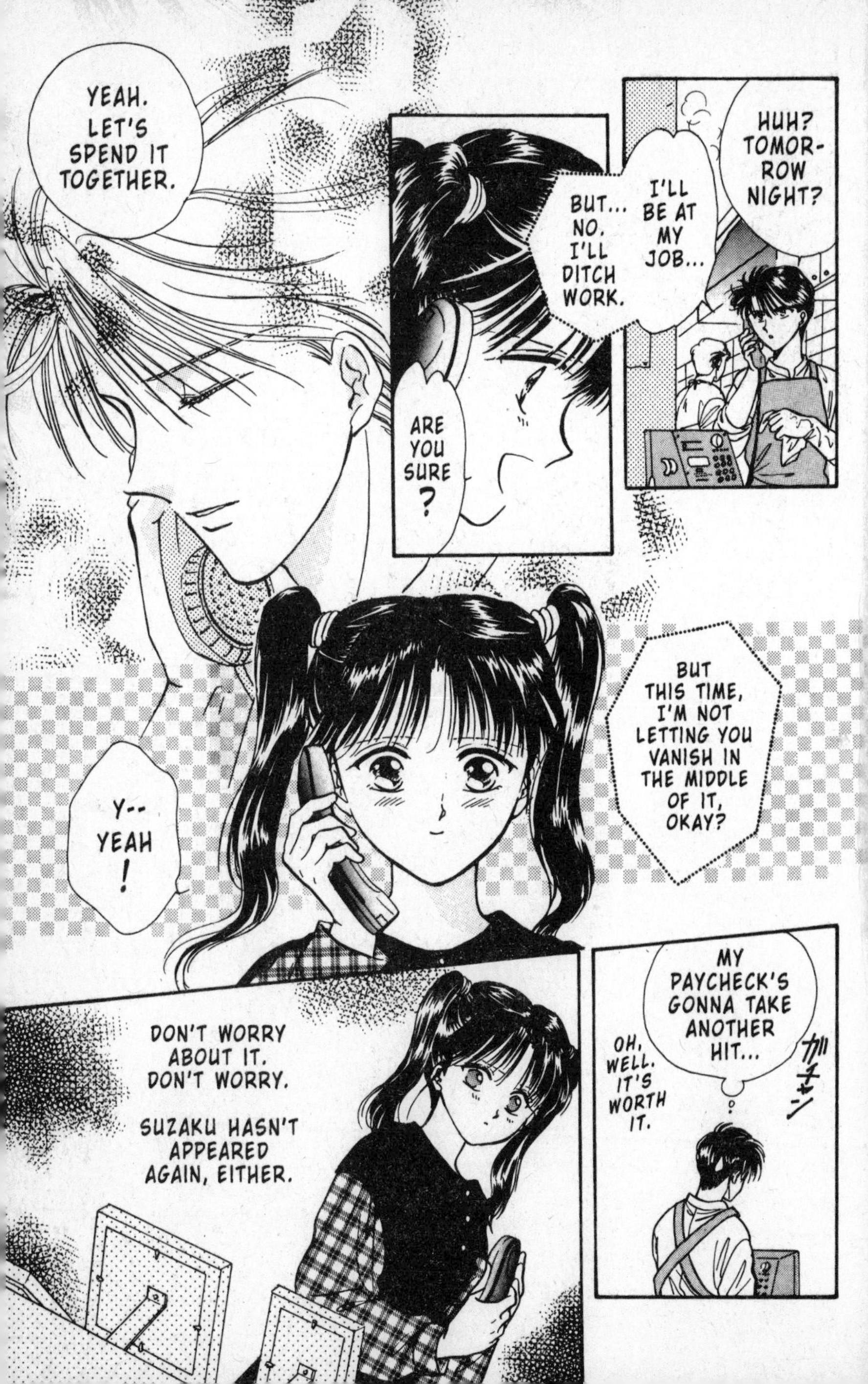
HUH? TOMOR-ROW NIGHT?
I'LL BE AT MY JOB...
BUT... NO. I'LL DITCH WORK.
ARE YOU SURE?
YEAH. LET'S SPEND IT TOGETHER.
BUT THIS TIME, I'M NOT LETTING YOU VANISH IN THE MIDDLE OF IT, OKAY?
Y-- YEAH!
MY PAYCHECK'S GONNA TAKE ANOTHER HIT...
OH, WELL. IT'S WORTH IT.
ガチャン
DON'T WORRY ABOUT IT. DON'T WORRY.
SUZAKU HASN'T APPEARED AGAIN, EITHER.

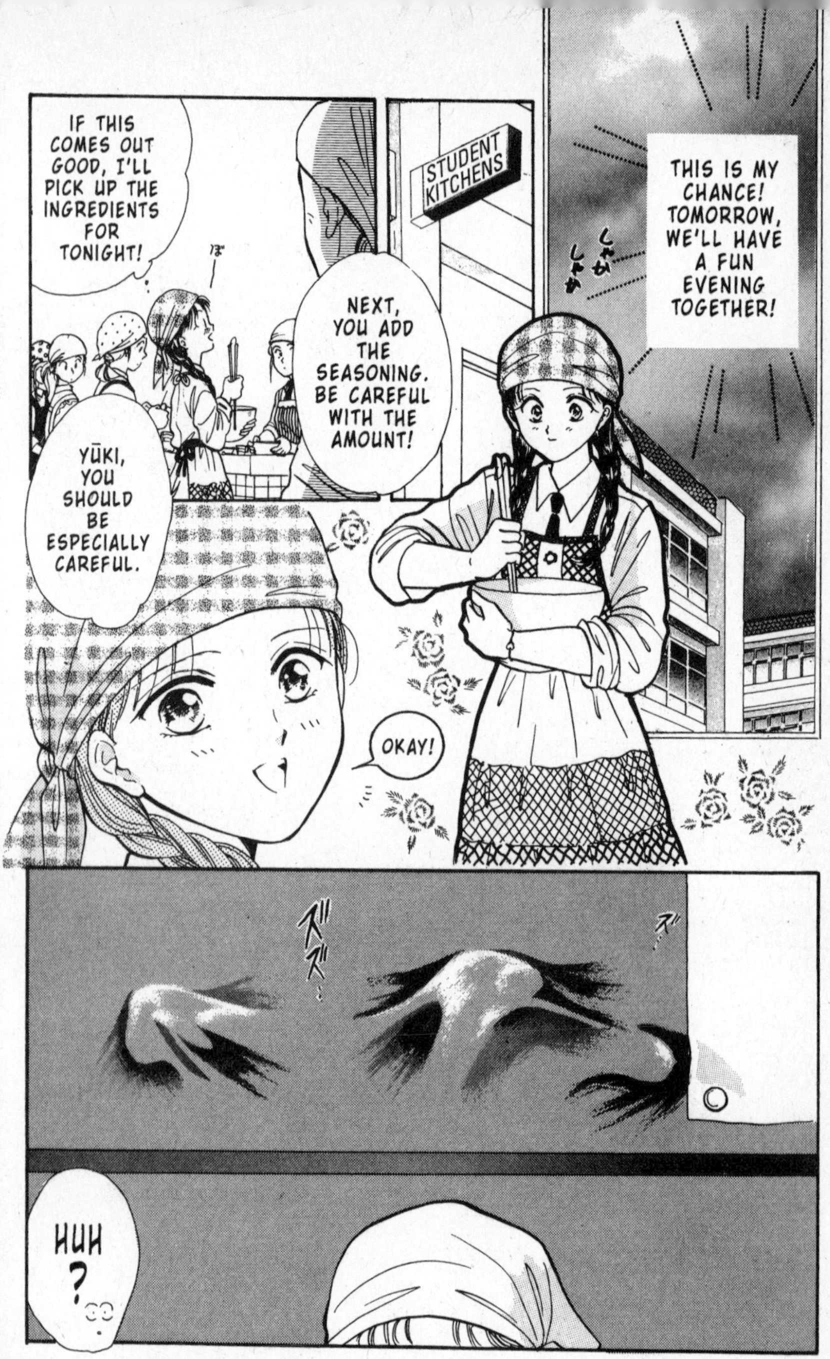
THIS IS MY CHANCE! TOMORROW, WE'LL HAVE A FUN EVENING TOGETHER!
しゃか しゃか
NEXT, YOU ADD THE SEASONING. BE CAREFUL WITH THE AMOUNT!
STUDENT KITCHENS
IF THIS COMES OUT GOOD, I'LL PICK UP THE INGREDIENTS FOR TONIGHT!
ぽー
YŪKI, YOU SHOULD BE ESPECIALLY CAREFUL.
OKAY!
ズ…
ズズ…
HUH?

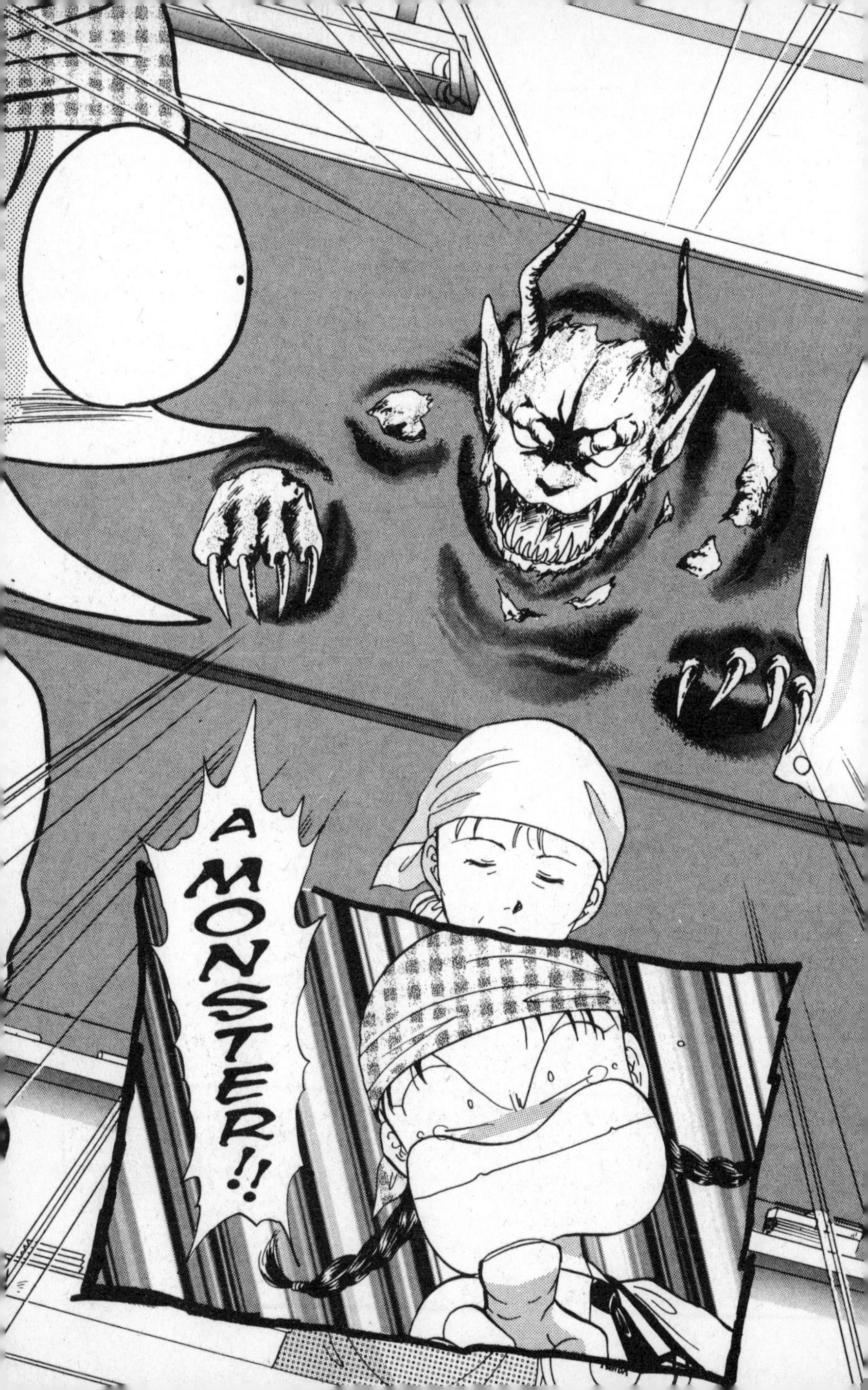
A MONSTER!!

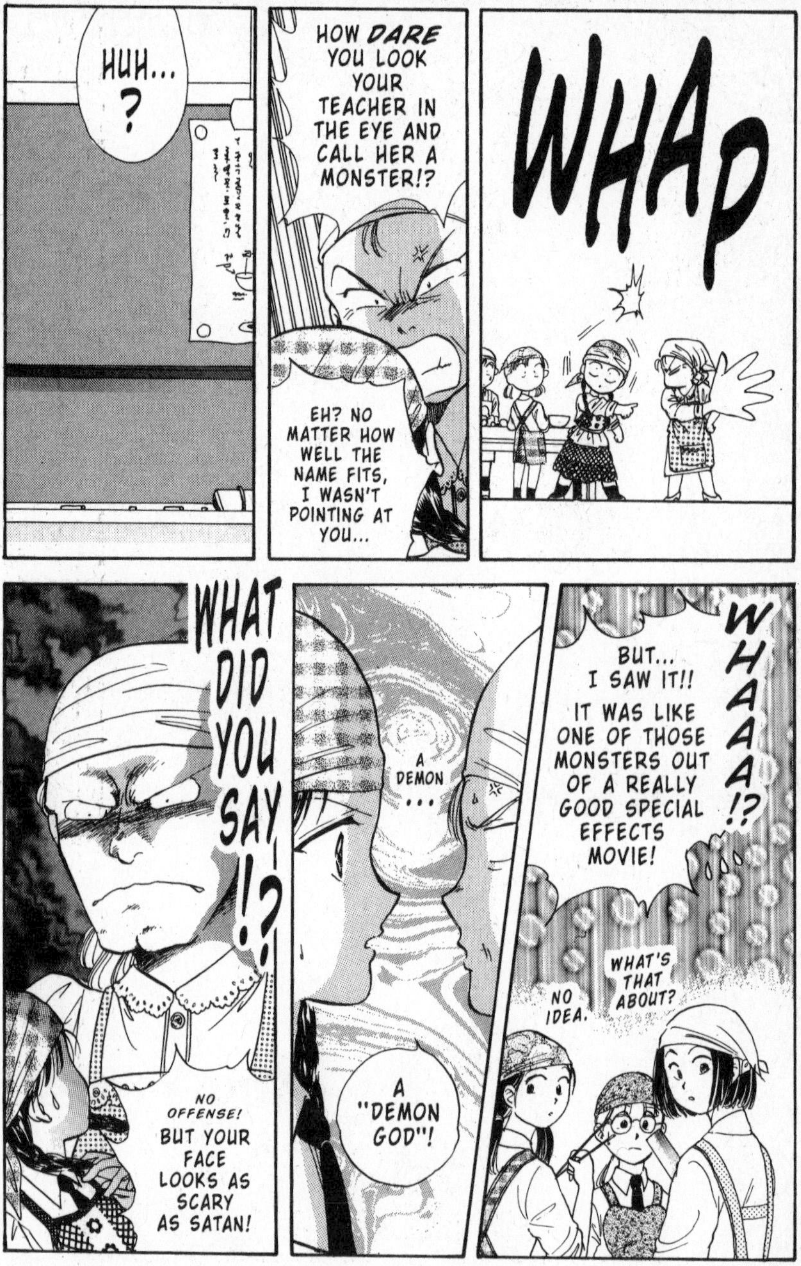
WHAP
HOW DARE YOU LOOK YOUR TEACHER IN THE EYE AND CALL HER A MONSTER!?
EH? NO MATTER HOW WELL THE NAME FITS, I WASN'T POINTING AT YOU...
HUH... ?
WHAAAA!?
BUT... I SAW IT!! IT WAS LIKE ONE OF THOSE MONSTERS OUT OF A REALLY GOOD SPECIAL EFFECTS MOVIE!
WHAT'S THAT ABOUT?
NO IDEA.
A DEMON ...
A "DEMON GOD"!
WHAT DID YOU SAY!?
NO OFFENSE! BUT YOUR FACE LOOKS AS SCARY AS SATAN!

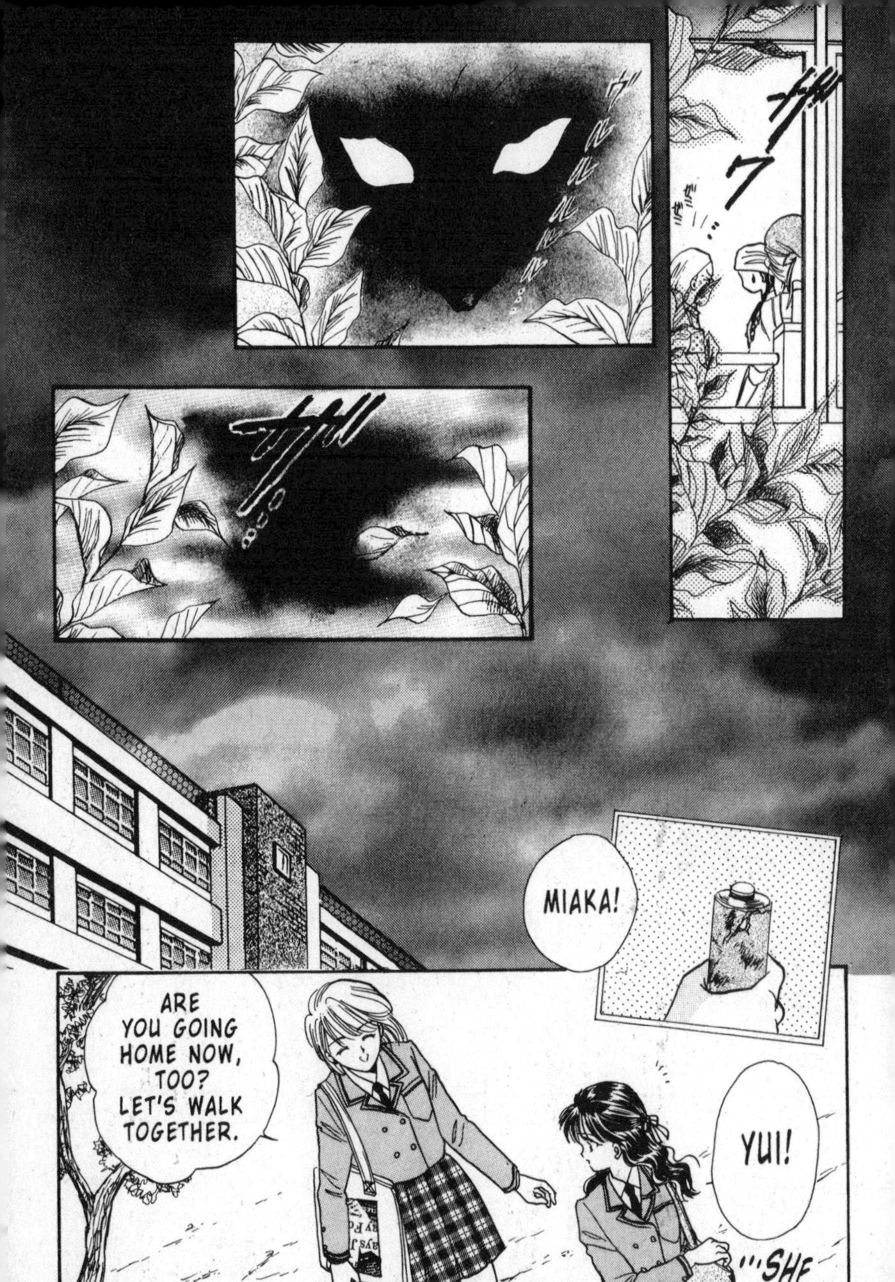
MIAKA!
YUI!
ARE YOU GOING HOME NOW, TOO? LET'S WALK TOGETHER.
...SHF

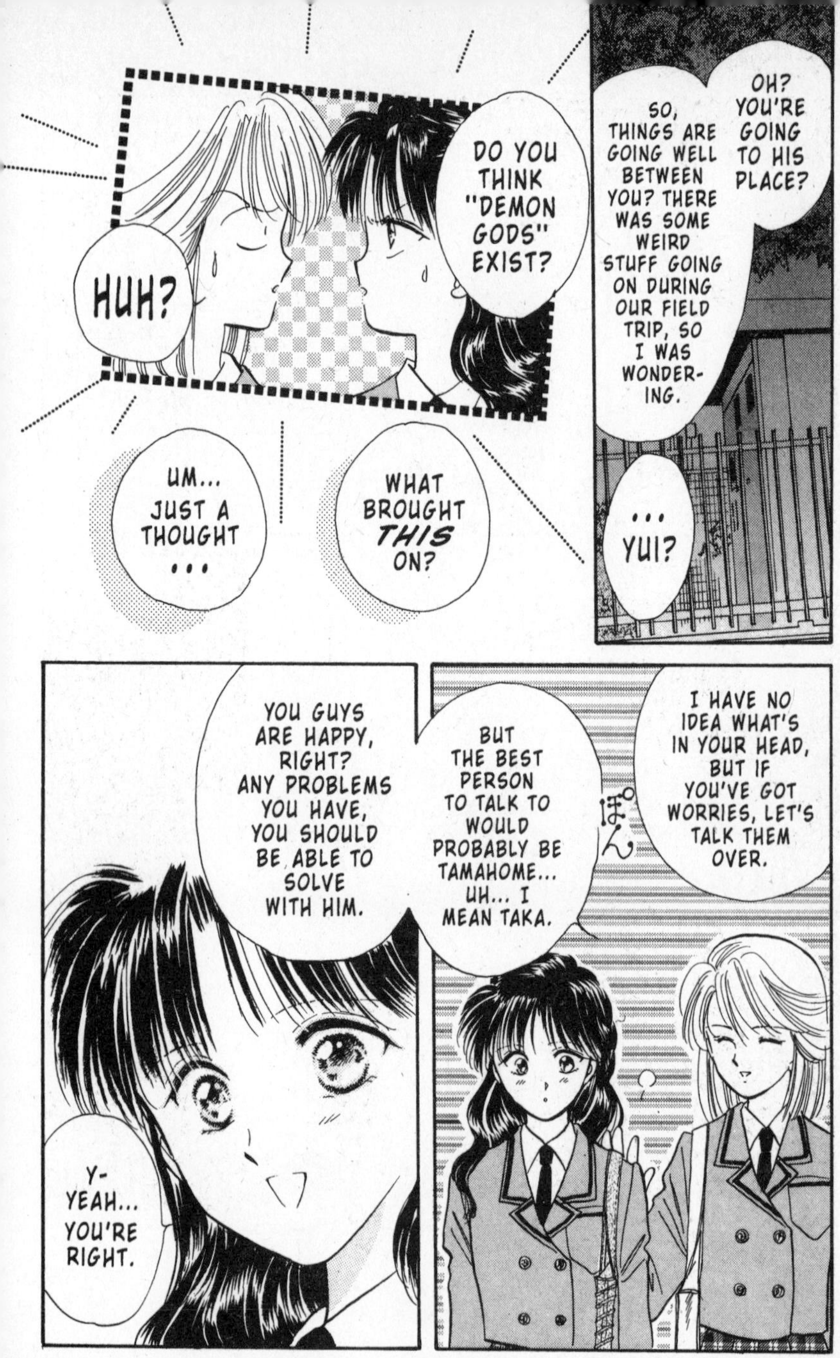
OH? YOU'RE GOING TO HIS PLACE?
SO, THINGS ARE GOING WELL BETWEEN YOU? THERE WAS SOME WEIRD STUFF GOING ON DURING OUR FIELD TRIP, SO I WAS WONDER-ING.
... YUI?
DO YOU THINK "DEMON GODS" EXIST?
HUH?
WHAT BROUGHT *THIS* ON?
UM... JUST A THOUGHT ...
I HAVE NO IDEA WHAT'S IN YOUR HEAD, BUT IF YOU'VE GOT WORRIES, LET'S TALK THEM OVER.
ぽん
BUT THE BEST PERSON TO TALK TO WOULD PROBABLY BE TAMAHOME... UH... I MEAN TAKA.
YOU GUYS ARE HAPPY, RIGHT? ANY PROBLEMS YOU HAVE, YOU SHOULD BE ABLE TO SOLVE WITH HIM.
Y-YEAH... YOU'RE RIGHT.

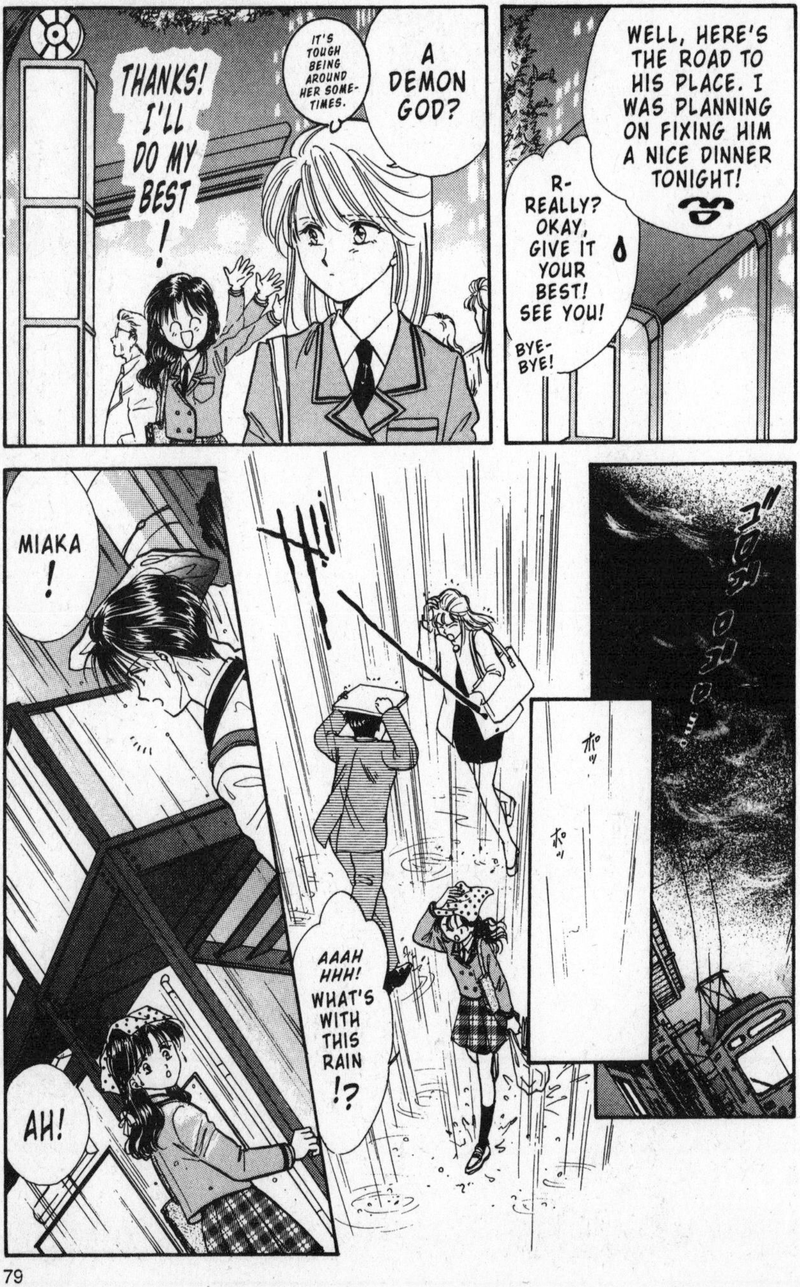
WELL, HERE'S THE ROAD TO HIS PLACE. I WAS PLANNING ON FIXING HIM A NICE DINNER TONIGHT!
R-REALLY? OKAY, GIVE IT YOUR BEST! SEE YOU!
BYE-BYE!
A DEMON GOD?
IT'S TOUGH BEING AROUND HER SOMETIMES.
THANKS! I'LL DO MY BEST!
ゴロゴロゴロ……
ポツ
ポツ
AAAHHH! WHAT'S WITH THIS RAIN!?
MIAKA!
AH!

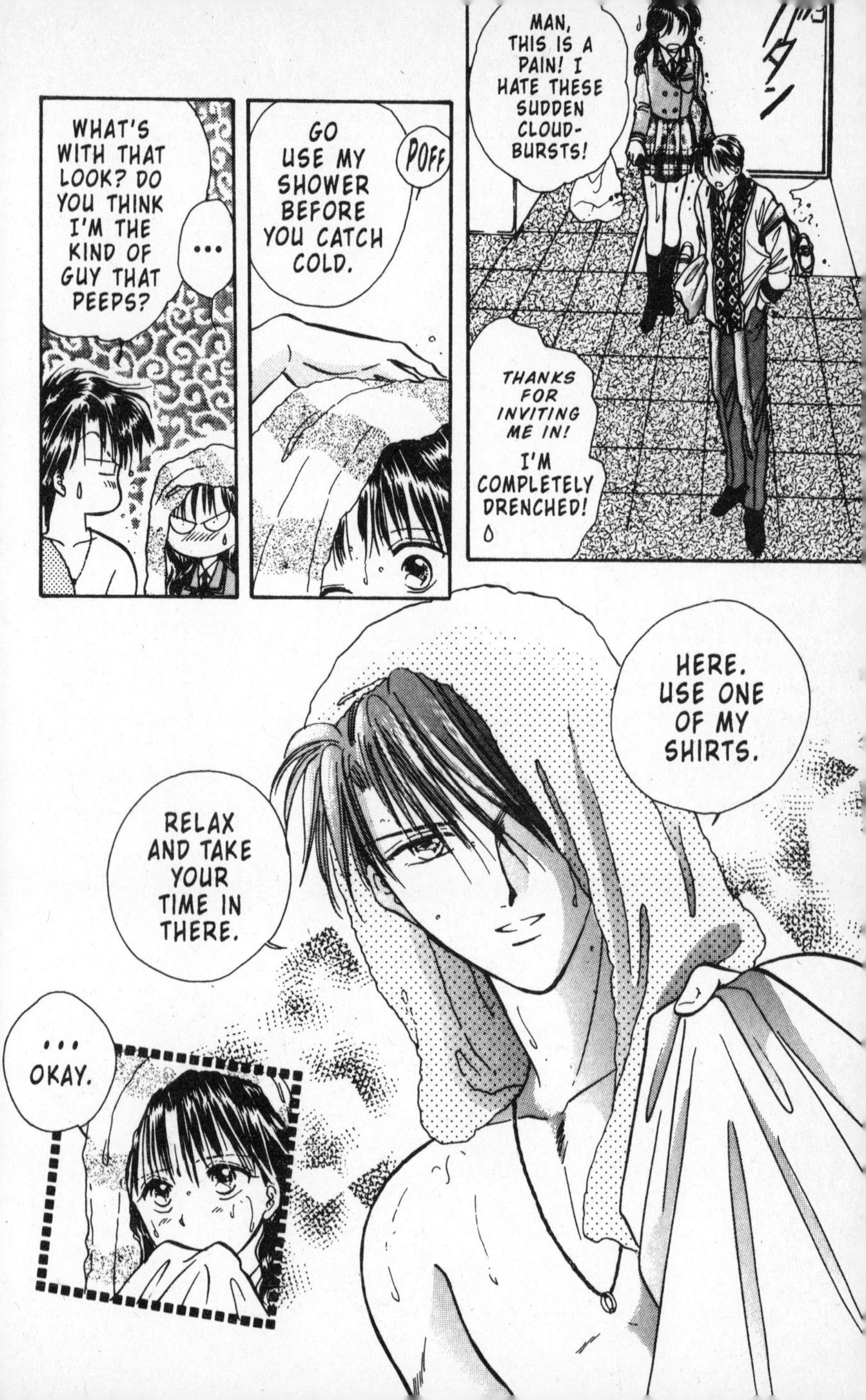
MAN, THIS IS A PAIN! I HATE THESE SUDDEN CLOUD-BURSTS!
THANKS FOR INVITING ME IN! I'M COMPLETELY DRENCHED!
POFF
GO USE MY SHOWER BEFORE YOU CATCH COLD.
...
WHAT'S WITH THAT LOOK? DO YOU THINK I'M THE KIND OF GUY THAT PEEPS?
HERE. USE ONE OF MY SHIRTS.
RELAX AND TAKE YOUR TIME IN THERE.
... OKAY.

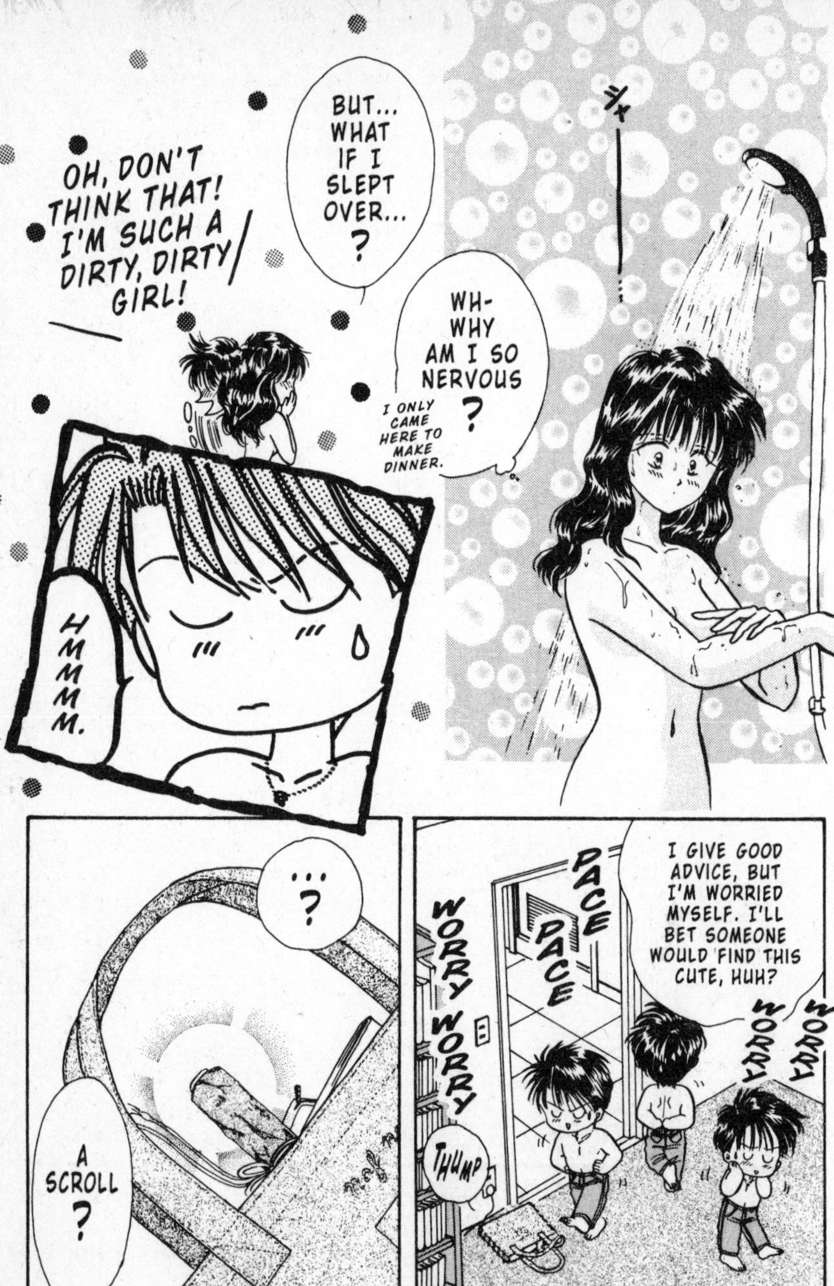
シャ
WH-WHY AM I SO NERVOUS?
I ONLY CAME HERE TO MAKE DINNER.
BUT... WHAT IF I SLEPT OVER...?
OH, DON'T THINK THAT! I'M SUCH A DIRTY, DIRTY GIRL!
HMMMMM.
I GIVE GOOD ADVICE, BUT I'M WORRIED MYSELF. I'LL BET SOMEONE WOULD FIND THIS CUTE, HUH?
WORRY WORRY
PACE PACE
WORRY WORRY
THUMP
...?
A SCROLL?

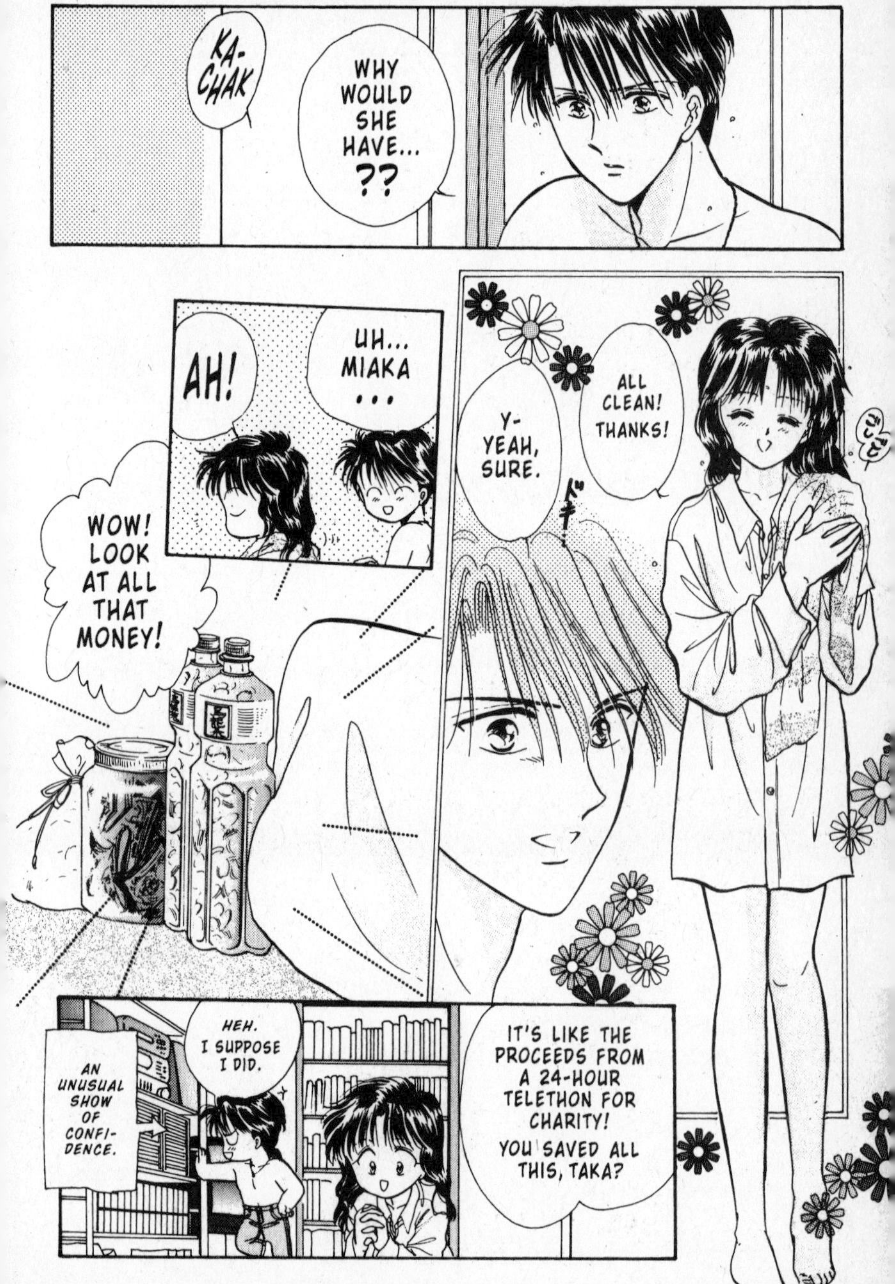
WHY WOULD SHE HAVE... ??
KA-CHAK
ALL CLEAN! THANKS!
Y-YEAH, SURE.
UH... MIAKA...
AH!
WOW! LOOK AT ALL THAT MONEY!
IT'S LIKE THE PROCEEDS FROM A 24-HOUR TELETHON FOR CHARITY!
YOU SAVED ALL THIS, TAKA?
HEH. I SUPPOSE I DID.
AN UNUSUAL SHOW OF CONFI-DENCE.

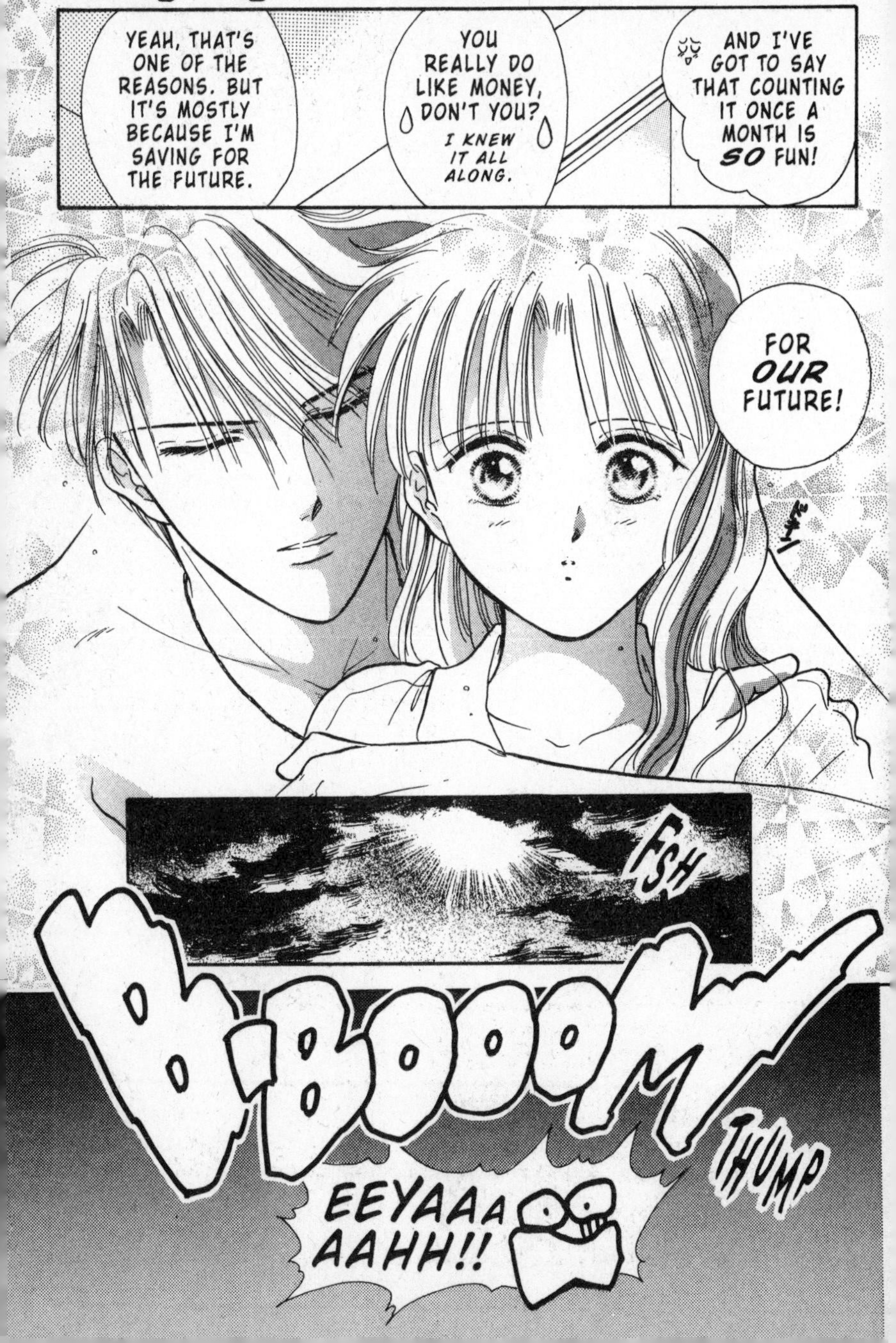
AND I'VE GOT TO SAY THAT COUNTING IT ONCE A MONTH IS **SO** FUN!
YOU REALLY DO LIKE MONEY, DON'T YOU?
I KNEW IT ALL ALONG.
YEAH, THAT'S ONE OF THE REASONS. BUT IT'S MOSTLY BECAUSE I'M SAVING FOR THE FUTURE.
FOR **OUR** FUTURE!
FSH
B-BOOOM
THUMP
EEYAAAA AAHH!!

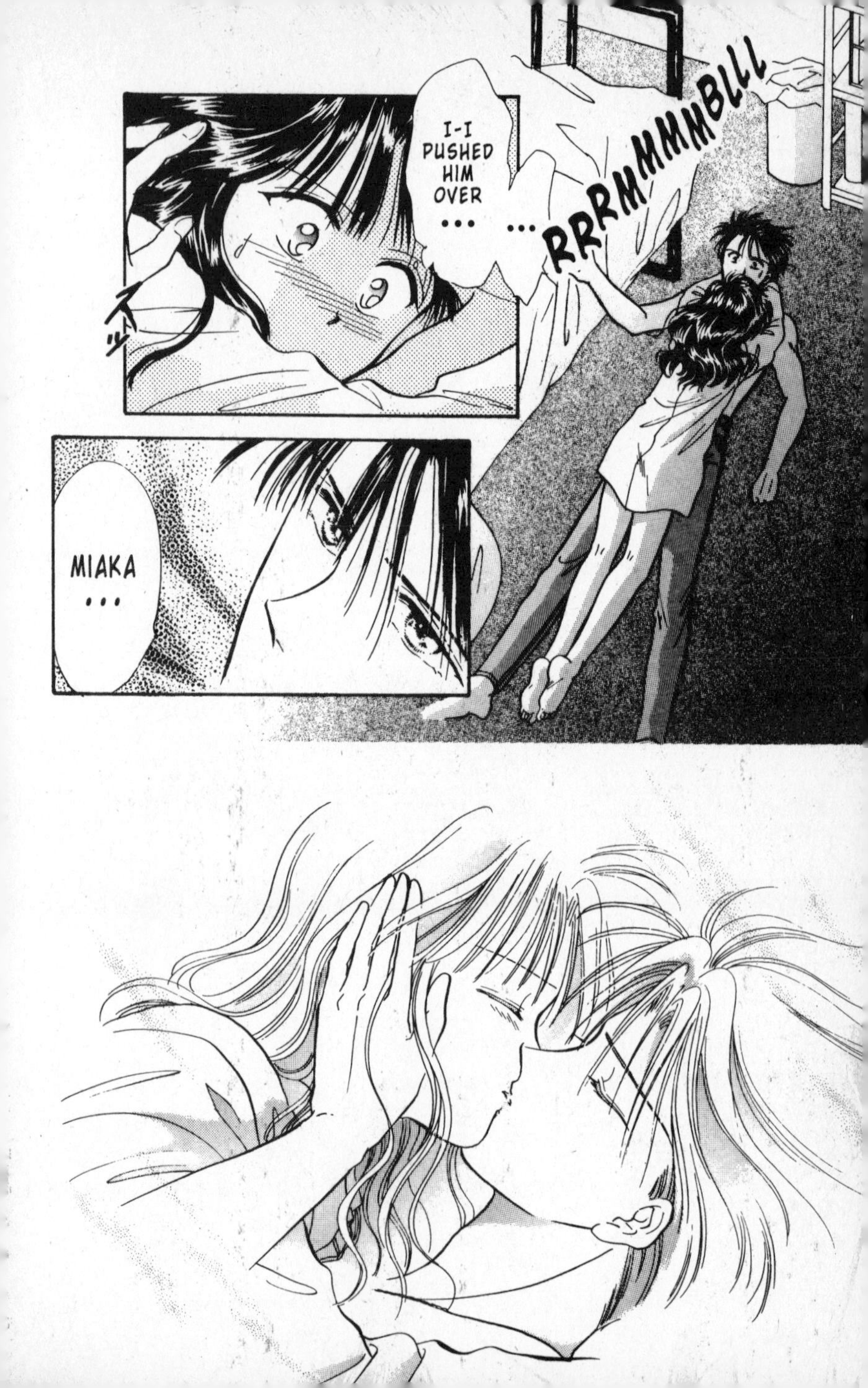
RRRMMMMBLLL
...
I-I PUSHED HIM OVER ...
MIAKA ...

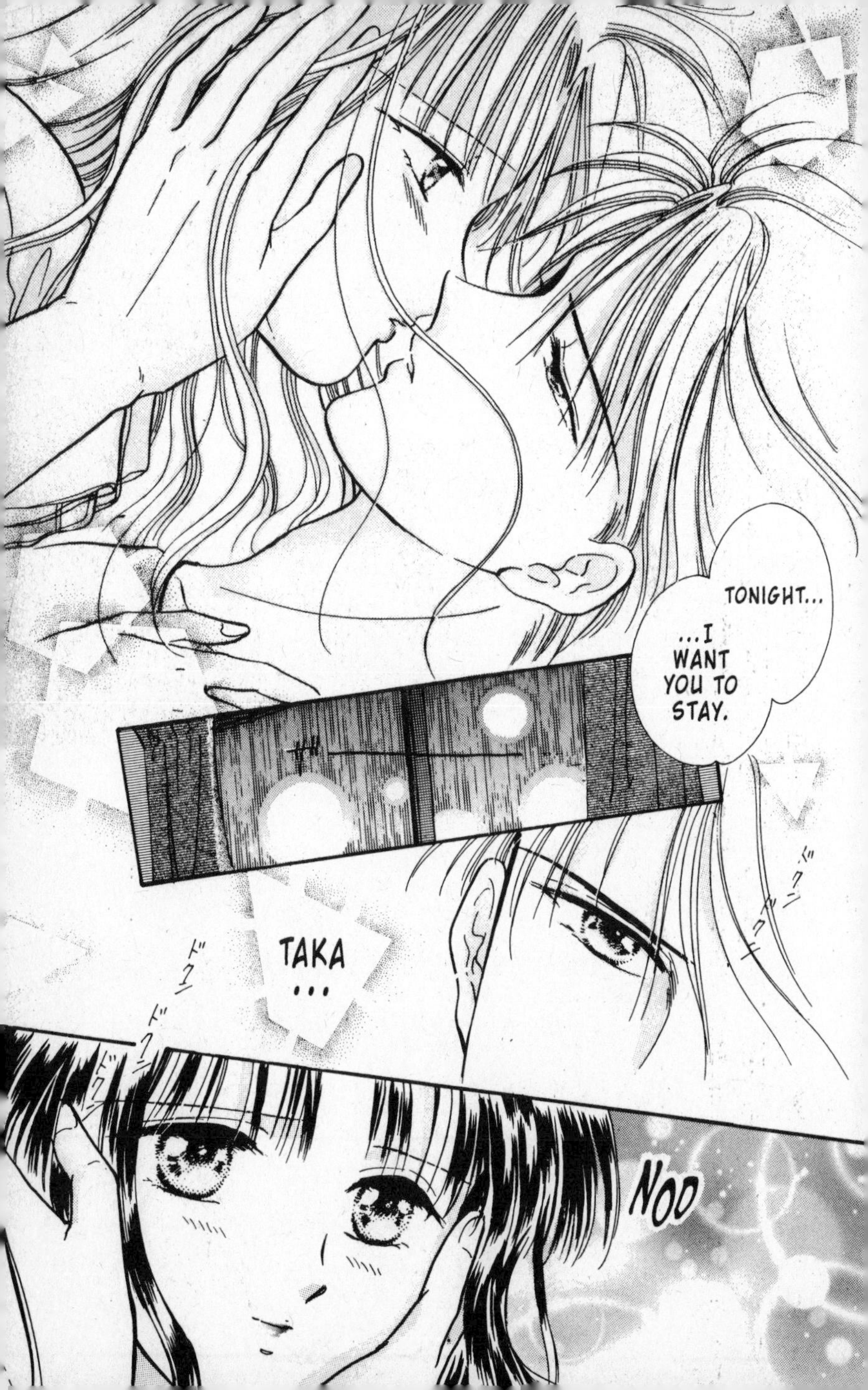
TONIGHT...
...I WANT YOU TO STAY.
TAKA...
NOD

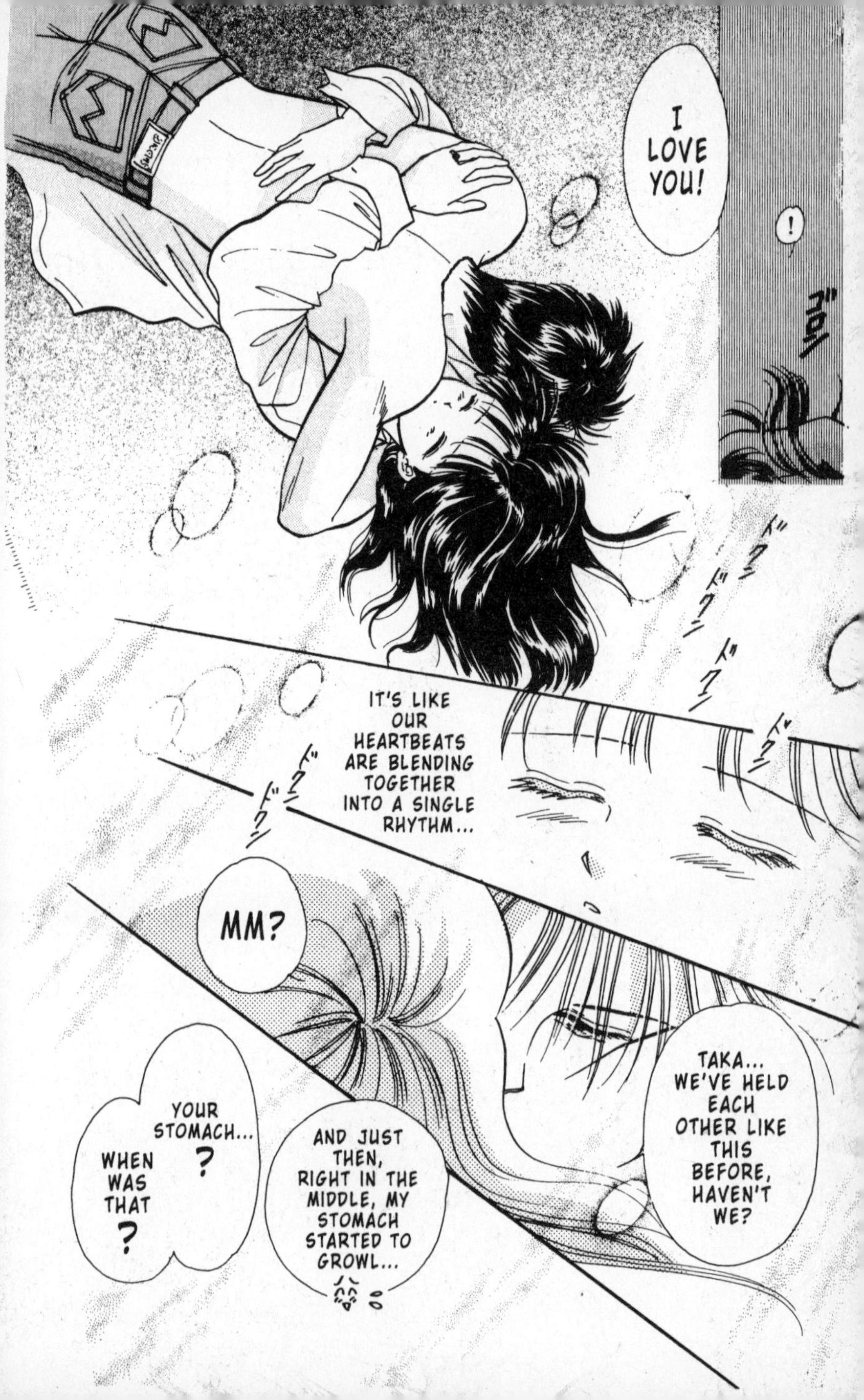
I LOVE YOU!
!
IT'S LIKE OUR HEARTBEATS ARE BLENDING TOGETHER INTO A SINGLE RHYTHM...
MM?
TAKA... WE'VE HELD EACH OTHER LIKE THIS BEFORE, HAVEN'T WE?
AND JUST THEN, RIGHT IN THE MIDDLE, MY STOMACH STARTED TO GROWL...
YOUR STOMACH...?
WHEN WAS THAT?

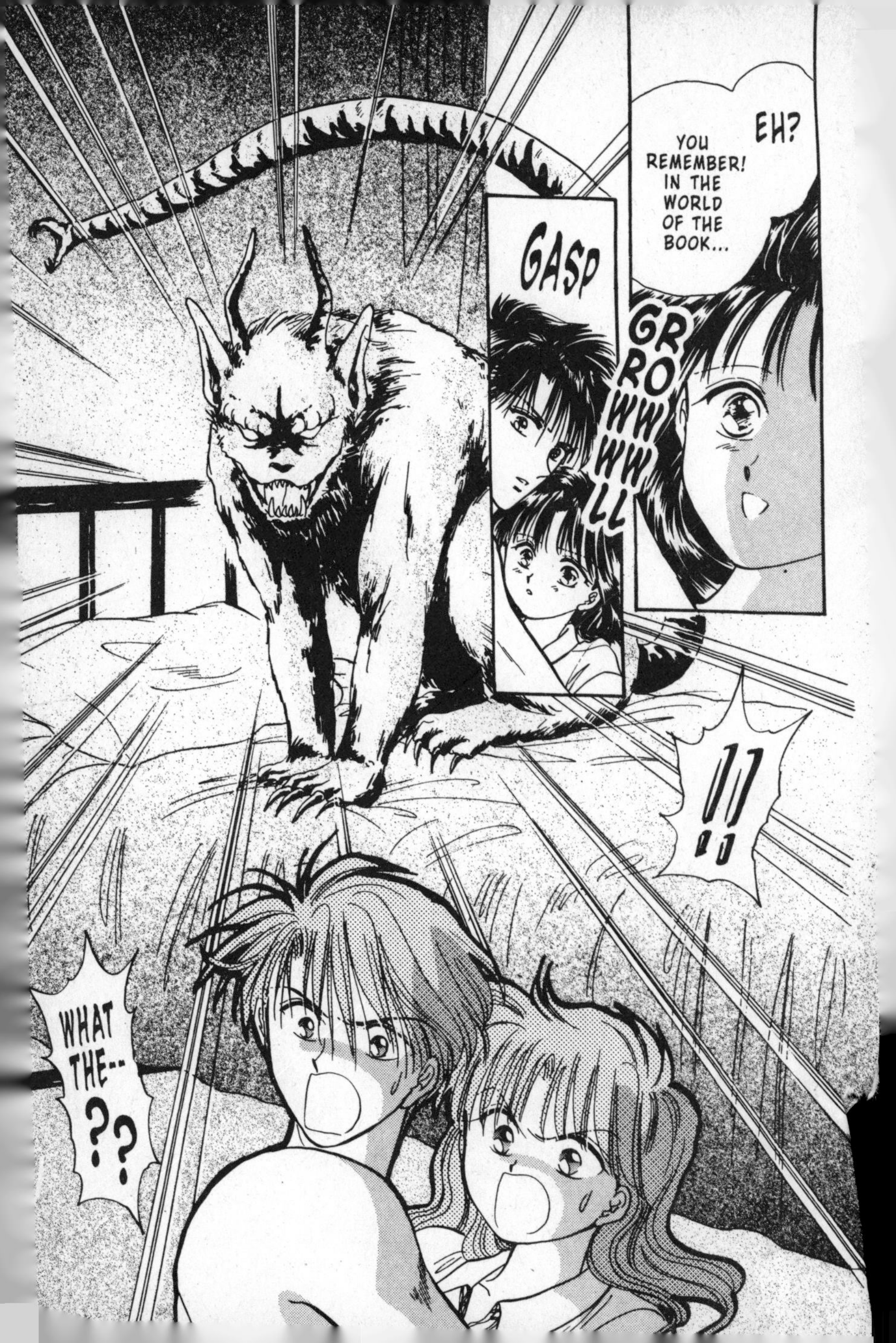
EH?
YOU REMEMBER! IN THE WORLD OF THE BOOK...
GRROWWWWLL
GASP
!!
WHAT THE--??

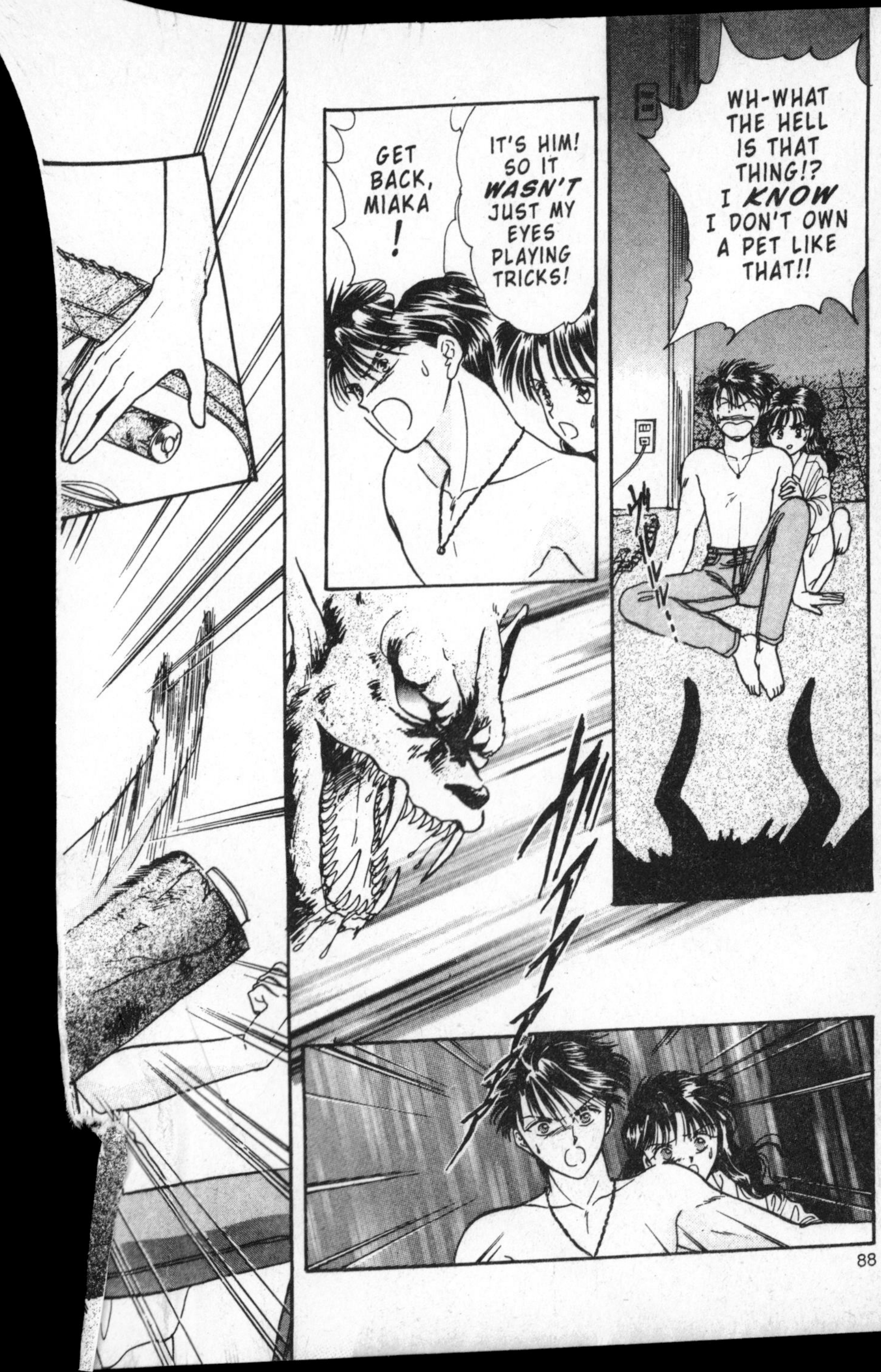
WH-WHAT THE HELL IS THAT THING!? I *KNOW* I DON'T OWN A PET LIKE THAT!!
IT'S HIM! SO IT *WASN'T* JUST MY EYES PLAYING TRICKS!
GET BACK, MIAKA!

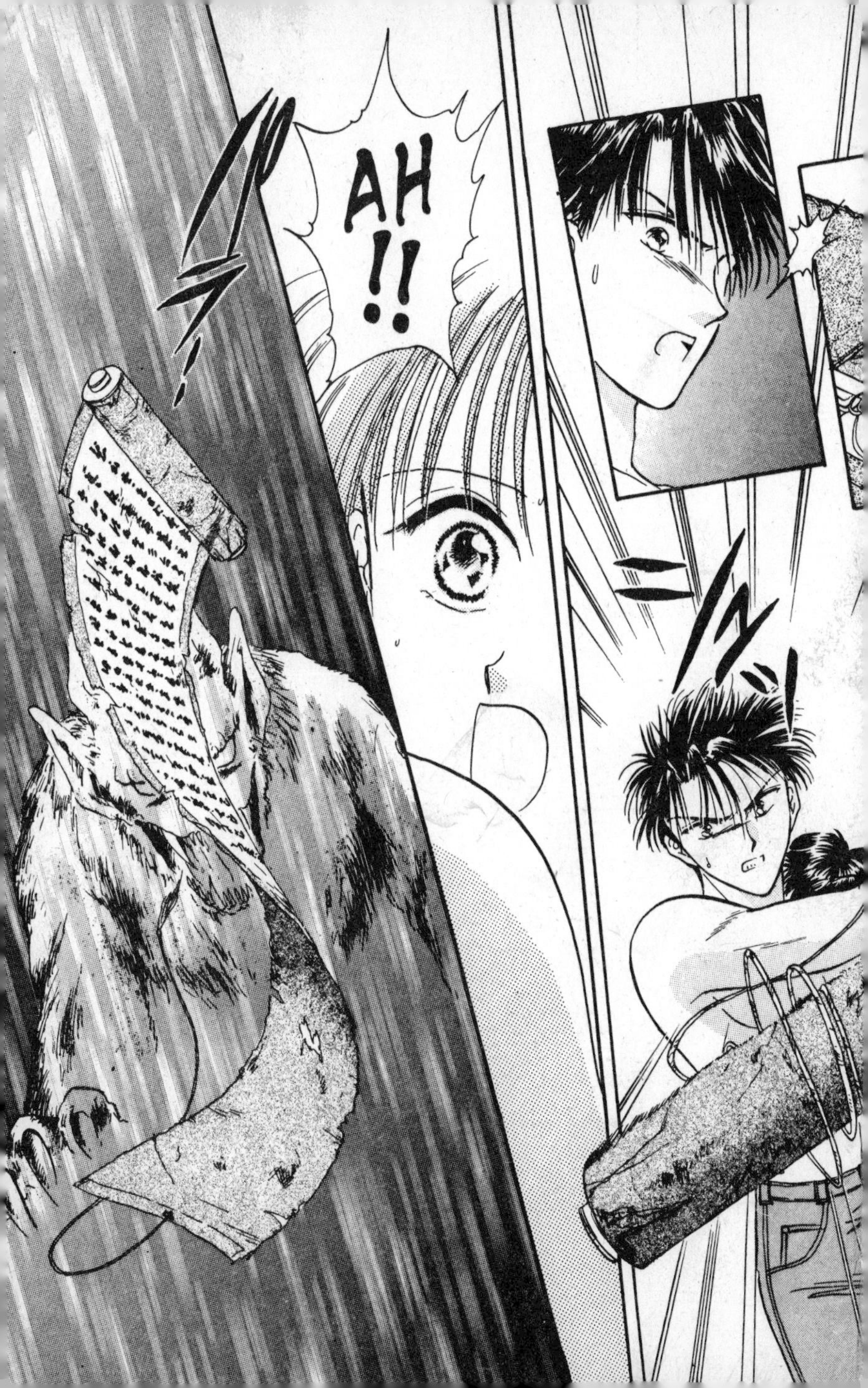
AH !!

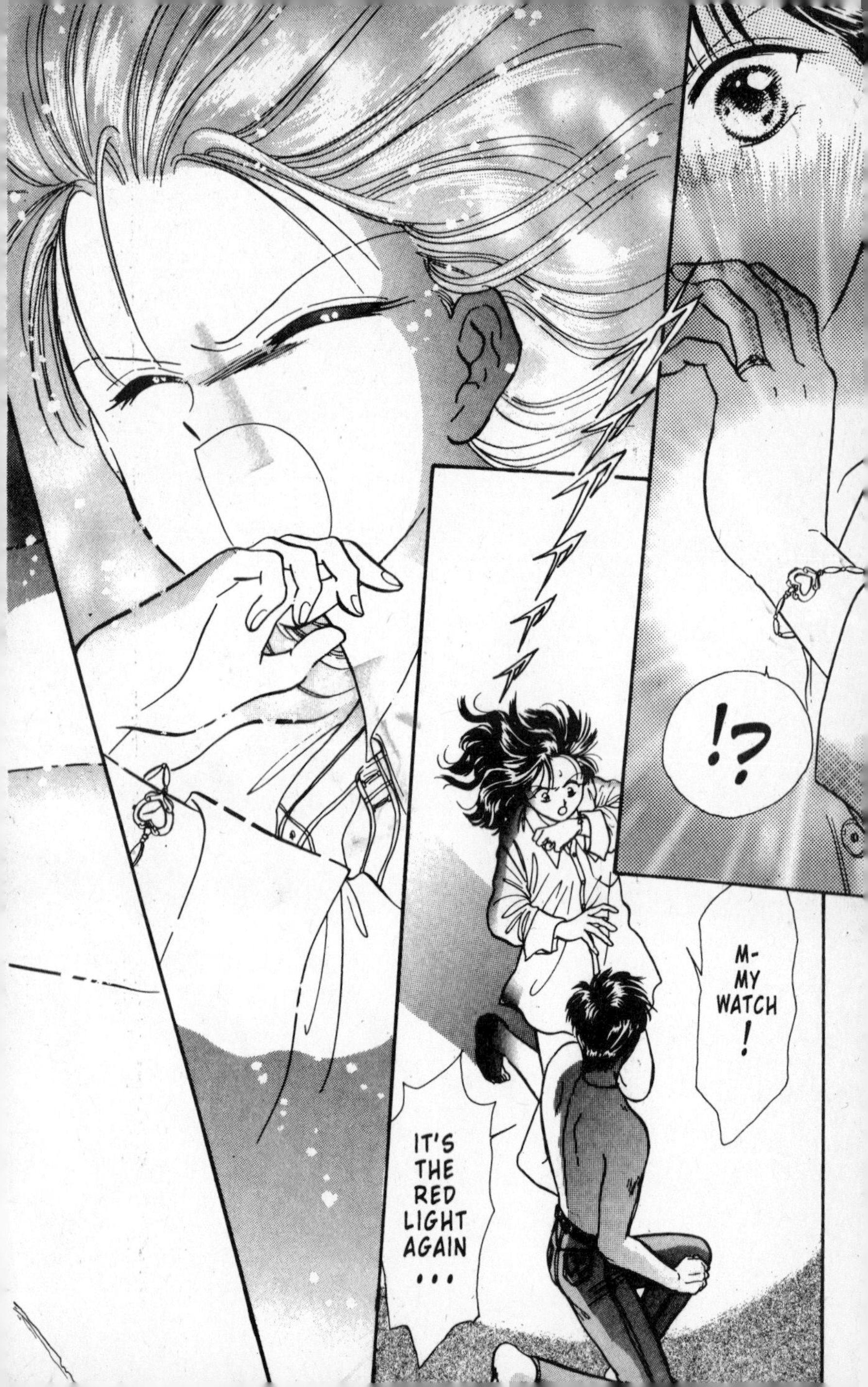
!?
M-MY WATCH!
IT'S THE RED LIGHT AGAIN...

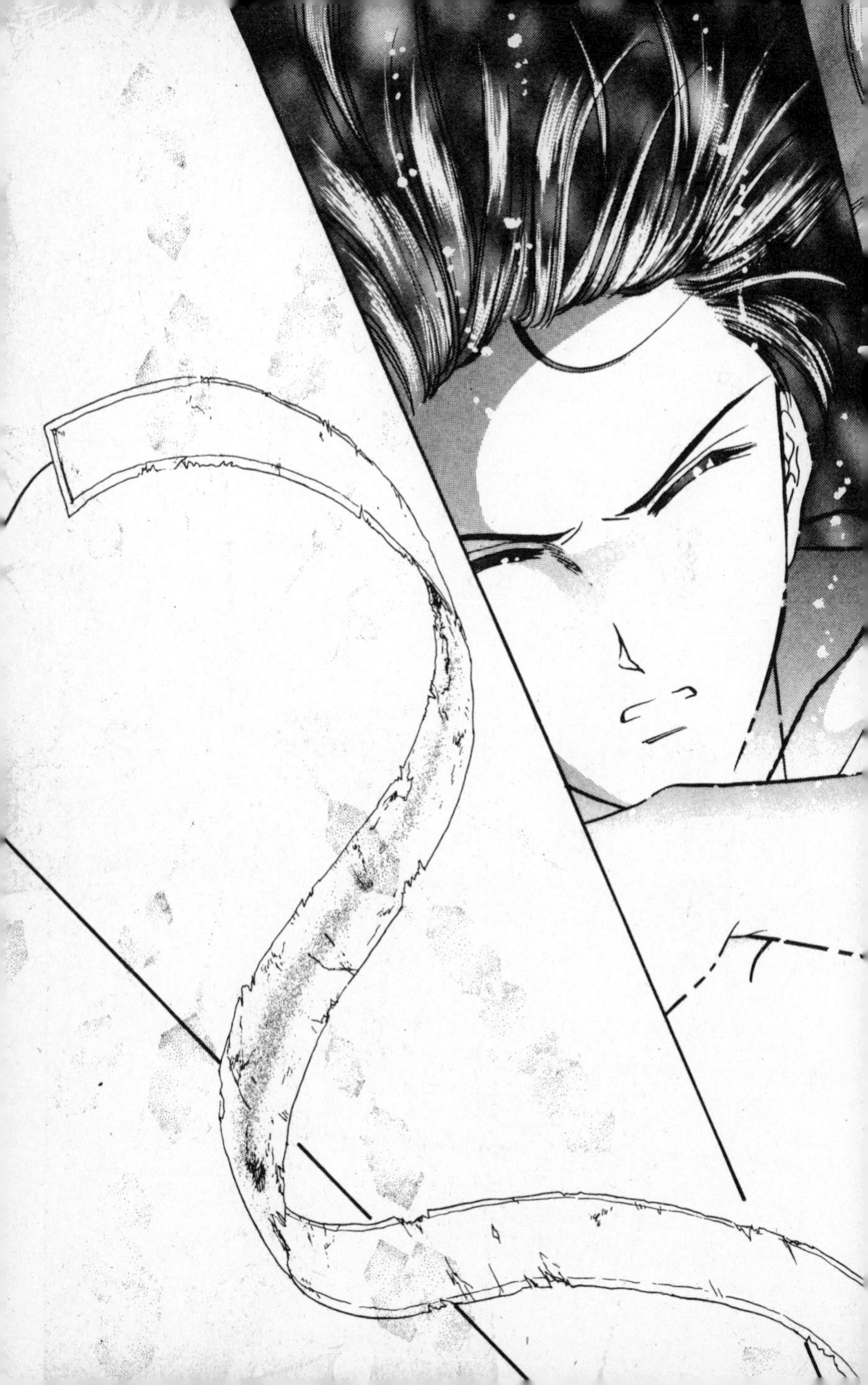

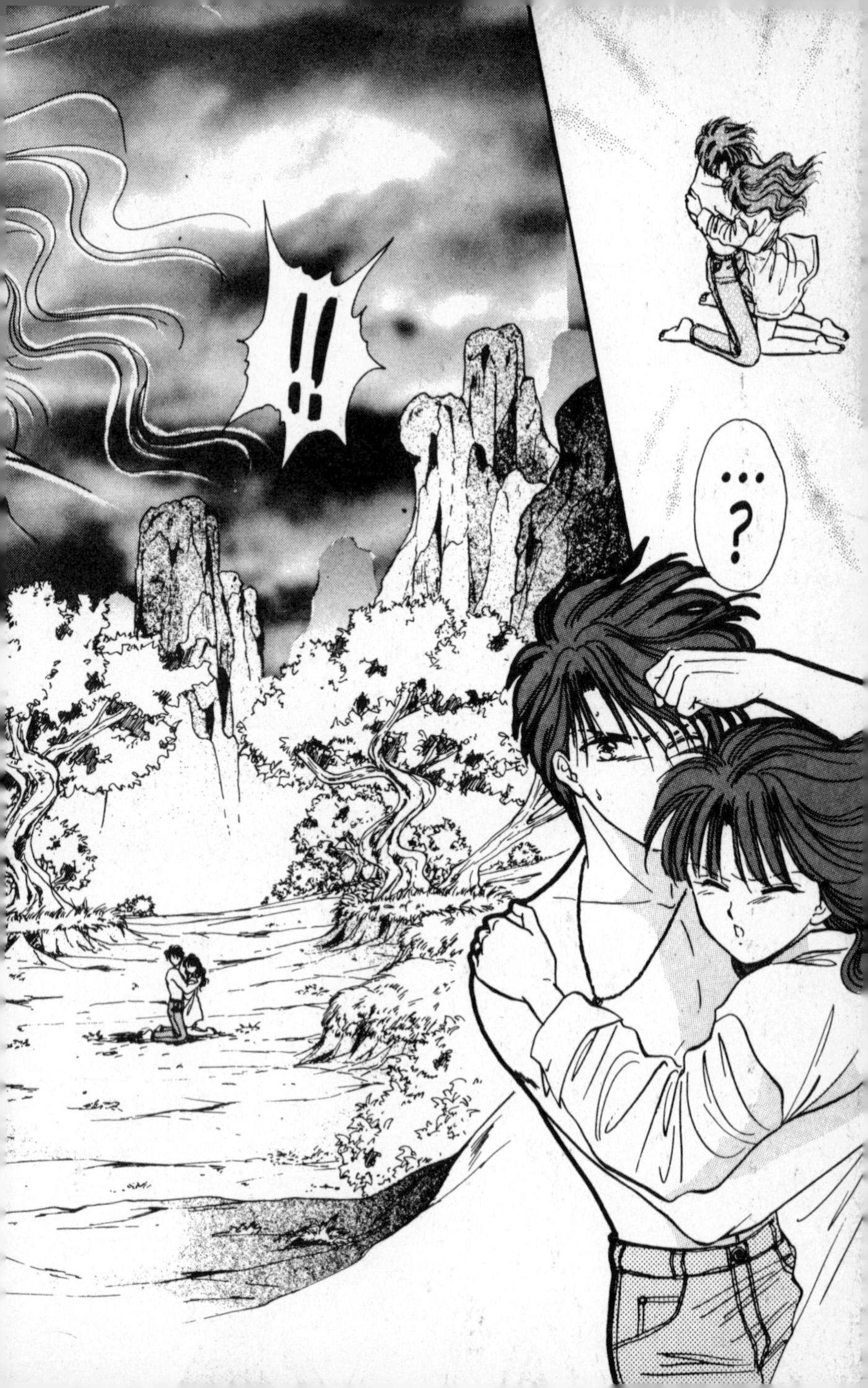

...?
!!

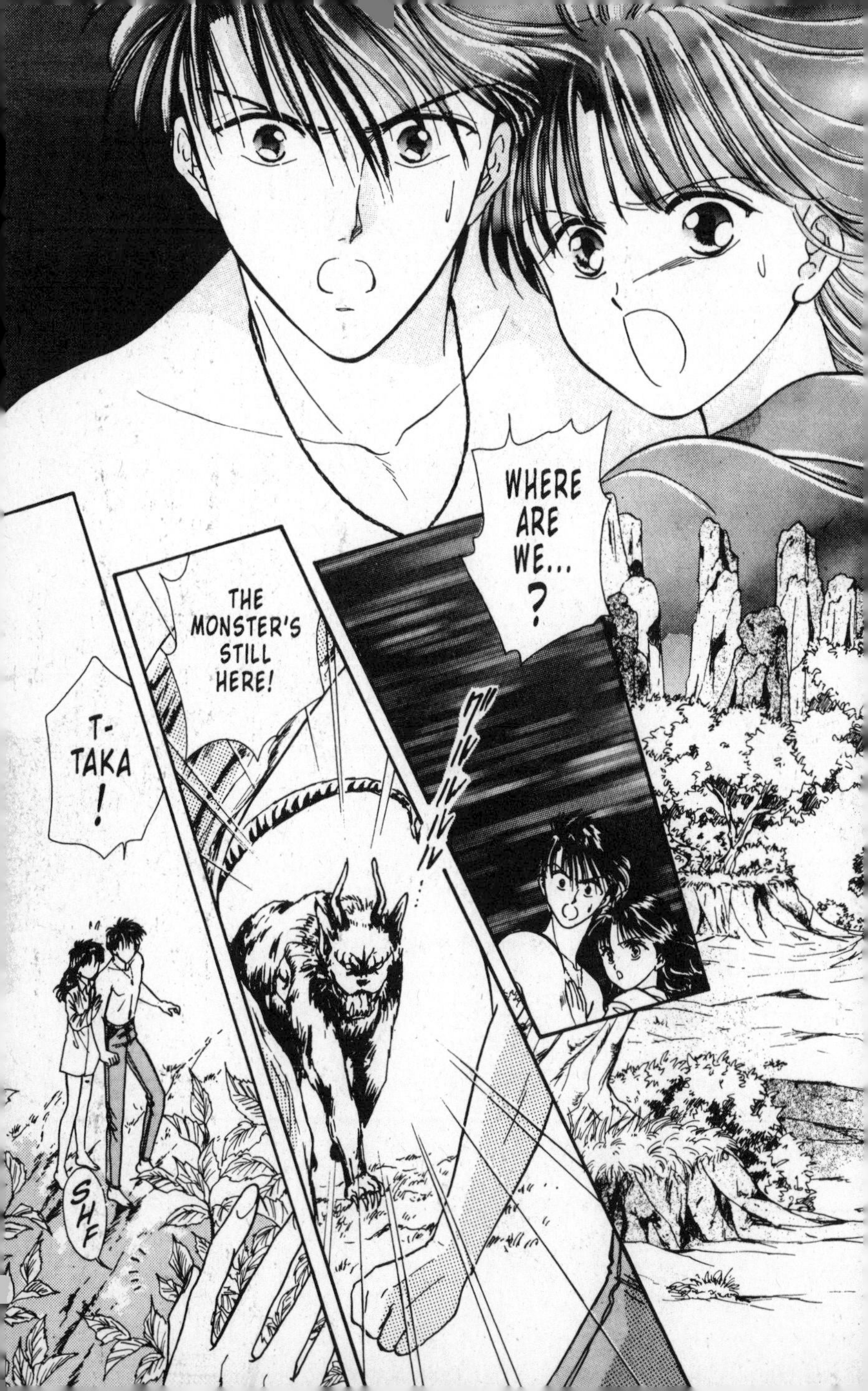
WHERE ARE WE...?
THE MONSTER'S STILL HERE!
T-TAKA!
SHF

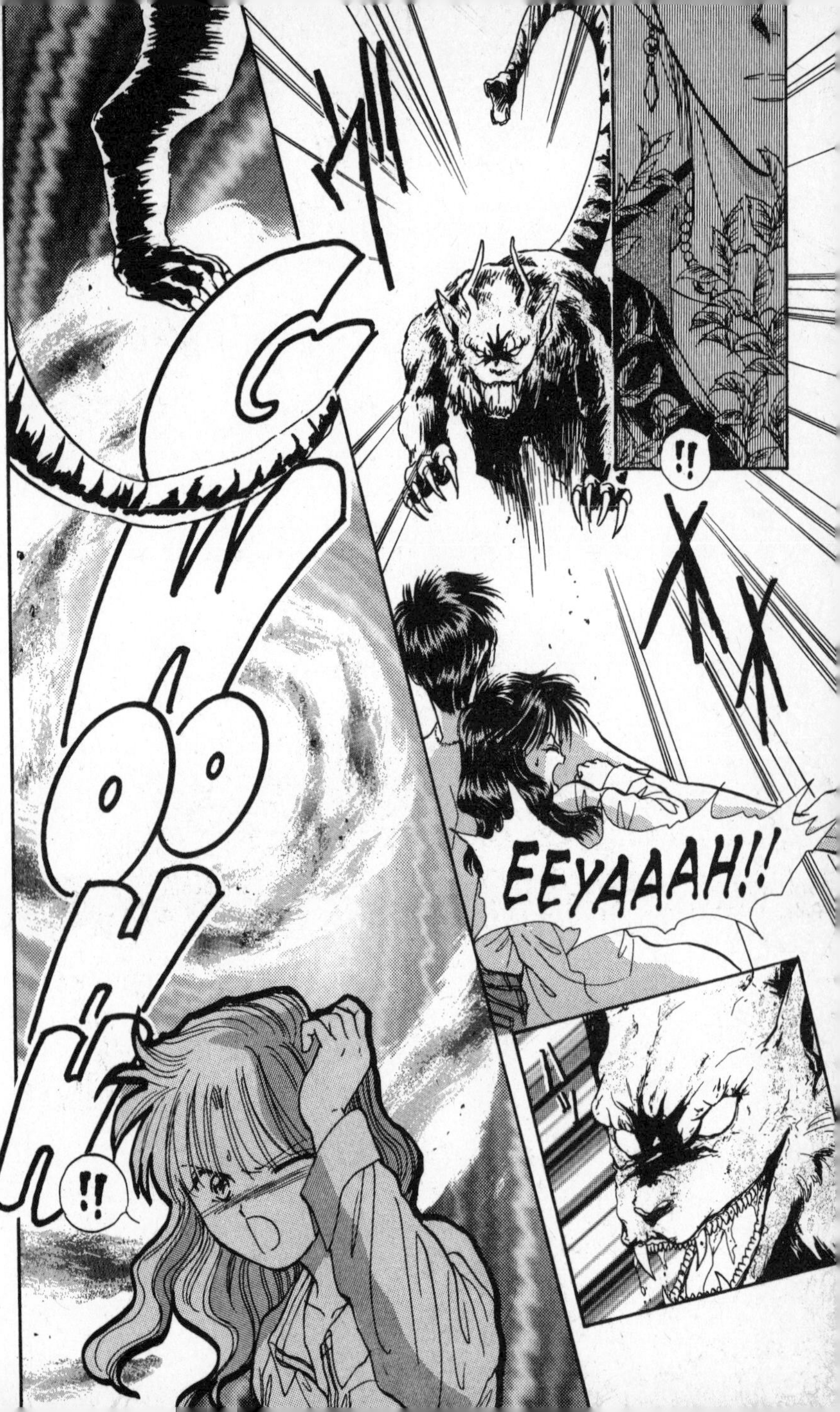
!!
EEYAAAH!!
!!

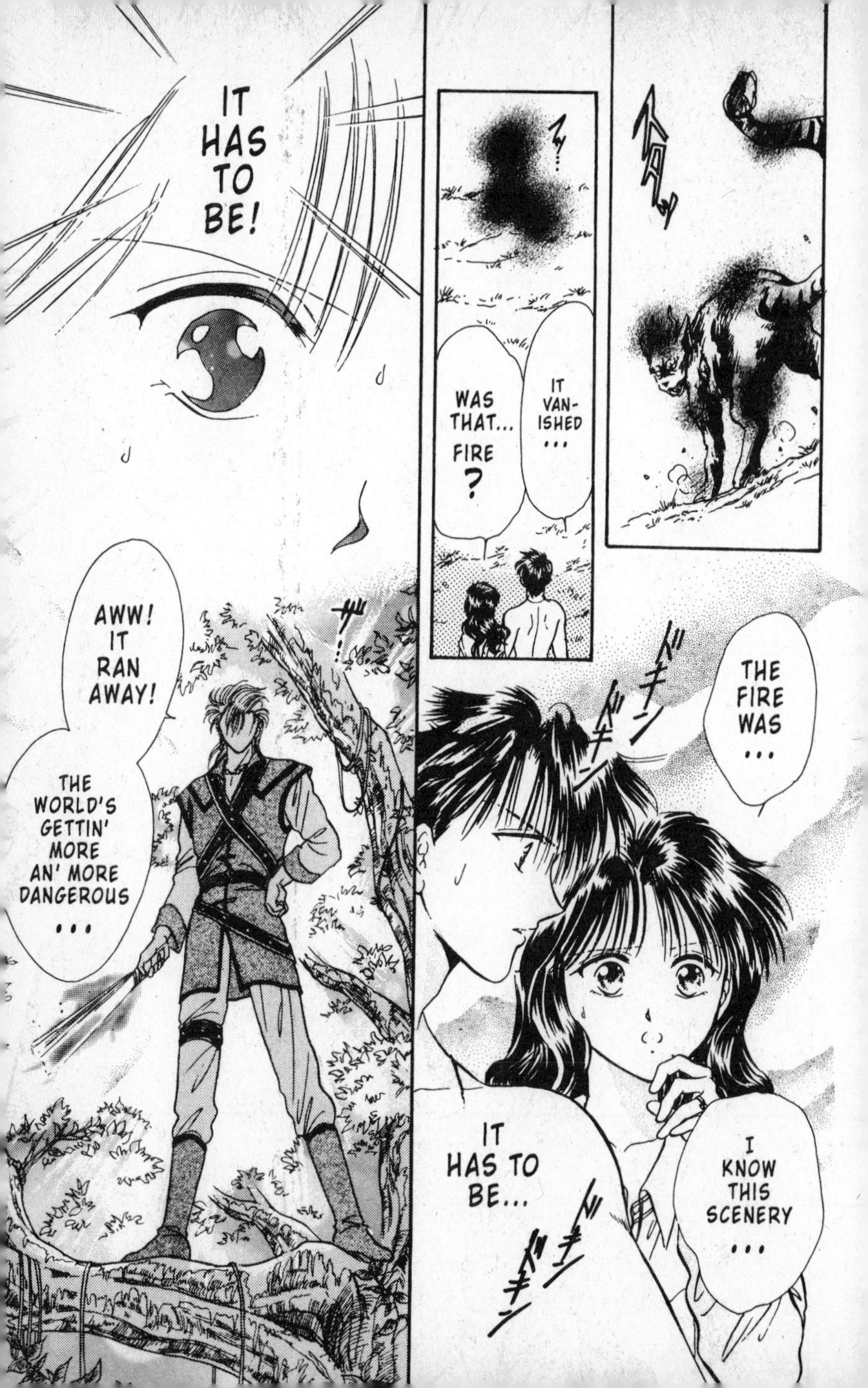
IT VANISHED...
WAS THAT... FIRE?
THE FIRE WAS...
I KNOW THIS SCENERY...
IT HAS TO BE...
IT HAS TO BE!
AWW! IT RAN AWAY!
THE WORLD'S GETTIN' MORE AN' MORE DANGEROUS...

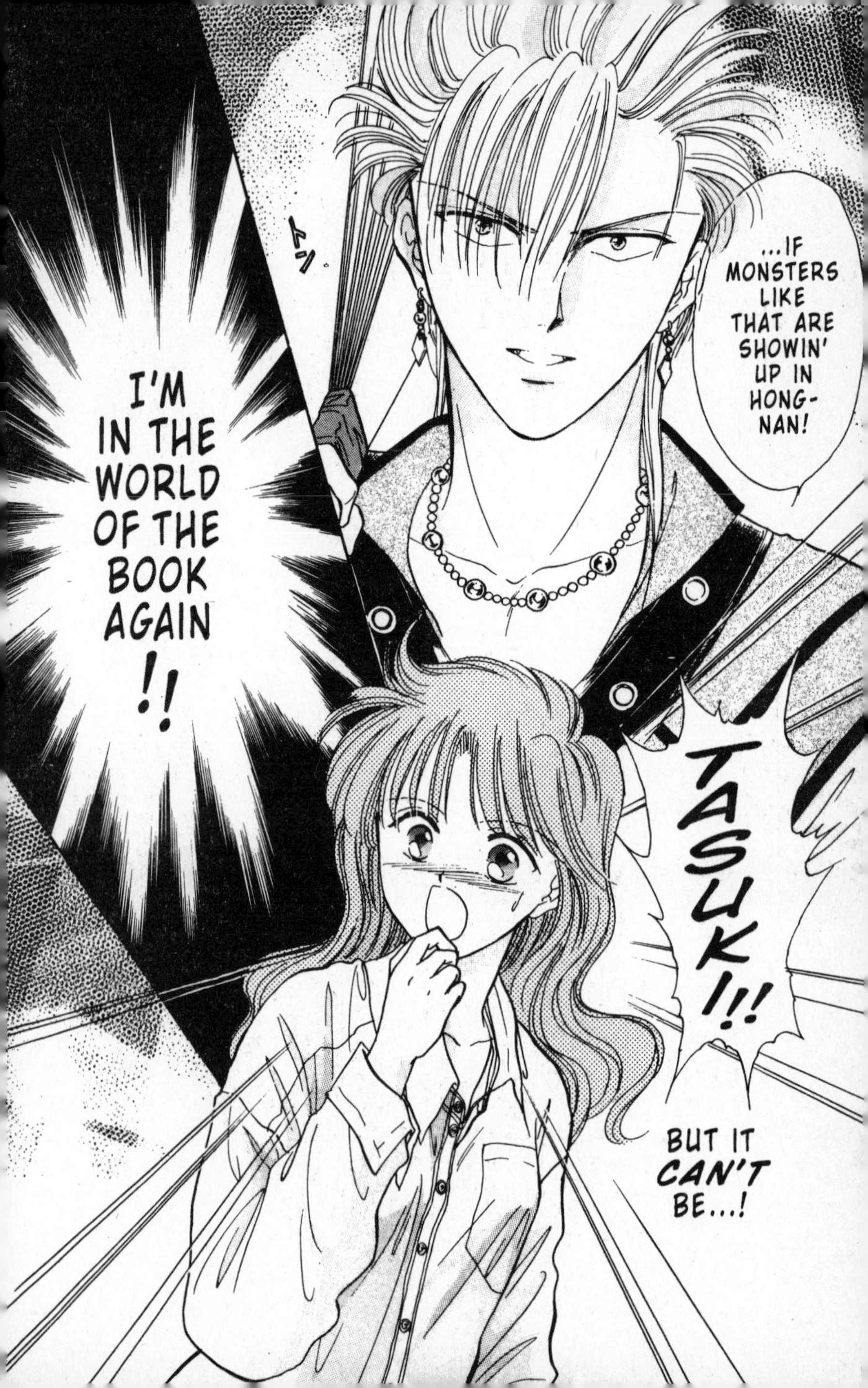

...IF MONSTERS LIKE THAT ARE SHOWIN' UP IN HONG-NAN!
I'M IN THE WORLD OF THE BOOK AGAIN!!
TASUKI!!
BUT IT *CAN'T* BE...!

CHAPTER EIGHTY
THE LOST HEART

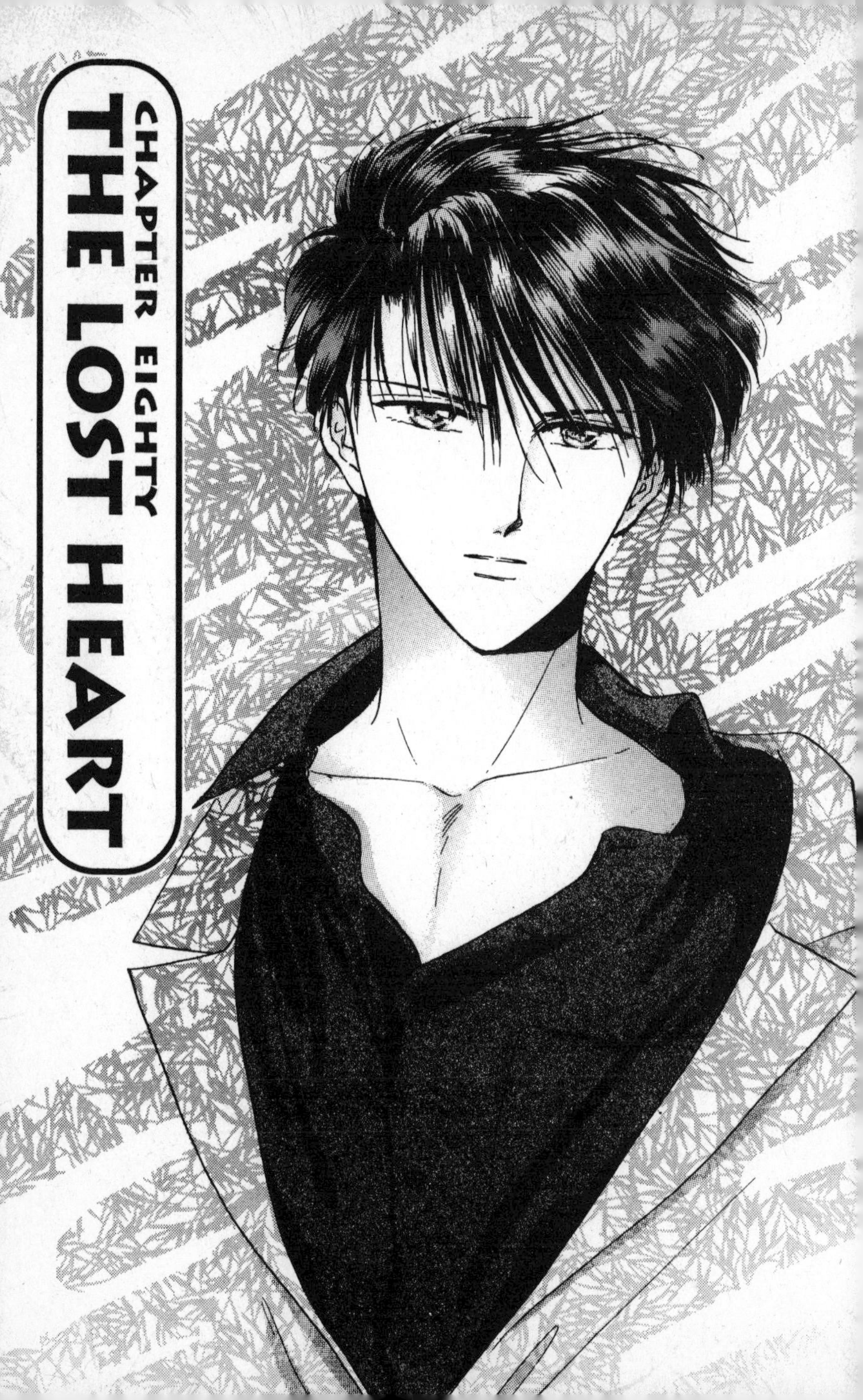

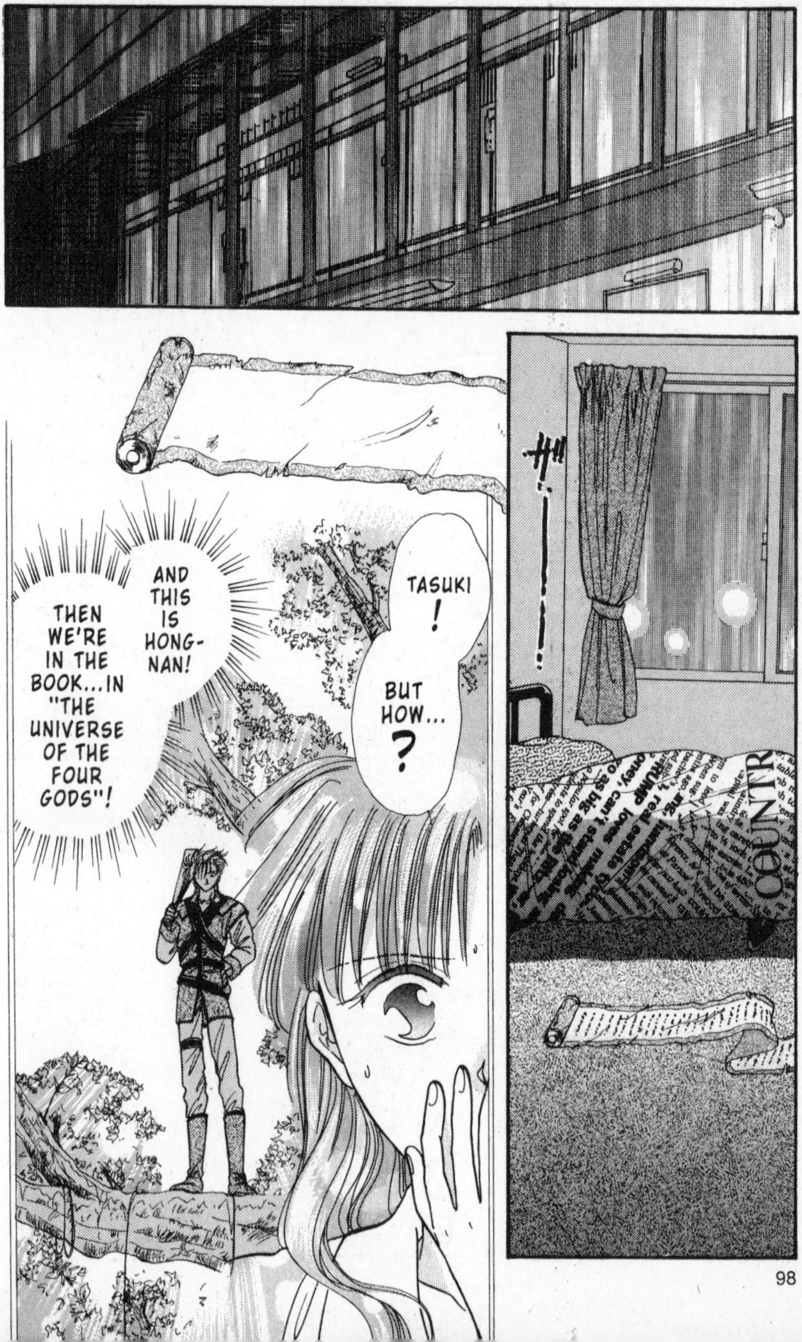
TASUKI!
BUT HOW...?
AND THIS IS HONG-NAN!
THEN WE'RE IN THE BOOK...IN "THE UNIVERSE OF THE FOUR GODS"!

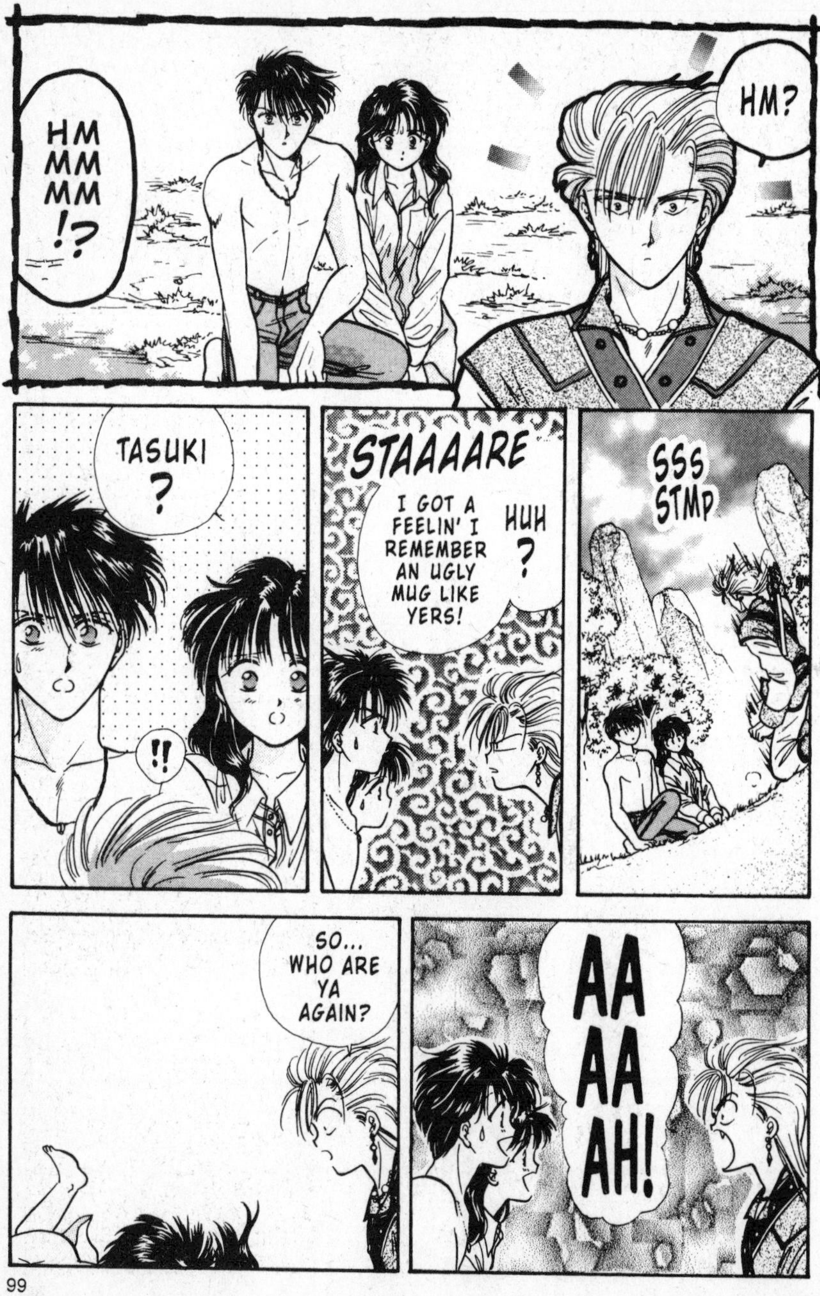
HM?
HMMMMM!?
SSS STMP
STAAAARE
HUH?
I GOT A FEELIN' I REMEMBER AN UGLY MUG LIKE YERS!
TASUKI?
!!
AAAAAAH!
SO... WHO ARE YA AGAIN?

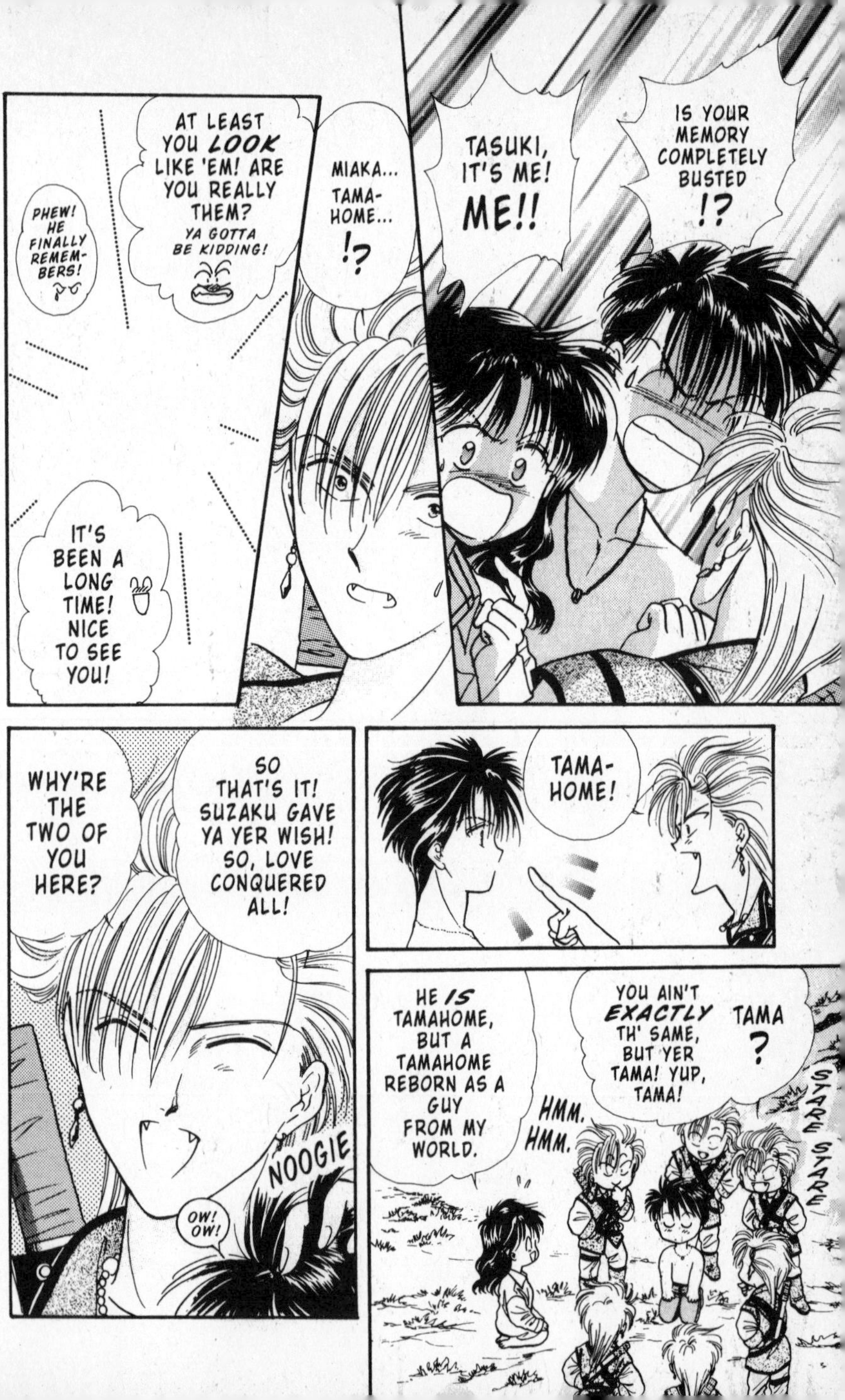
IS YOUR MEMORY COMPLETELY BUSTED !?
TASUKI, IT'S ME! ME!!
MIAKA... TAMA-HOME... !?
AT LEAST YOU LOOK LIKE 'EM! ARE YOU REALLY THEM?
YA GOTTA BE KIDDING!
PHEW! HE FINALLY REMEMBERS!
IT'S BEEN A LONG TIME! NICE TO SEE YOU!
TAMA-HOME!
TAMA ?
YOU AIN'T EXACTLY TH' SAME, BUT YER TAMA! YUP, TAMA!
STARE STARE
HMM. HMM.
HE IS TAMAHOME, BUT A TAMAHOME REBORN AS A GUY FROM MY WORLD.
SO THAT'S IT! SUZAKU GAVE YA YER WISH! SO, LOVE CONQUERED ALL!
WHY'RE THE TWO OF YOU HERE?
NOOGIE
OW! OW!

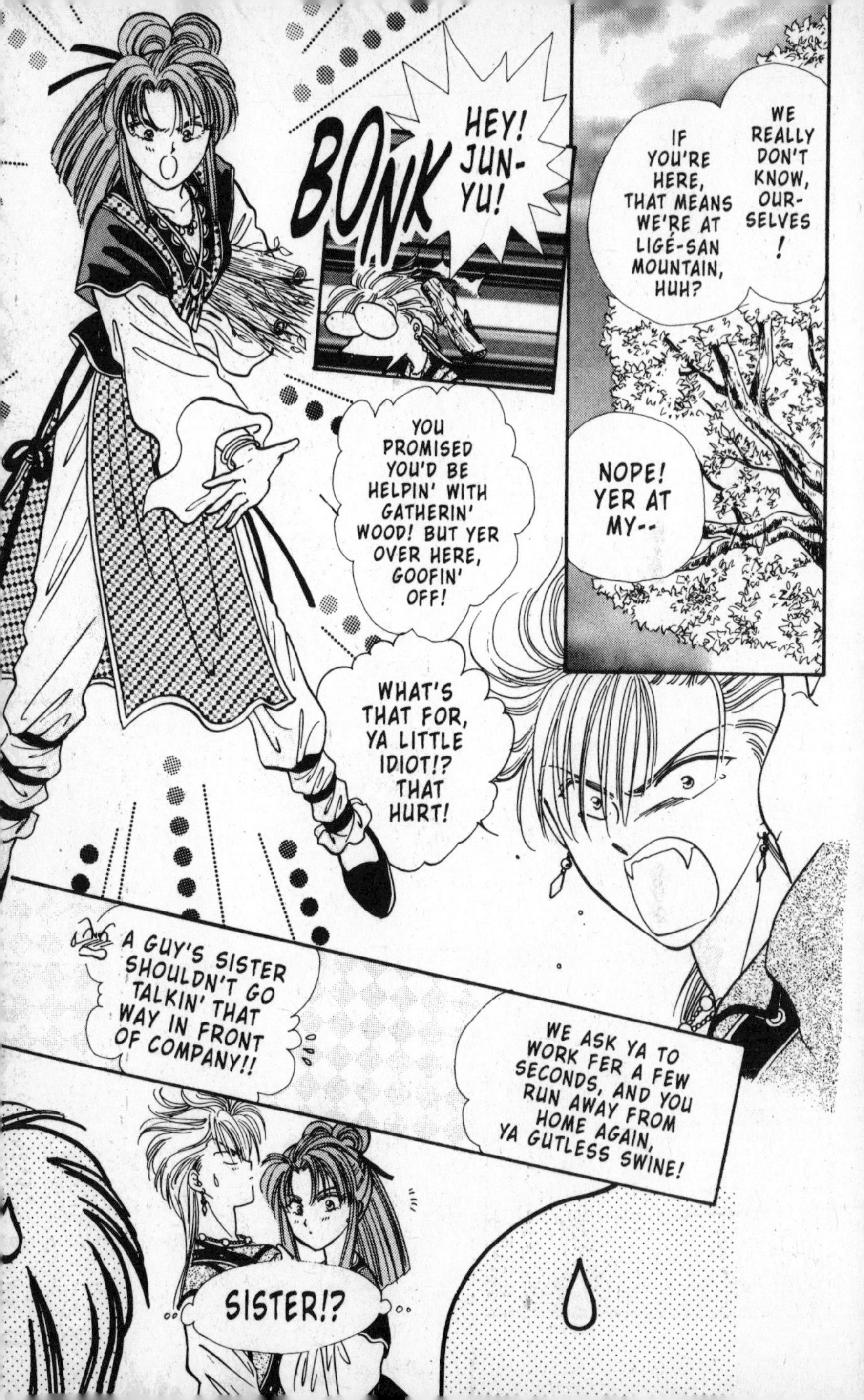
WE REALLY DON'T KNOW, OURSELVES!
IF YOU'RE HERE, THAT MEANS WE'RE AT LIGÉ-SAN MOUNTAIN, HUH?
NOPE! YER AT MY--
HEY! JUN-YU!
BONK
YOU PROMISED YOU'D BE HELPIN' WITH GATHERIN' WOOD! BUT YER OVER HERE, GOOFIN' OFF!
WHAT'S THAT FOR, YA LITTLE IDIOT!? THAT HURT!
WE ASK YA TO WORK FER A FEW SECONDS, AND YOU RUN AWAY FROM HOME AGAIN, YA GUTLESS SWINE!
A GUY'S SISTER SHOULDN'T GO TALKIN' THAT WAY IN FRONT OF COMPANY!!
SISTER!?

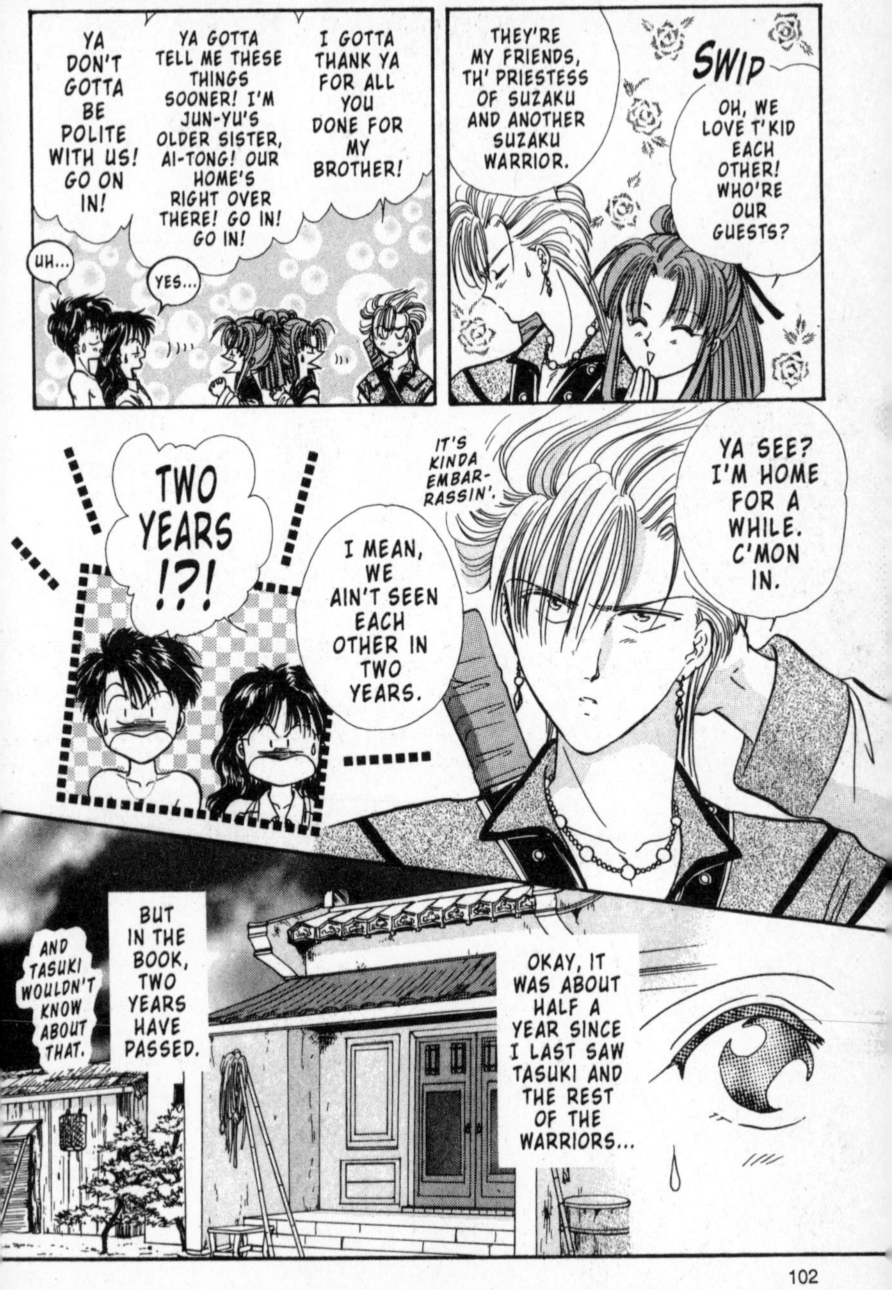
SWIP
OH, WE LOVE T'KID EACH OTHER! WHO'RE OUR GUESTS?
THEY'RE MY FRIENDS, TH' PRIESTESS OF SUZAKU AND ANOTHER SUZAKU WARRIOR.
I GOTTA THANK YA FOR ALL YOU DONE FOR MY BROTHER!
YA GOTTA TELL ME THESE THINGS SOONER! I'M JUN-YU'S OLDER SISTER, AI-TONG! OUR HOME'S RIGHT OVER THERE! GO IN! GO IN!
YA DON'T GOTTA BE POLITE WITH US! GO ON IN!
YES...
UH...
YA SEE? I'M HOME FOR A WHILE. C'MON IN.
IT'S KINDA EMBARRASSIN'.
I MEAN, WE AIN'T SEEN EACH OTHER IN TWO YEARS.
TWO YEARS !?!
OKAY, IT WAS ABOUT HALF A YEAR SINCE I LAST SAW TASUKI AND THE REST OF THE WARRIORS...
BUT IN THE BOOK, TWO YEARS HAVE PASSED.
AND TASUKI WOULDN'T KNOW ABOUT THAT.

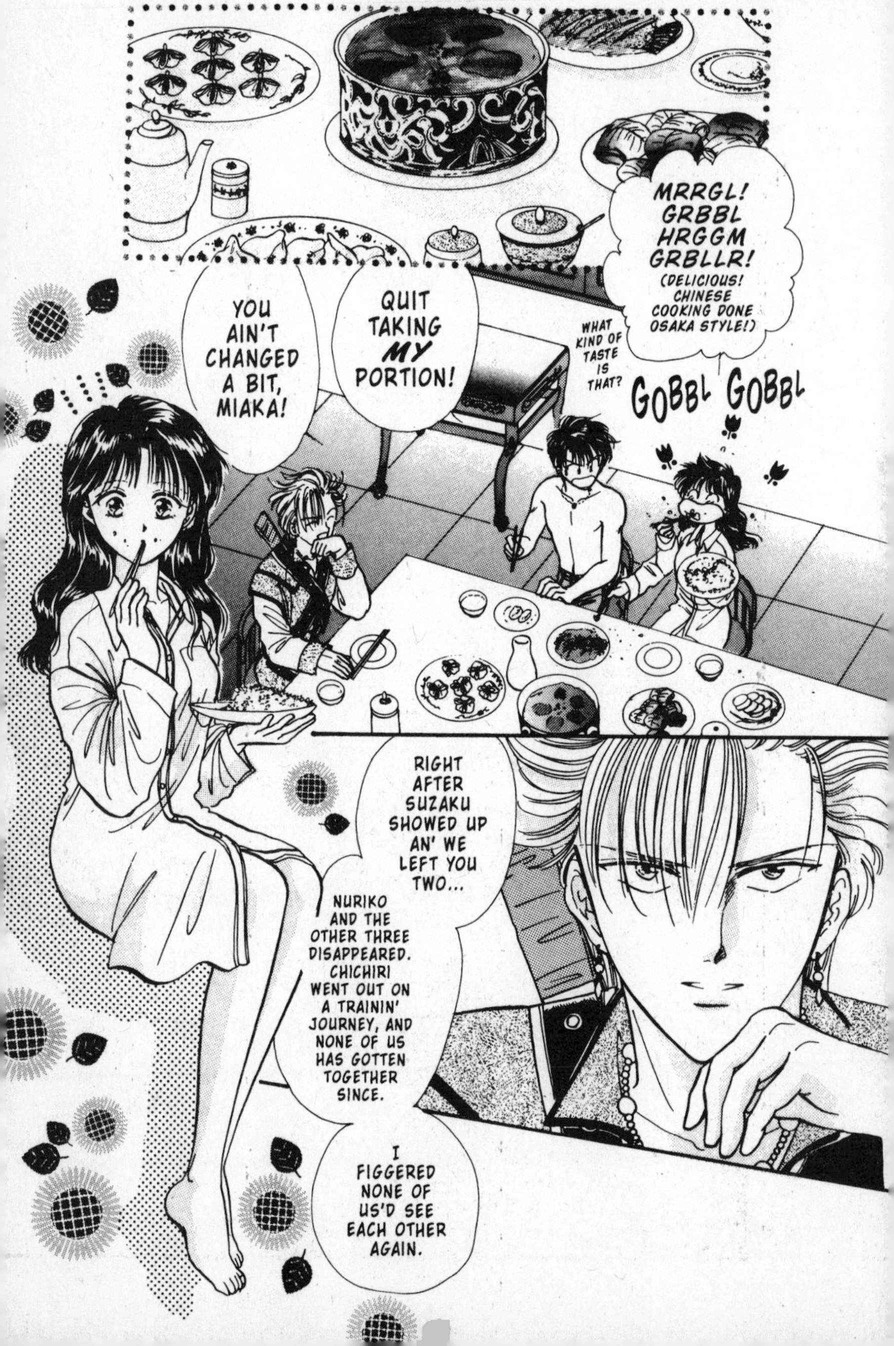
MRRGL! GRBBL HRGGM GRBLLR! (DELICIOUS! CHINESE COOKING DONE OSAKA STYLE!)
WHAT KIND OF TASTE IS THAT?
GOBBL GOBBL
QUIT TAKING MY PORTION!
YOU AIN'T CHANGED A BIT, MIAKA!
RIGHT AFTER SUZAKU SHOWED UP AN' WE LEFT YOU TWO...
NURIKO AND THE OTHER THREE DISAPPEARED. CHICHIRI WENT OUT ON A TRAININ' JOURNEY, AND NONE OF US HAS GOTTEN TOGETHER SINCE.
I FIGGERED NONE OF US'D SEE EACH OTHER AGAIN.

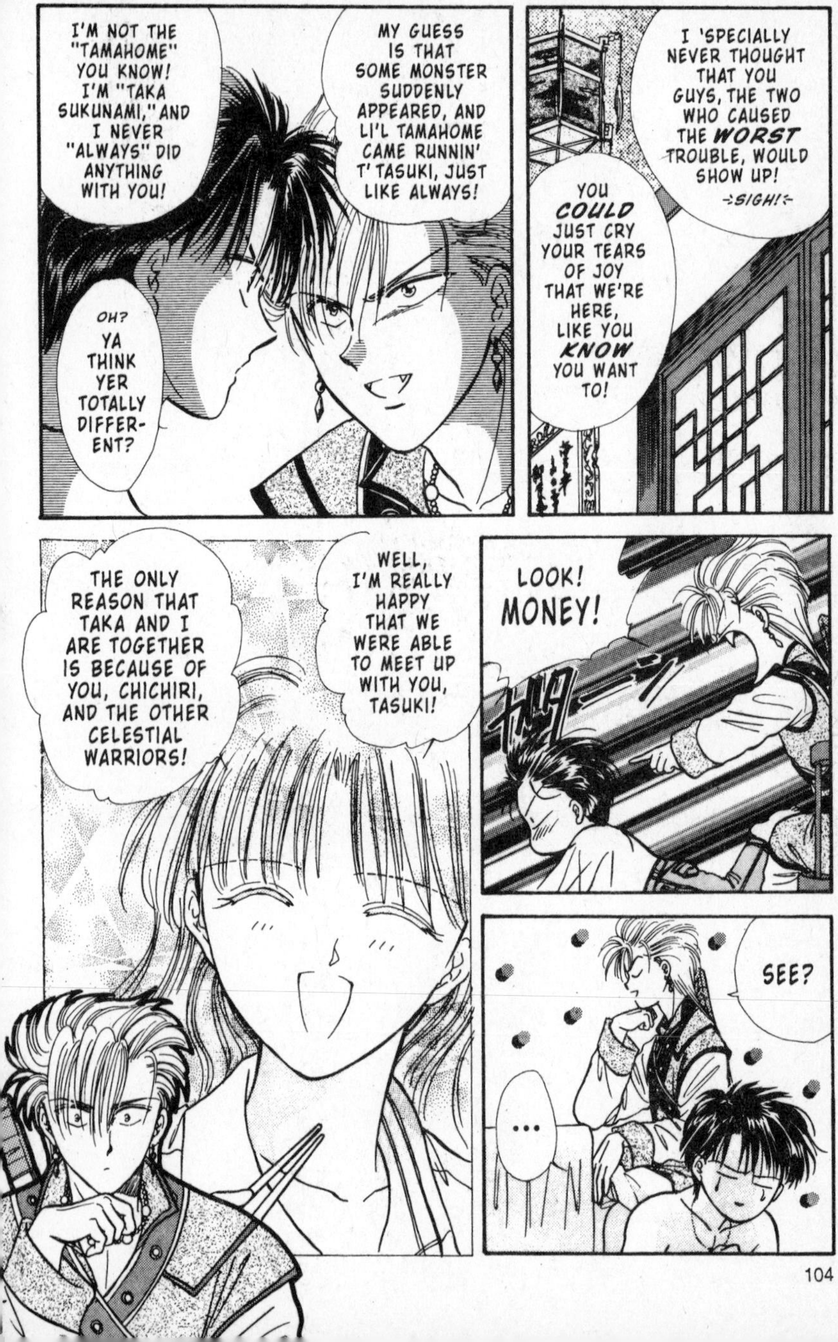
I 'SPECIALLY NEVER THOUGHT THAT YOU GUYS, THE TWO WHO CAUSED THE WORST TROUBLE, WOULD SHOW UP!
SIGH!
YOU COULD JUST CRY YOUR TEARS OF JOY THAT WE'RE HERE, LIKE YOU KNOW YOU WANT TO!
MY GUESS IS THAT SOME MONSTER SUDDENLY APPEARED, AND LI'L TAMAHOME CAME RUNNIN' T' TASUKI, JUST LIKE ALWAYS!
I'M NOT THE "TAMAHOME" YOU KNOW! I'M "TAKA SUKUNAMI," AND I NEVER "ALWAYS" DID ANYTHING WITH YOU!
OH? YA THINK YER TOTALLY DIFFER-ENT?
LOOK! MONEY!
SEE?
...
WELL, I'M REALLY HAPPY THAT WE WERE ABLE TO MEET UP WITH YOU, TASUKI!
THE ONLY REASON THAT TAKA AND I ARE TOGETHER IS BECAUSE OF YOU, CHICHIRI, AND THE OTHER CELESTIAL WARRIORS!

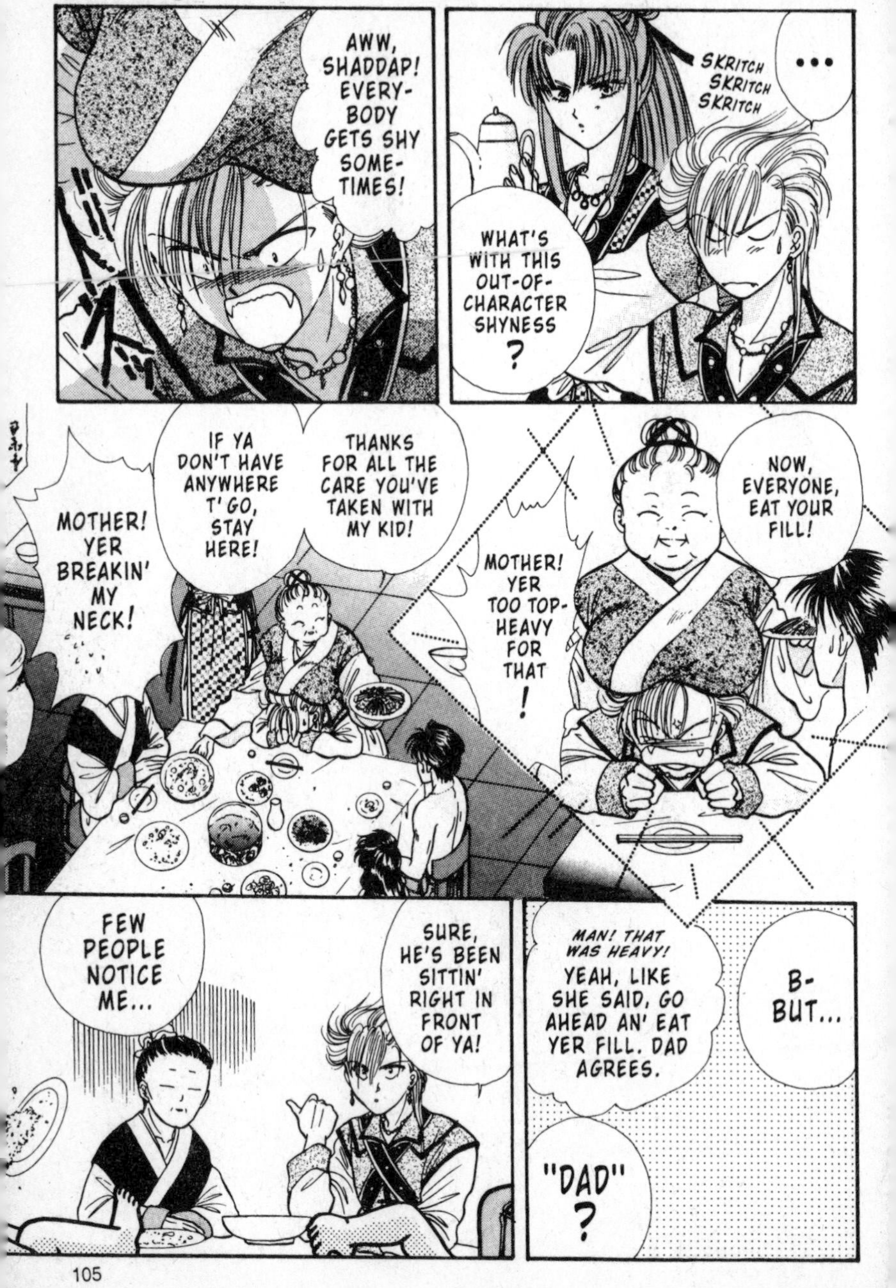
...
SKRITCH SKRITCH SKRITCH
WHAT'S WITH THIS OUT-OF-CHARACTER SHYNESS?
AWW, SHADDAP! EVERYBODY GETS SHY SOMETIMES!
NOW, EVERYONE, EAT YOUR FILL!
MOTHER! YER TOO TOP-HEAVY FOR THAT!
THANKS FOR ALL THE CARE YOU'VE TAKEN WITH MY KID!
IF YA DON'T HAVE ANYWHERE T' GO, STAY HERE!
MOTHER! YER BREAKIN' MY NECK!
B-BUT...
MAN! THAT WAS HEAVY!
YEAH, LIKE SHE SAID, GO AHEAD AN' EAT YER FILL. DAD AGREES.
"DAD"?
FEW PEOPLE NOTICE ME...
SURE, HE'S BEEN SITTIN' RIGHT IN FRONT OF YA!

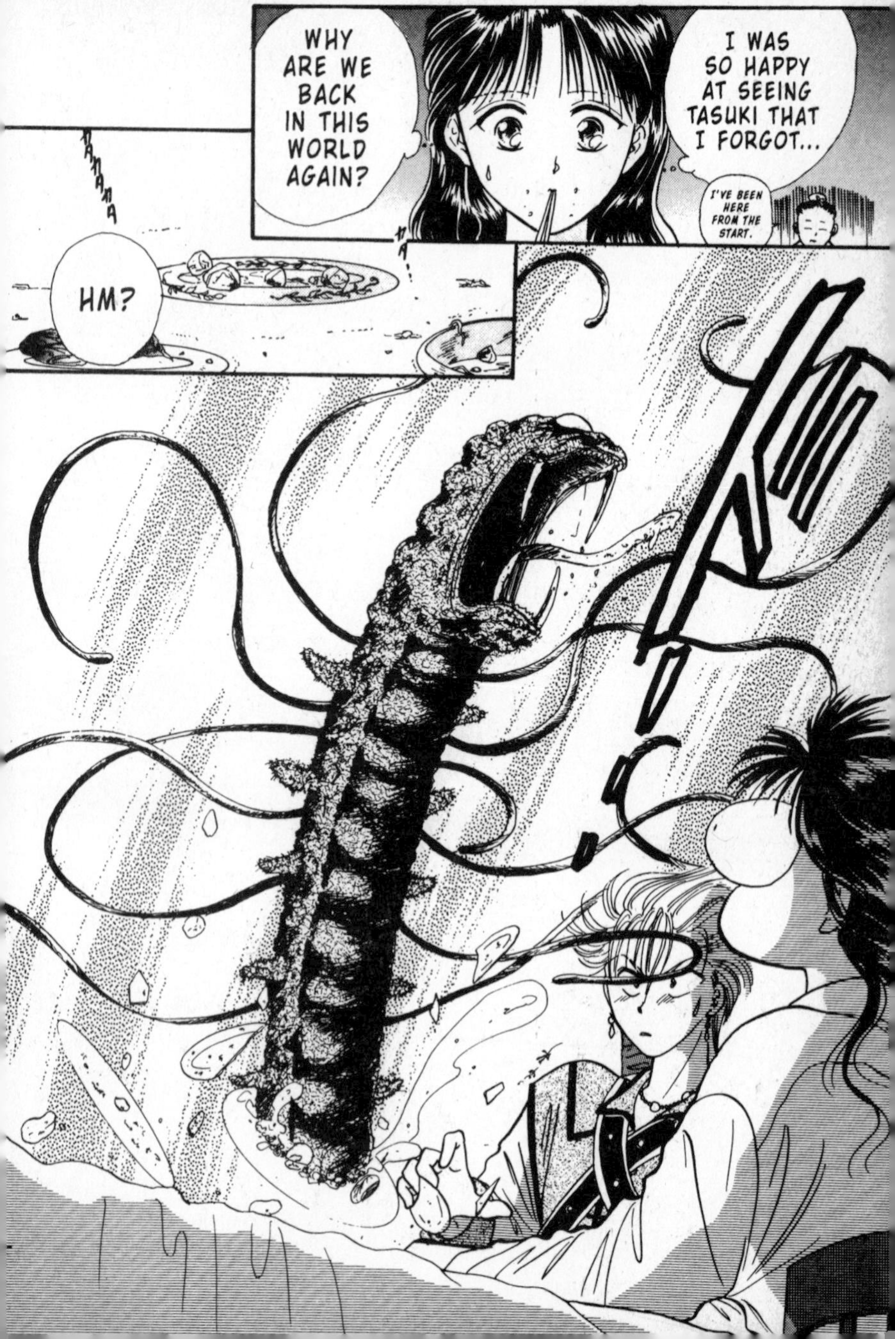
I WAS SO HAPPY AT SEEING TASUKI THAT I FORGOT...
WHY ARE WE BACK IN THIS WORLD AGAIN?
I'VE BEEN HERE FROM THE START.
HM?

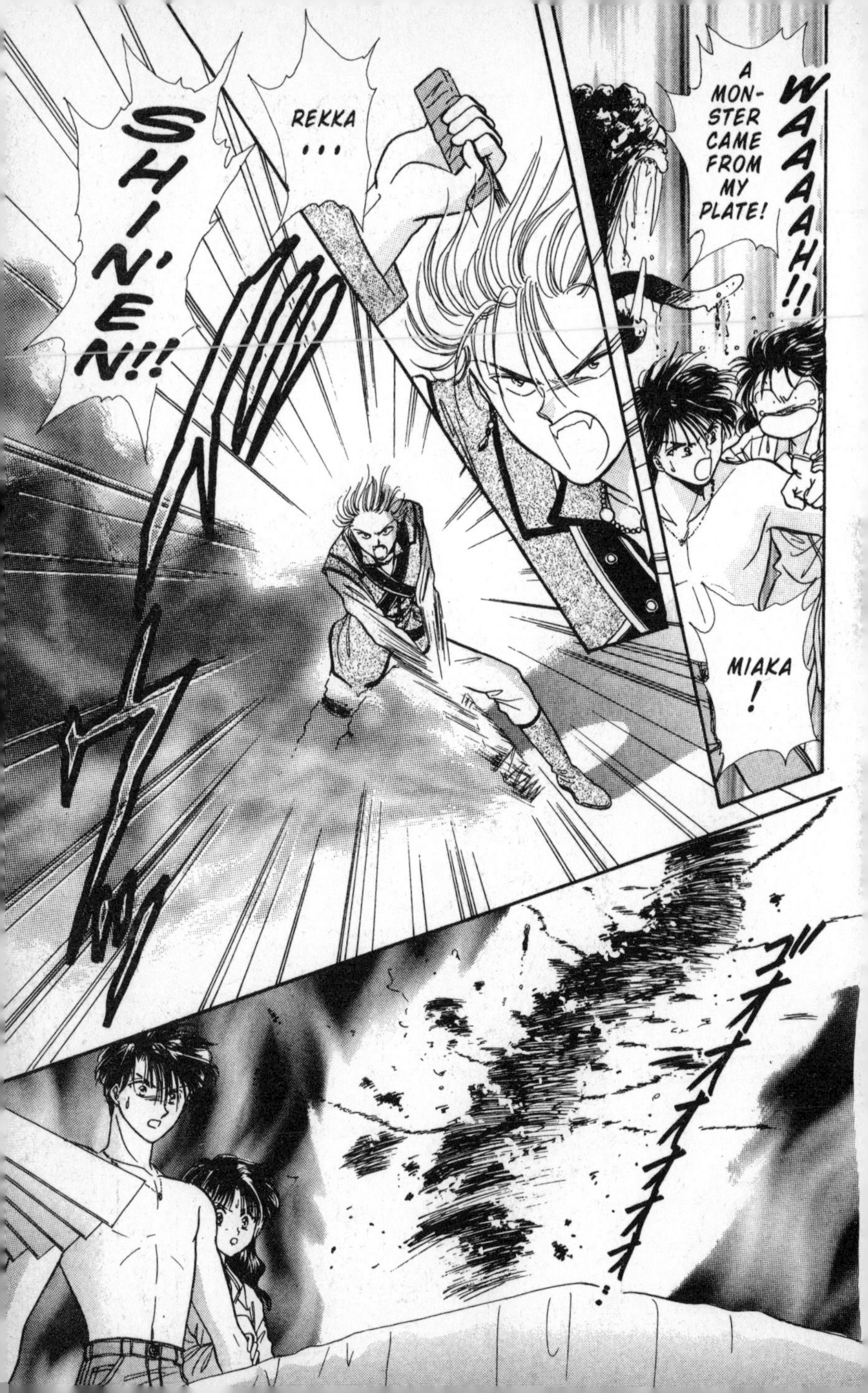
WAAAAAH!!
A MON-STER CAME FROM MY PLATE!
MIAKA!
REKKA...
SHIN'EN!!

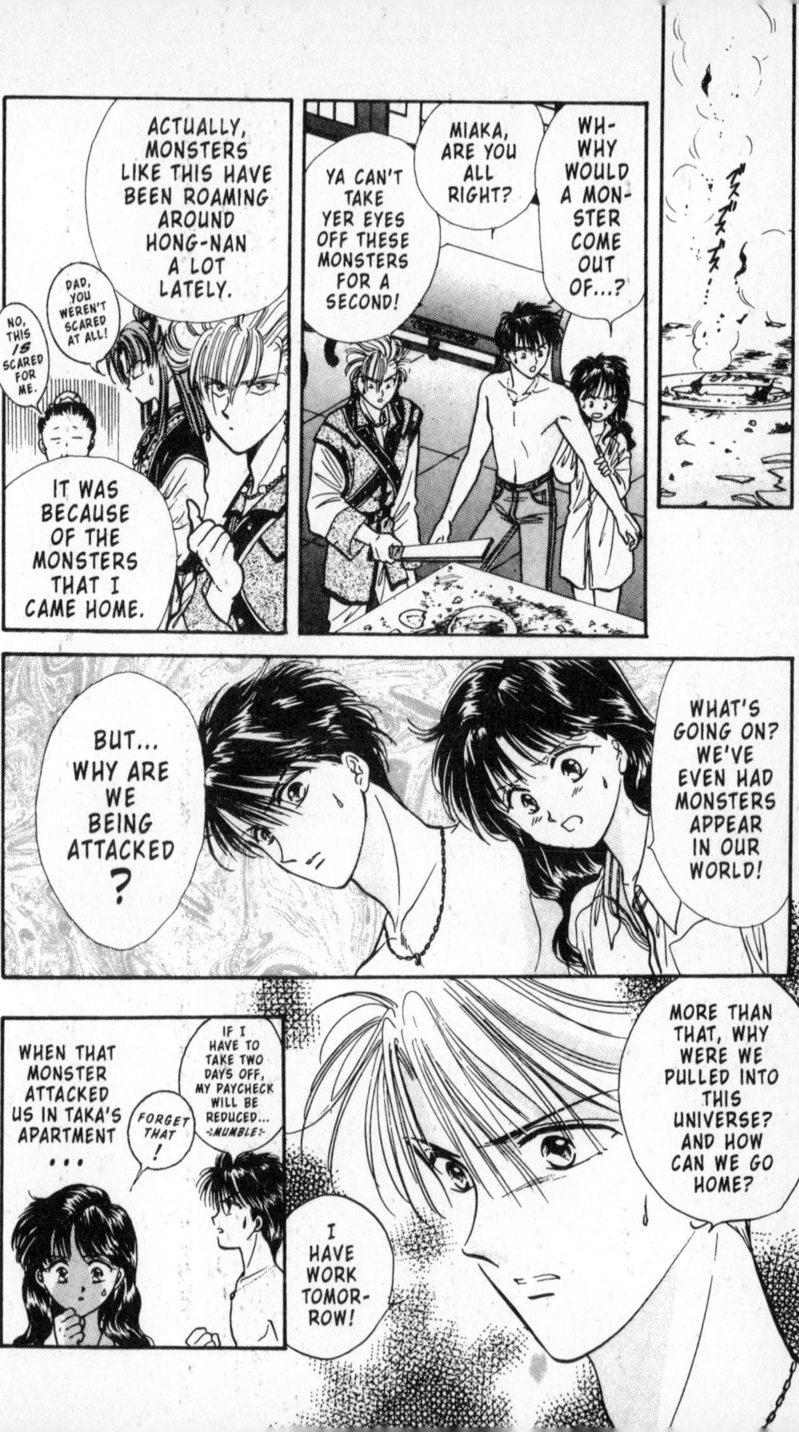
ズズズズ…
WH-WHY WOULD A MONSTER COME OUT OF...?
MIAKA, ARE YOU ALL RIGHT?
YA CAN'T TAKE YER EYES OFF THESE MONSTERS FOR A SECOND!
ACTUALLY, MONSTERS LIKE THIS HAVE BEEN ROAMING AROUND HONG-NAN A LOT LATELY.
DAD, YOU WEREN'T SCARED AT ALL!
NO, THIS *IS* SCARED FOR ME.
IT WAS BECAUSE OF THE MONSTERS THAT I CAME HOME.
WHAT'S GOING ON? WE'VE EVEN HAD MONSTERS APPEAR IN OUR WORLD!
BUT... WHY ARE WE BEING ATTACKED?
MORE THAN THAT, WHY WERE WE PULLED INTO THIS UNIVERSE? AND HOW CAN WE GO HOME?
I HAVE WORK TOMORROW!
IF I HAVE TO TAKE TWO DAYS OFF, MY PAYCHECK WILL BE REDUCED... MUMBLE
FORGET THAT!
WHEN THAT MONSTER ATTACKED US IN TAKA'S APARTMENT ...

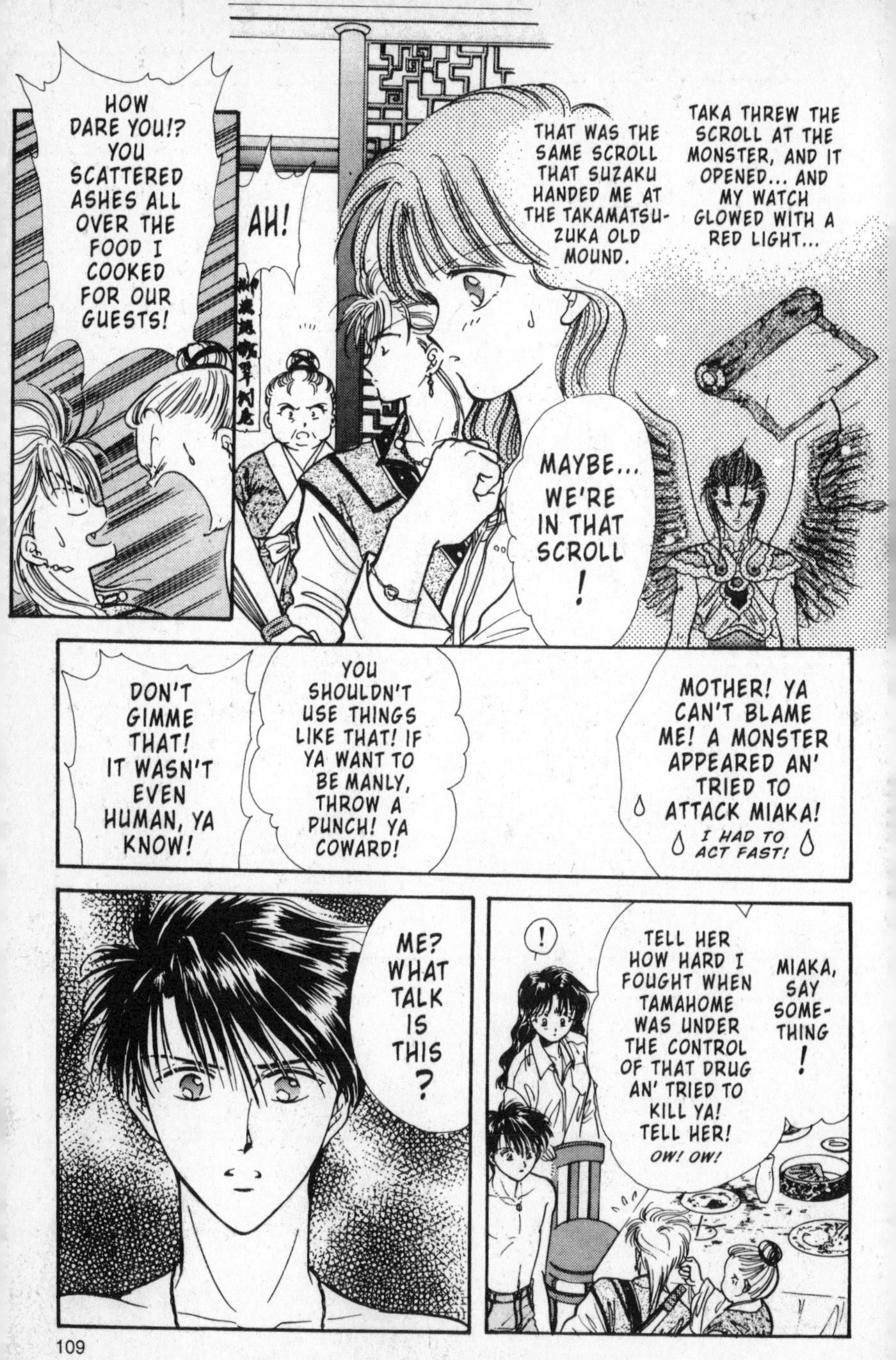
TAKA THREW THE SCROLL AT THE MONSTER, AND IT OPENED... AND MY WATCH GLOWED WITH A RED LIGHT...
THAT WAS THE SAME SCROLL THAT SUZAKU HANDED ME AT THE TAKAMATSU-ZUKA OLD MOUND.
MAYBE... WE'RE IN THAT SCROLL!
AH!
HOW DARE YOU!? YOU SCATTERED ASHES ALL OVER THE FOOD I COOKED FOR OUR GUESTS!
MOTHER! YA CAN'T BLAME ME! A MONSTER APPEARED AN' TRIED TO ATTACK MIAKA!
I HAD TO ACT FAST!
YOU SHOULDN'T USE THINGS LIKE THAT! IF YA WANT TO BE MANLY, THROW A PUNCH! YA COWARD!
DON'T GIMME THAT! IT WASN'T EVEN HUMAN, YA KNOW!
MIAKA, SAY SOMETHING!
TELL HER HOW HARD I FOUGHT WHEN TAMAHOME WAS UNDER THE CONTROL OF THAT DRUG AN' TRIED TO KILL YA! TELL HER!
OW! OW!
!
ME? WHAT TALK IS THIS?

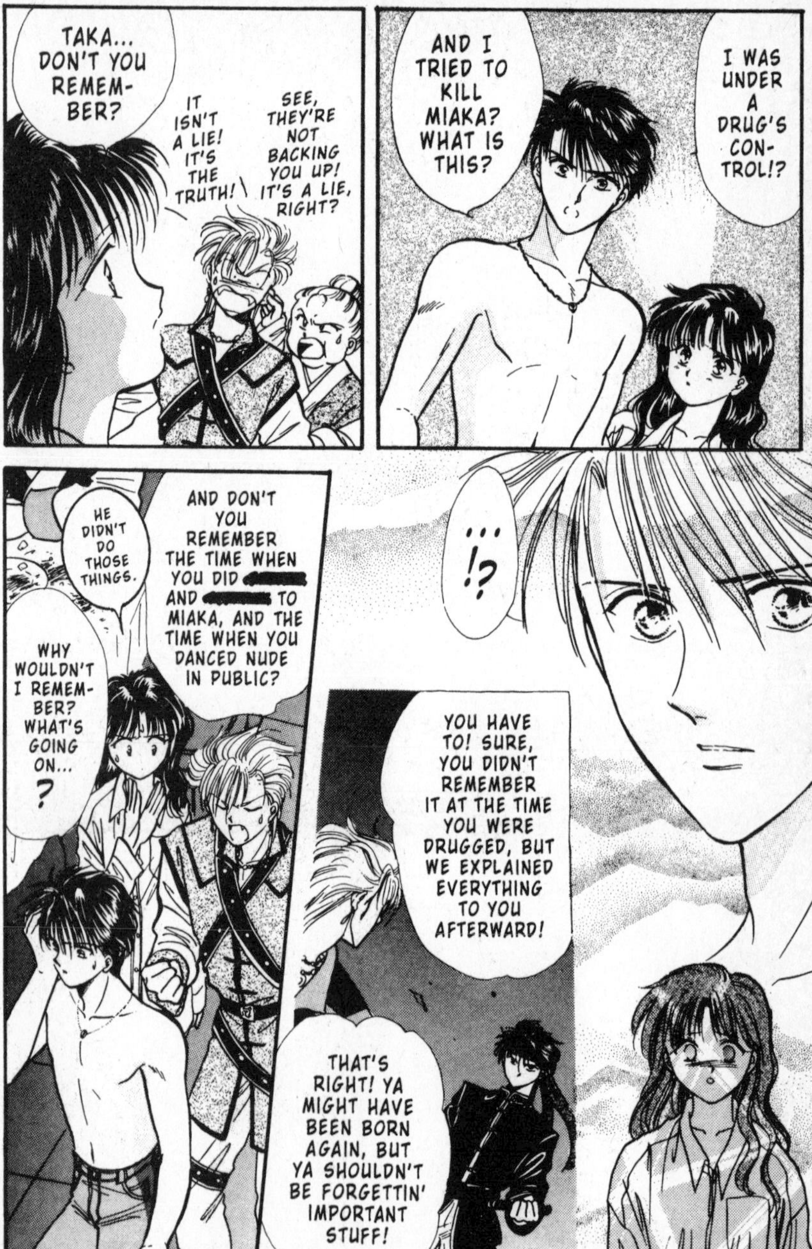
I WAS UNDER A DRUG'S CON-TROL!?
AND I TRIED TO KILL MIAKA? WHAT IS THIS?
TAKA... DON'T YOU REMEM-BER?
SEE, THEY'RE NOT BACKING YOU UP! IT'S A LIE, RIGHT?
IT ISN'T A LIE! IT'S THE TRUTH!
...!?
AND DON'T YOU REMEMBER THE TIME WHEN YOU DID [redacted] AND [redacted] TO MIAKA, AND THE TIME WHEN YOU DANCED NUDE IN PUBLIC?
HE DIDN'T DO THOSE THINGS.
WHY WOULDN'T I REMEM-BER? WHAT'S GOING ON...?
YOU HAVE TO! SURE, YOU DIDN'T REMEMBER IT AT THE TIME YOU WERE DRUGGED, BUT WE EXPLAINED EVERYTHING TO YOU AFTERWARD!
THAT'S RIGHT! YA MIGHT HAVE BEEN BORN AGAIN, BUT YA SHOULDN'T BE FORGETTIN' IMPORTANT STUFF!

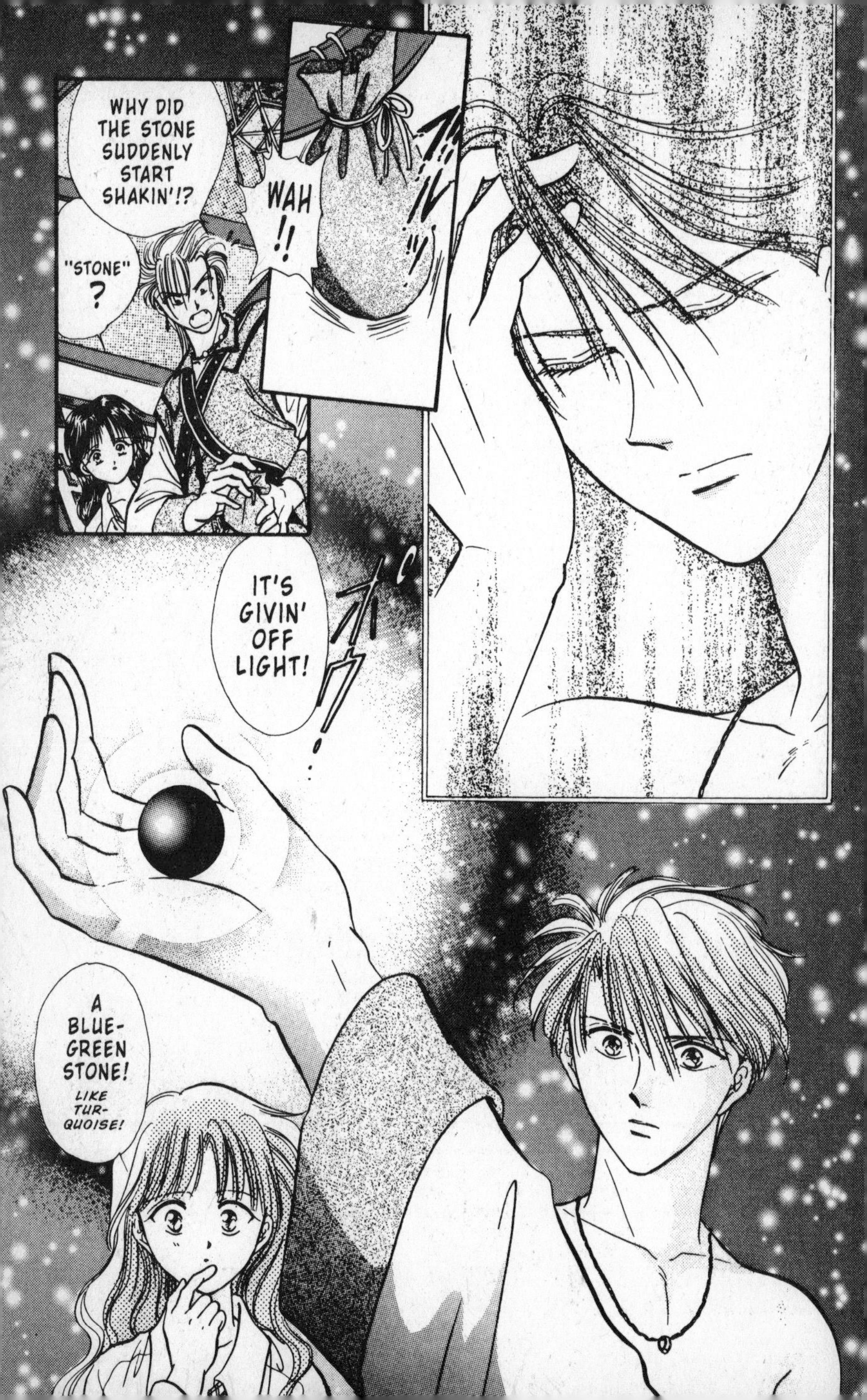
WAH!!
WHY DID THE STONE SUDDENLY START SHAKIN'!?
"STONE"?
IT'S GIVIN' OFF LIGHT!
A BLUE-GREEN STONE!
LIKE TURQUOISE!

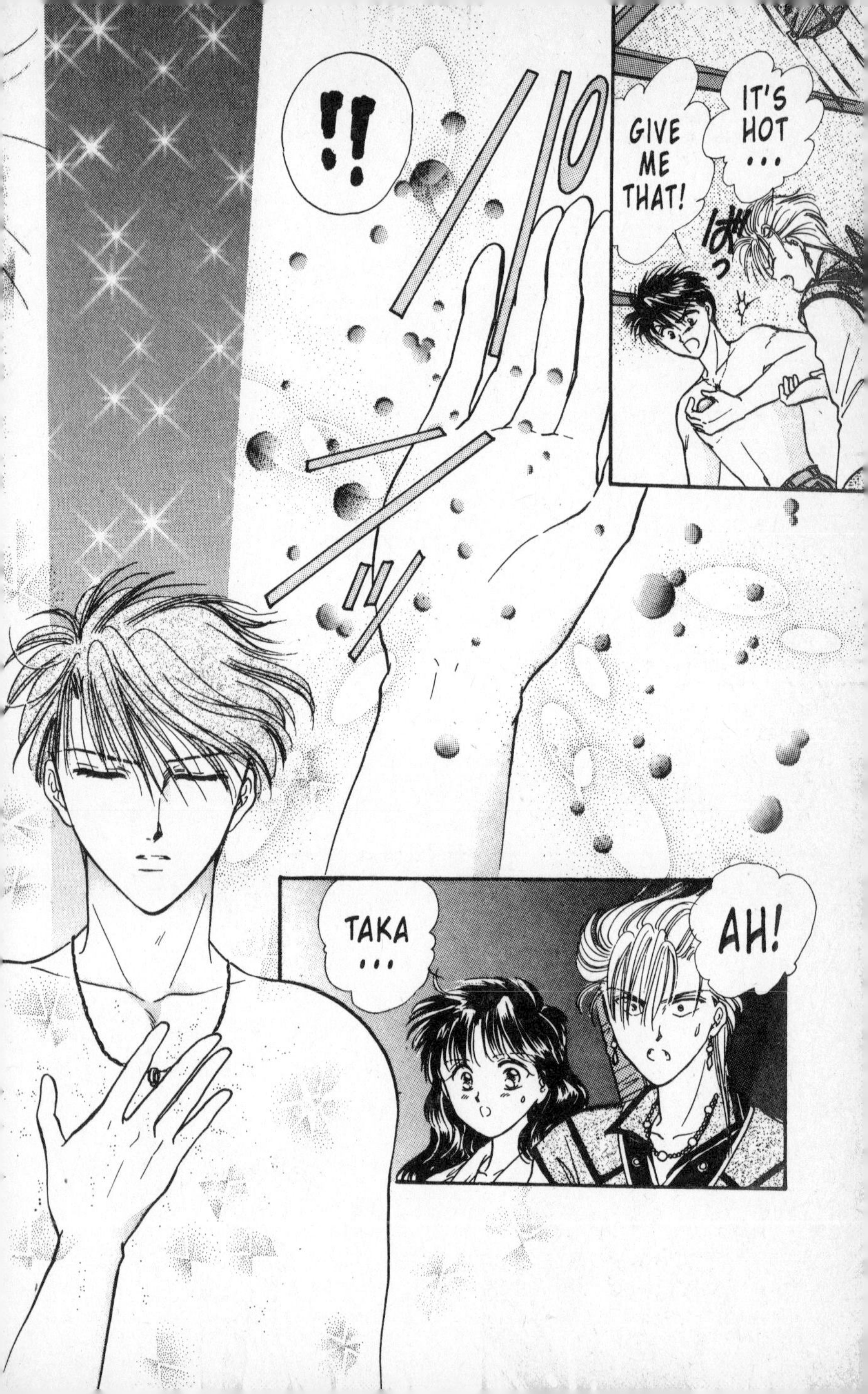
IT'S HOT ...
GIVE ME THAT!
!!
AH!
TAKA ...

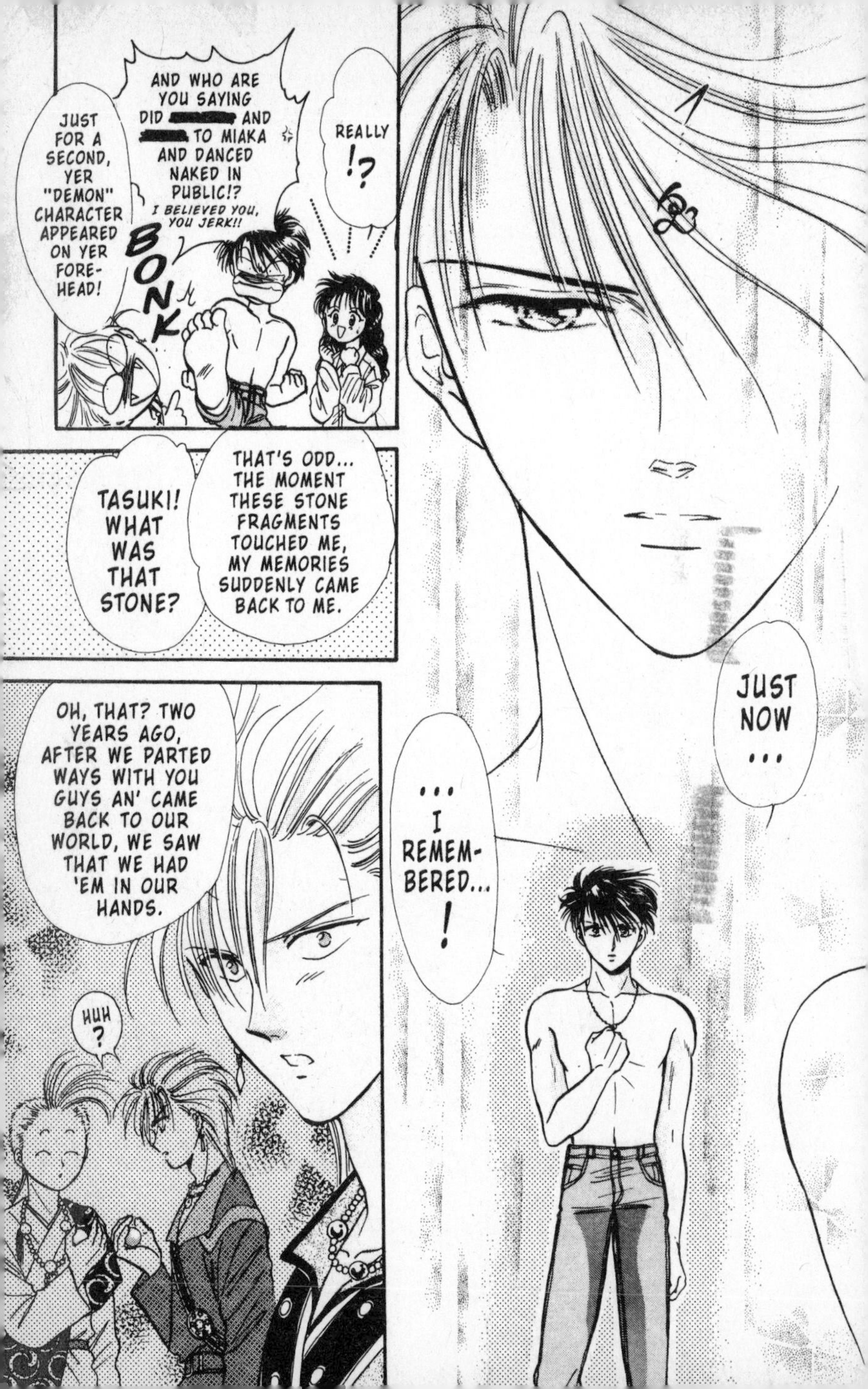

JUST NOW ...
... I REMEMBERED... !
REALLY !?
AND WHO ARE YOU SAYING DID [redacted] AND [redacted] TO MIAKA AND DANCED NAKED IN PUBLIC!?
JUST FOR A SECOND, YER "DEMON" CHARACTER APPEARED ON YER FOREHEAD!
I BELIEVED YOU, YOU JERK!!
BONK
THAT'S ODD... THE MOMENT THESE STONE FRAGMENTS TOUCHED ME, MY MEMORIES SUDDENLY CAME BACK TO ME.
TASUKI! WHAT WAS THAT STONE?
OH, THAT? TWO YEARS AGO, AFTER WE PARTED WAYS WITH YOU GUYS AN' CAME BACK TO OUR WORLD, WE SAW THAT WE HAD 'EM IN OUR HANDS.
HUH ?

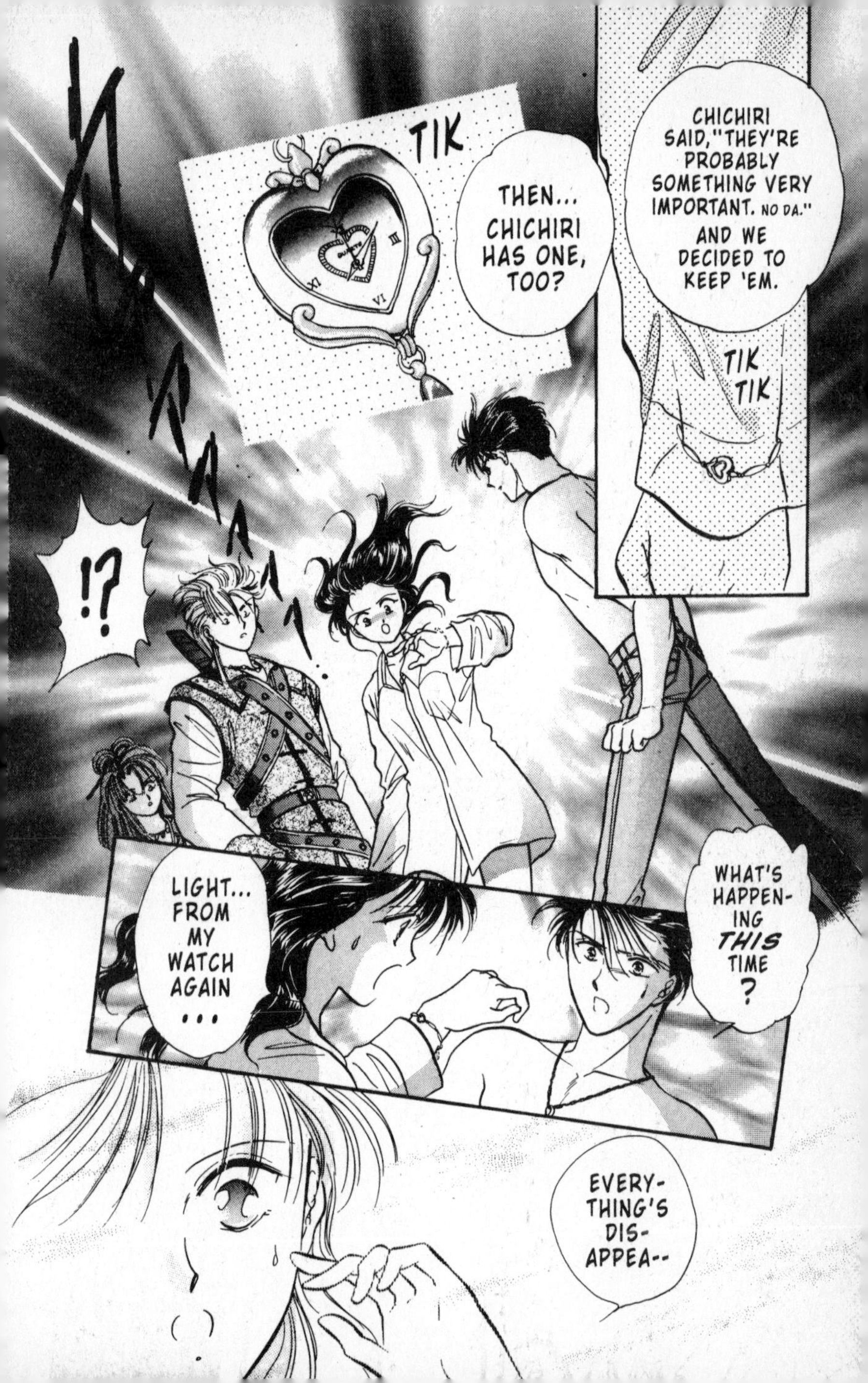
CHICHIRI SAID, "THEY'RE PROBABLY SOMETHING VERY IMPORTANT. NO DA."
AND WE DECIDED TO KEEP 'EM.
TIK TIK
TIK
THEN... CHICHIRI HAS ONE, TOO?
!?
WHAT'S HAPPEN-ING *THIS* TIME?
LIGHT... FROM MY WATCH AGAIN...
EVERY-THING'S DIS-APPEA--

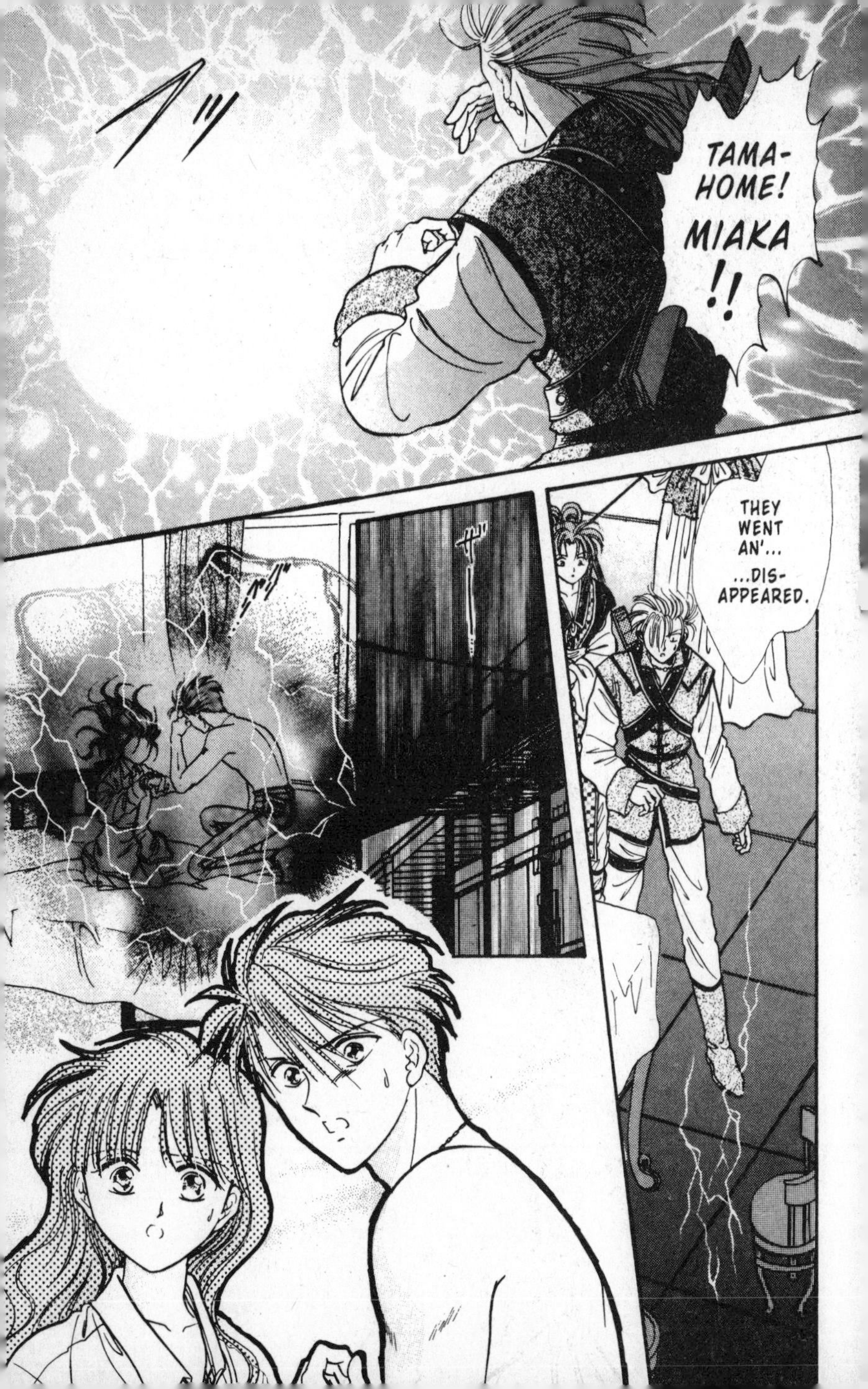
TAMA-HOME! MIAKA!!
ハッ
THEY WENT AN'...
...DIS-APPEARED.

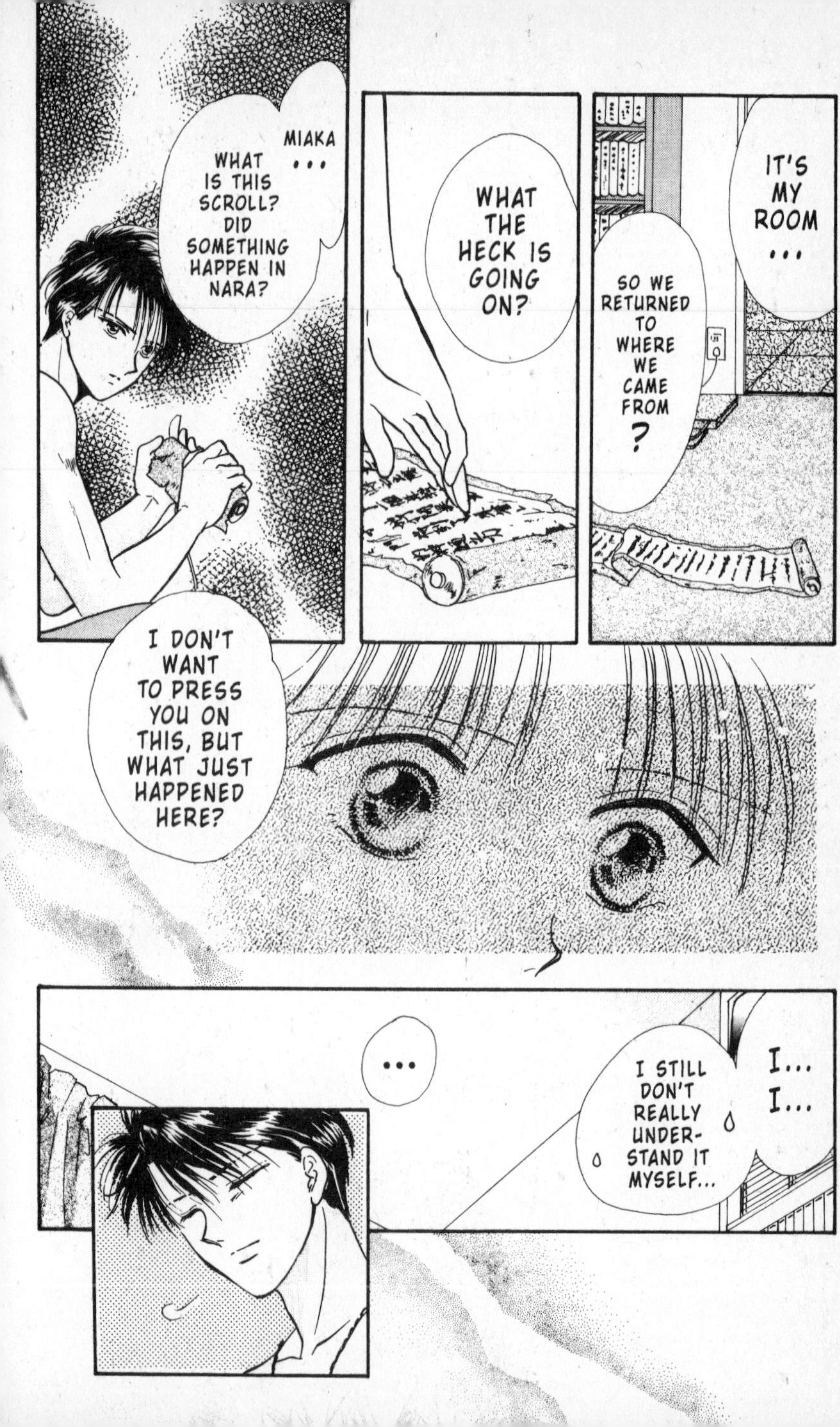
IT'S MY ROOM...
SO WE RETURNED TO WHERE WE CAME FROM?
WHAT THE HECK IS GOING ON?
MIAKA...
WHAT IS THIS SCROLL? DID SOMETHING HAPPEN IN NARA?
I DON'T WANT TO PRESS YOU ON THIS, BUT WHAT JUST HAPPENED HERE?
I... I...
I STILL DON'T REALLY UNDER-STAND IT MYSELF...
...

Continued...

If you think I'm obsessed with Tamahome, you're wrong... actually it's Hotohori! ☺ I'm not very good at drawing either of them (Hey! Hey!!), so how did the anime company manage to draw them so beautifully? ☺ You see, when I saw the anime, it was the first time I was able to look at Fushigi objectively, and the thought that came to mind was, "Miaka!! You have it too good, damn you!" ☺ I never once thought anything like that during the more than three years of drawing the comic! (Okay, I thought it a little when Nakago came into the story. ☺ But now, every week I see a video--only a short time before the rest of you see it--and I'm so shocked at the skill that I say, "Wow!"

When Miaka walks in front of Tamahome, I wave my arms at her saying, "Miaka! You're in the way! Move!" And when Hotohori puts the moves on Miaka, I'm saying, "Stop! Don't go for her! I'm the one you want!" *Yes, I am an idiot.* And when Nakago finally appears, you're just going to have to forgive me because I'll be fainting. (So far, I've only seen sketches, so I'm still okay.) *I was so picky when it came to Nakago! I think it must be love!* I may be (well, I almost certainly am) doing this because it's someone else's Fushigi. I'm not really involved in the production of the anime. (Sometimes production people ask advice, but since manga and anime are two entirely different businesses, I'm not actually a part of the anime.) Just like you, I only see it after the production is finished. (I see the storyboards and things like that, but since they're anime professionals and I'm not, I nearly always go with their suggestions.) *I know nothing!* But also, since the manga and anime are separate things, I get an unusually objective look at the story. I've never looked at my own drawing and screamed at how good they look. In fact, I get sick of them pretty quickly. Oh, and the reason that Tamahome's hair isn't cut until the fourth episode is because I asked them to do it that way. *I thought that cutting it was such a shame!*

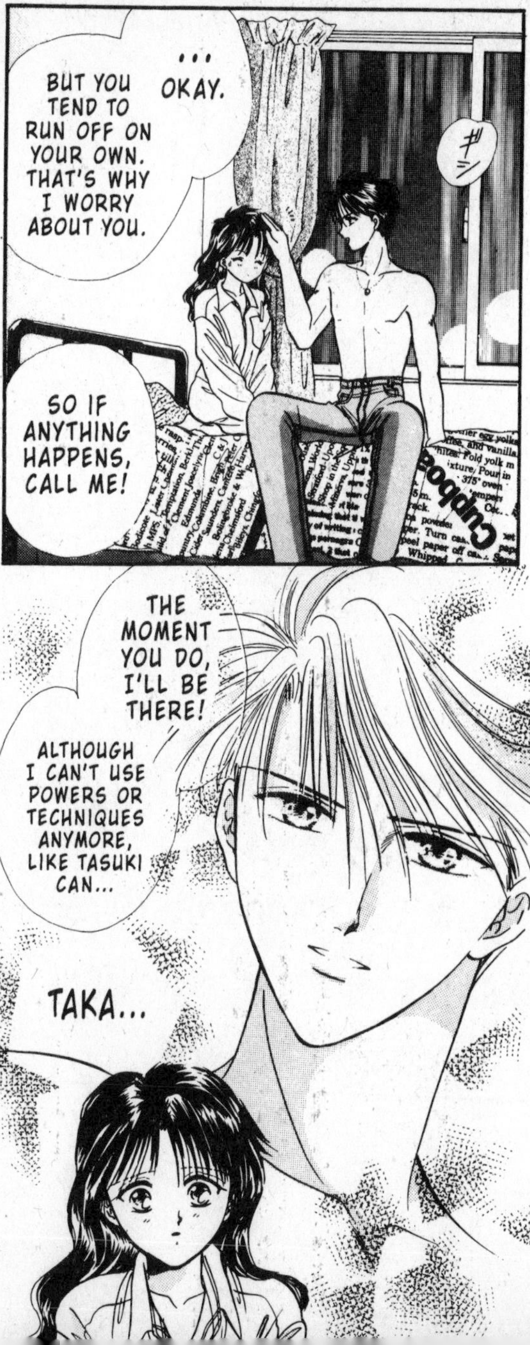
... OKAY.
BUT YOU TEND TO RUN OFF ON YOUR OWN. THAT'S WHY I WORRY ABOUT YOU.
SO IF ANYTHING HAPPENS, CALL ME!
THE MOMENT YOU DO, I'LL BE THERE!
ALTHOUGH I CAN'T USE POWERS OR TECHNIQUES ANYMORE, LIKE TASUKI CAN...
TAKA...

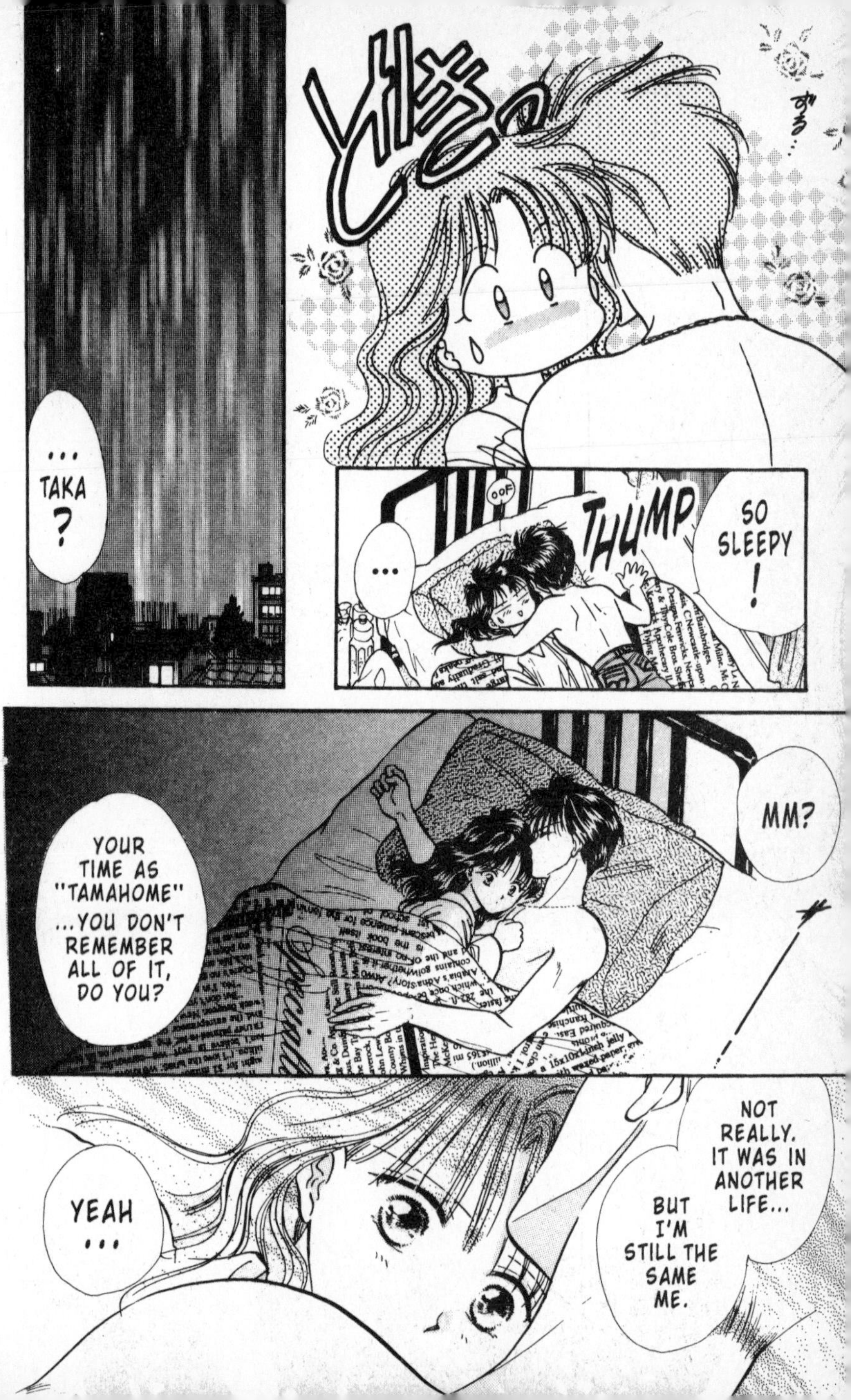

どきっ
ずる…
SO SLEEPY!
THUMP
OOF
...
...TAKA?
MM?
YOUR TIME AS "TAMAHOME" ...YOU DON'T REMEMBER ALL OF IT, DO YOU?
NOT REALLY. IT WAS IN ANOTHER LIFE...
BUT I'M STILL THE SAME ME.
YEAH...

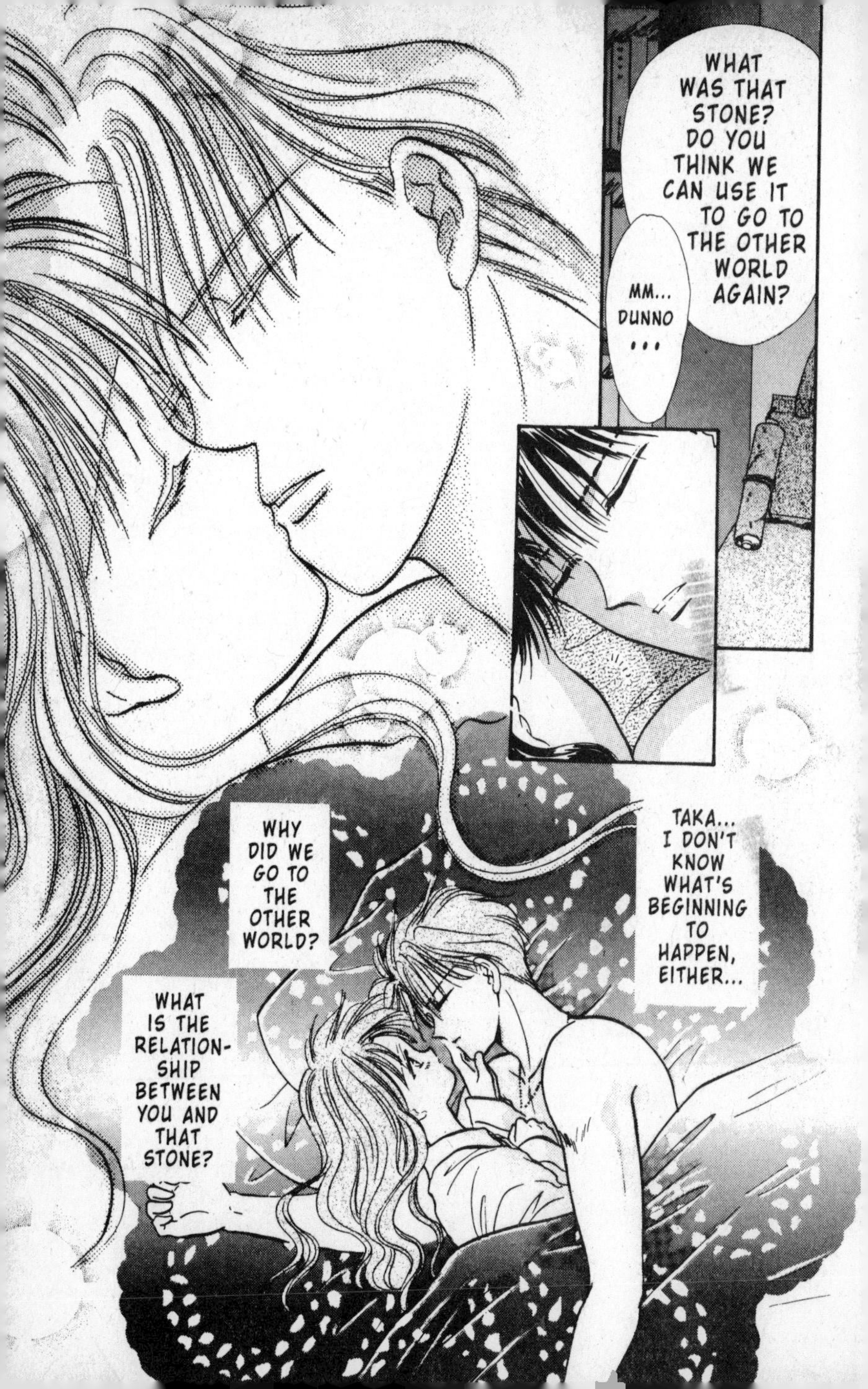
WHAT WAS THAT STONE? DO YOU THINK WE CAN USE IT TO GO TO THE OTHER WORLD AGAIN?
MM... DUNNO ...
TAKA... I DON'T KNOW WHAT'S BEGINNING TO HAPPEN, EITHER...
WHY DID WE GO TO THE OTHER WORLD?
WHAT IS THE RELATION-SHIP BETWEEN YOU AND THAT STONE?

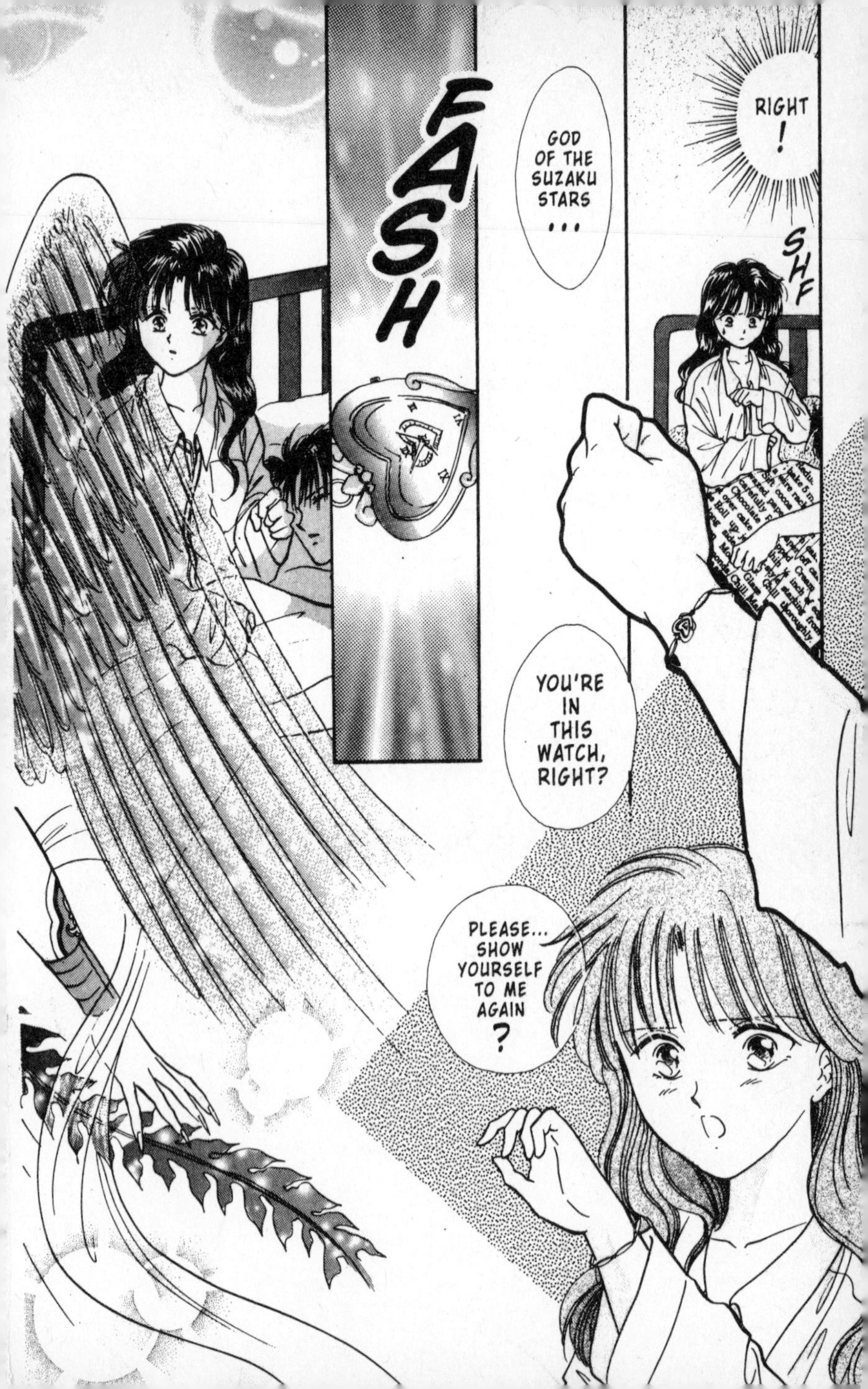
RIGHT!
SHF
YOU'RE IN THIS WATCH, RIGHT?
PLEASE... SHOW YOURSELF TO ME AGAIN?
GOD OF THE SUZAKU STARS...
FASH

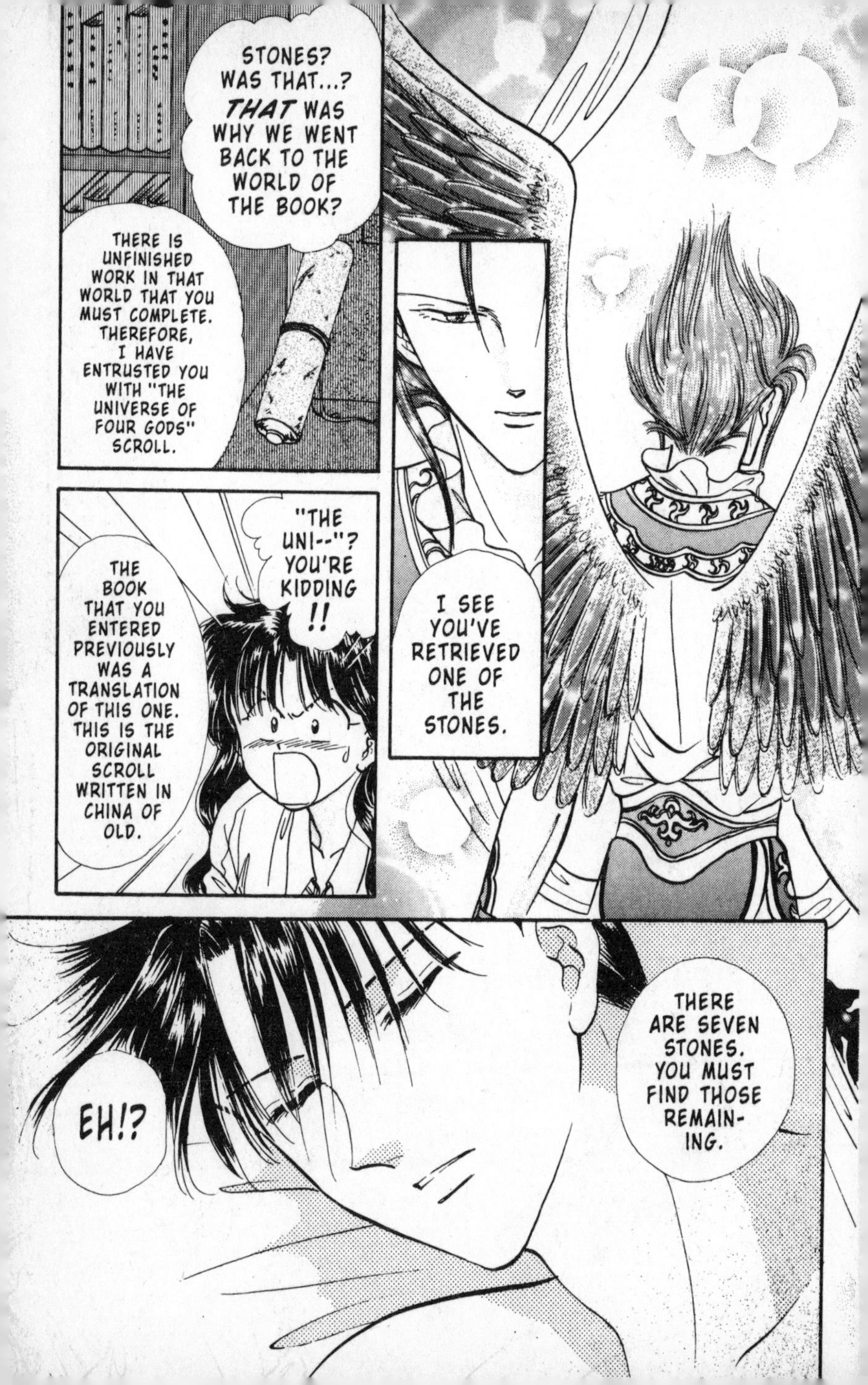
I SEE YOU'VE RETRIEVED ONE OF THE STONES.
STONES? WAS THAT...? *THAT* WAS WHY WE WENT BACK TO THE WORLD OF THE BOOK?
THERE IS UNFINISHED WORK IN THAT WORLD THAT YOU MUST COMPLETE. THEREFORE, I HAVE ENTRUSTED YOU WITH "THE UNIVERSE OF FOUR GODS" SCROLL.
"THE UNI--"? YOU'RE KIDDING !!
THE BOOK THAT YOU ENTERED PREVIOUSLY WAS A TRANSLATION OF THIS ONE. THIS IS THE ORIGINAL SCROLL WRITTEN IN CHINA OF OLD.
THERE ARE SEVEN STONES. YOU MUST FIND THOSE REMAIN-ING.
EH!?

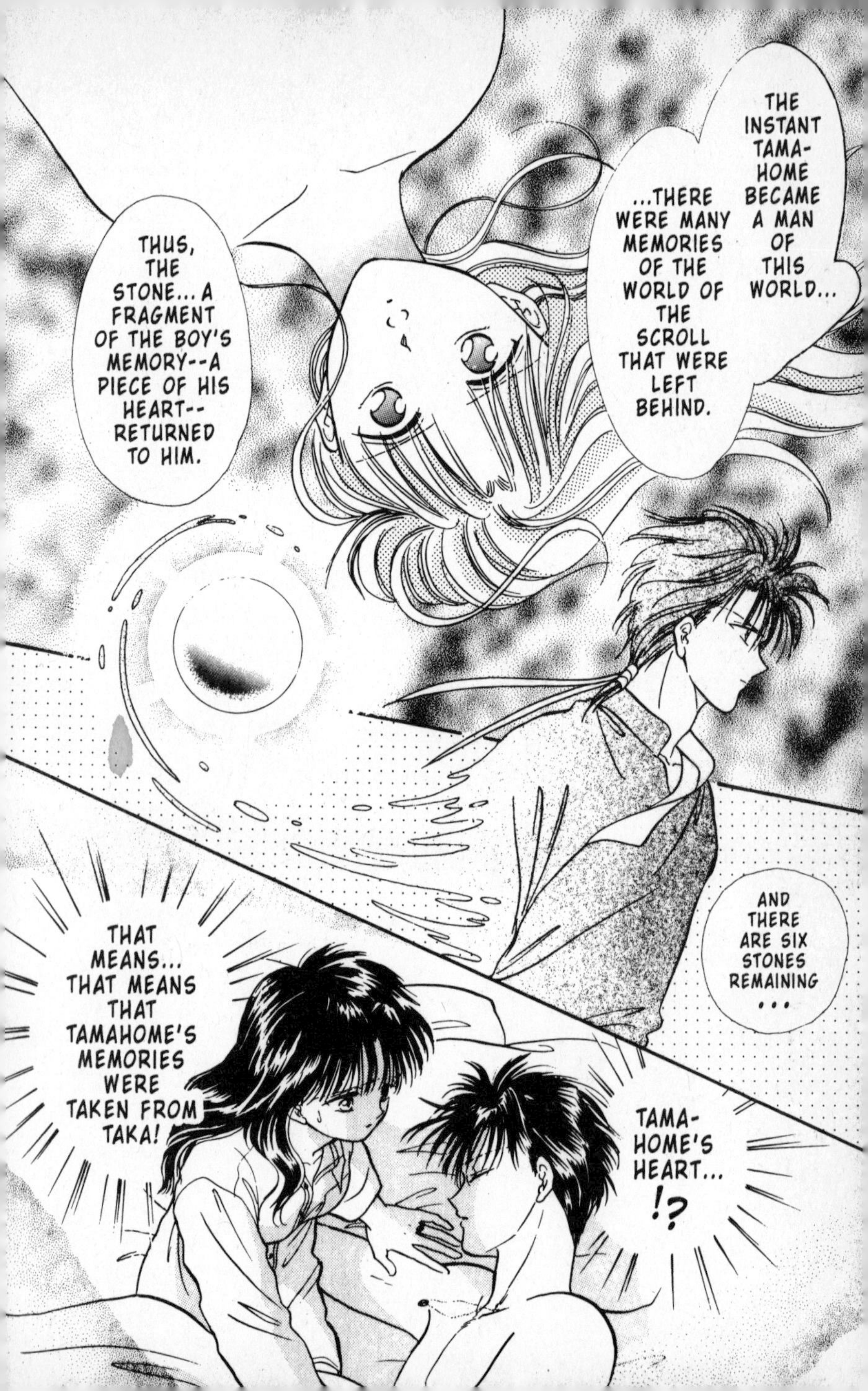
THE INSTANT TAMA-HOME BECAME A MAN OF THIS WORLD...
...THERE WERE MANY MEMORIES OF THE WORLD OF THE SCROLL THAT WERE LEFT BEHIND.
THUS, THE STONE... A FRAGMENT OF THE BOY'S MEMORY--A PIECE OF HIS HEART--RETURNED TO HIM.
AND THERE ARE SIX STONES REMAINING...
TAMA-HOME'S HEART...!?
THAT MEANS... THAT MEANS THAT TAMAHOME'S MEMORIES WERE TAKEN FROM TAKA!

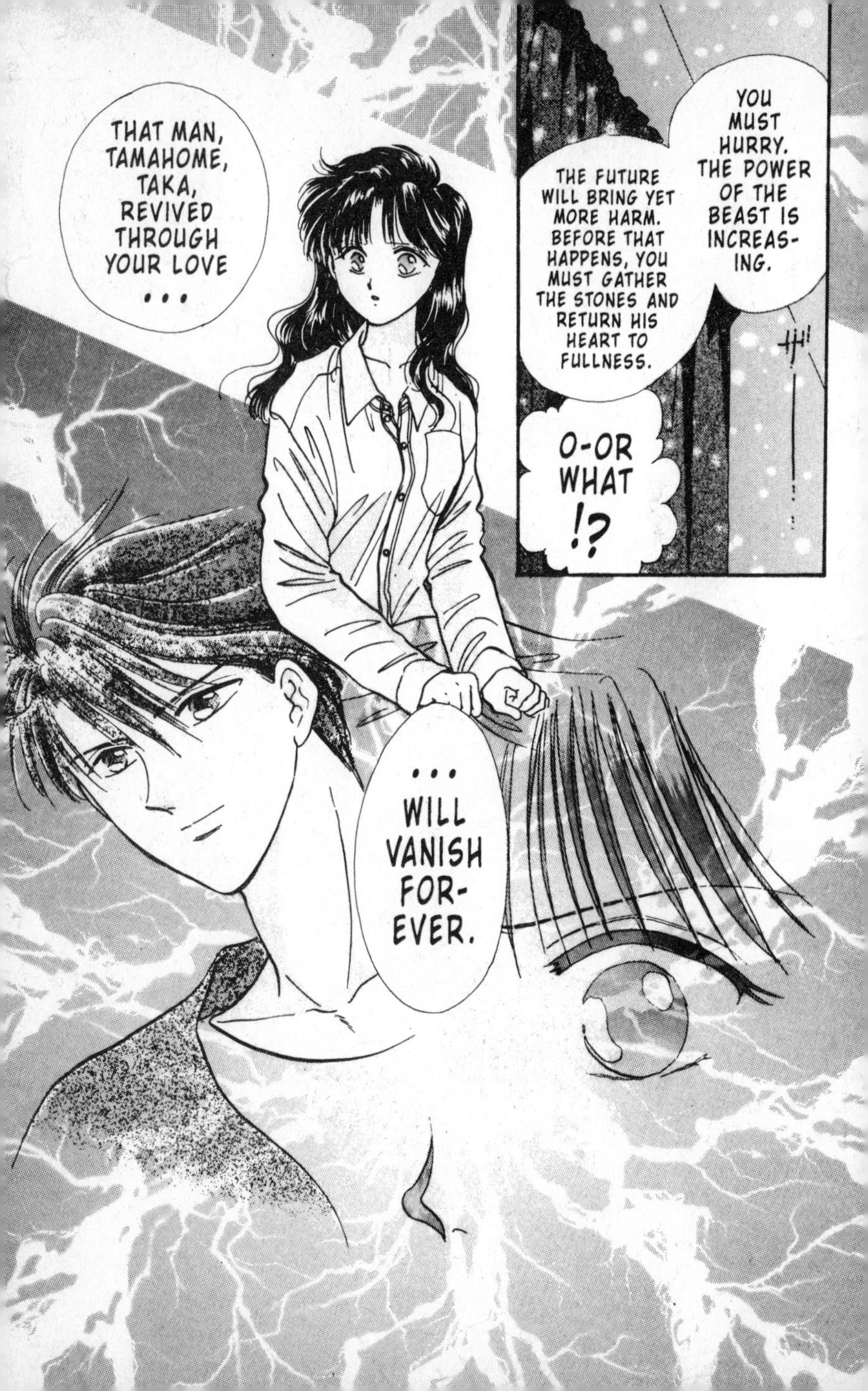
YOU MUST HURRY. THE POWER OF THE BEAST IS INCREAS-ING.
THE FUTURE WILL BRING YET MORE HARM. BEFORE THAT HAPPENS, YOU MUST GATHER THE STONES AND RETURN HIS HEART TO FULLNESS.
O-OR WHAT !?
THAT MAN, TAMAHOME, TAKA, REVIVED THROUGH YOUR LOVE ...
... WILL VANISH FOR-EVER.

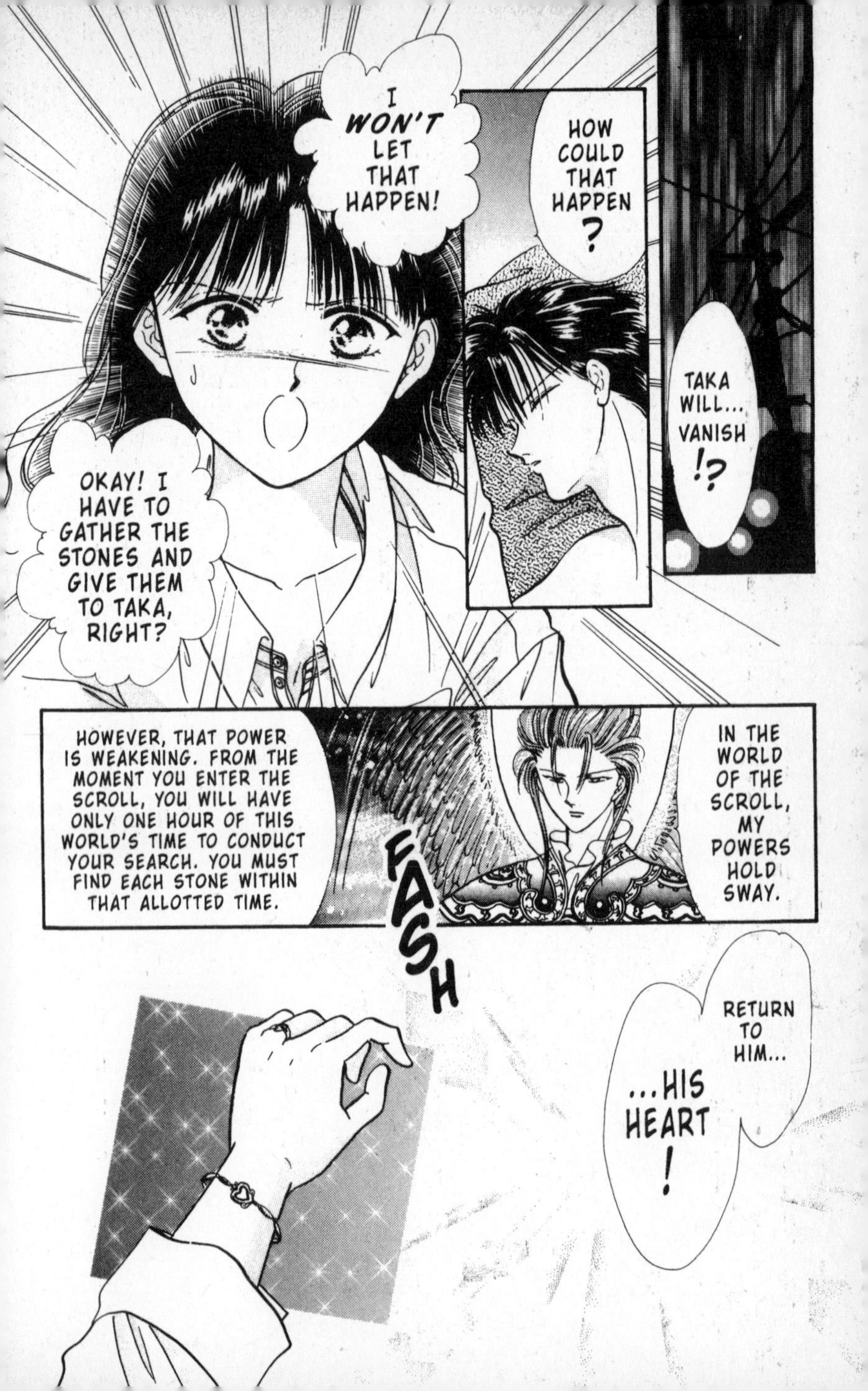
TAKA WILL... VANISH!?
HOW COULD THAT HAPPEN?
I WON'T LET THAT HAPPEN!
OKAY! I HAVE TO GATHER THE STONES AND GIVE THEM TO TAKA, RIGHT?
IN THE WORLD OF THE SCROLL, MY POWERS HOLD SWAY.
HOWEVER, THAT POWER IS WEAKENING. FROM THE MOMENT YOU ENTER THE SCROLL, YOU WILL HAVE ONLY ONE HOUR OF THIS WORLD'S TIME TO CONDUCT YOUR SEARCH. YOU MUST FIND EACH STONE WITHIN THAT ALLOTTED TIME.
FASH
RETURN TO HIM...
...HIS HEART!

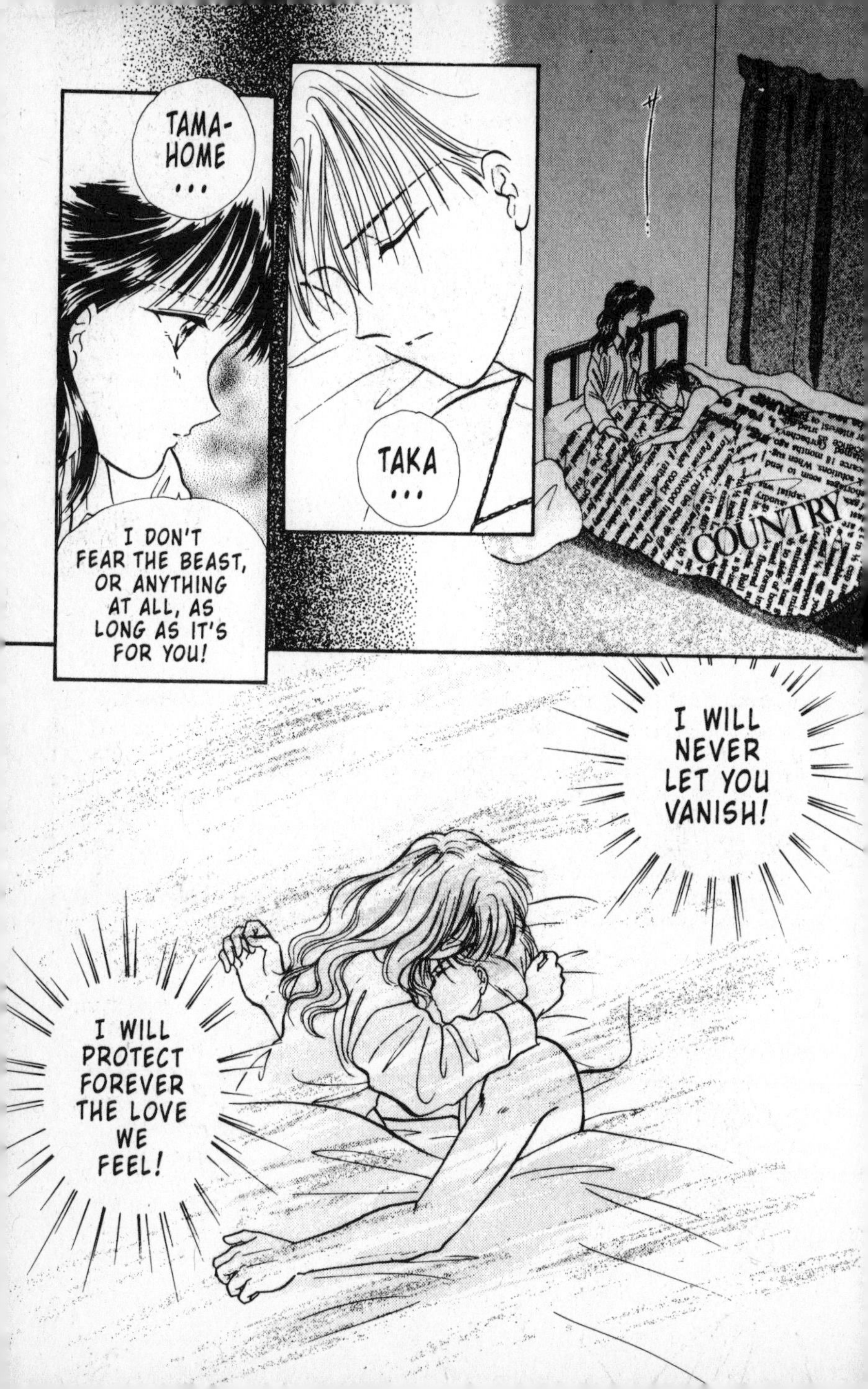
COUNTRY
TAKA ...
TAMA-HOME ...
I DON'T FEAR THE BEAST, OR ANYTHING AT ALL, AS LONG AS IT'S FOR YOU!
I WILL NEVER LET YOU VANISH!
I WILL PROTECT FOREVER THE LOVE WE FEEL!

SOME KIND OF CORNER FOR TALKING ABOUT A WHOLE LOT OF THINGS (What's that supposed to mean?)

• CD Book 4 is coming out! The voice actors are the same as with the previous releases. This time "135" wrote the music and lyrics for songs for Miaka and Tamahome, AND they did the background music (and produced it, too!) *Wheeee! I'm so happy!* *There's even a great chorus!* And because of that, I was able to meet them! (But unfortunately, at the time, I got a little motion-sick from the ride there, and my head was pounding!) I was so surprised at how such fun people were able to produce such dramatic music! There are really party-hard types of tunes ⇦ (Just my opinion, but I think those words match them exactly!) along with some nice soft music in there! Be sure to listen for it!

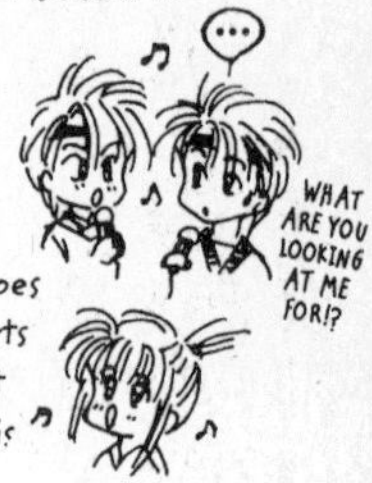
WHAT ARE YOU LOOKING AT ME FOR!?

But! The Amiboshi and Suboshi song on this album is a song that implies that they're... a couple. *I love Mr. Nagai's music, and I think that Mr. Anri Hibi's lyrics are just wonderful!* It took me listening to it two or three times on my headphones to realize it. Even so, I get the feeling (this isn't confirmed or anything) that Mr. Iwanaga tried to make two distinct voices when he sang the song. You really can make out two personalities! It goes "Ami," "Su," "Ami," "Su," "Ami." When he sings "Futatsu no Kodooooo ♫♫" ("Two Hearts Beating"), I can only imagine Suboshi singing it while he gazes at Amiboshi! (Is it just my imagination?) Mr. Iwanaga, you are amazing!! What if I'm wrong!? But no, it is definitely a duet!

The song for Chiriko is composed by a brand new talent, but it's very sad and made my chest tighten up when I heard it. Ms. Orikasa's voice sounds just like a young boy's, and it made me shout, "Chirikoooo!" and want to hug him! *Ohhhh!!* Be sure to listen to it!

...they say that Book 5 will have a Nakago song! *Ha ha ha!* BONK

• Also... A Summer (1995) Shôjo Comic special will contain a bonus Fushigi CD Single! I don't know what issue it's in, but you have to buy the magazine or you'll never get it! (By the same people who brought you the CD Books!) This one is about Miaka and the seven warriors going to an onsen hot springs resort, and it's really funny! I read the script at work and started laughing manically! I laughed until I cried! *Don't look, people!* Episode three is the best! You get an idea of just how manly Tasuki and Chichiri are. And fans of Mitsukake will hear an unusual side of his personality. It's a great piece, and the only thing you can criticize about it is that it's too short! *Wa ha ha ha!*

• Watase has decided that Fushigi Side Story novels will be written!! When? Dunno! Watase's free time? Zero. I really want to write them as manga, but there is no magazine to carry them, and it would make them too short! I wanted to write the "Priestess of Genbu" and the "Priestess of Byakko" as two different series! *I want to introduce all of the Celestial Warriors!* Anyway, they will come out, so please be patient! *(The author seems to lack self-confidence.)*

SMALL REQUEST CORNER

• Please don't send me letters saying, "The books and illustrations (etc.) I want aren't available! So please make it!" Some people even send money! Please don't! I'm not the person who decides what is going to be published. Nor do I decide on merchandising or bonus gifts or prizes, or any of that! So even if you ask me... *that is the job of the editorial and licensing departments of the publisher.* (Also, I can't return your sign-boards, so please don't send them to me!) I have nothing to do with the anime, so if you send me letters saying, "I don't get the broadcast in my area. Please do something about it!" I can't do anything about it! Contact your area TV stations! *Also, don't ask me to change the anime production!* A manga artist's job is doing manga and illustrations, and that's it! ANYTHING else is the job of other people! I'm a person who really tries to do as much as I can at all times, but when I have requests to do things that I can't do, it just adds to my stress factor! ☺

• Finally, when you write letters, can you try to write them in the usual way? Writing them on hearts or something like that is cute, but when we open the mail, it's a real problem! Time is always scarce, so... please!

CHAPTER EIGHTY-ONE
SEVEN DESTINATIONS

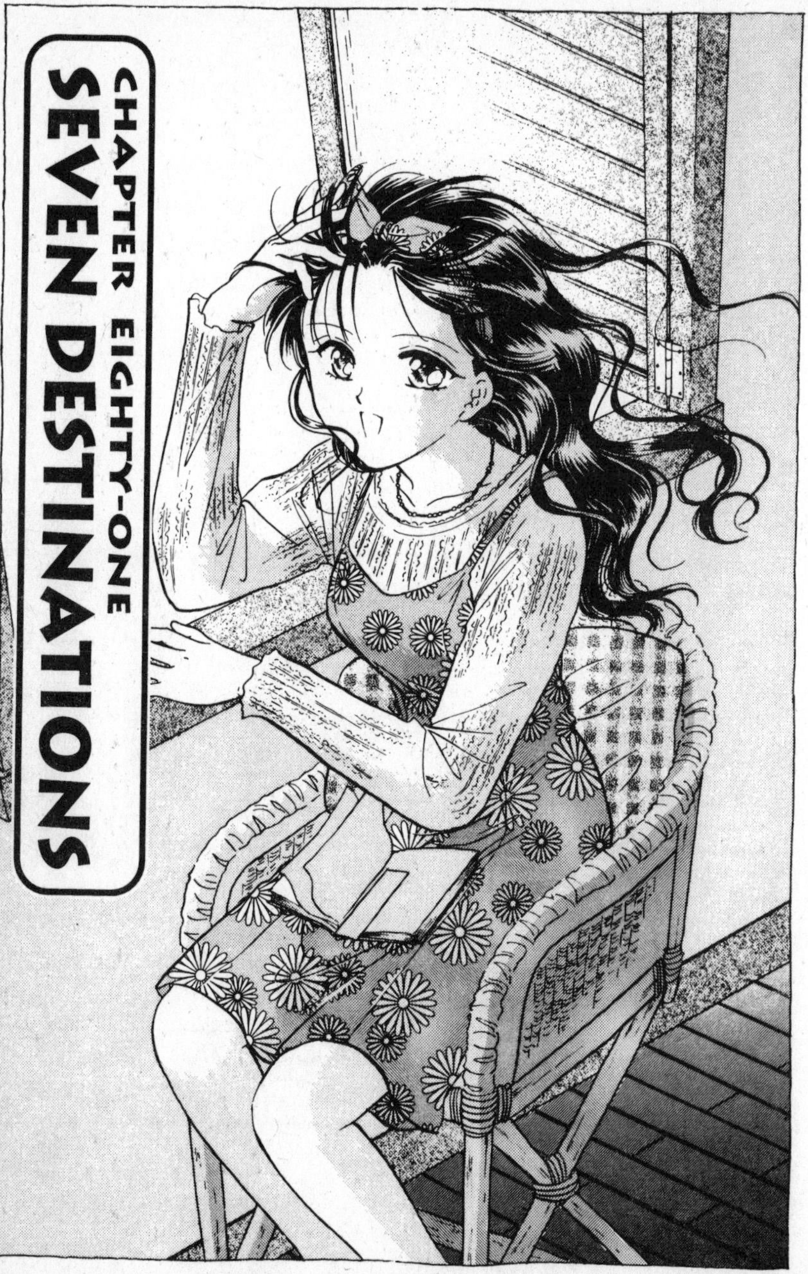

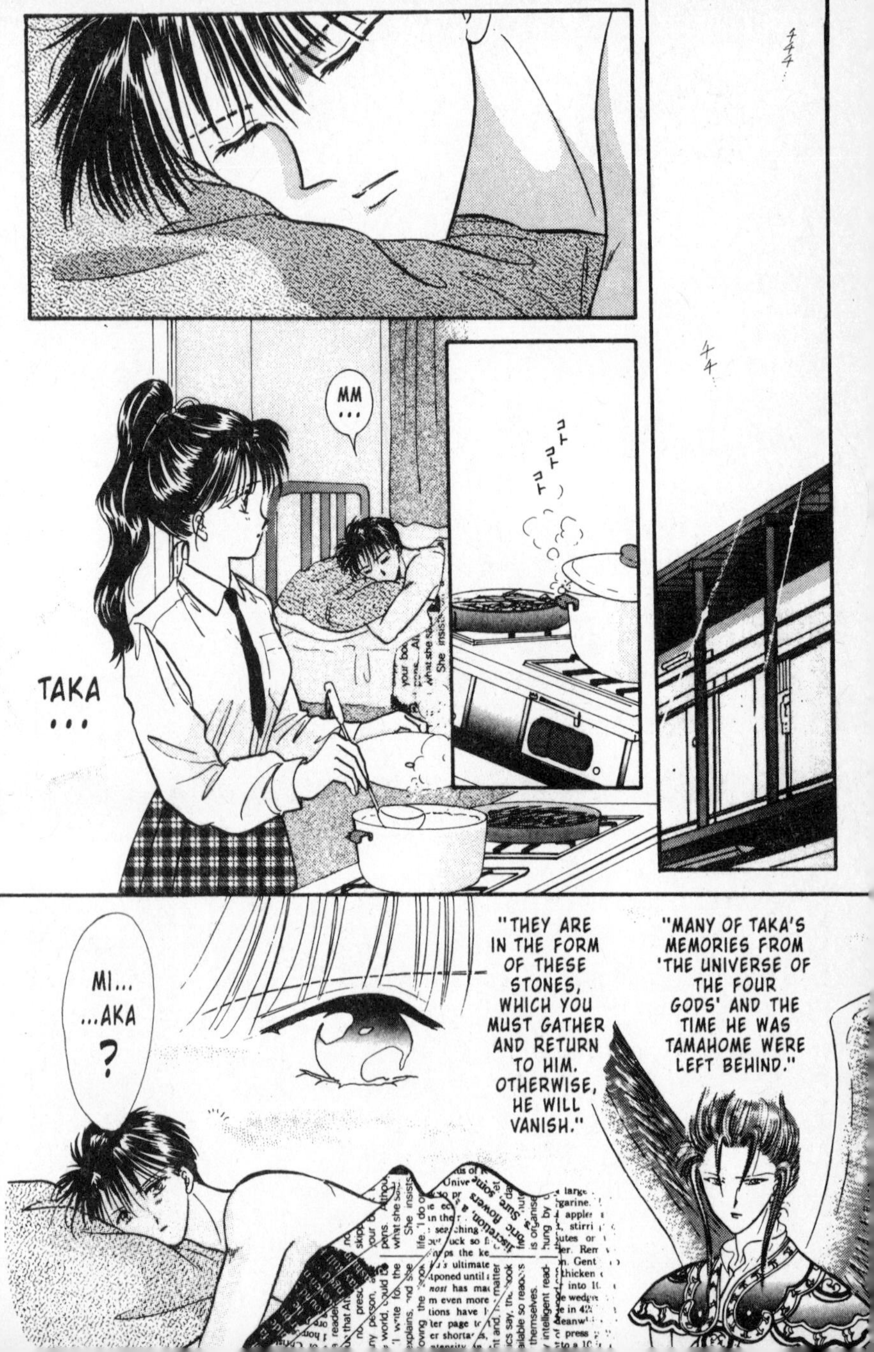
MM...
TAKA...
"MANY OF TAKA'S MEMORIES FROM 'THE UNIVERSE OF THE FOUR GODS' AND THE TIME HE WAS TAMAHOME WERE LEFT BEHIND."
"THEY ARE IN THE FORM OF THESE STONES, WHICH YOU MUST GATHER AND RETURN TO HIM. OTHERWISE, HE WILL VANISH."
MI... ...AKA ?

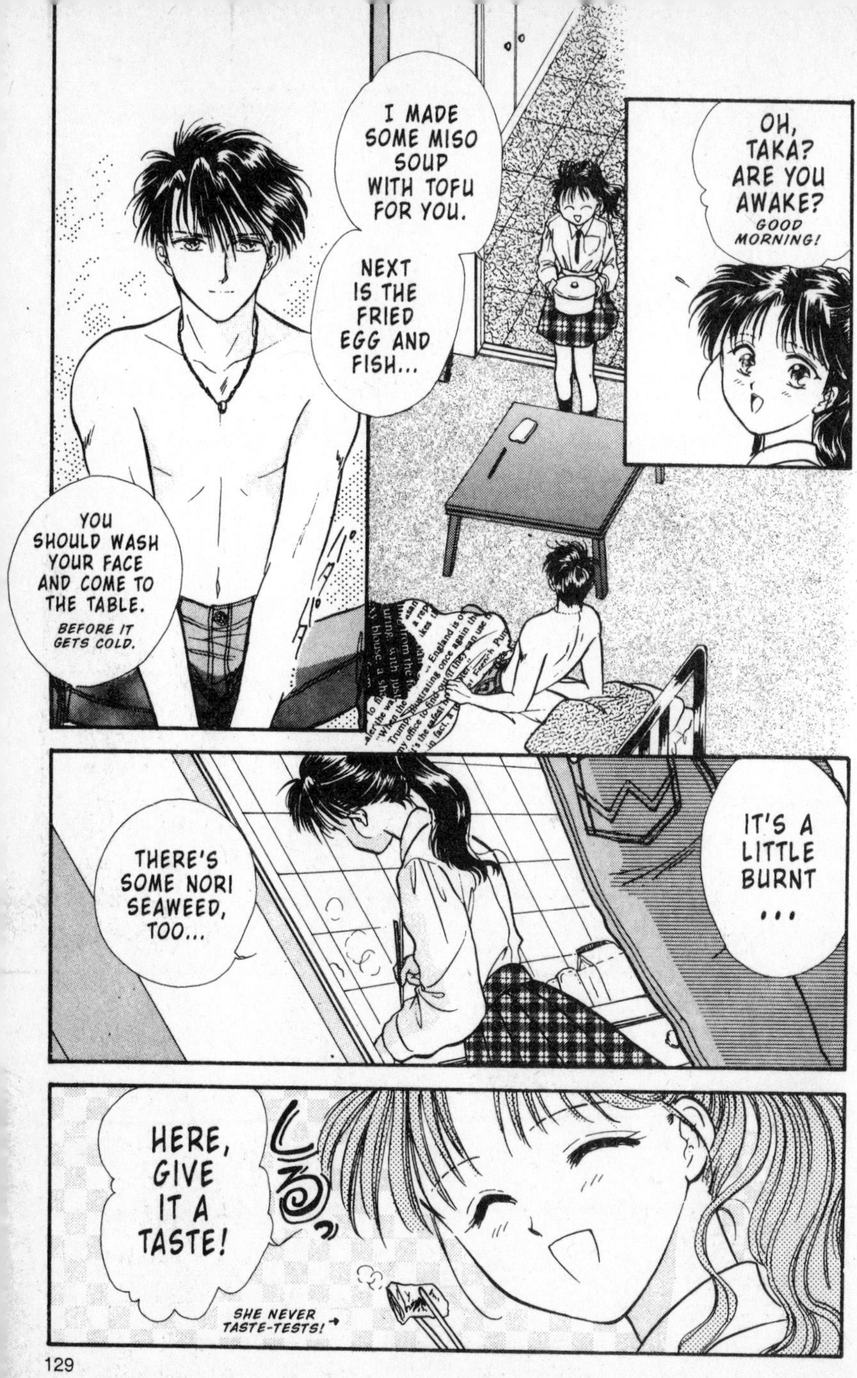

OH, TAKA? ARE YOU AWAKE?
GOOD MORNING!
I MADE SOME MISO SOUP WITH TOFU FOR YOU.
NEXT IS THE FRIED EGG AND FISH...
YOU SHOULD WASH YOUR FACE AND COME TO THE TABLE.
BEFORE IT GETS COLD.
IT'S A LITTLE BURNT ...
THERE'S SOME NORI SEAWEED, TOO...
HERE, GIVE IT A TASTE!
SHE NEVER TASTE-TESTS!

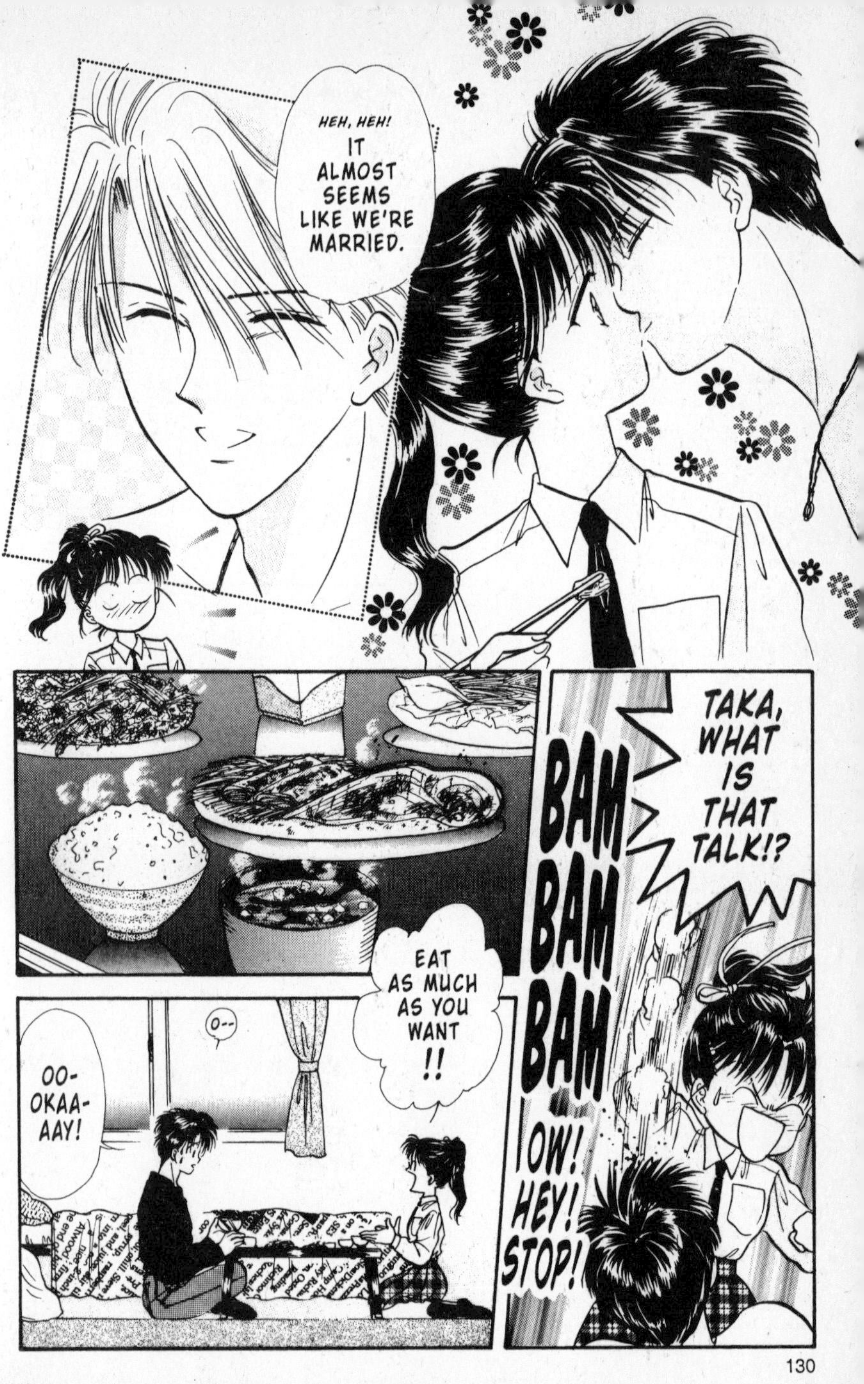
HEH, HEH!
IT ALMOST SEEMS LIKE WE'RE MARRIED.
TAKA, WHAT IS THAT TALK!?
BAM BAM BAM BAM
OW! HEY! STOP!
EAT AS MUCH AS YOU WANT !!
O--
OO-OKAAA-AAY!

Prophet

As research for Part 2, I took a trip to the Takamatsu-Zuka Old Mound. Of course, the only thing I could do was walk around for a bit. (The museum was closed!) They didn't let anyone into the mound itself, but I could pretty much see all of the sights. They had all the 28 constellations on display (Well, they ARE real constellations...), but it was fascinating to see all of those familiar names lined up like that! "Tamahome" and "Chichiri" and such are all Japanese pronunciations. I wonder how Tasuki's name (for example) would be pronounced in Chinese? The constellations were painted on the ceiling of the Old Mound chamber, and on the four walls were the four gods. (There really is a hole in Suzaku's wall, so we don't know what that fresco looked like.) I could only think about what a wonderful grave it was! I really wonder who was buried there. Whoever it is, I apologize for drawing a manga about it without permission! Still, I love anything about the ancients! (That's not to say that I know all that much about it.) I was looking around for a setting, and I'm happy I found such a romantic one.
Long before it was decided that FUSHIGI YUGI would be serialized, I saw a TV program called SHIJIN DENSETSU ("The Myths of the Four Gods"). It showed pictures of places in Japan with a connection to their worship, but it was only when I saw it later that I realized that it also had pictures of the Old Mound. Come to think of it, there was a TAKOYAKI (fried octopus) vendor in Asuka (When I looked around I saw that he also sells DANGO... and he doesn't pan fry the takoyaki, it's deep fried in oil) whose takoyaki was soooo delicious! I want to go back and try it again, but it's an odd way of cooking them.
I guess it should be called "TAKOAGE."

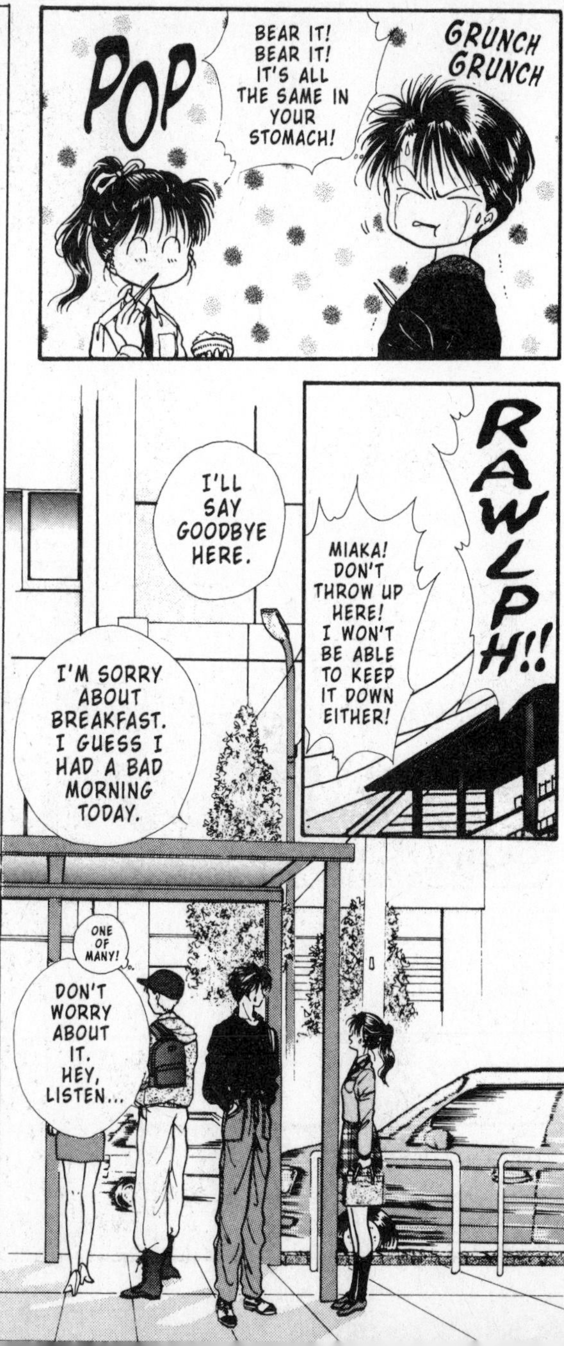
GRUNCH GRUNCH
BEAR IT! BEAR IT! IT'S ALL THE SAME IN YOUR STOMACH!
POP
RAWLPH!!
MIAKA! DON'T THROW UP HERE! I WON'T BE ABLE TO KEEP IT DOWN EITHER!
I'LL SAY GOODBYE HERE.
I'M SORRY ABOUT BREAKFAST. I GUESS I HAD A BAD MORNING TODAY.
ONE OF MANY!
DON'T WORRY ABOUT IT. HEY, LISTEN...

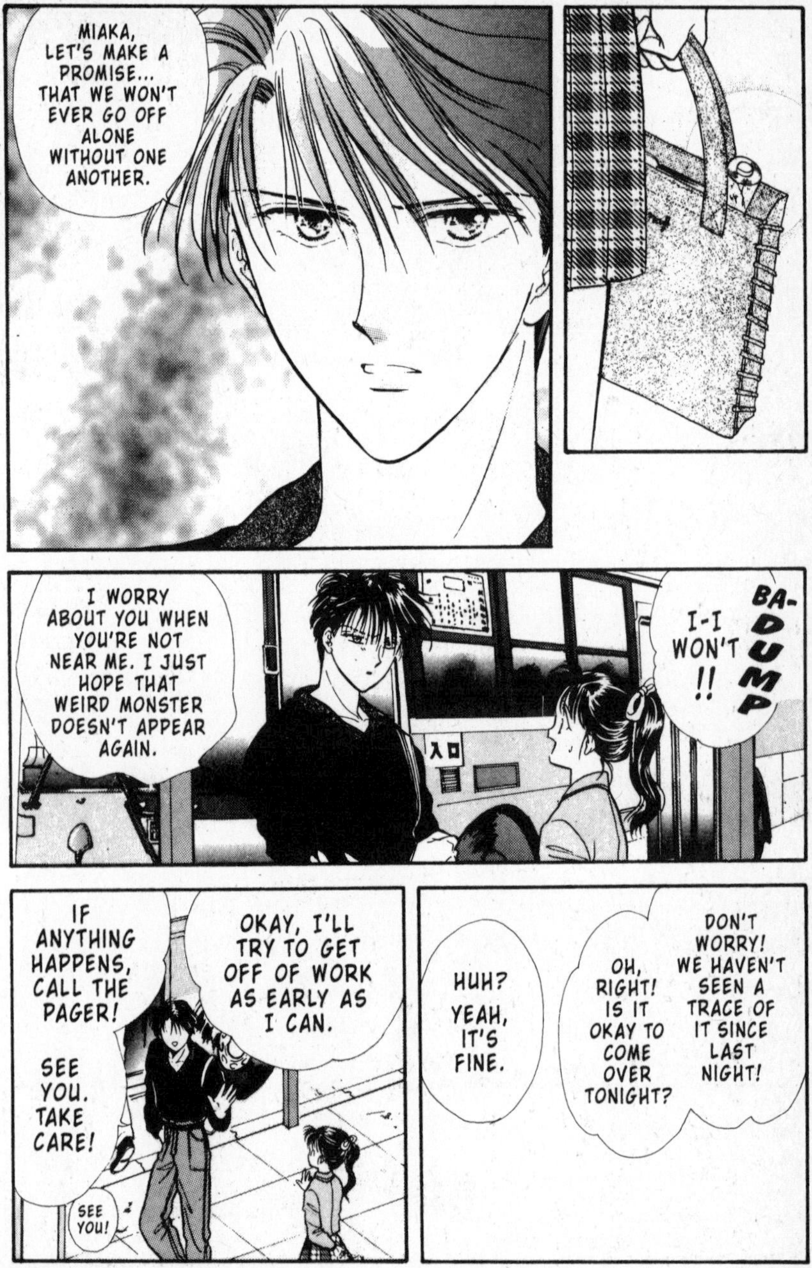
MIAKA, LET'S MAKE A PROMISE... THAT WE WON'T EVER GO OFF ALONE WITHOUT ONE ANOTHER.
I-I WON'T !!
BA-DUMP
I WORRY ABOUT YOU WHEN YOU'RE NOT NEAR ME. I JUST HOPE THAT WEIRD MONSTER DOESN'T APPEAR AGAIN.
DON'T WORRY! WE HAVEN'T SEEN A TRACE OF IT SINCE LAST NIGHT!
OH, RIGHT! IS IT OKAY TO COME OVER TONIGHT?
HUH? YEAH, IT'S FINE.
OKAY, I'LL TRY TO GET OFF OF WORK AS EARLY AS I CAN.
IF ANYTHING HAPPENS, CALL THE PAGER!
SEE YOU. TAKE CARE!
SEE YOU!

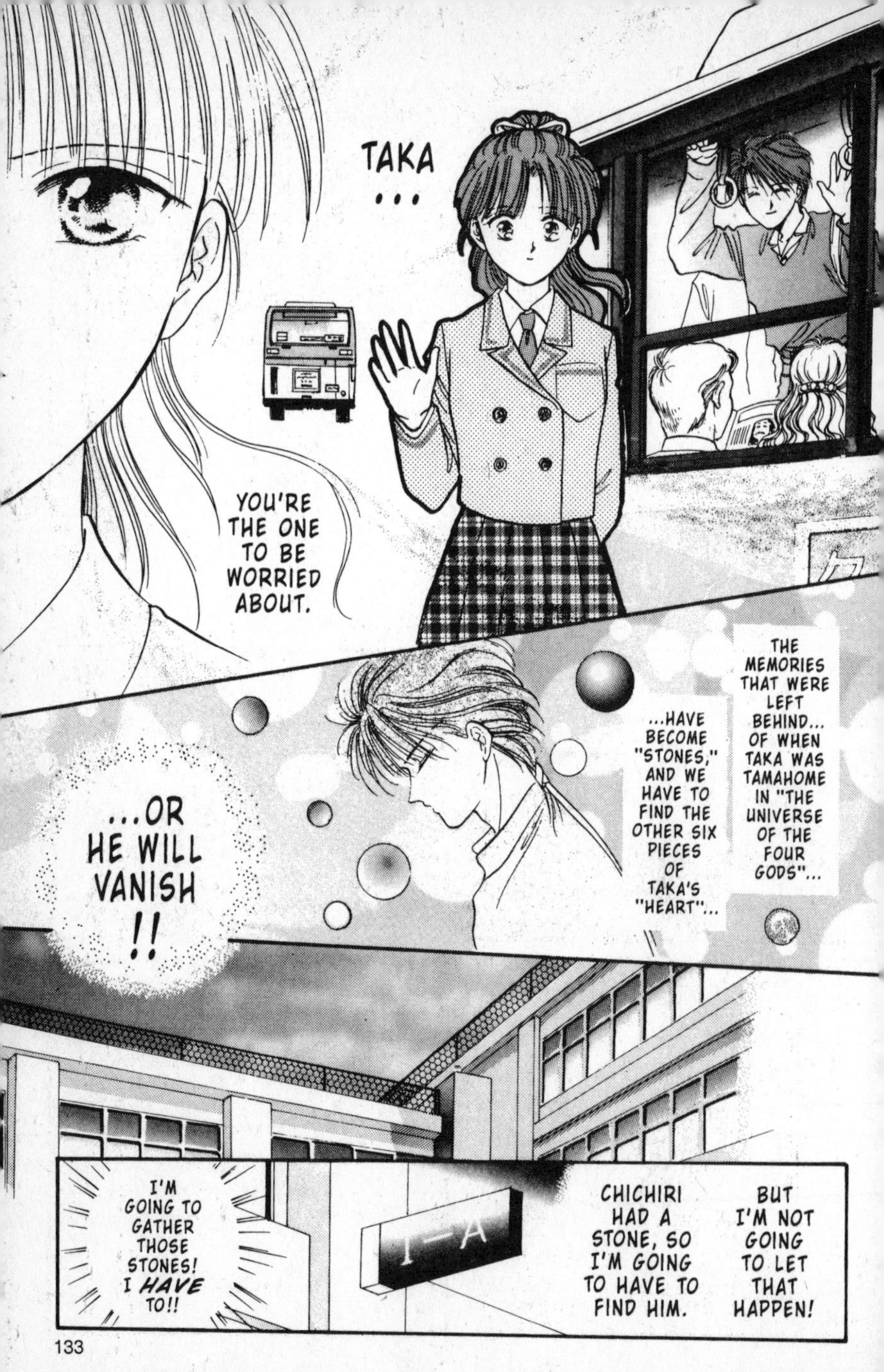

TAKA ...
YOU'RE THE ONE TO BE WORRIED ABOUT.
THE MEMORIES THAT WERE LEFT BEHIND... OF WHEN TAKA WAS TAMAHOME IN "THE UNIVERSE OF THE FOUR GODS"...
...HAVE BECOME "STONES," AND WE HAVE TO FIND THE OTHER SIX PIECES OF TAKA'S "HEART"...
...OR HE WILL VANISH !!
BUT I'M NOT GOING TO LET THAT HAPPEN!
CHICHIRI HAD A STONE, SO I'M GOING TO HAVE TO FIND HIM.
1-A
I'M GOING TO GATHER THOSE STONES! I *HAVE* TO!!

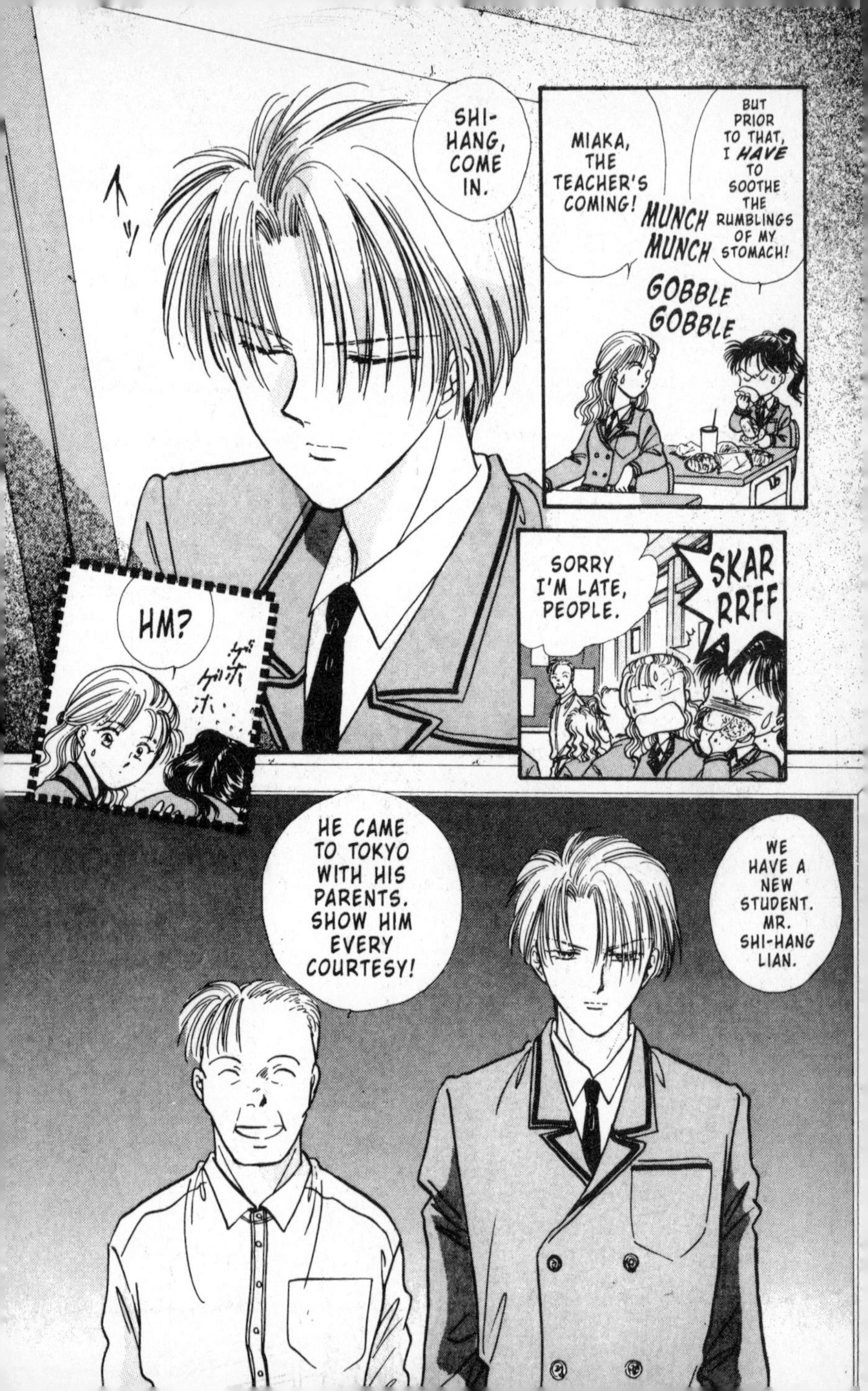
MIAKA, THE TEACHER'S COMING!
BUT PRIOR TO THAT, I *HAVE* TO SOOTHE THE RUMBLINGS OF MY STOMACH!
MUNCH MUNCH
GOBBLE GOBBLE
SKAR RRFF
SORRY I'M LATE, PEOPLE.
SHI-HANG, COME IN.
HM?
WE HAVE A NEW STUDENT. MR. SHI-HANG LIAN.
HE CAME TO TOKYO WITH HIS PARENTS. SHOW HIM EVERY COURTESY!

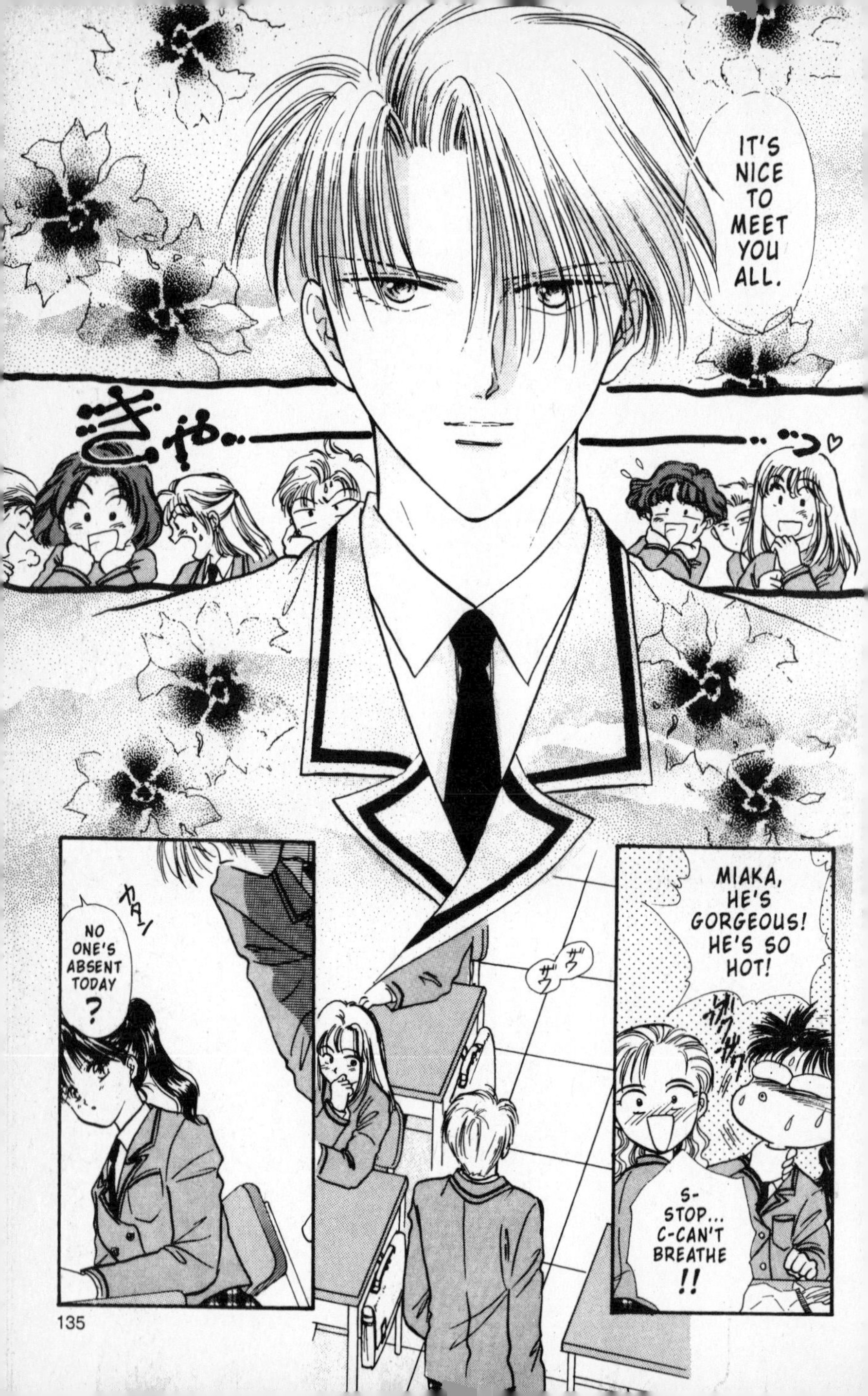
IT'S NICE TO MEET YOU ALL.
ぎゃ‥
MIAKA, HE'S GORGEOUS! HE'S SO HOT!
S-STOP... C-CAN'T BREATHE!!
ザワ ザワ
NO ONE'S ABSENT TODAY?

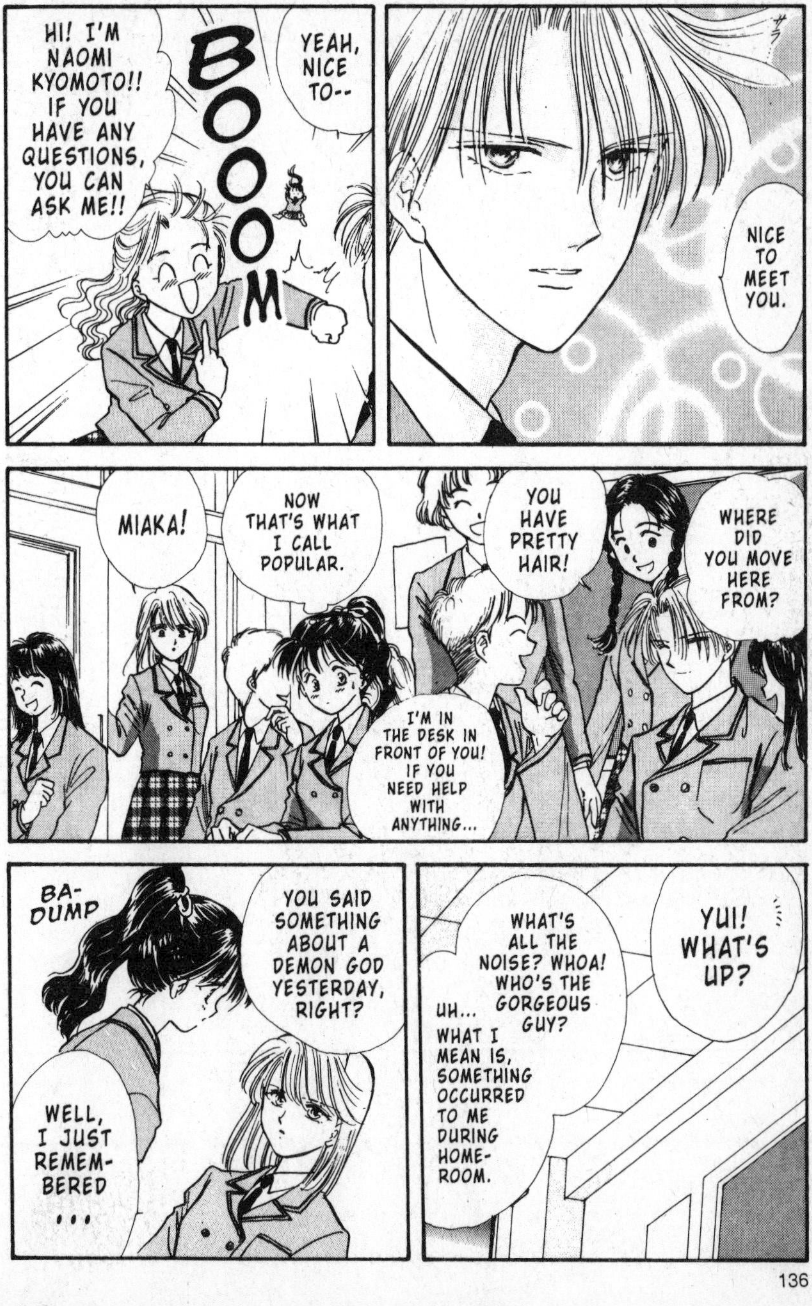
NICE TO MEET YOU.
YEAH, NICE TO--
HI! I'M NAOMI KYOMOTO!! IF YOU HAVE ANY QUESTIONS, YOU CAN ASK ME!!
BOOOM
WHERE DID YOU MOVE HERE FROM?
YOU HAVE PRETTY HAIR!
I'M IN THE DESK IN FRONT OF YOU! IF YOU NEED HELP WITH ANYTHING...
NOW THAT'S WHAT I CALL POPULAR.
MIAKA!
YUI! WHAT'S UP?
WHAT'S ALL THE NOISE? WHOA! WHO'S THE GORGEOUS GUY?
UH... WHAT I MEAN IS, SOMETHING OCCURRED TO ME DURING HOME-ROOM.
YOU SAID SOMETHING ABOUT A DEMON GOD YESTERDAY, RIGHT?
BA-DUMP
WELL, I JUST REMEM-BERED ...

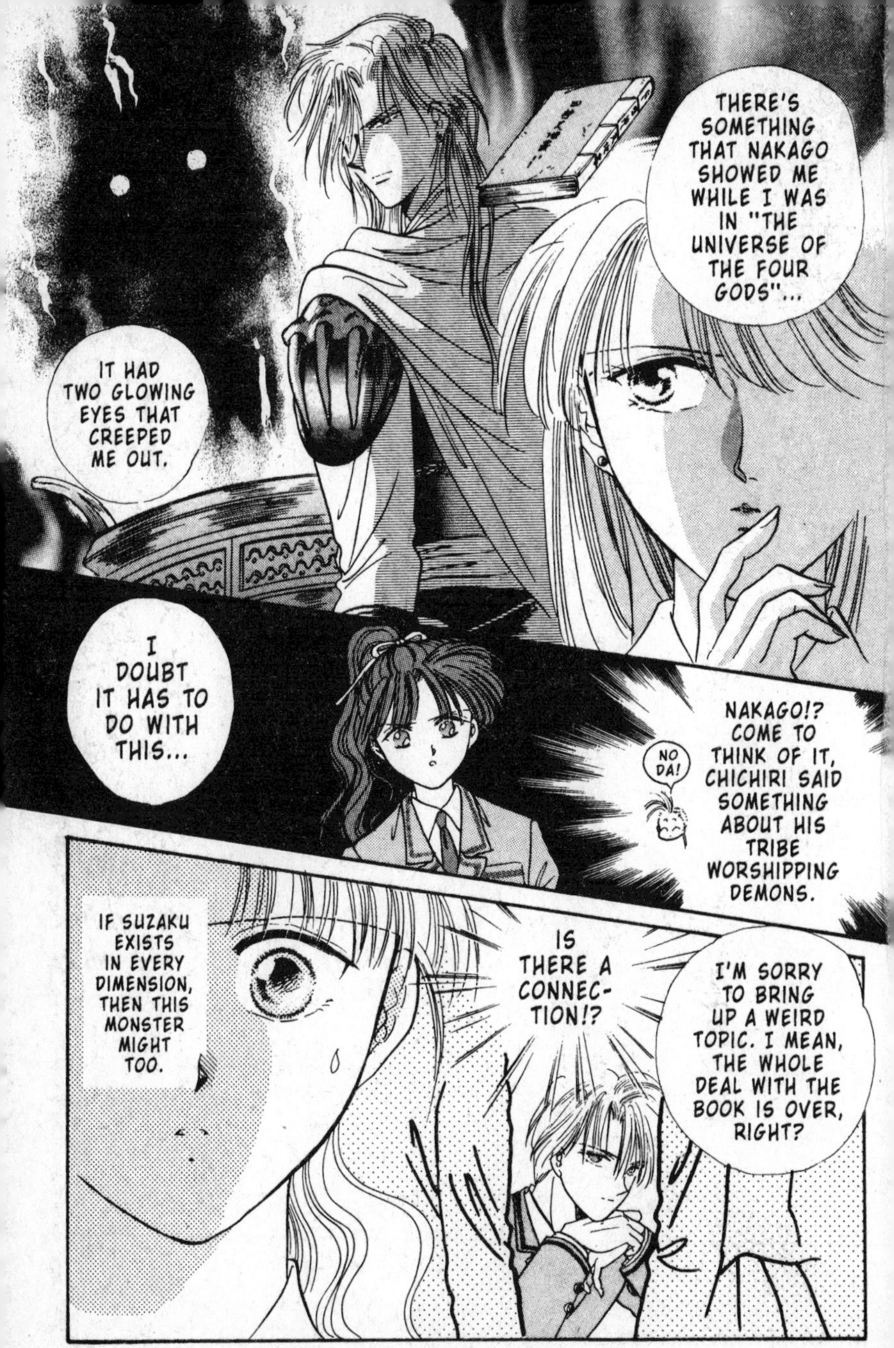
THERE'S SOMETHING THAT NAKAGO SHOWED ME WHILE I WAS IN "THE UNIVERSE OF THE FOUR GODS"...
IT HAD TWO GLOWING EYES THAT CREEPED ME OUT.
NAKAGO!? COME TO THINK OF IT, CHICHIRI SAID SOMETHING ABOUT HIS TRIBE WORSHIPPING DEMONS.
NO DA!
I DOUBT IT HAS TO DO WITH THIS...
I'M SORRY TO BRING UP A WEIRD TOPIC. I MEAN, THE WHOLE DEAL WITH THE BOOK IS OVER, RIGHT?
IS THERE A CONNEC-TION!?
IF SUZAKU EXISTS IN EVERY DIMENSION, THEN THIS MONSTER MIGHT TOO.

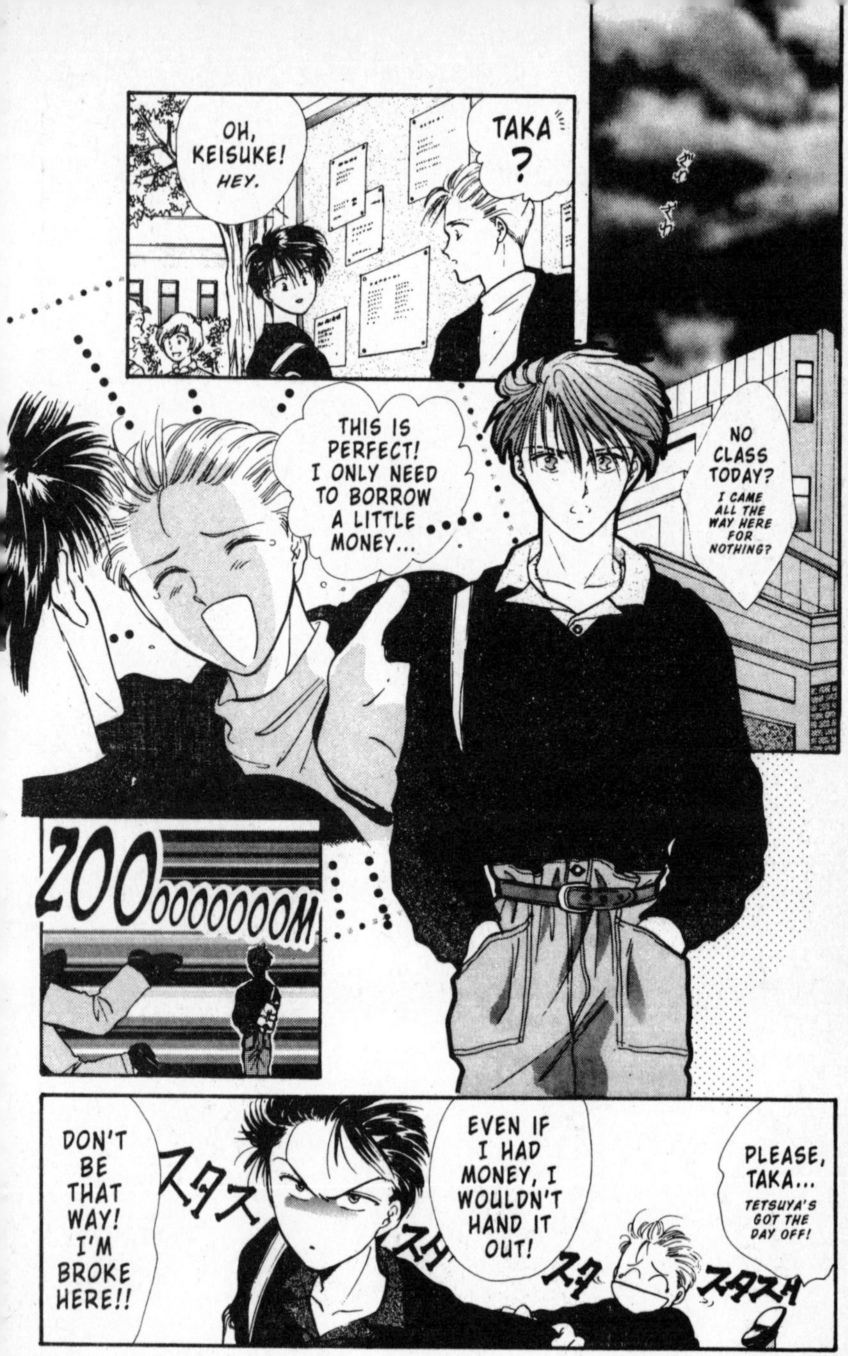
NO CLASS TODAY?
I CAME ALL THE WAY HERE FOR NOTHING?
TAKA ?
OH, KEISUKE! HEY.
THIS IS PERFECT! I ONLY NEED TO BORROW A LITTLE MONEY...
ZOOOOOOOOOM
PLEASE, TAKA...
TETSUYA'S GOT THE DAY OFF!
スタスタ
EVEN IF I HAD MONEY, I WOULDN'T HAND IT OUT!
スタ
スタス
DON'T BE THAT WAY! I'M BROKE HERE!!

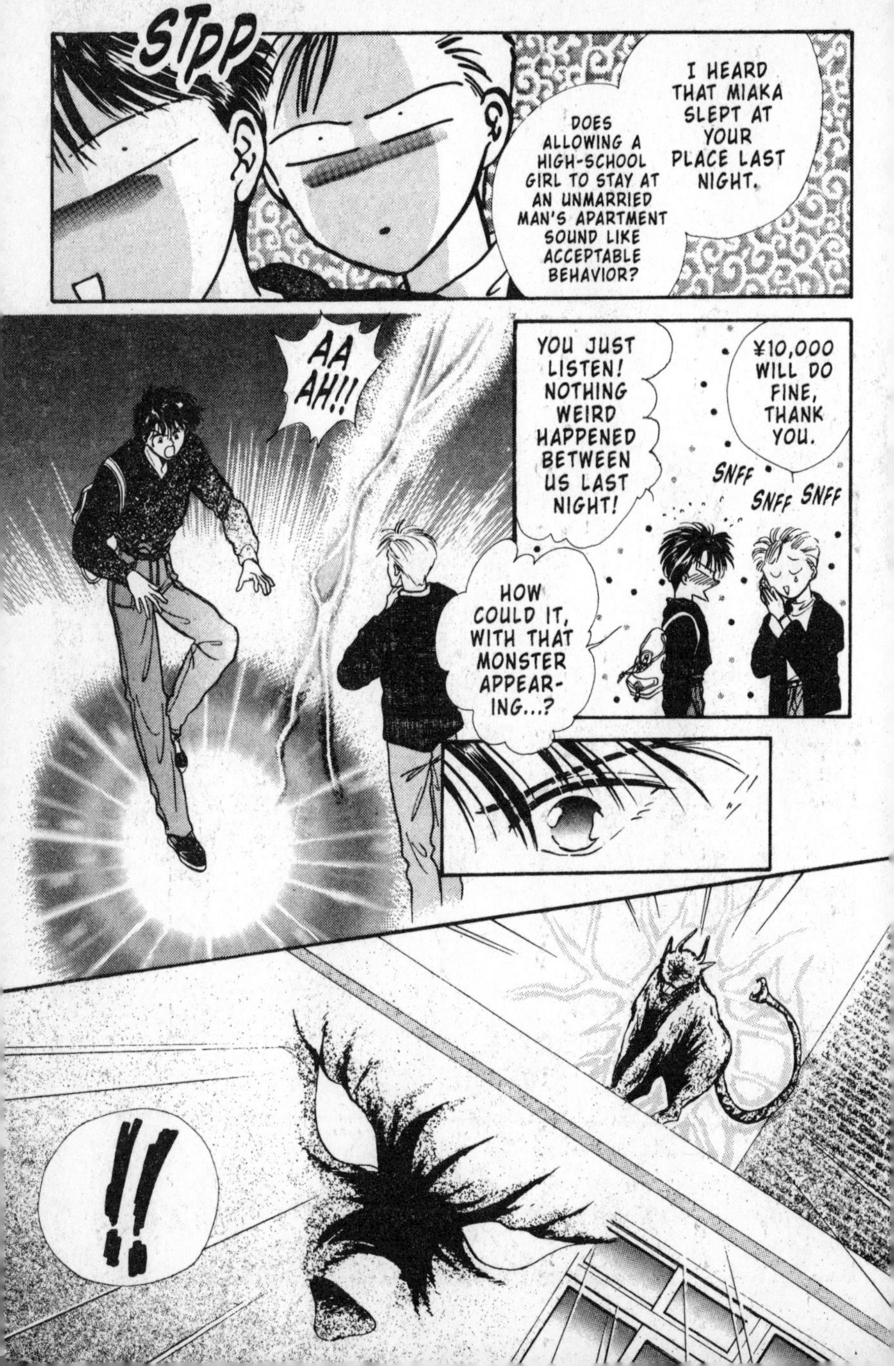
I HEARD THAT MIAKA SLEPT AT YOUR PLACE LAST NIGHT.
DOES ALLOWING A HIGH-SCHOOL GIRL TO STAY AT AN UNMARRIED MAN'S APARTMENT SOUND LIKE ACCEPTABLE BEHAVIOR?
STPP
¥10,000 WILL DO FINE, THANK YOU.
SNFF
SNFF SNFF
YOU JUST LISTEN! NOTHING WEIRD HAPPENED BETWEEN US LAST NIGHT!
HOW COULD IT, WITH THAT MONSTER APPEARING...?
AA AH!!
!!

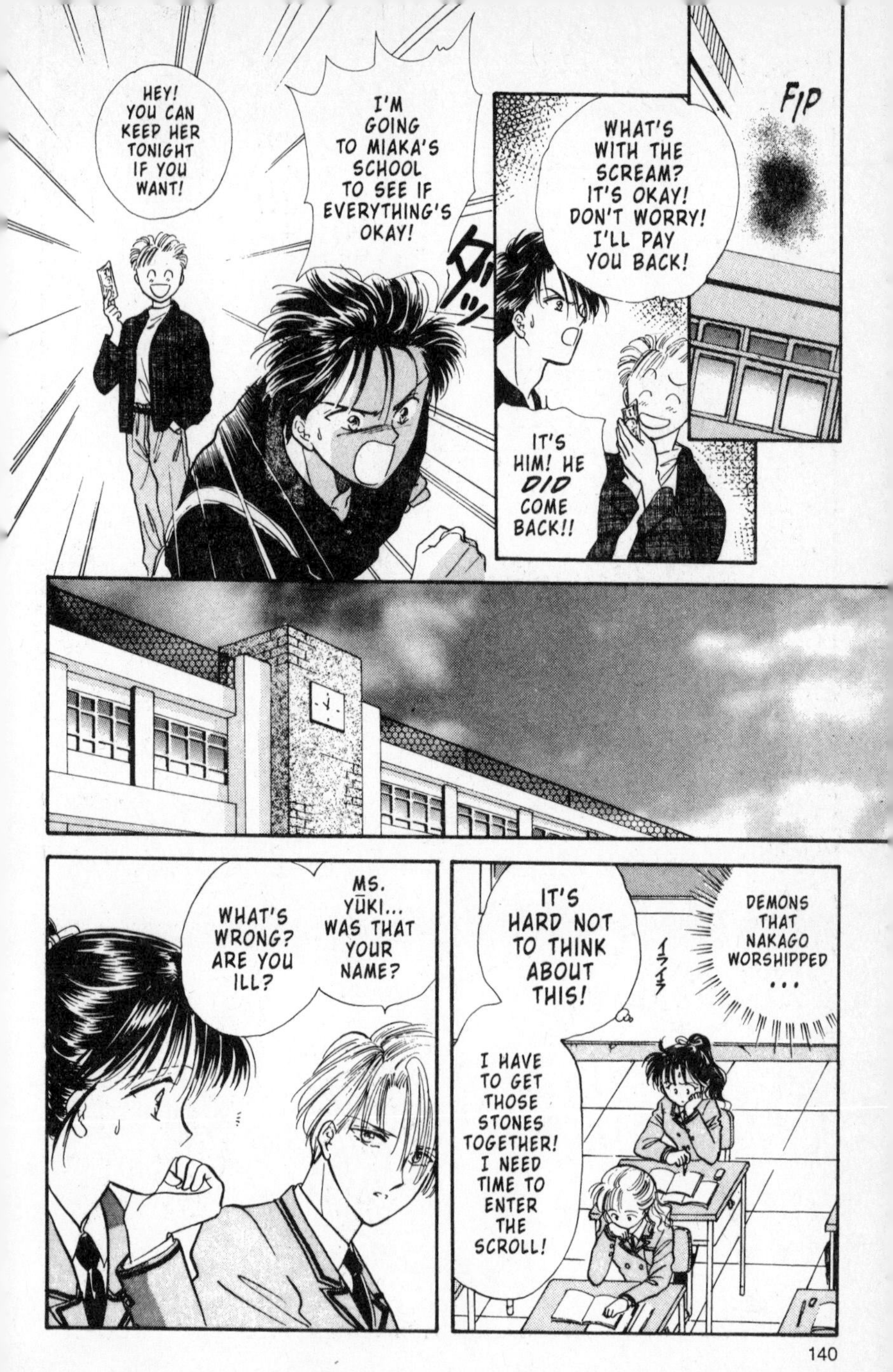
FIP
WHAT'S WITH THE SCREAM? IT'S OKAY! DON'T WORRY! I'LL PAY YOU BACK!
IT'S HIM! HE *DID* COME BACK!!
I'M GOING TO MIAKA'S SCHOOL TO SEE IF EVERYTHING'S OKAY!
ダッ
HEY! YOU CAN KEEP HER TONIGHT IF YOU WANT!
DEMONS THAT NAKAGO WORSHIPPED ...
IT'S HARD NOT TO THINK ABOUT THIS!
イライラ
I HAVE TO GET THOSE STONES TOGETHER! I NEED TIME TO ENTER THE SCROLL!
MS. YŪKI... WAS THAT YOUR NAME?
WHAT'S WRONG? ARE YOU ILL?

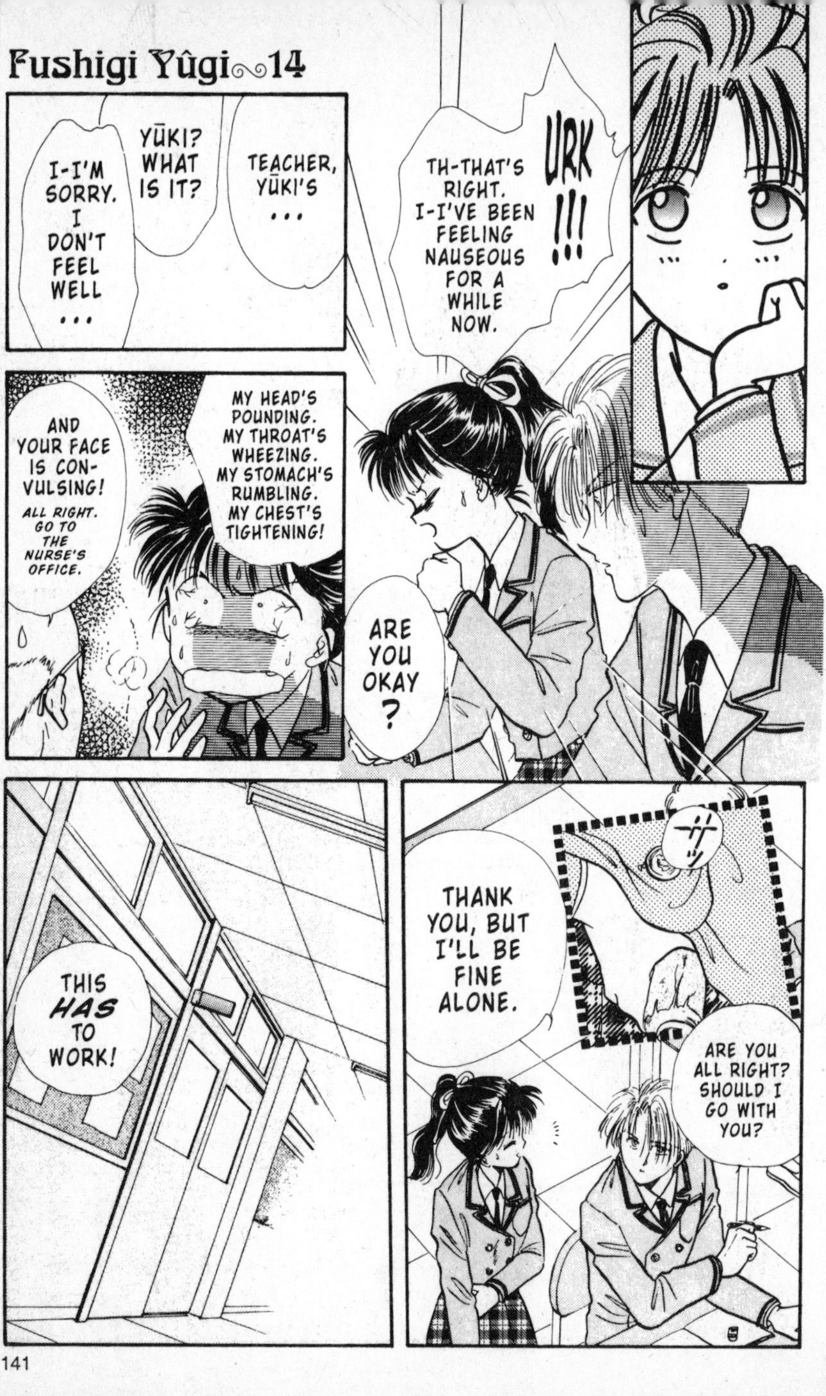
TEACHER, YŪKI'S ...
YŪKI? WHAT IS IT?
I-I'M SORRY. I DON'T FEEL WELL ...
TH-THAT'S RIGHT. I-I'VE BEEN FEELING NAUSEOUS FOR A WHILE NOW.
URK !!!
MY HEAD'S POUNDING. MY THROAT'S WHEEZING. MY STOMACH'S RUMBLING. MY CHEST'S TIGHTENING!
AND YOUR FACE IS CON-VULSING!
ALL RIGHT. GO TO THE NURSE'S OFFICE.
ARE YOU OKAY ?
ARE YOU ALL RIGHT? SHOULD I GO WITH YOU?
ガタッ
THANK YOU, BUT I'LL BE FINE ALONE.
THIS *HAS* TO WORK!

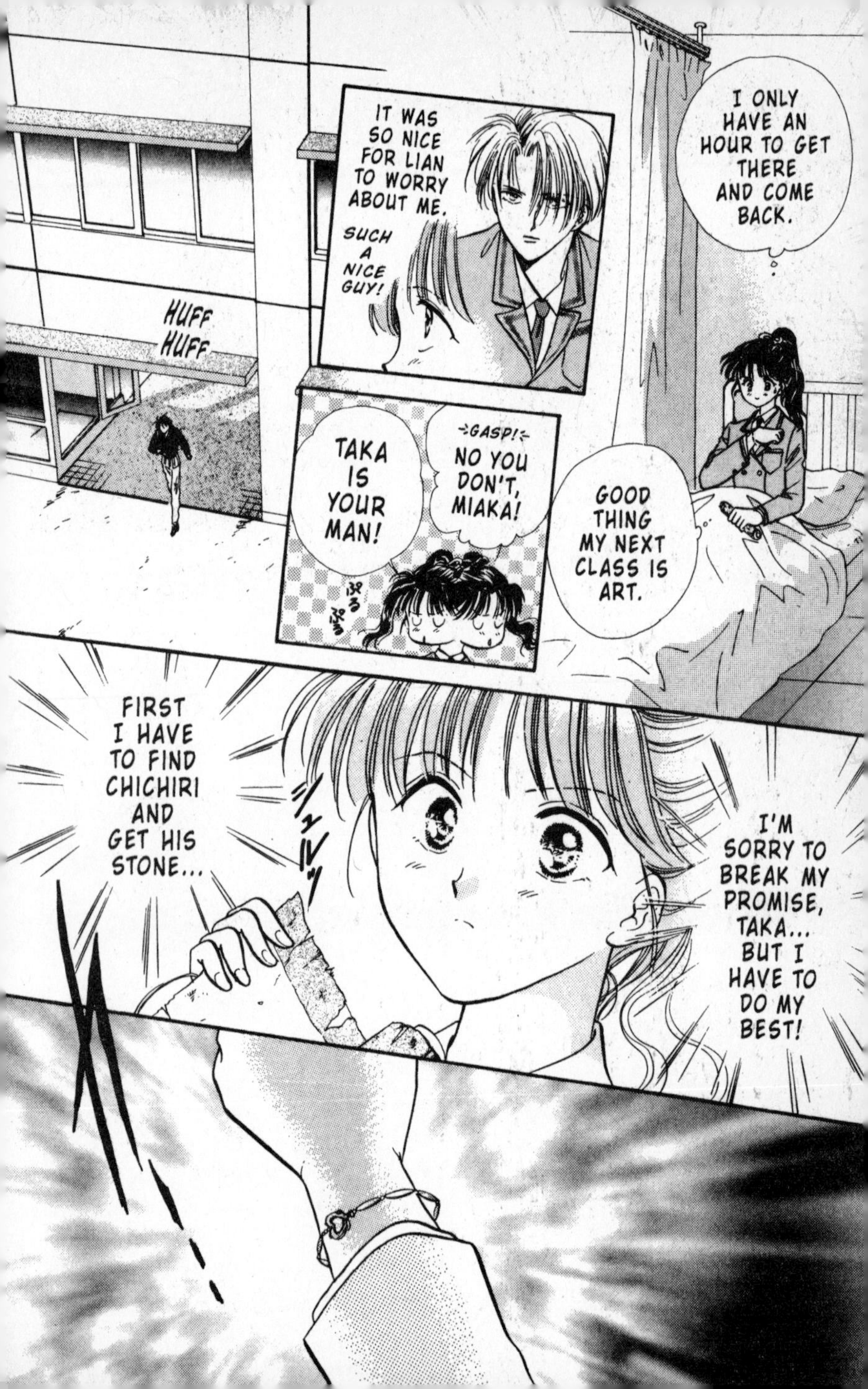
I ONLY HAVE AN HOUR TO GET THERE AND COME BACK.
GOOD THING MY NEXT CLASS IS ART.
IT WAS SO NICE FOR LIAN TO WORRY ABOUT ME.
SUCH A NICE GUY!
GASP!
NO YOU DON'T, MIAKA!
TAKA IS YOUR MAN!
ぷるぷる
HUFF HUFF
I'M SORRY TO BREAK MY PROMISE, TAKA... BUT I HAVE TO DO MY BEST!
FIRST I HAVE TO FIND CHICHIRI AND GET HIS STONE...

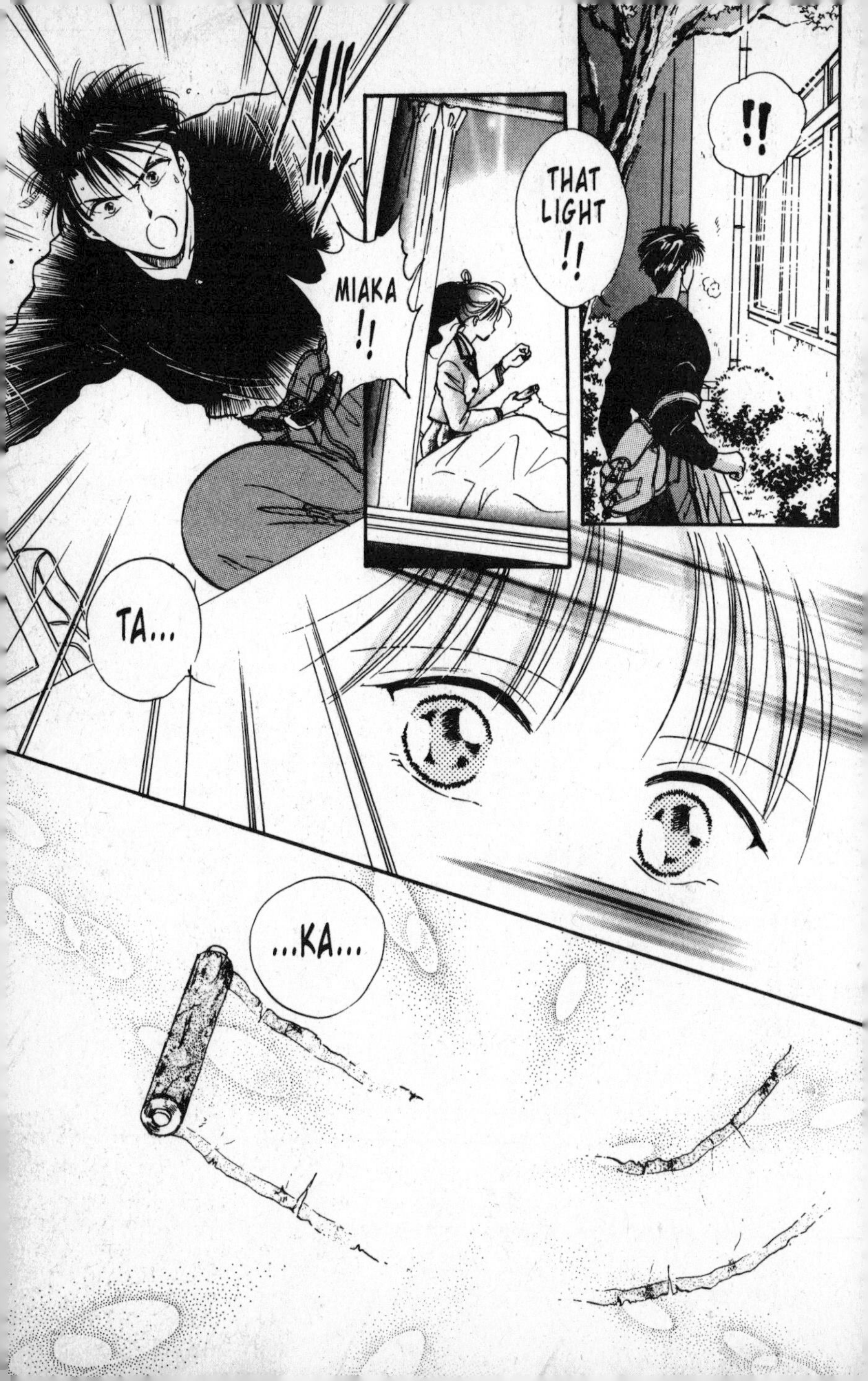
!!
THAT LIGHT !!
MIAKA !!
TA...
...KA...

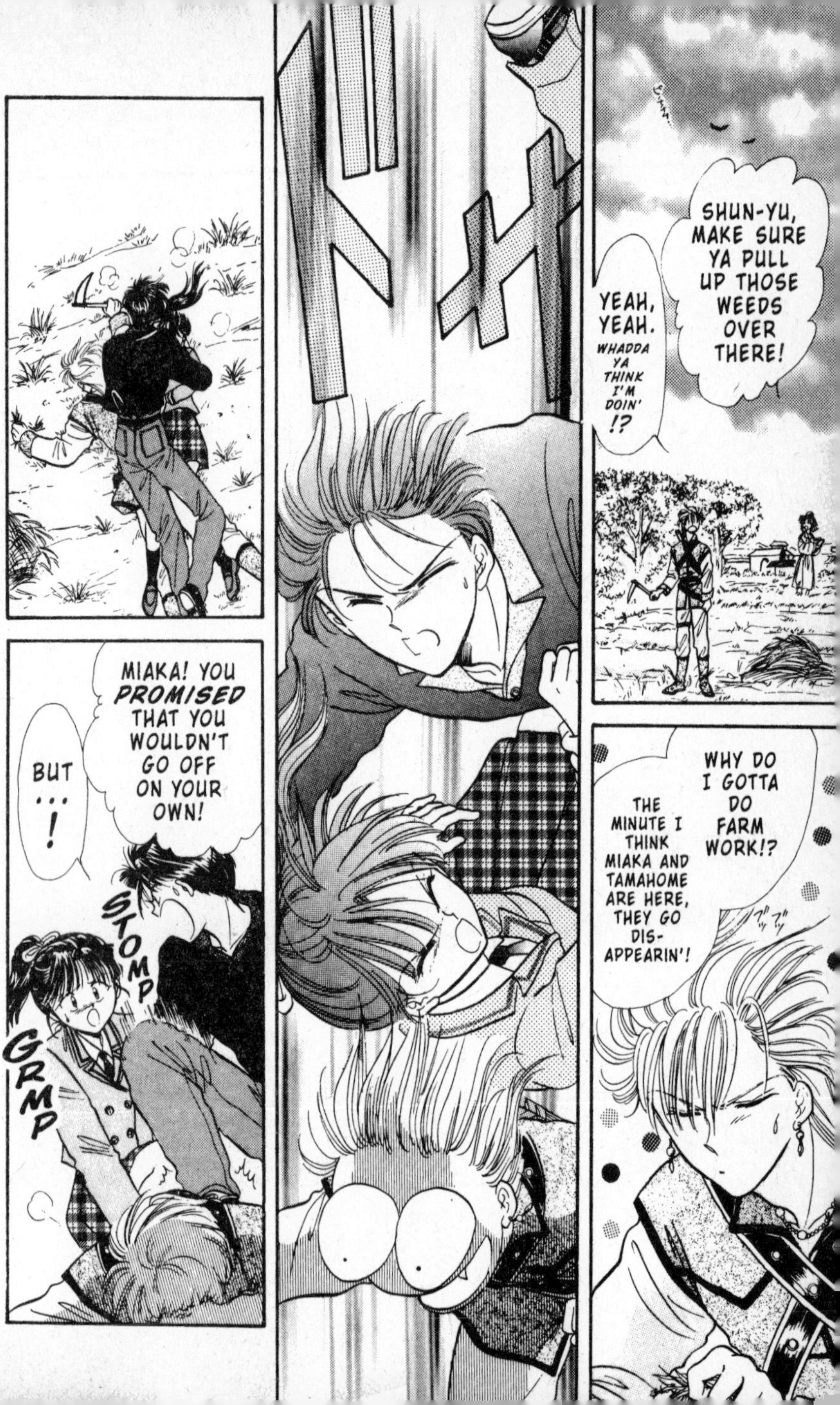
SHUN-YU, MAKE SURE YA PULL UP THOSE WEEDS OVER THERE!
YEAH, YEAH. WHADDA YA THINK I'M DOIN' !?
WHY DO I GOTTA DO FARM WORK!?
THE MINUTE I THINK MIAKA AND TAMAHOME ARE HERE, THEY GO DIS-APPEARIN'!
MIAKA! YOU PROMISED THAT YOU WOULDN'T GO OFF ON YOUR OWN!
BUT ...!
STOMP
GRMP

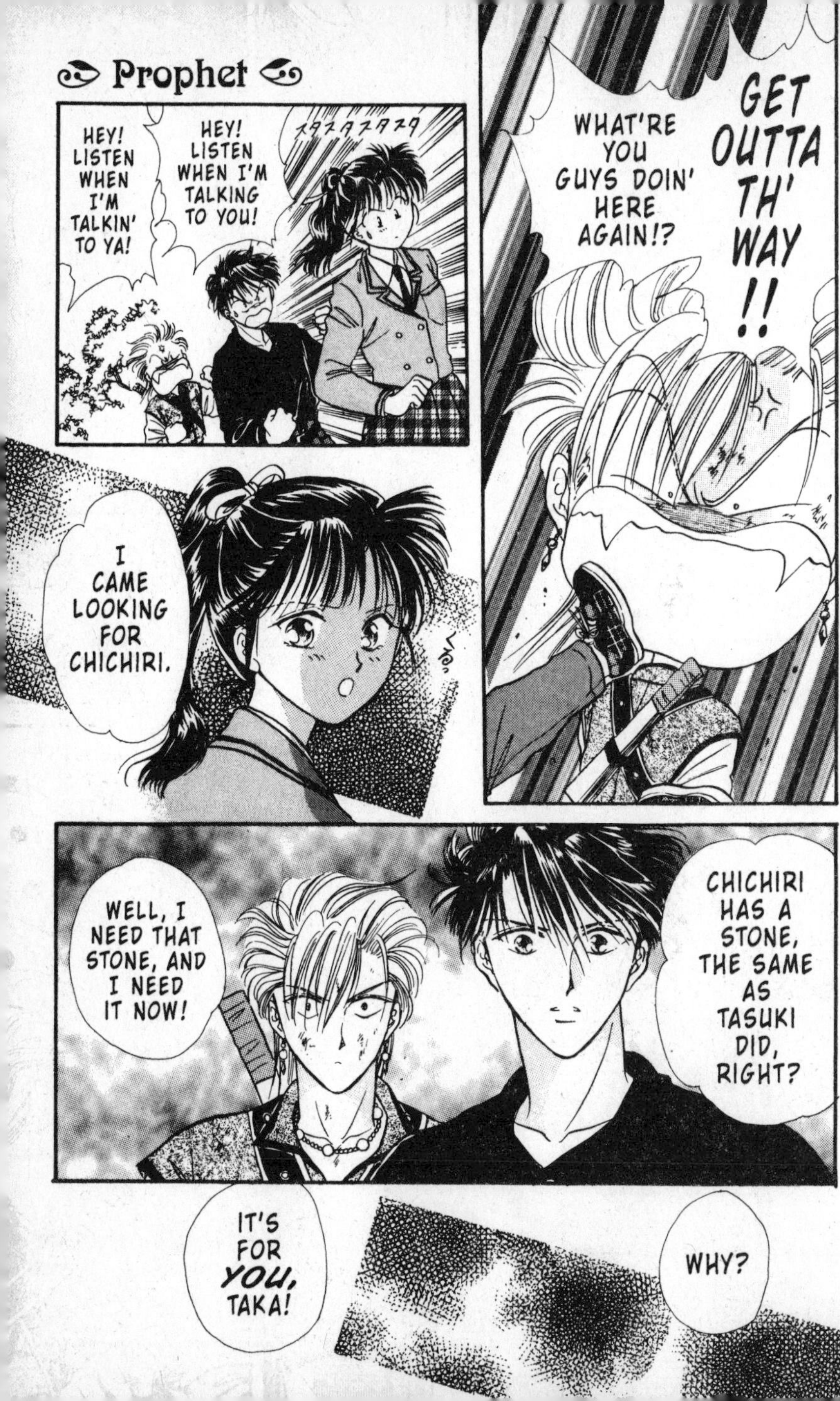
GET OUTTA TH' WAY!!
WHAT'RE YOU GUYS DOIN' HERE AGAIN!?
スタスタスタスタ
HEY! LISTEN WHEN I'M TALKING TO YOU!
HEY! LISTEN WHEN I'M TALKIN' TO YA!
I CAME LOOKING FOR CHICHIRI.
CHICHIRI HAS A STONE, THE SAME AS TASUKI DID, RIGHT?
WELL, I NEED THAT STONE, AND I NEED IT NOW!
WHY?
IT'S FOR YOU, TAKA!

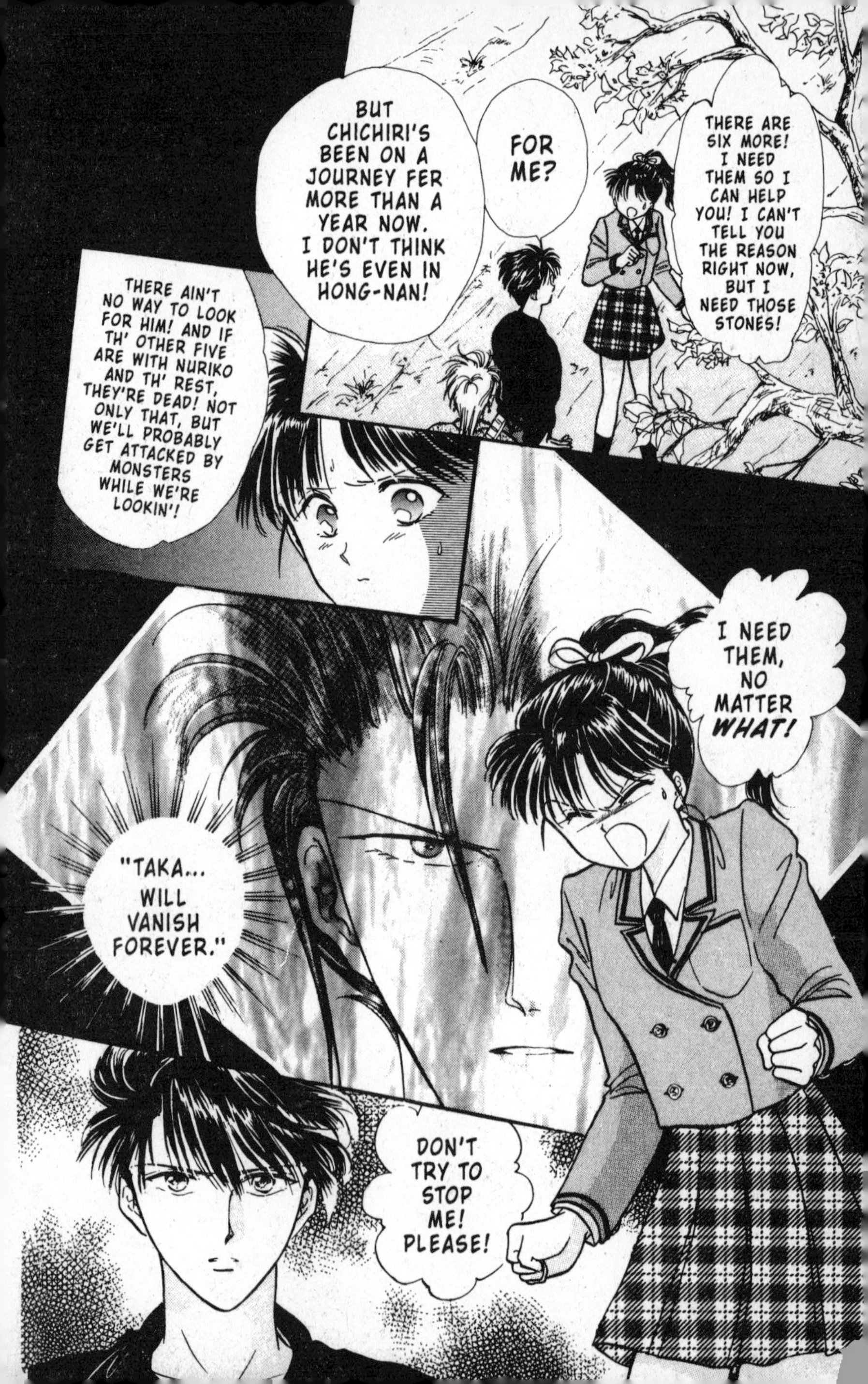
THERE ARE SIX MORE! I NEED THEM SO I CAN HELP YOU! I CAN'T TELL YOU THE REASON RIGHT NOW, BUT I NEED THOSE STONES!
FOR ME?
BUT CHICHIRI'S BEEN ON A JOURNEY FER MORE THAN A YEAR NOW. I DON'T THINK HE'S EVEN IN HONG-NAN!
THERE AIN'T NO WAY TO LOOK FOR HIM! AND IF TH' OTHER FIVE ARE WITH NURIKO AND TH' REST, THEY'RE DEAD! NOT ONLY THAT, BUT WE'LL PROBABLY GET ATTACKED BY MONSTERS WHILE WE'RE LOOKIN'!
I NEED THEM, NO MATTER ***WHAT!***
"TAKA... WILL VANISH FOREVER."
DON'T TRY TO STOP ME! PLEASE!

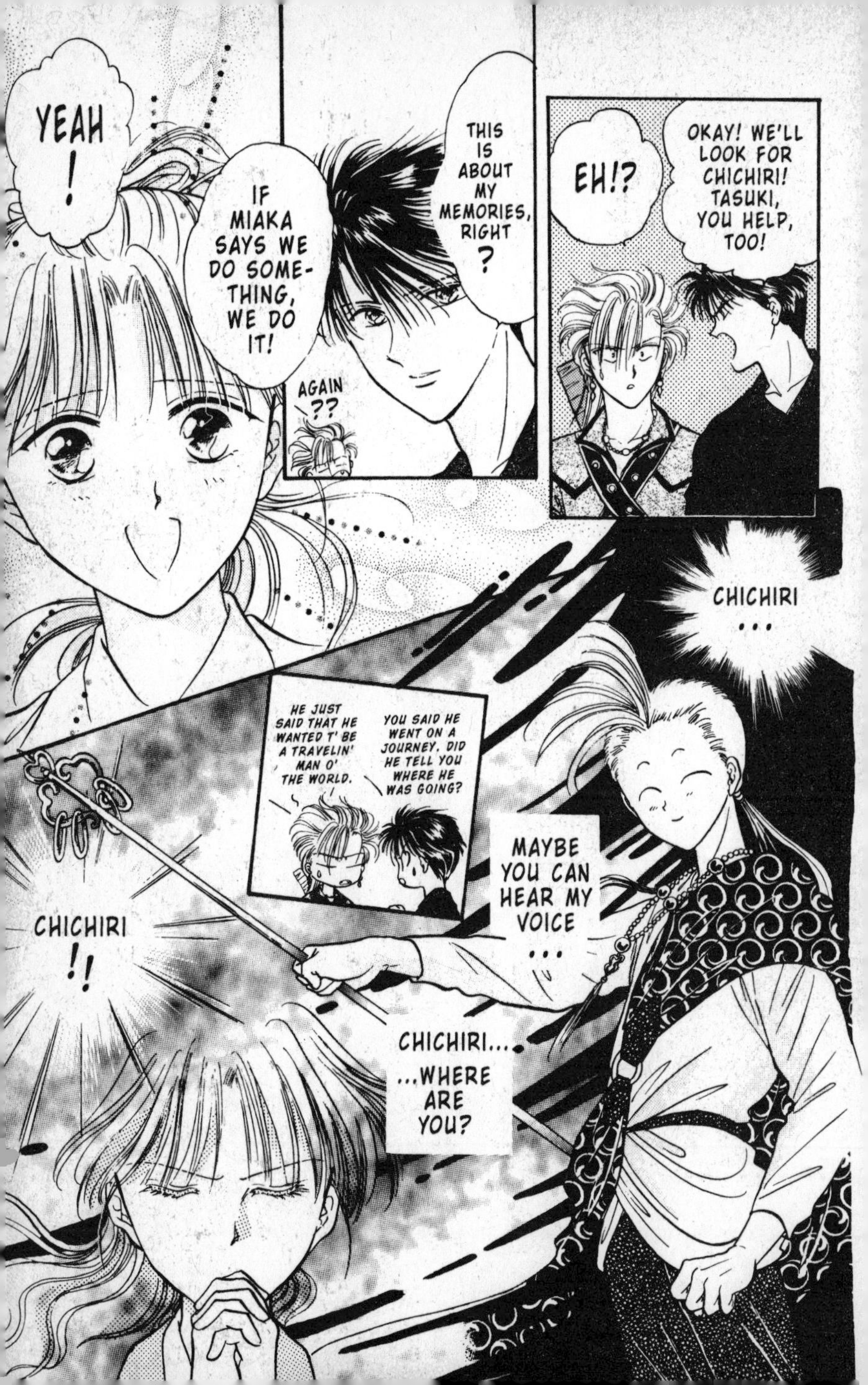
OKAY! WE'LL LOOK FOR CHICHIRI! TASUKI, YOU HELP, TOO!
EH!?
THIS IS ABOUT MY MEMORIES, RIGHT?
IF MIAKA SAYS WE DO SOMETHING, WE DO IT!
AGAIN??
YEAH!
CHICHIRI...
YOU SAID HE WENT ON A JOURNEY. DID HE TELL YOU WHERE HE WAS GOING?
HE JUST SAID THAT HE WANTED T' BE A TRAVELIN' MAN O' THE WORLD.
MAYBE YOU CAN HEAR MY VOICE...
CHICHIRI... ...WHERE ARE YOU?
CHICHIRI!!

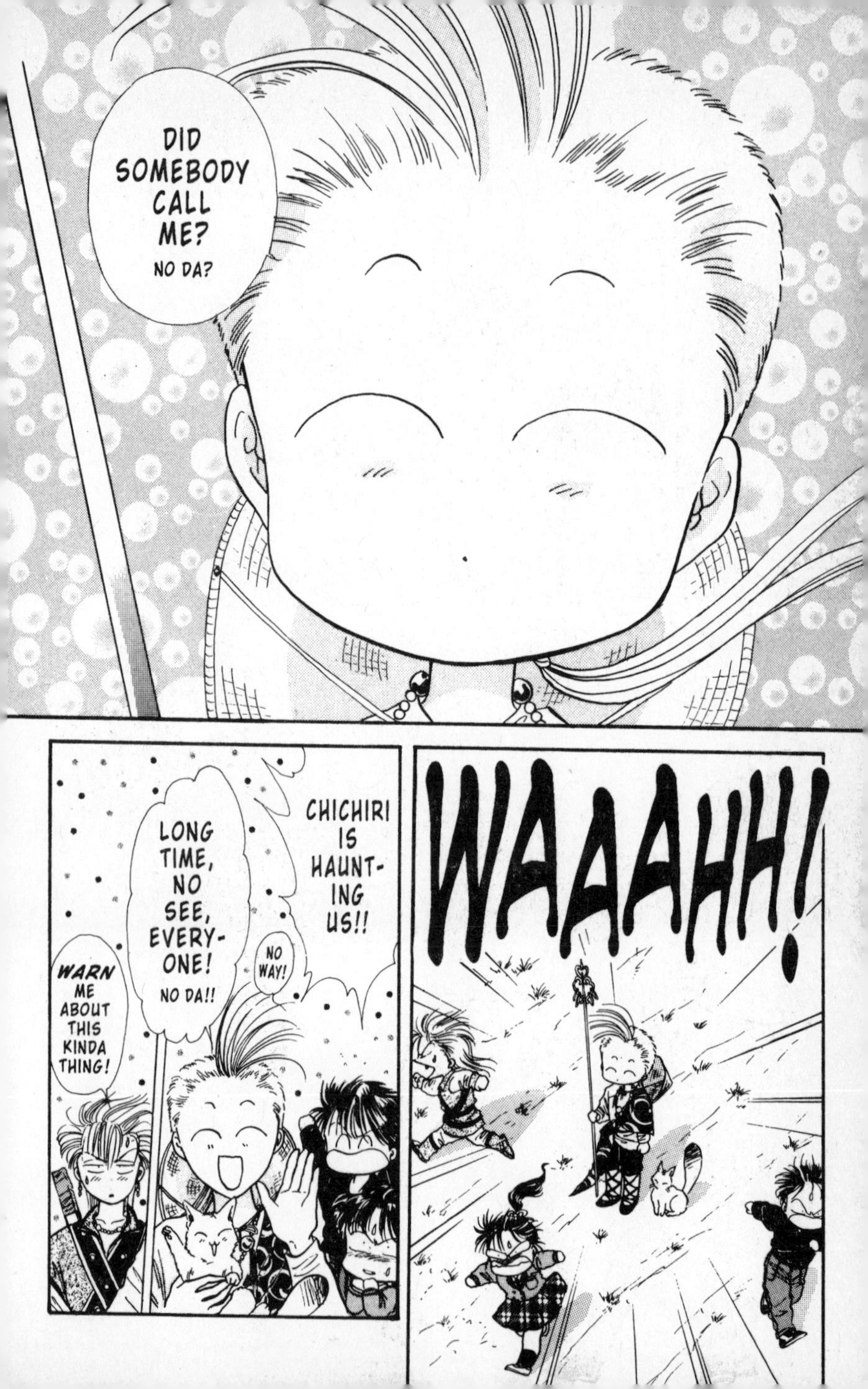
DID SOMEBODY CALL ME? NO DA?
WAAAHH!
CHICHIRI IS HAUNT-ING US!!
LONG TIME, NO SEE, EVERY-ONE! NO DA!!
NO WAY!
WARN ME ABOUT THIS KINDA THING!

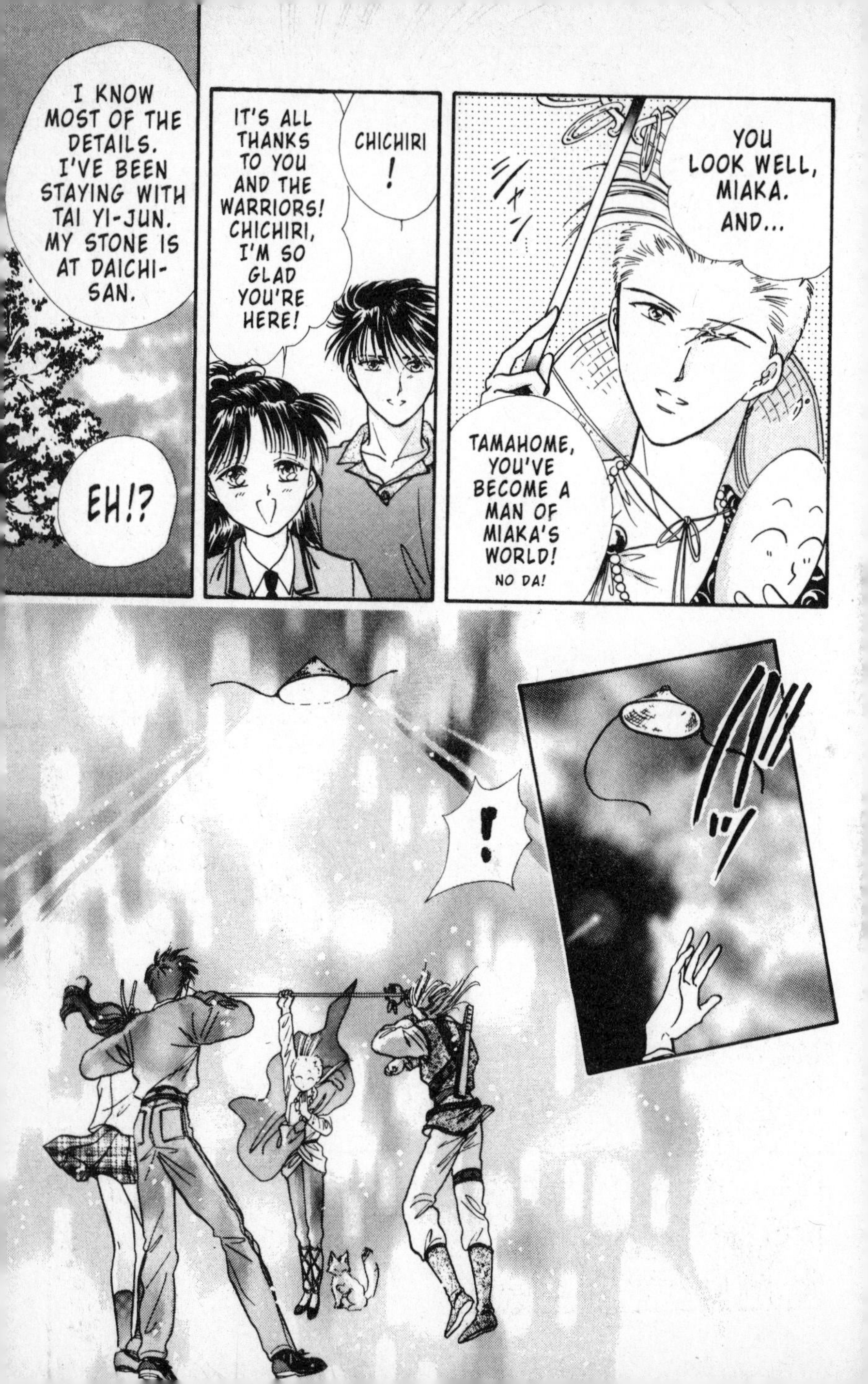

YOU LOOK WELL, MIAKA. AND...
シャン
TAMAHOME, YOU'VE BECOME A MAN OF MIAKA'S WORLD! NO DA!
CHICHIRI!
IT'S ALL THANKS TO YOU AND THE WARRIORS! CHICHIRI, I'M SO GLAD YOU'RE HERE!
I KNOW MOST OF THE DETAILS. I'VE BEEN STAYING WITH TAI YI-JUN. MY STONE IS AT DAICHI-SAN.
EH!?
!

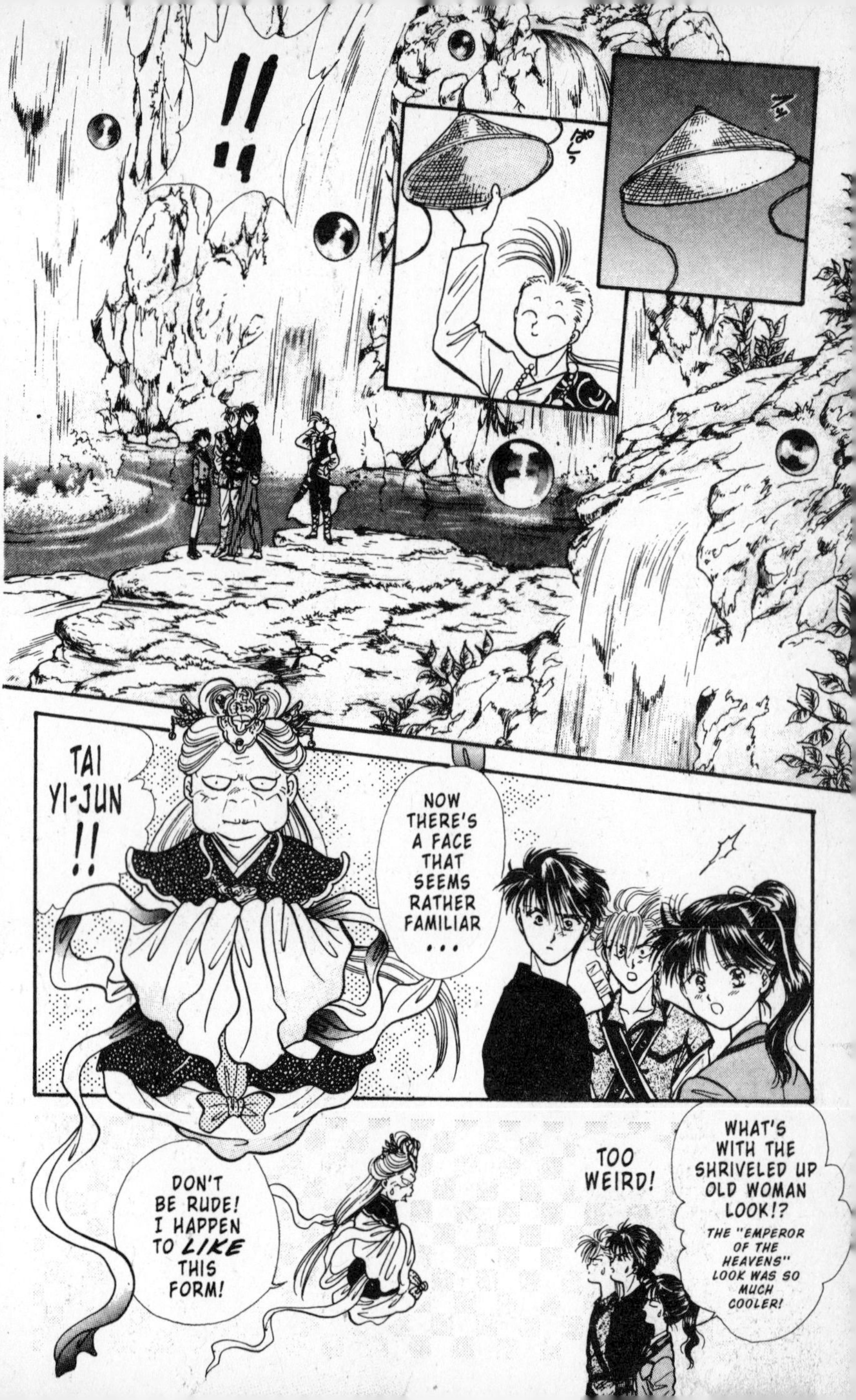
!!
NOW THERE'S A FACE THAT SEEMS RATHER FAMILIAR...
TAI YI-JUN !!
WHAT'S WITH THE SHRIVELED UP OLD WOMAN LOOK!?
THE "EMPEROR OF THE HEAVENS" LOOK WAS SO MUCH COOLER!
TOO WEIRD!
DON'T BE RUDE! I HAPPEN TO *LIKE* THIS FORM!

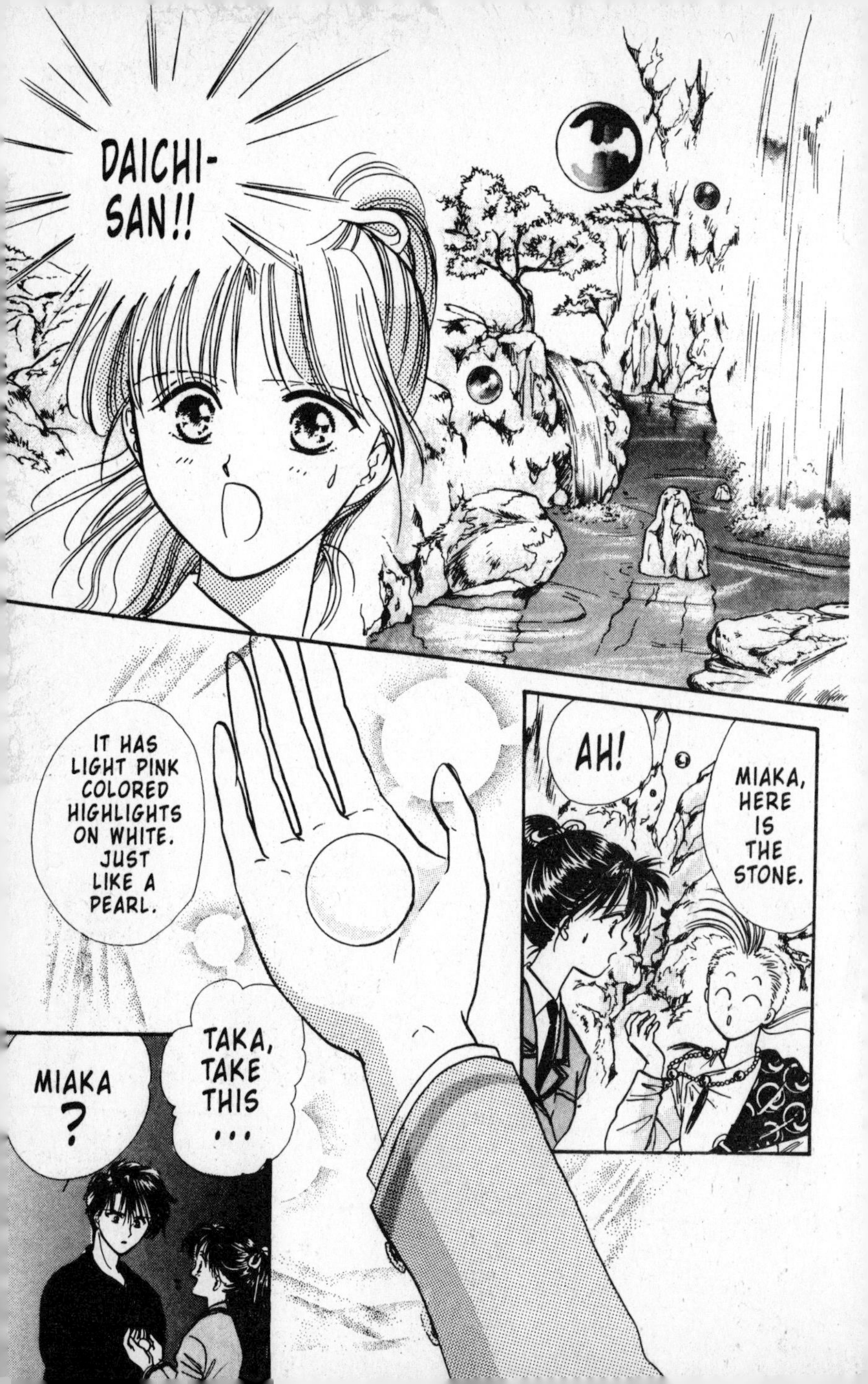
DAICHI-SAN!!
MIAKA, HERE IS THE STONE.
AH!
IT HAS LIGHT PINK COLORED HIGHLIGHTS ON WHITE. JUST LIKE A PEARL.
TAKA, TAKE THIS...
MIAKA?

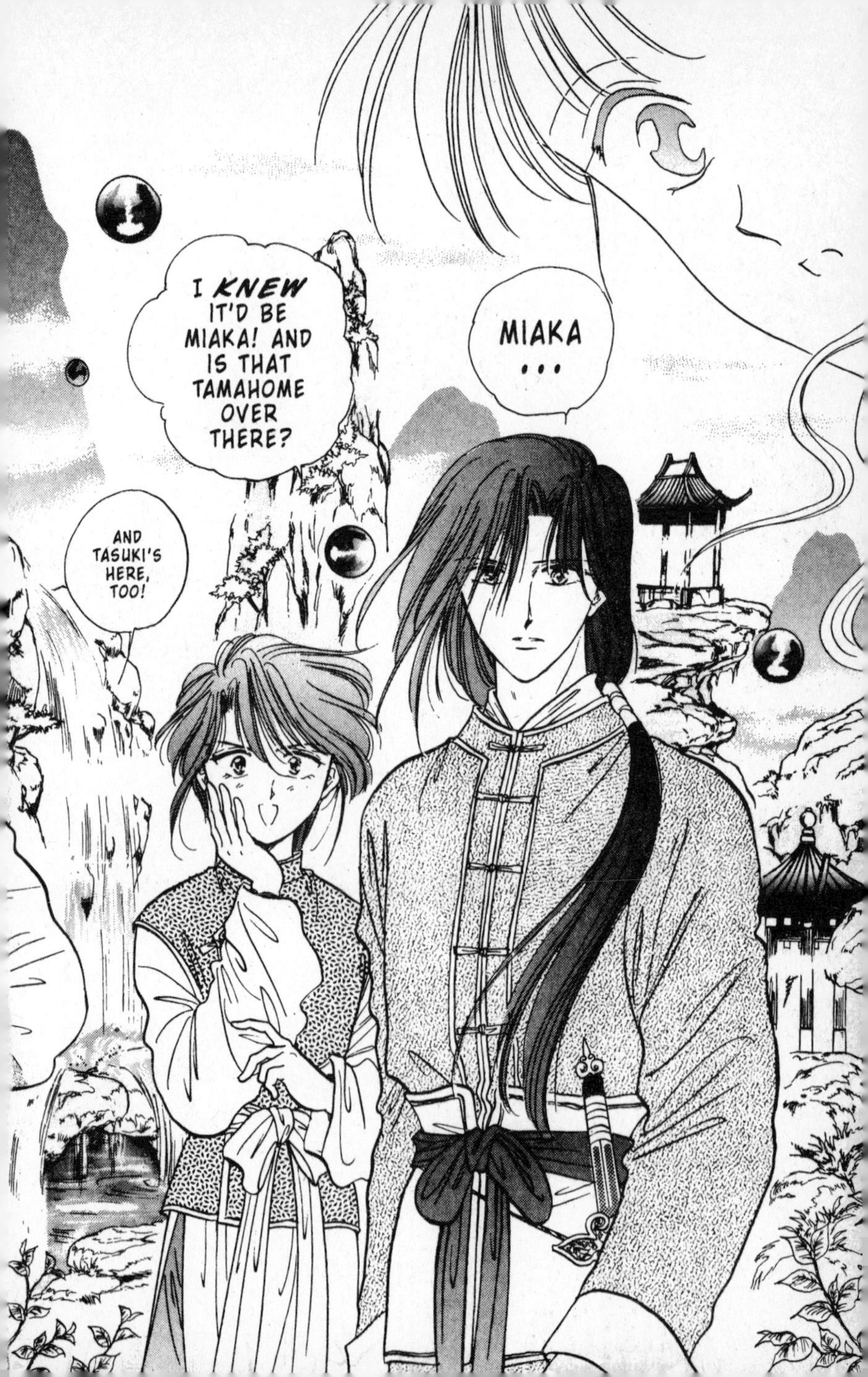
MIAKA ...
I *KNEW* IT'D BE MIAKA! AND IS THAT TAMAHOME OVER THERE?
AND TASUKI'S HERE, TOO!

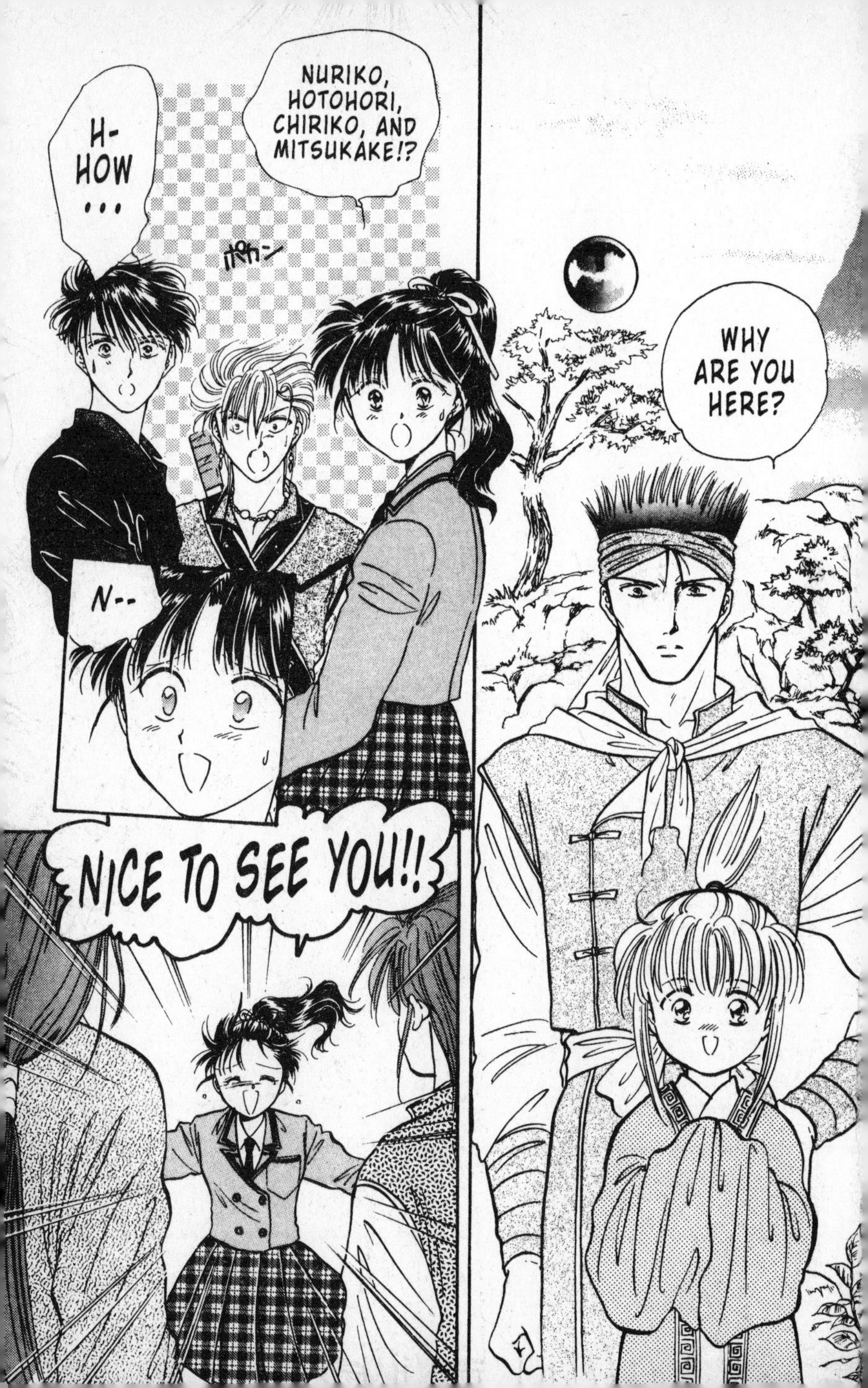
WHY ARE YOU HERE?
NURIKO, HOTOHORI, CHIRIKO, AND MITSUKAKE!?
H- HOW ...
N--
NICE TO SEE YOU!!

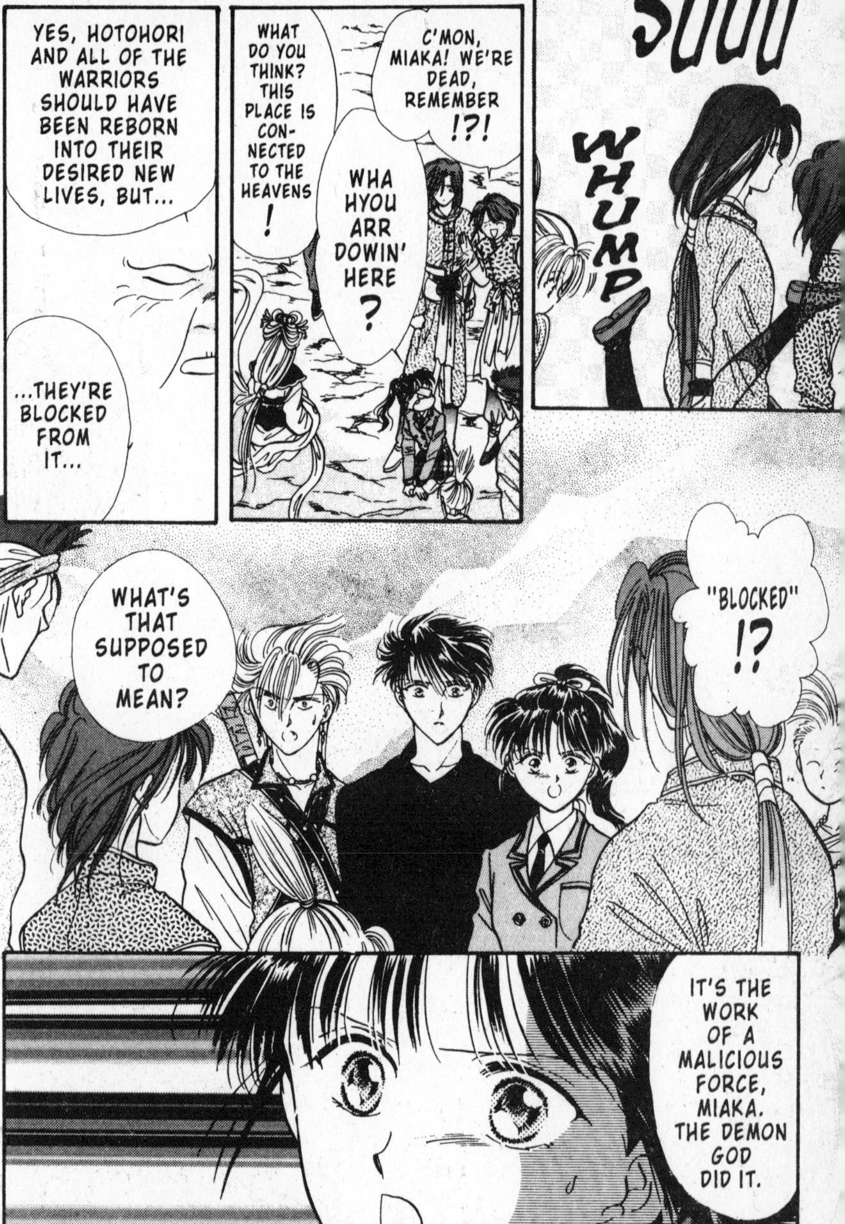
SUUU
WHUMP
C'MON, MIAKA! WE'RE DEAD, REMEMBER !?!
WHAT DO YOU THINK? THIS PLACE IS CON-NECTED TO THE HEAVENS !
WHA HYOU ARR DOWIN' HERE ?
YES, HOTOHORI AND ALL OF THE WARRIORS SHOULD HAVE BEEN REBORN INTO THEIR DESIRED NEW LIVES, BUT...
...THEY'RE BLOCKED FROM IT...
"BLOCKED" !?
WHAT'S THAT SUPPOSED TO MEAN?
IT'S THE WORK OF A MALICIOUS FORCE, MIAKA. THE DEMON GOD DID IT.

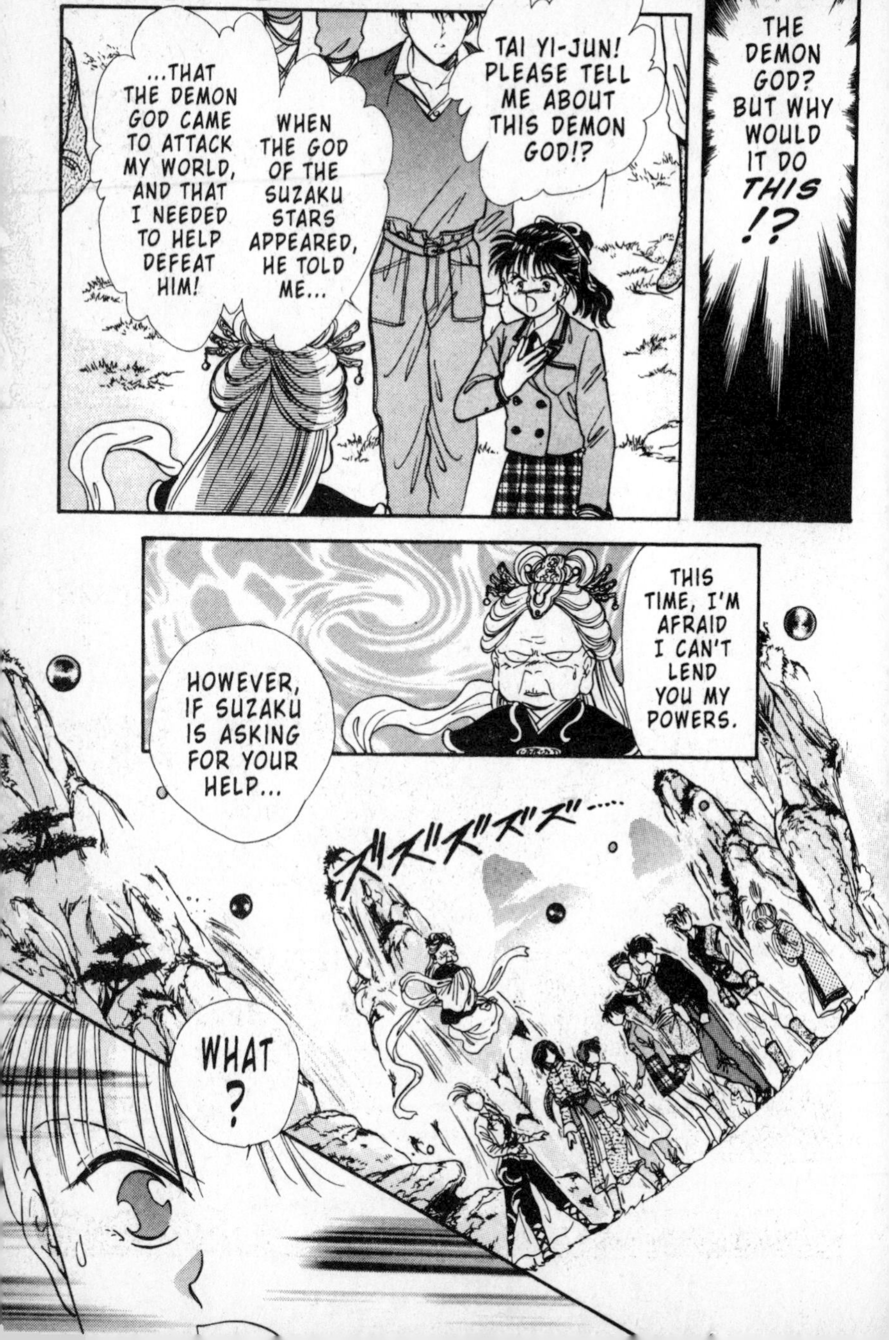
THE DEMON GOD? BUT WHY WOULD IT DO THIS!?
TAI YI-JUN! PLEASE TELL ME ABOUT THIS DEMON GOD!?
WHEN THE GOD OF THE SUZAKU STARS APPEARED, HE TOLD ME...
...THAT THE DEMON GOD CAME TO ATTACK MY WORLD, AND THAT I NEEDED TO HELP DEFEAT HIM!
THIS TIME, I'M AFRAID I CAN'T LEND YOU MY POWERS.
HOWEVER, IF SUZAKU IS ASKING FOR YOUR HELP...
ズズズズ.....
WHAT?

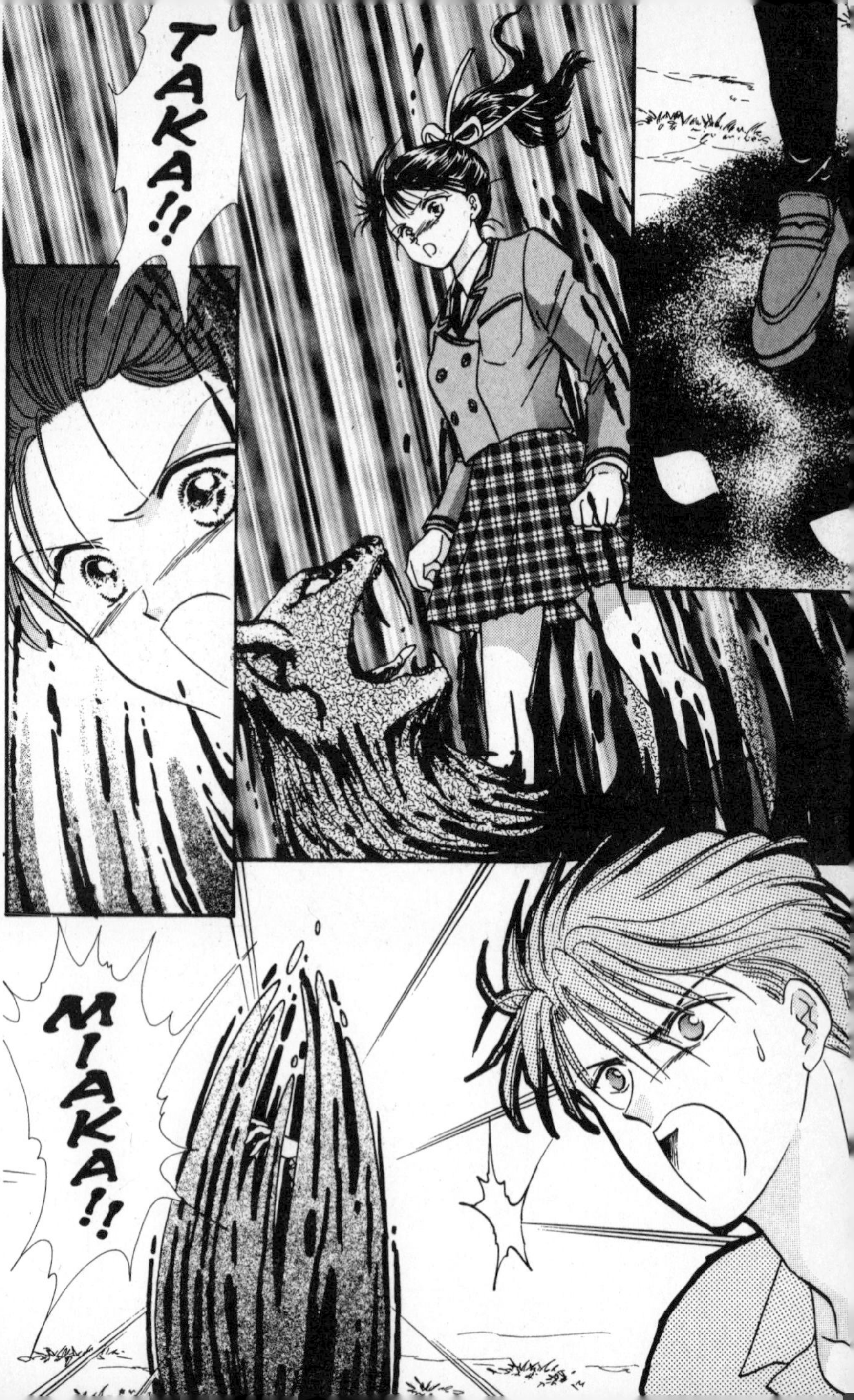
TAKA!!
MIAKA!!

ふしぎ悪戯
FUSHIGI AKUGI
THE MALICIOUS PLAY (11)

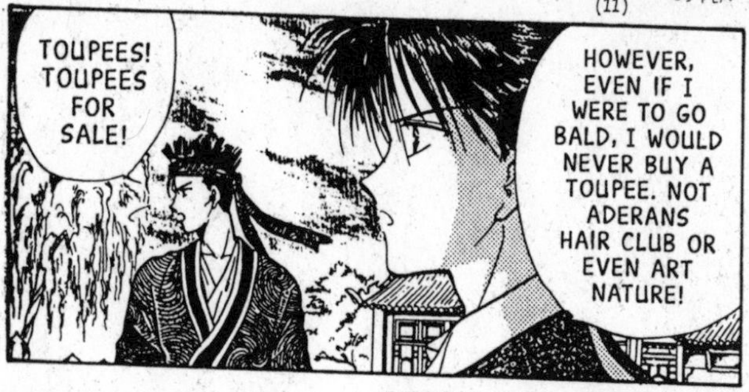
HOWEVER, EVEN IF I WERE TO GO BALD, I WOULD NEVER BUY A TOUPEE. NOT ADERANS HAIR CLUB OR EVEN ART NATURE!
TOUPEES! TOUPEES FOR SALE!

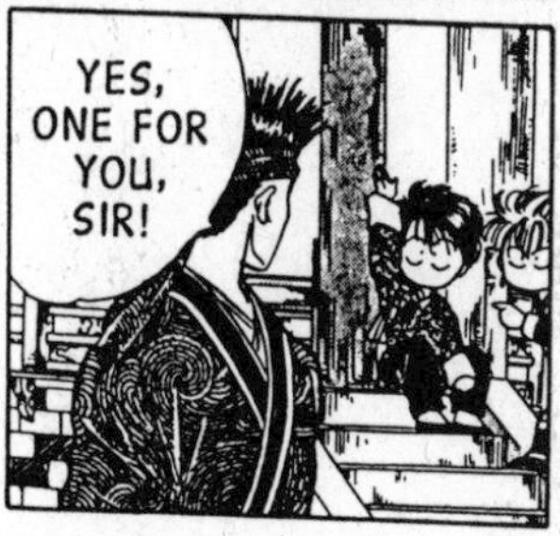
YES, ONE FOR YOU, SIR!

Suggested by: A valued reader.

These panels weren't meant to be used for Fushigi Akugi, but it was so funny, I couldn't help it! (So remember, now wig jokes are out!) By the way, the people in the office were coming up with other "wig play" story lines that broke up the whole room.

Like... To Taka's shock, the Emperor of the Heavens prophesized that he was going to lose his hair! Or that the contents of the "stones" weren't Taka's memories but his hair.

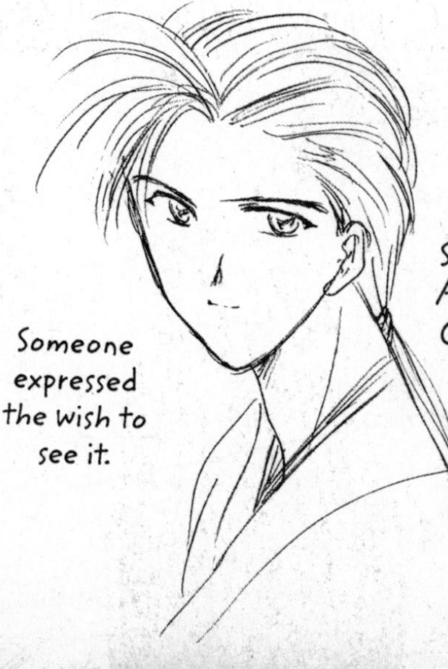

Suddenly... A teenage Chichiri!!

Someone expressed the wish to see it.

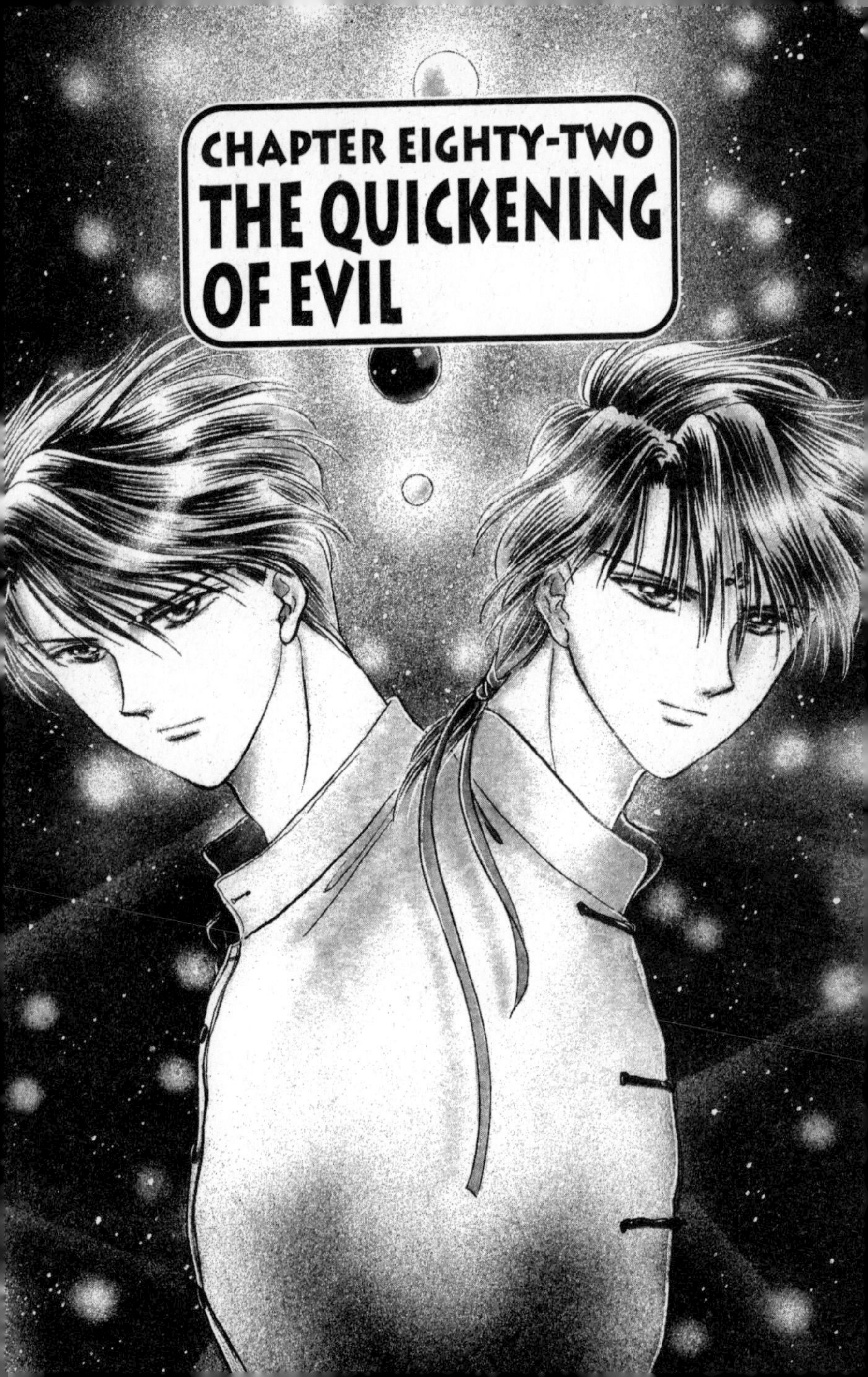
CHAPTER EIGHTY-TWO
THE QUICKENING OF EVIL

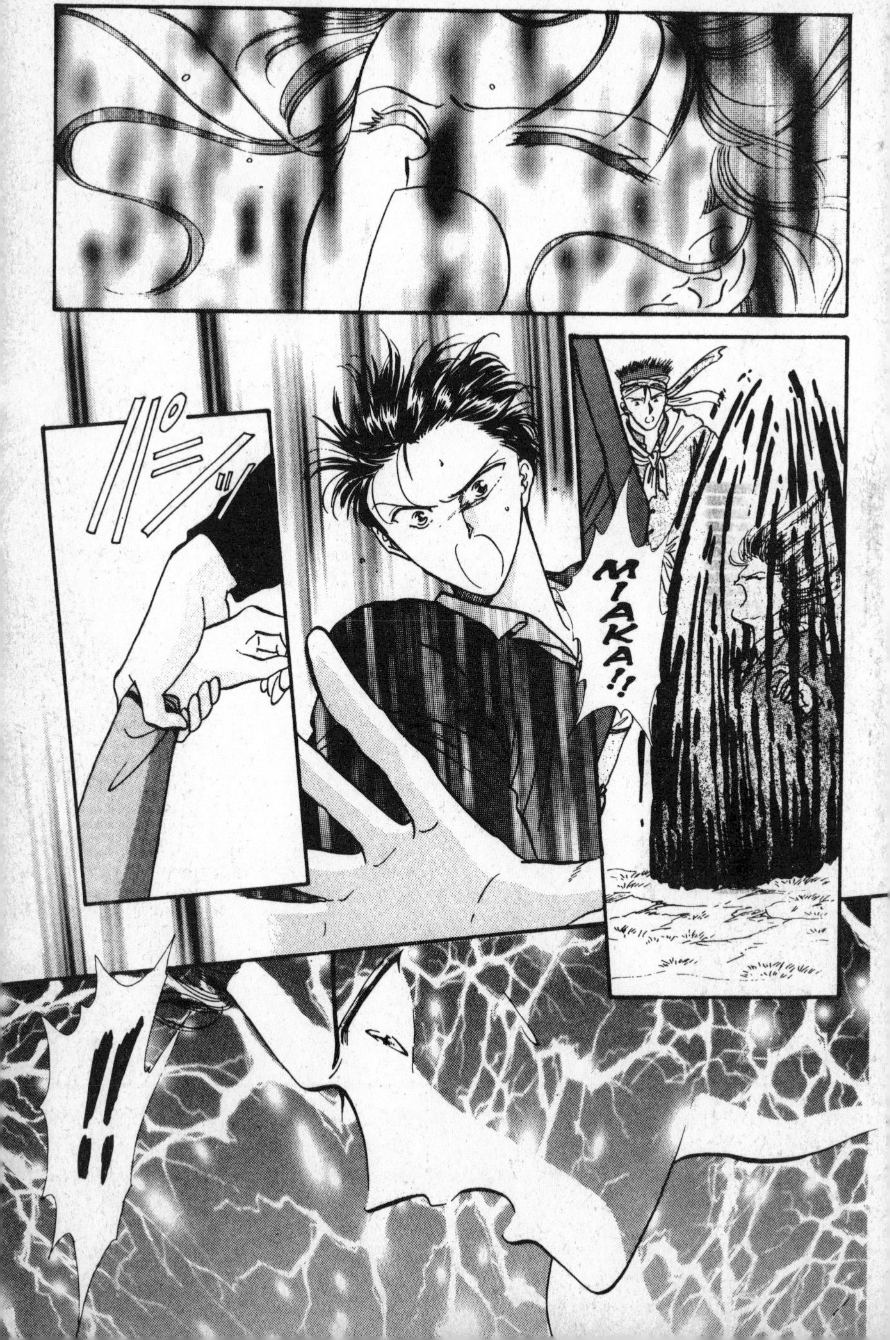
MIAKA!!
パシッ
!!

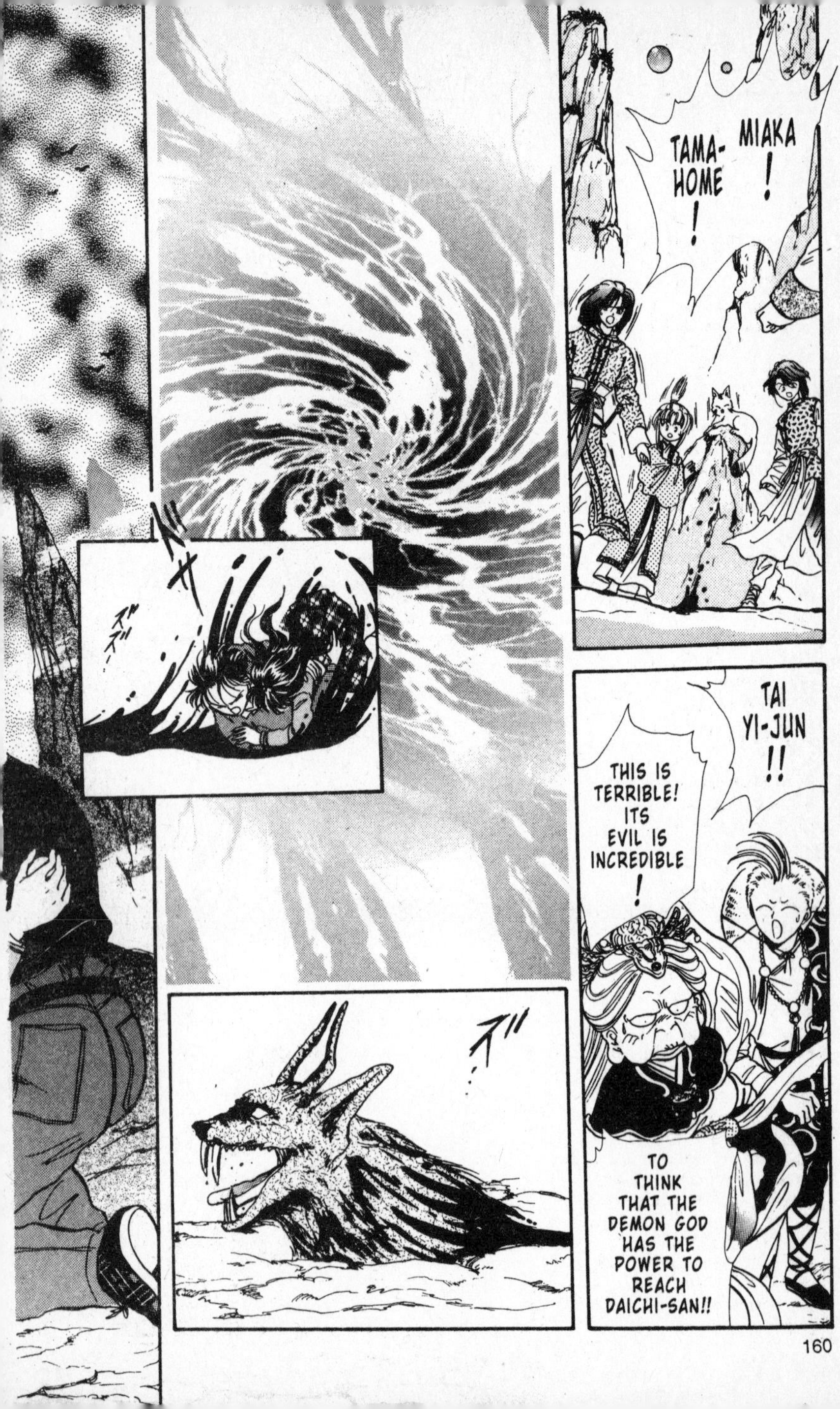
MIAKA!
TAMA-HOME!
TAI YI-JUN!!
THIS IS TERRIBLE! ITS EVIL IS INCREDIBLE!
TO THINK THAT THE DEMON GOD HAS THE POWER TO REACH DAICHI-SAN!!

And the final column. This time, because the first chapter of the book was so long, we only had five chapters in this book. (Volume 10 was the same way...)
With the release of Volume 13, I received a lot of reader mail, but as a result of the anime, I was surprised at how many people in their 20s and 30s were writing in! Some wrote, "Since I had the money, I bought volumes 1 through 13 all at once!" and I think that is just wonderful!
It seems that since volume 13 ended so satisfyingly, there are some people who find it hard to read Part 2! (Besides, it won't include Nakago!☺) What can I say? I'm just happy that people can enjoy anything that I've drawn! ☺ Well, the setting for Part 1 was inside the book, and since this part is in both the "real world" and "inside the scroll," I'm drawing on and on until I just keel over!
By the way, about the "stones," I have all sorts of ideas about what all the "treasure stones" should look like. *A Power Stone. I wonder how this story will turn out!*

RIGHT × × ×

Now, there are all sorts of fannish things (like novels) being sent to me, and it's making my eyes sparkle! I was looking forward to just seeing illustrations, but now that the work has expanded to manga and stuff, I'm so happy!! Don't ask me what they're about!! But you know that if it has anything to do with Nakago, it's okay by me! Same with Amiboshi and Suboshi! ☺ To everyone in the Seiryō Gakuen High School club who sent me their magazine every issue... You're all girls, right? (Of course they are! What would boys be doing in a group like that?) Also to the people of the Tamahome Committee of "Yū-like Yūgi," I'm sorry I couldn't reply to all of your postcards, but they were really cute! ♥♥♥ It's like there is a true potpourri of creators and readers! Ow! I seem a little pressed for time recently. (How odd.) Am I drawing too much manga? If I get inflammation of the tendons, I won't be able to draw anymore! So I'll leave off here... *Tmp tmp tmp tmp tmp tmp tmp (the sound of running away!)*

'95. 6/5

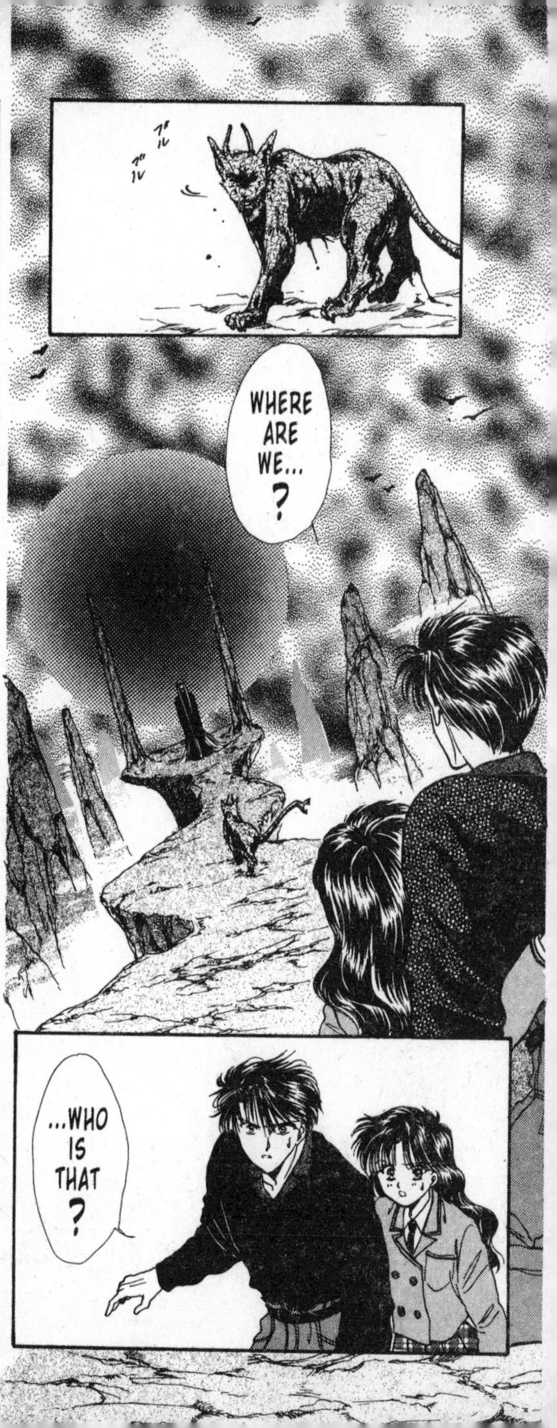
WHERE ARE WE...?
...WHO IS THAT?

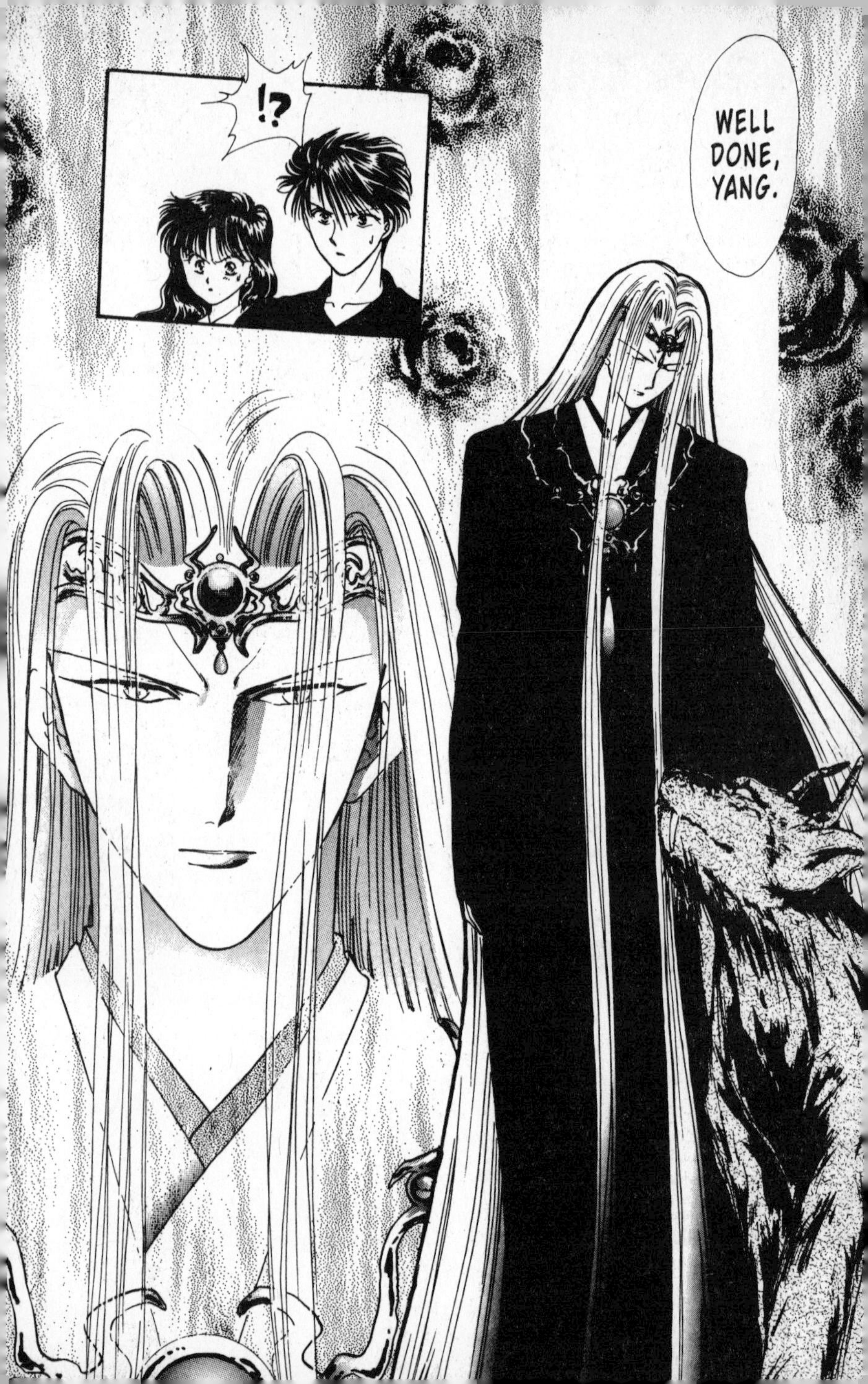
WELL DONE, YANG.
!?

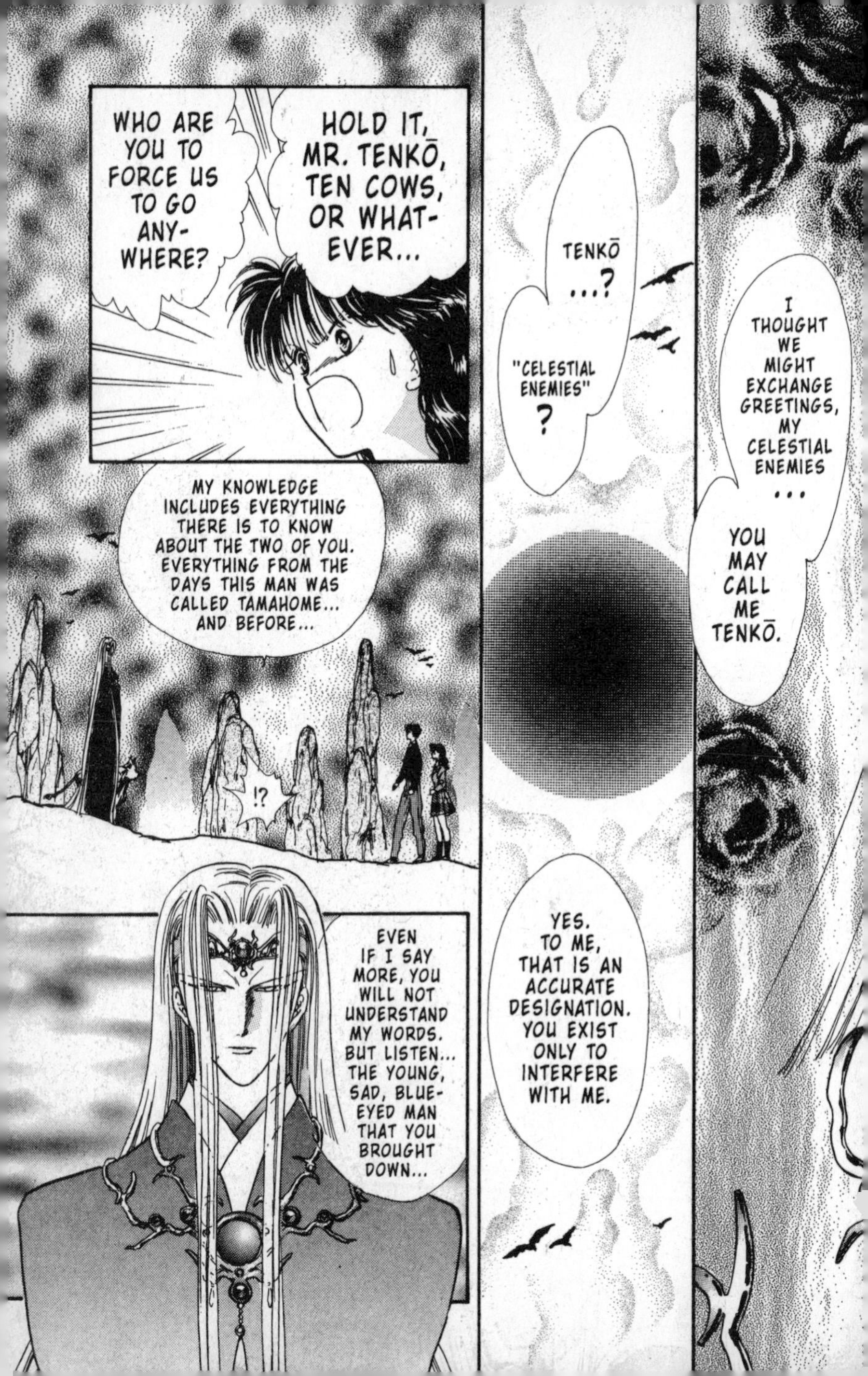
I THOUGHT WE MIGHT EXCHANGE GREETINGS, MY CELESTIAL ENEMIES...
YOU MAY CALL ME TENKŌ.
TENKŌ ...?
"CELESTIAL ENEMIES" ?
YES. TO ME, THAT IS AN ACCURATE DESIGNATION. YOU EXIST ONLY TO INTERFERE WITH ME.
HOLD IT, MR. TENKŌ, TEN COWS, OR WHAT-EVER...
WHO ARE YOU TO FORCE US TO GO ANY-WHERE?
MY KNOWLEDGE INCLUDES EVERYTHING THERE IS TO KNOW ABOUT THE TWO OF YOU. EVERYTHING FROM THE DAYS THIS MAN WAS CALLED TAMAHOME... AND BEFORE...
!?
EVEN IF I SAY MORE, YOU WILL NOT UNDERSTAND MY WORDS. BUT LISTEN... THE YOUNG, SAD, BLUE-EYED MAN THAT YOU BROUGHT DOWN...

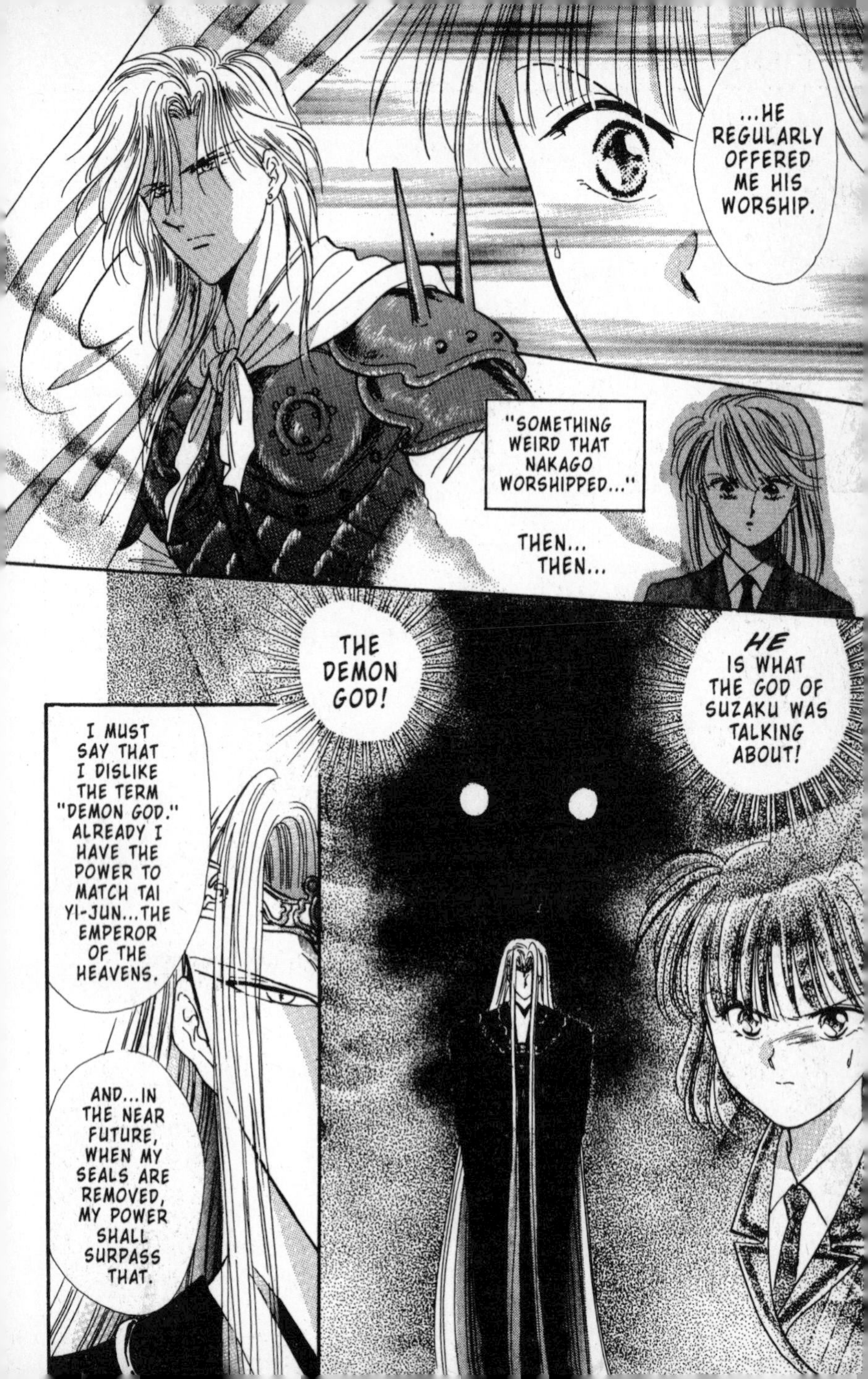
...HE REGULARLY OFFERED ME HIS WORSHIP.
"SOMETHING WEIRD THAT NAKAGO WORSHIPPED..."
THEN... THEN...
HE IS WHAT THE GOD OF SUZAKU WAS TALKING ABOUT!
THE DEMON GOD!
I MUST SAY THAT I DISLIKE THE TERM "DEMON GOD." ALREADY I HAVE THE POWER TO MATCH TAI YI-JUN...THE EMPEROR OF THE HEAVENS.
AND...IN THE NEAR FUTURE, WHEN MY SEALS ARE REMOVED, MY POWER SHALL SURPASS THAT.

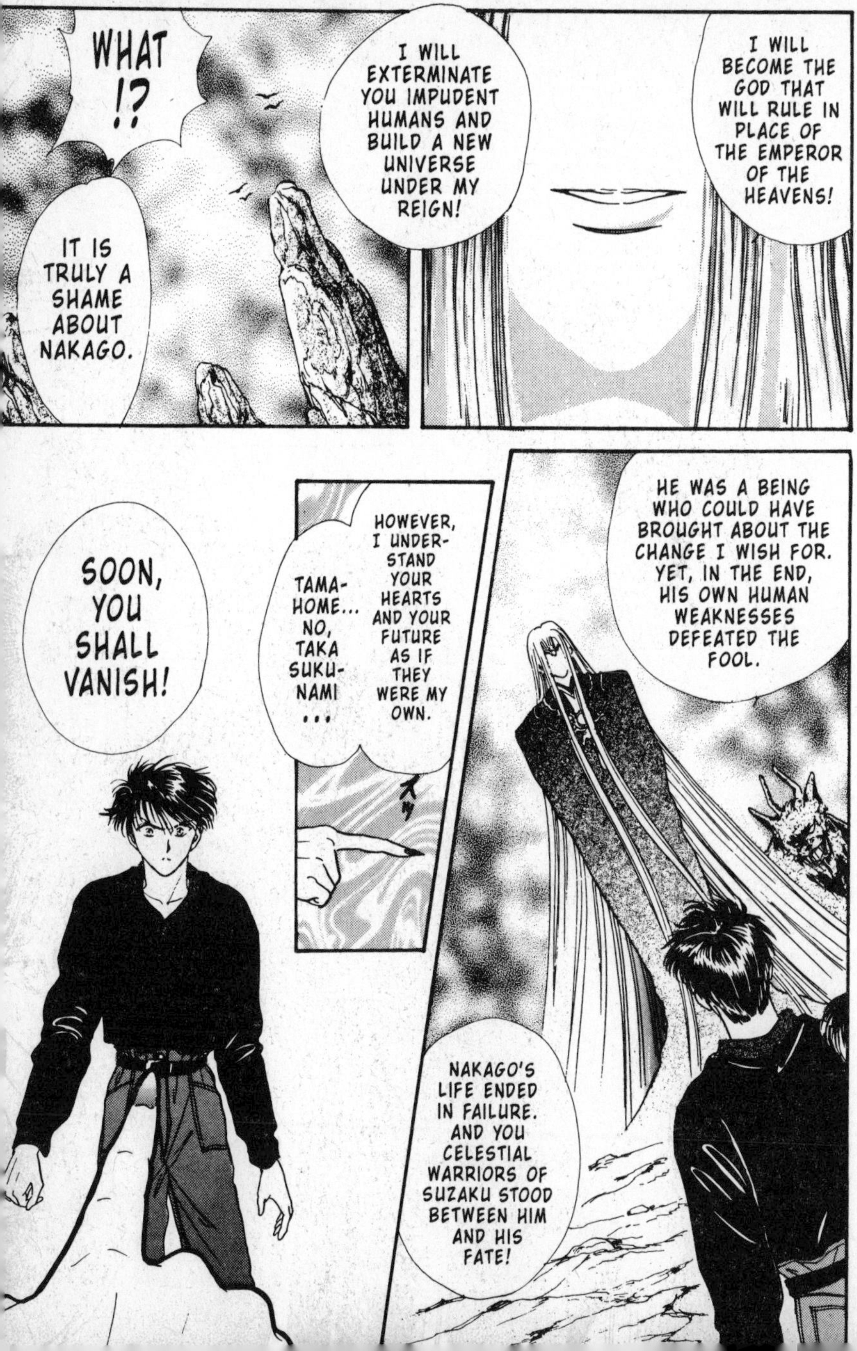
I WILL BECOME THE GOD THAT WILL RULE IN PLACE OF THE EMPEROR OF THE HEAVENS!
I WILL EXTERMINATE YOU IMPUDENT HUMANS AND BUILD A NEW UNIVERSE UNDER MY REIGN!
WHAT !?
IT IS TRULY A SHAME ABOUT NAKAGO.
HE WAS A BEING WHO COULD HAVE BROUGHT ABOUT THE CHANGE I WISH FOR. YET, IN THE END, HIS OWN HUMAN WEAKNESSES DEFEATED THE FOOL.
NAKAGO'S LIFE ENDED IN FAILURE. AND YOU CELESTIAL WARRIORS OF SUZAKU STOOD BETWEEN HIM AND HIS FATE!
HOWEVER, I UNDER-STAND YOUR HEARTS AND YOUR FUTURE AS IF THEY WERE MY OWN.
TAMA-HOME... NO, TAKA SUKU-NAMI ...
スッ
SOON, YOU SHALL VANISH!

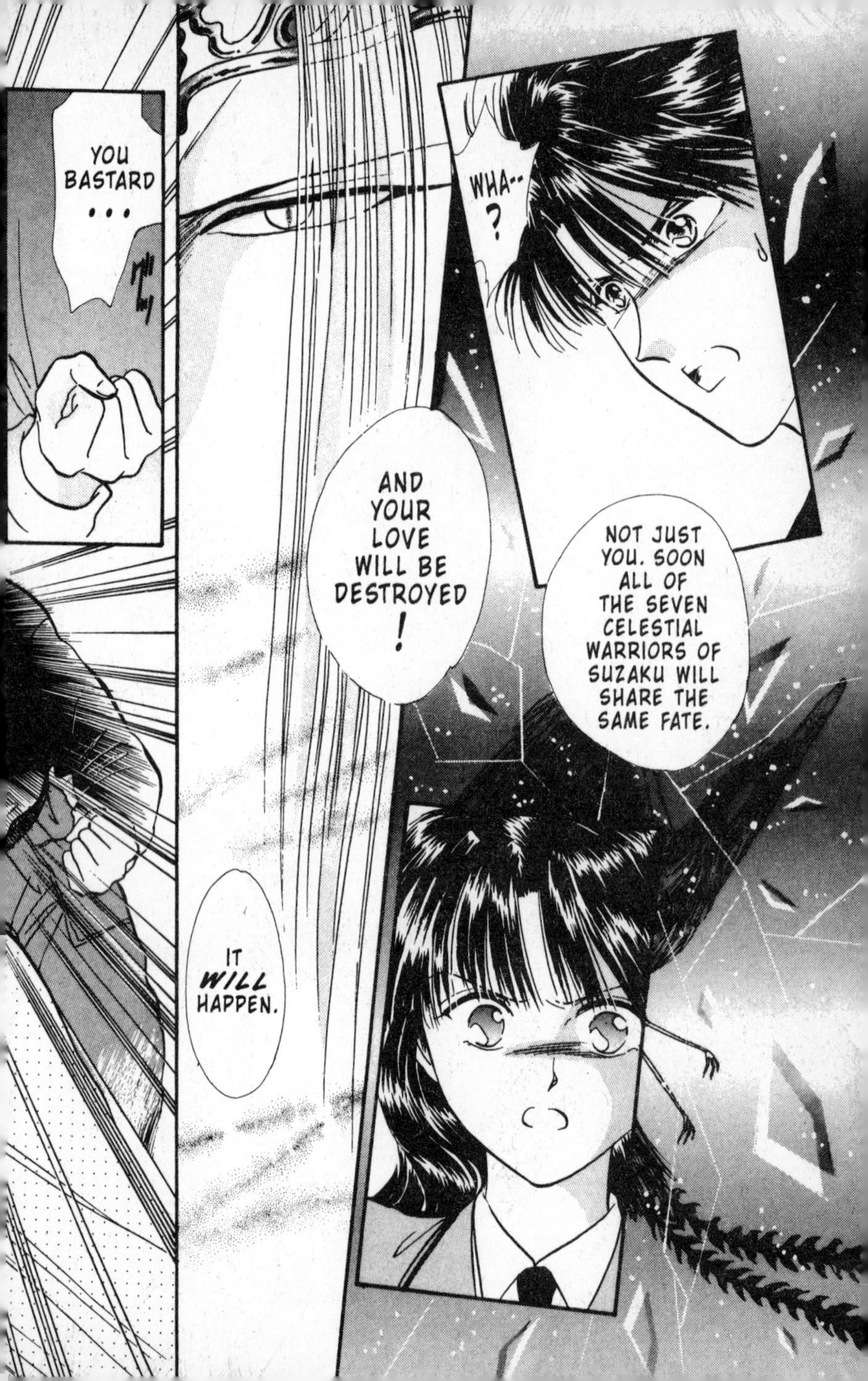
WHA-- ?
NOT JUST YOU. SOON ALL OF THE SEVEN CELESTIAL WARRIORS OF SUZAKU WILL SHARE THE SAME FATE.
AND YOUR LOVE WILL BE DESTROYED !
IT *WILL* HAPPEN.
YOU BASTARD ...

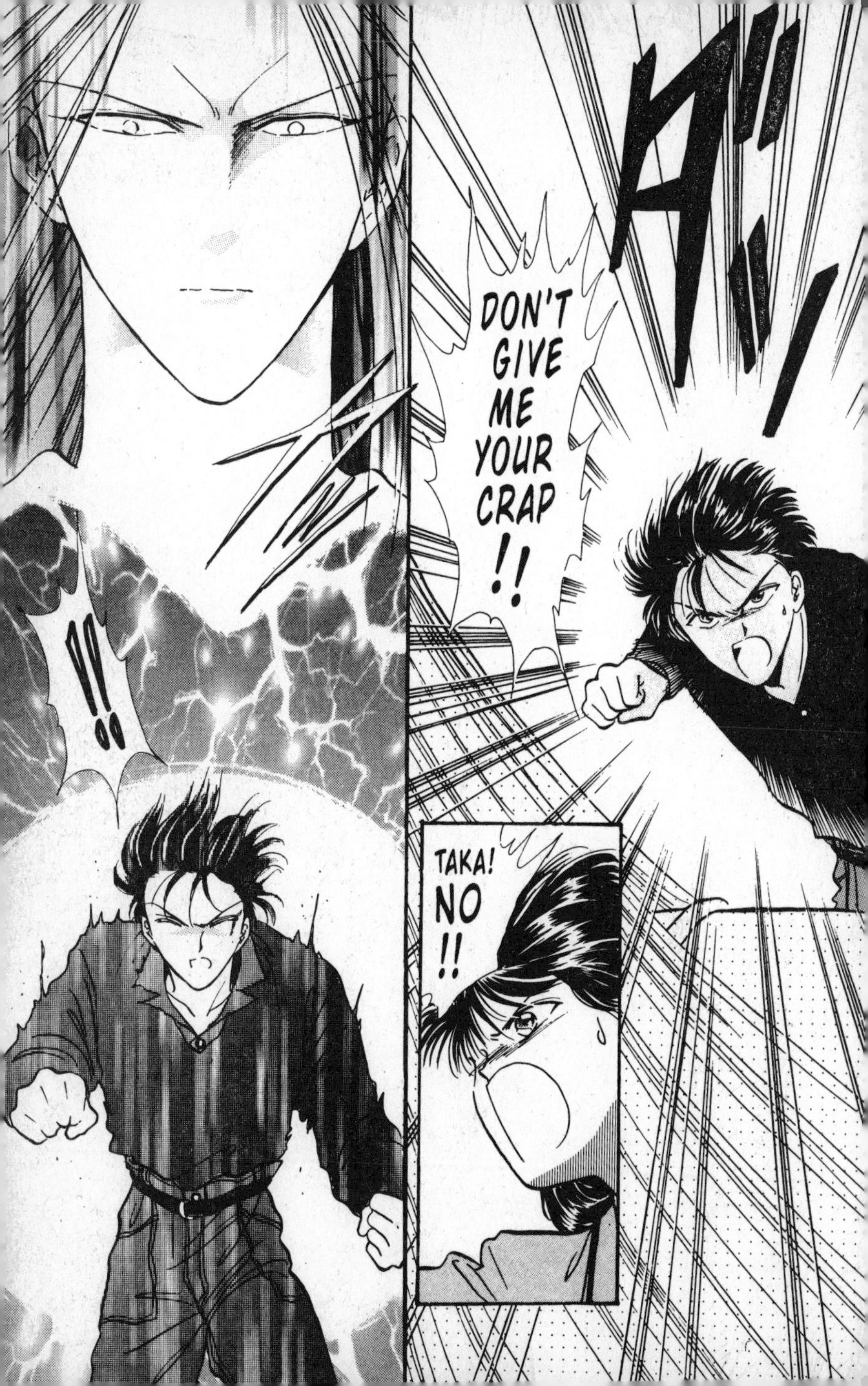
DON'T GIVE ME YOUR CRAP !!
TAKA! NO !!
!!

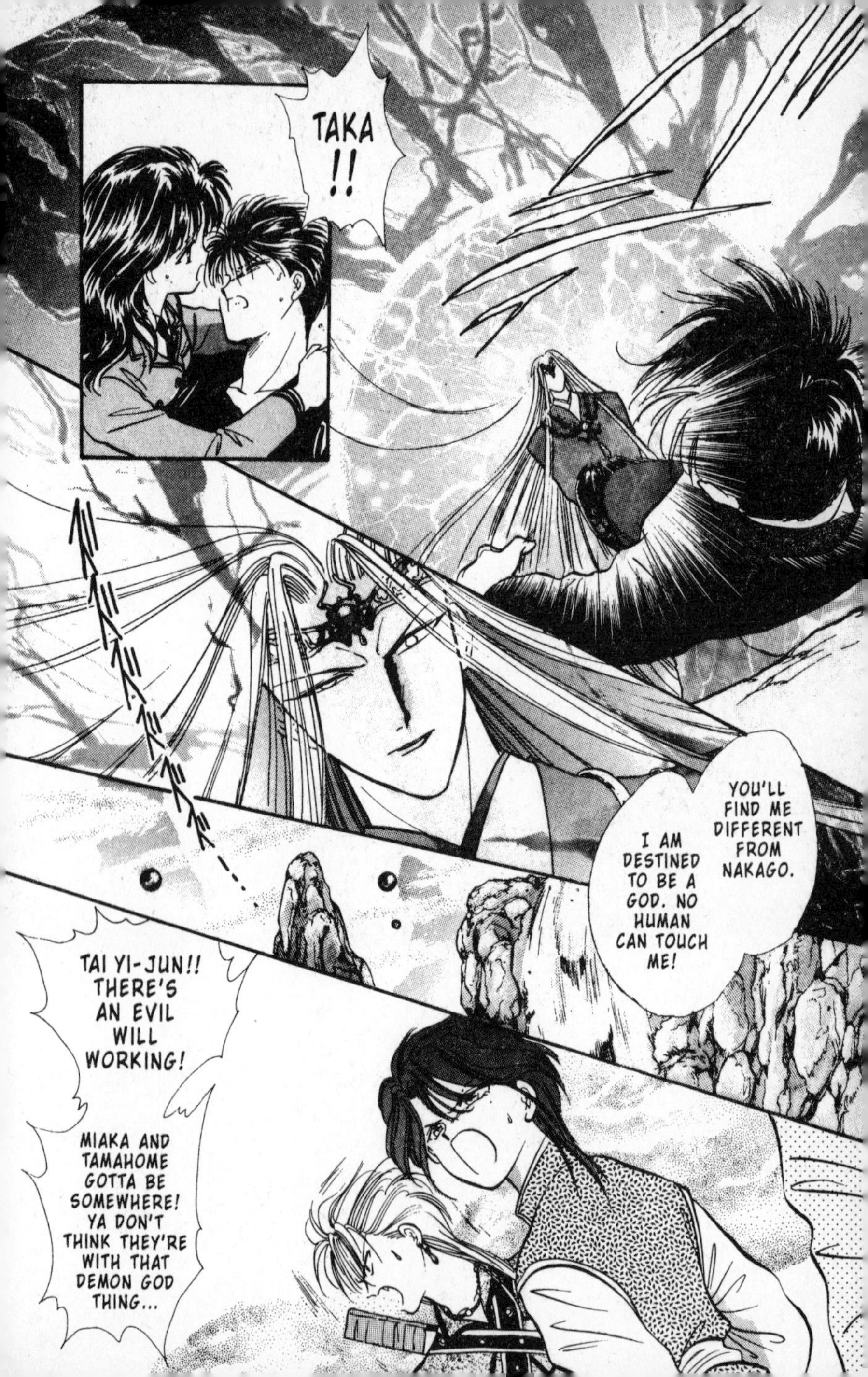
TAKA !!
YOU'LL FIND ME DIFFERENT FROM NAKAGO.
I AM DESTINED TO BE A GOD. NO HUMAN CAN TOUCH ME!
TAI YI-JUN!! THERE'S AN EVIL WILL WORKING!
MIAKA AND TAMAHOME GOTTA BE SOMEWHERE! YA DON'T THINK THEY'RE WITH THAT DEMON GOD THING...

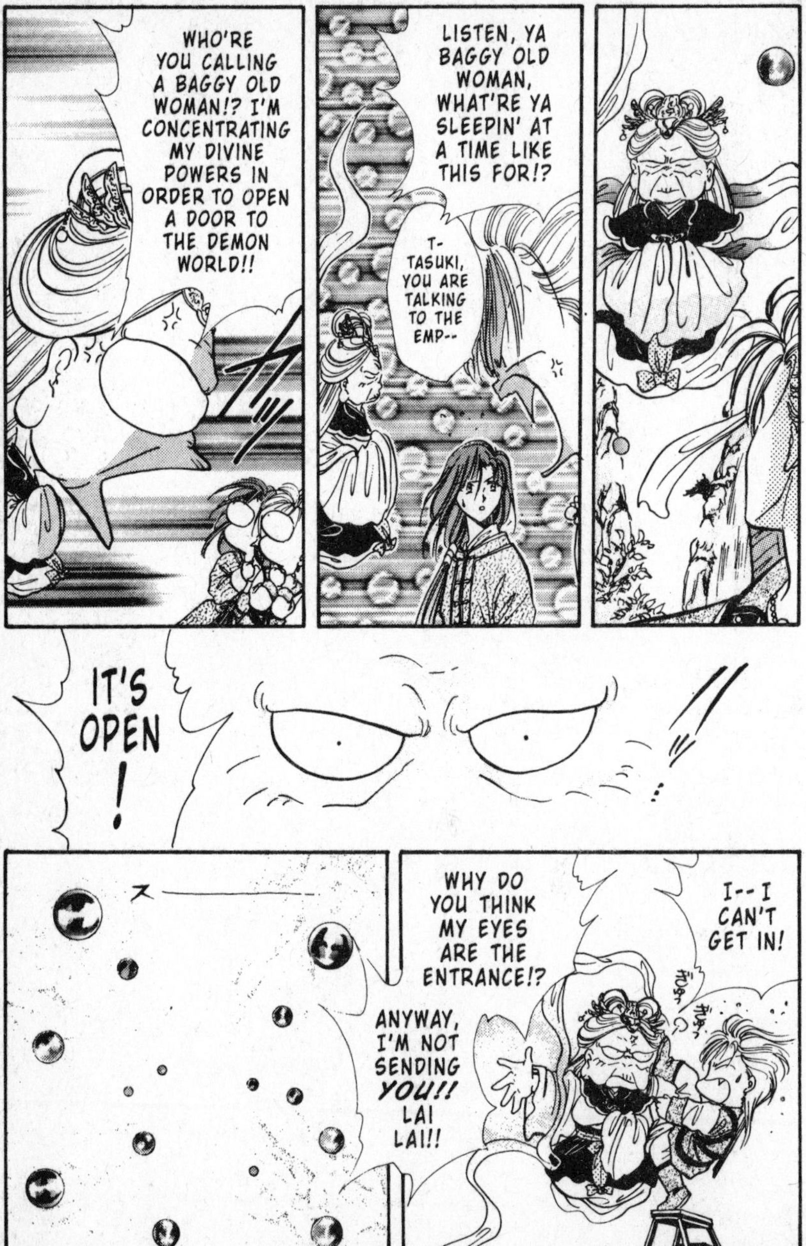
LISTEN, YA BAGGY OLD WOMAN, WHAT'RE YA SLEEPIN' AT A TIME LIKE THIS FOR!?
T-TASUKI, YOU ARE TALKING TO THE EMP--
WHO'RE YOU CALLING A BAGGY OLD WOMAN!? I'M CONCENTRATING MY DIVINE POWERS IN ORDER TO OPEN A DOOR TO THE DEMON WORLD!!
IT'S OPEN!
I-- I CAN'T GET IN!
WHY DO YOU THINK MY EYES ARE THE ENTRANCE!?
ANYWAY, I'M NOT SENDING *YOU!!* LAI LAI!!

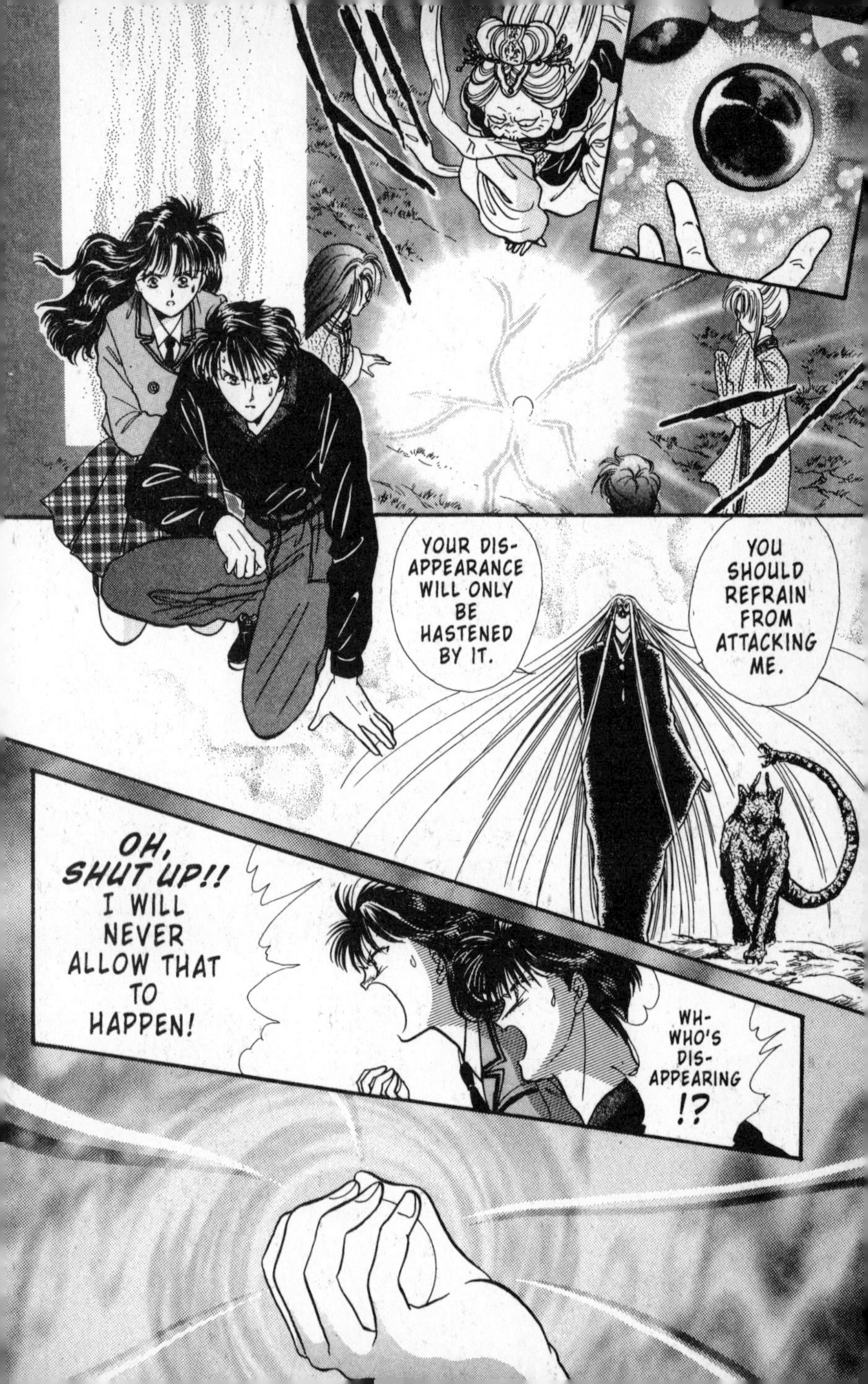
YOU SHOULD REFRAIN FROM ATTACKING ME.
YOUR DIS-APPEARANCE WILL ONLY BE HASTENED BY IT.
WH-WHO'S DIS-APPEARING !?
OH, SHUT UP!! I WILL NEVER ALLOW THAT TO HAPPEN!

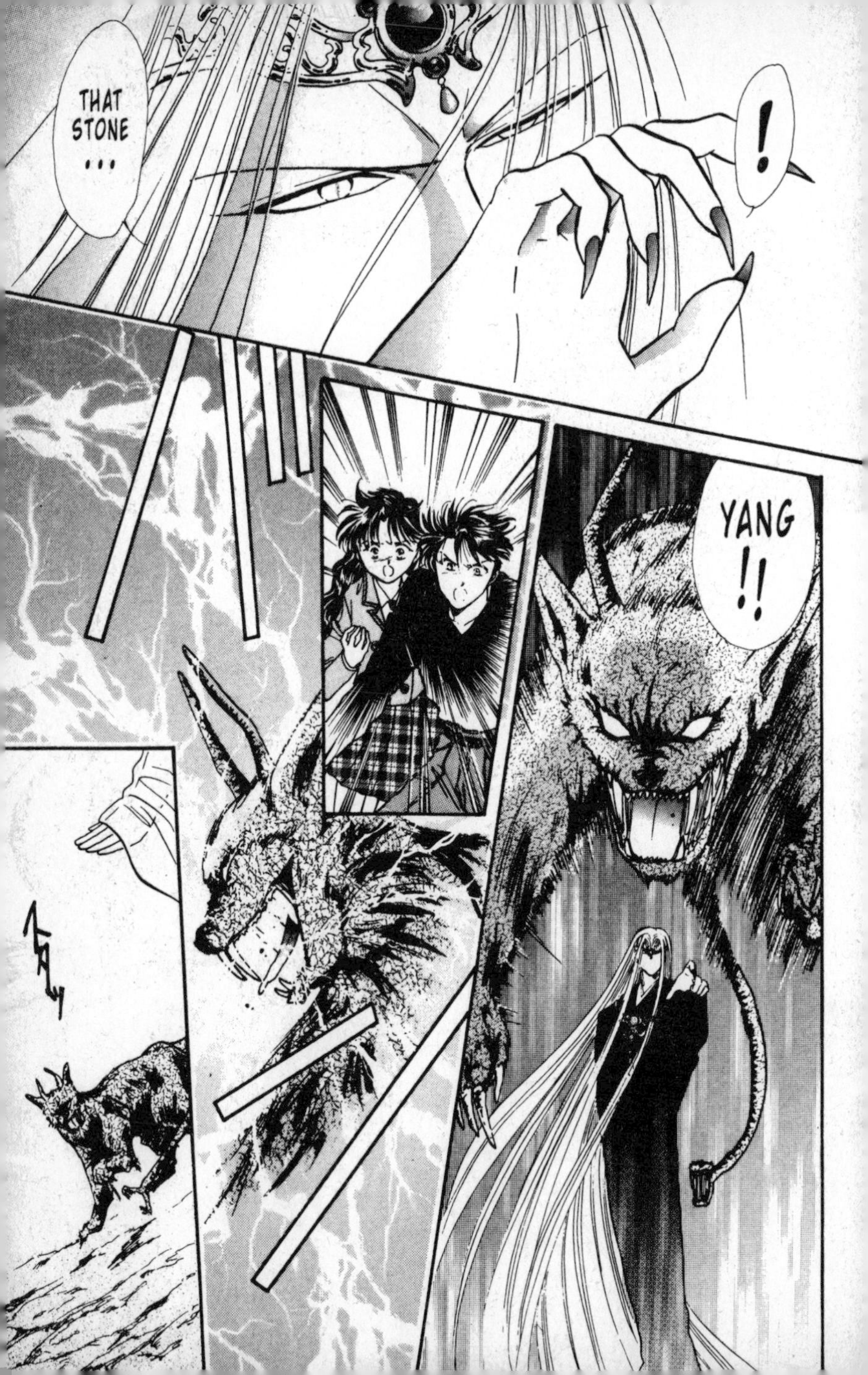
!
THAT STONE ...
YANG !!

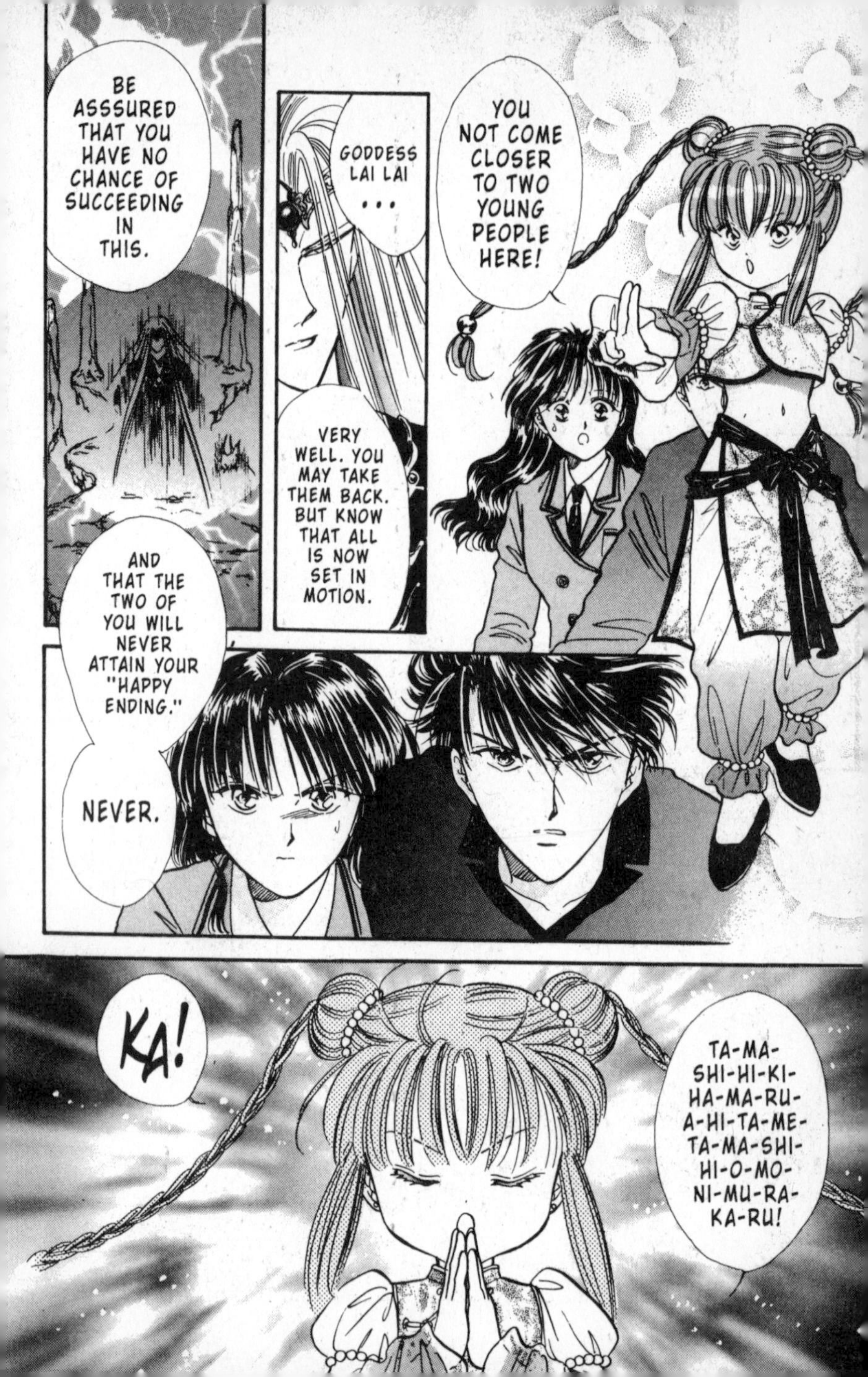
YOU NOT COME CLOSER TO TWO YOUNG PEOPLE HERE!
GODDESS LAI LAI ...
VERY WELL. YOU MAY TAKE THEM BACK. BUT KNOW THAT ALL IS NOW SET IN MOTION.
BE ASSSURED THAT YOU HAVE NO CHANCE OF SUCCEEDING IN THIS.
AND THAT THE TWO OF YOU WILL NEVER ATTAIN YOUR "HAPPY ENDING."
NEVER.
TA-MA-SHI-HI-KI-HA-MA-RU-A-HI-TA-ME-TA-MA-SHI-HI-O-MO-NI-MU-RA-KA-RU!
KA!

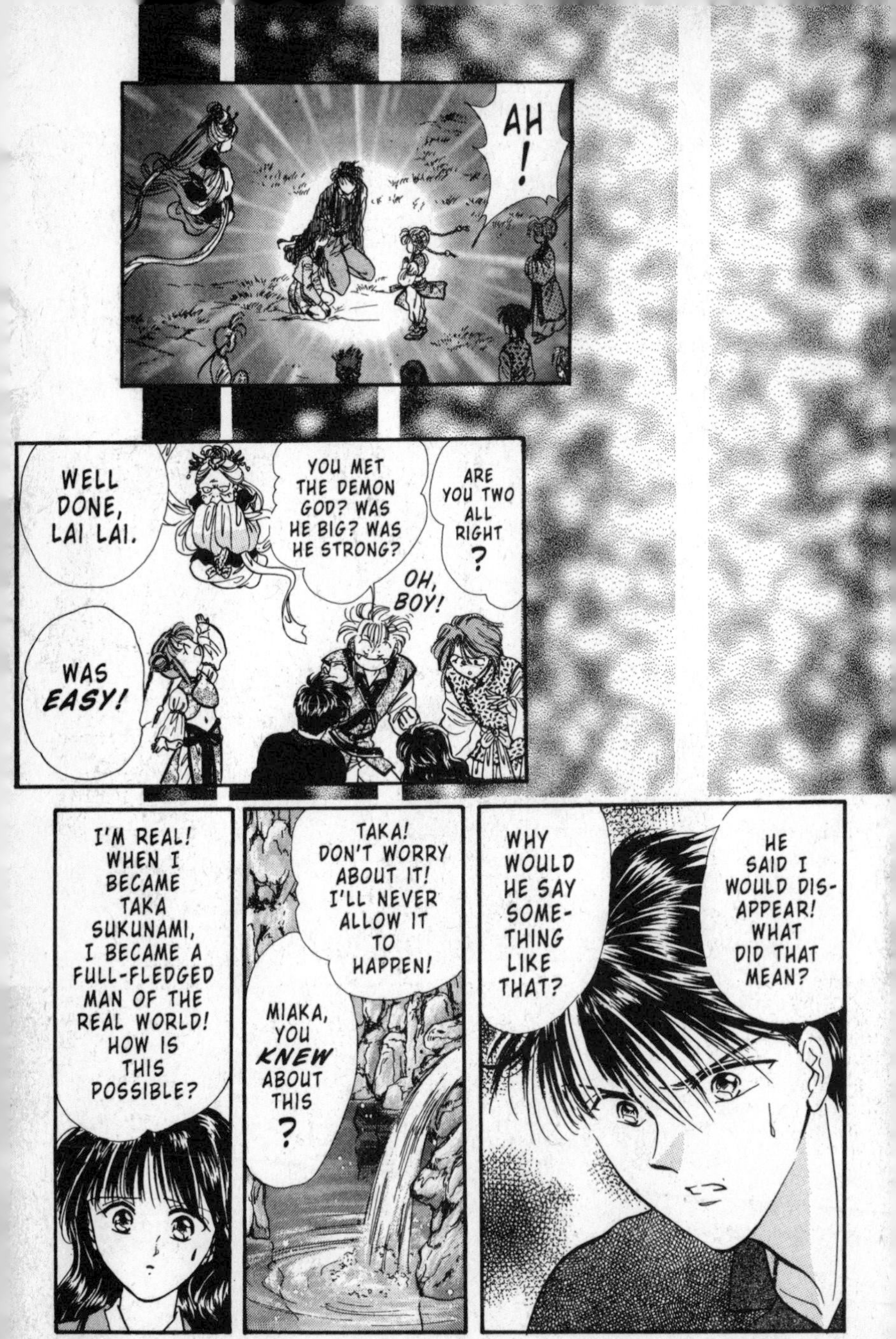
AH!
ARE YOU TWO ALL RIGHT?
YOU MET THE DEMON GOD? WAS HE BIG? WAS HE STRONG?
OH, BOY!
WELL DONE, LAI LAI.
WAS *EASY!*
HE SAID I WOULD DIS-APPEAR! WHAT DID THAT MEAN?
WHY WOULD HE SAY SOME-THING LIKE THAT?
TAKA! DON'T WORRY ABOUT IT! I'LL NEVER ALLOW IT TO HAPPEN!
MIAKA, YOU *KNEW* ABOUT THIS?
I'M REAL! WHEN I BECAME TAKA SUKUNAMI, I BECAME A FULL-FLEDGED MAN OF THE REAL WORLD! HOW IS THIS POSSIBLE?

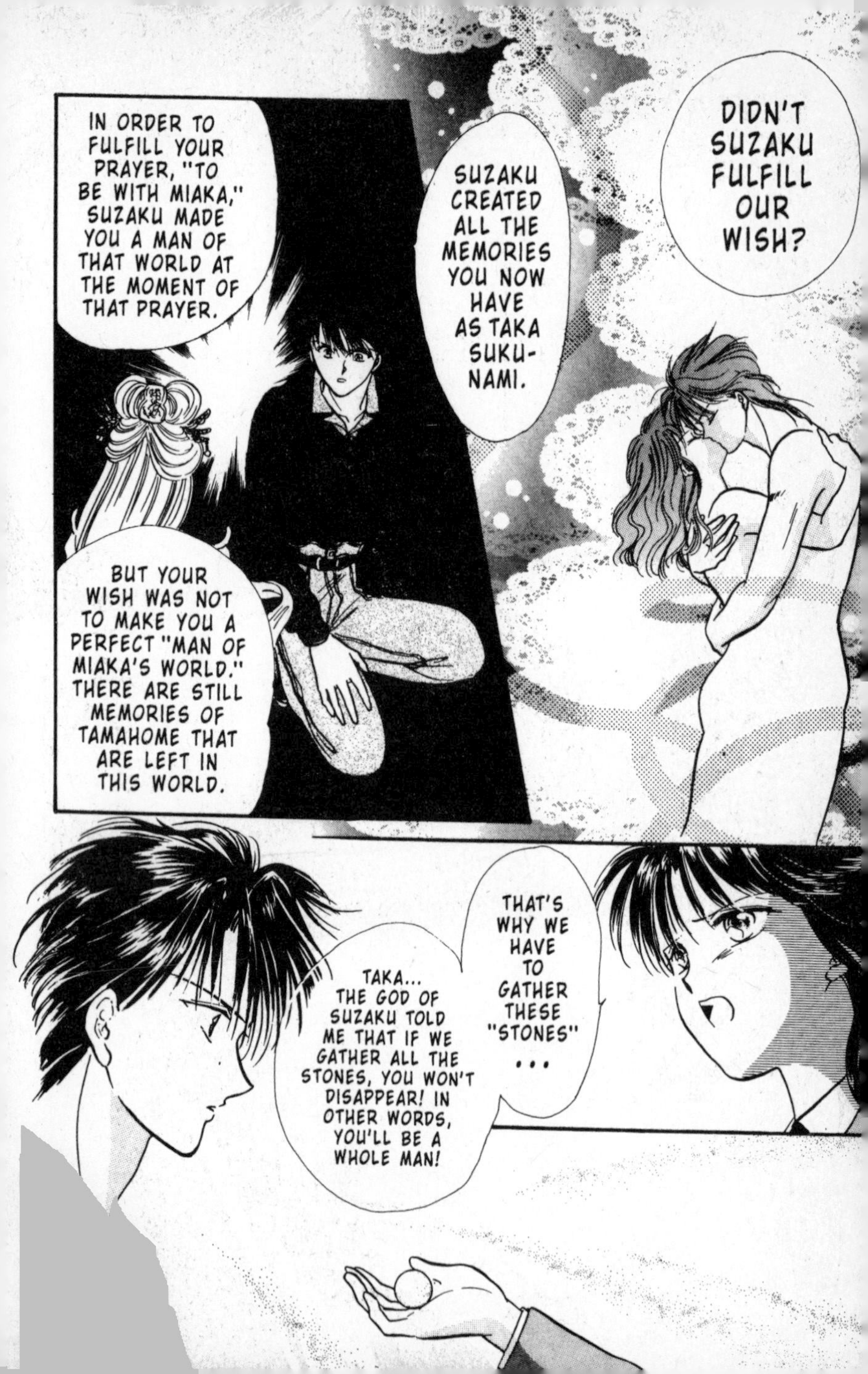
DIDN'T SUZAKU FULFILL OUR WISH?
SUZAKU CREATED ALL THE MEMORIES YOU NOW HAVE AS TAKA SUKU-NAMI.
IN ORDER TO FULFILL YOUR PRAYER, "TO BE WITH MIAKA," SUZAKU MADE YOU A MAN OF THAT WORLD AT THE MOMENT OF THAT PRAYER.
BUT YOUR WISH WAS NOT TO MAKE YOU A PERFECT "MAN OF MIAKA'S WORLD." THERE ARE STILL MEMORIES OF TAMAHOME THAT ARE LEFT IN THIS WORLD.
THAT'S WHY WE HAVE TO GATHER THESE "STONES"...
TAKA... THE GOD OF SUZAKU TOLD ME THAT IF WE GATHER ALL THE STONES, YOU WON'T DISAPPEAR! IN OTHER WORDS, YOU'LL BE A WHOLE MAN!

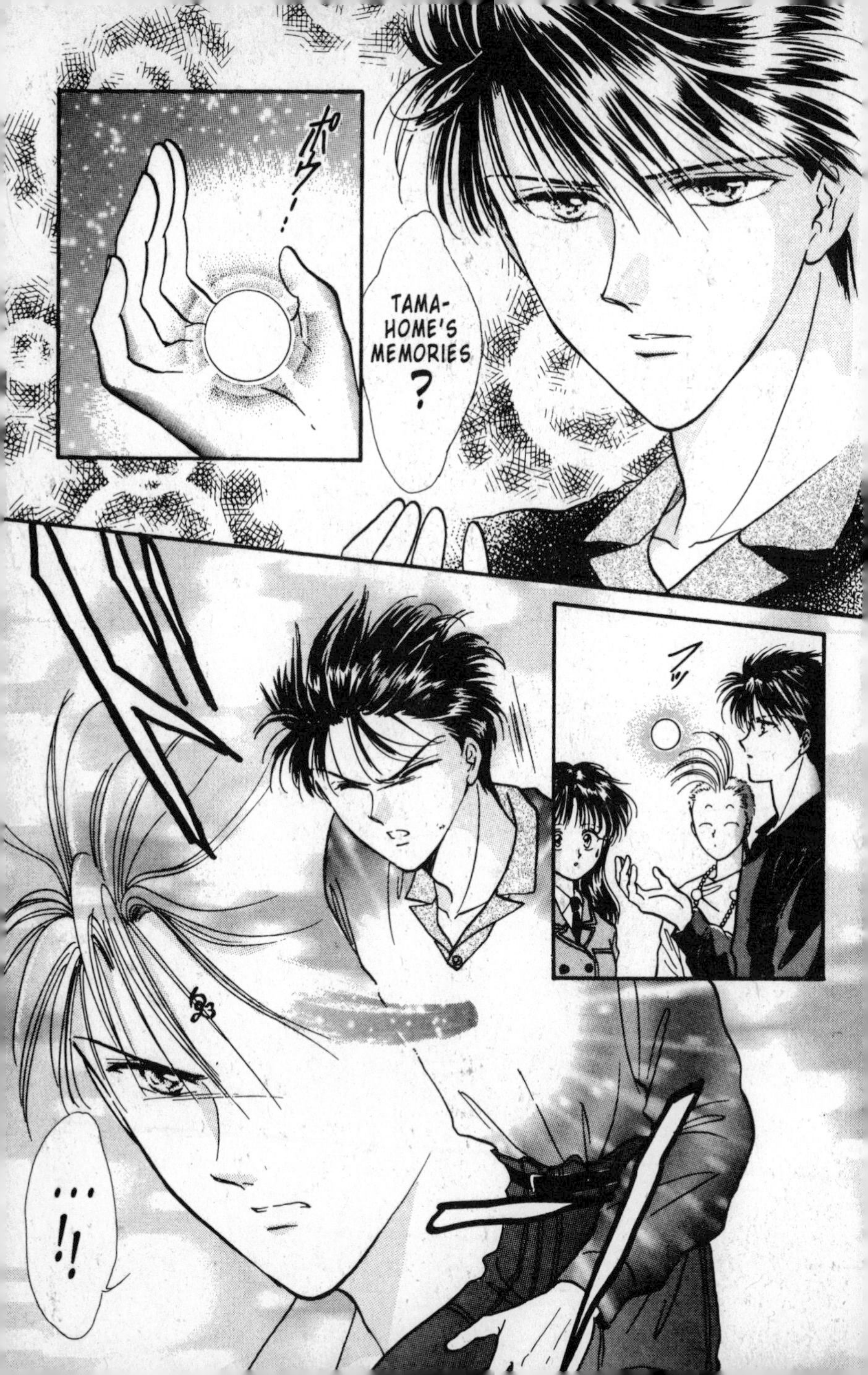
TAMA-HOME'S MEMORIES ?
...!!

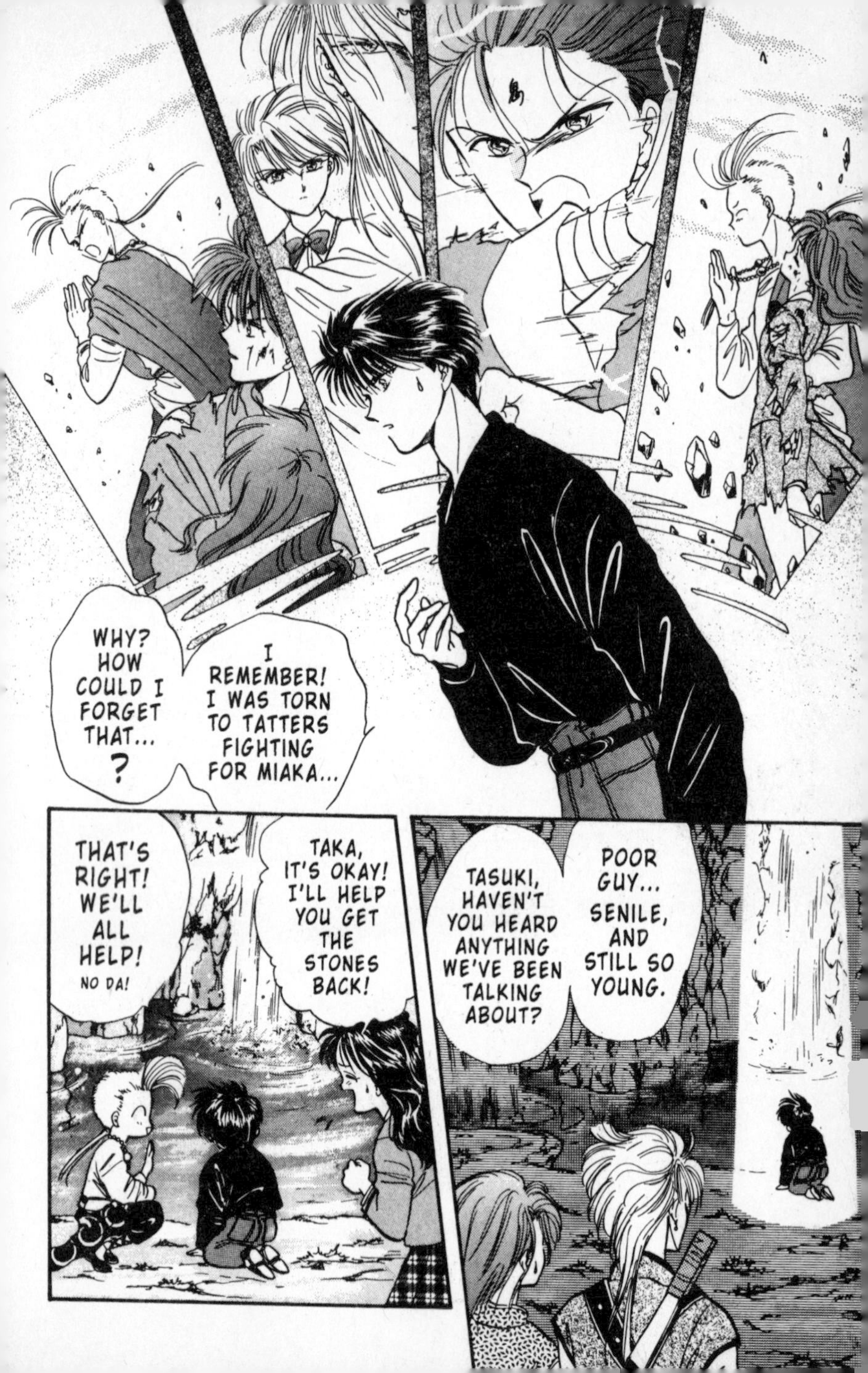
I REMEMBER! I WAS TORN TO TATTERS FIGHTING FOR MIAKA...
WHY? HOW COULD I FORGET THAT...?
POOR GUY... SENILE, AND STILL SO YOUNG.
TASUKI, HAVEN'T YOU HEARD ANYTHING WE'VE BEEN TALKING ABOUT?
TAKA, IT'S OKAY! I'LL HELP YOU GET THE STONES BACK!
THAT'S RIGHT! WE'LL ALL HELP! NO DA!

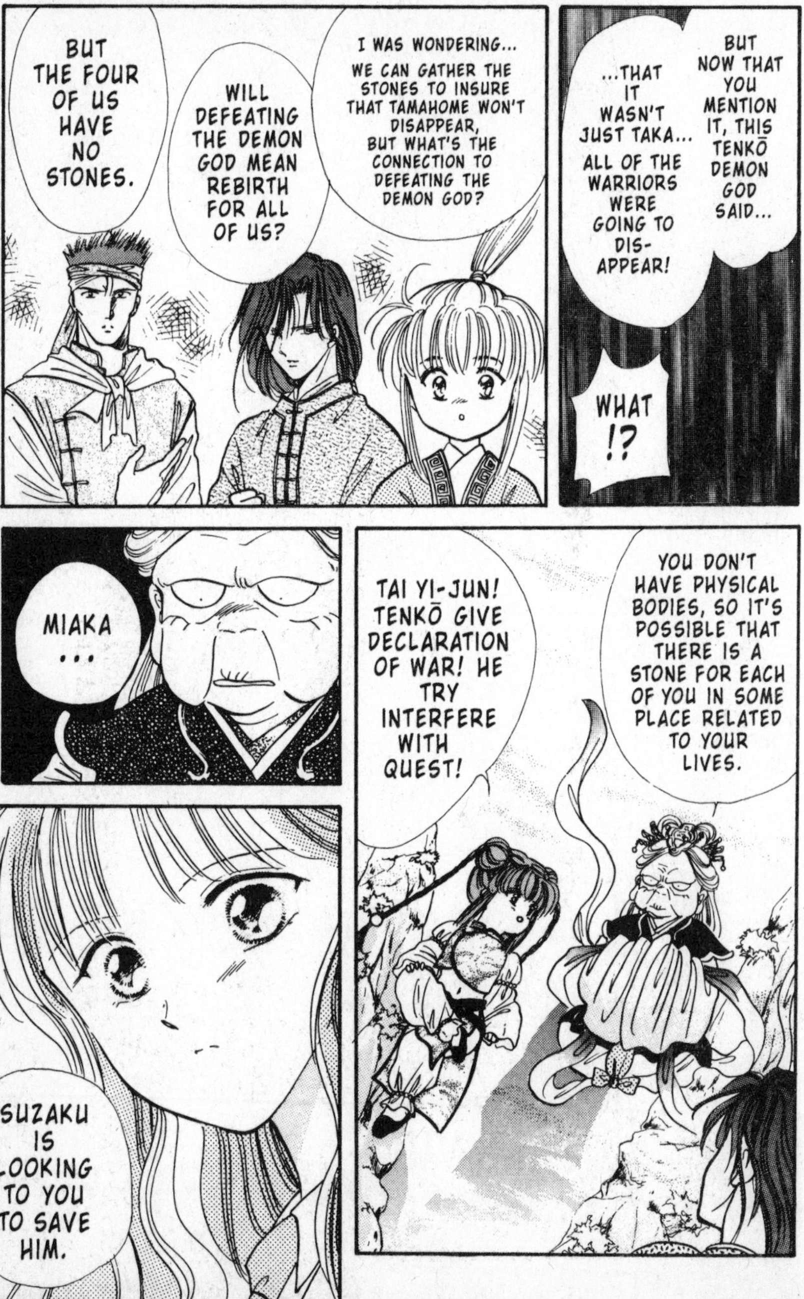
BUT NOW THAT YOU MENTION IT, THIS TENKŌ DEMON GOD SAID...
...THAT IT WASN'T JUST TAKA... ALL OF THE WARRIORS WERE GOING TO DIS-APPEAR!
WHAT!?
I WAS WONDERING... WE CAN GATHER THE STONES TO INSURE THAT TAMAHOME WON'T DISAPPEAR, BUT WHAT'S THE CONNECTION TO DEFEATING THE DEMON GOD?
WILL DEFEATING THE DEMON GOD MEAN REBIRTH FOR ALL OF US?
BUT THE FOUR OF US HAVE NO STONES.
YOU DON'T HAVE PHYSICAL BODIES, SO IT'S POSSIBLE THAT THERE IS A STONE FOR EACH OF YOU IN SOME PLACE RELATED TO YOUR LIVES.
TAI YI-JUN! TENKŌ GIVE DECLARATION OF WAR! HE TRY INTERFERE WITH QUEST!
MIAKA...
SUZAKU IS LOOKING TO YOU TO SAVE HIM.

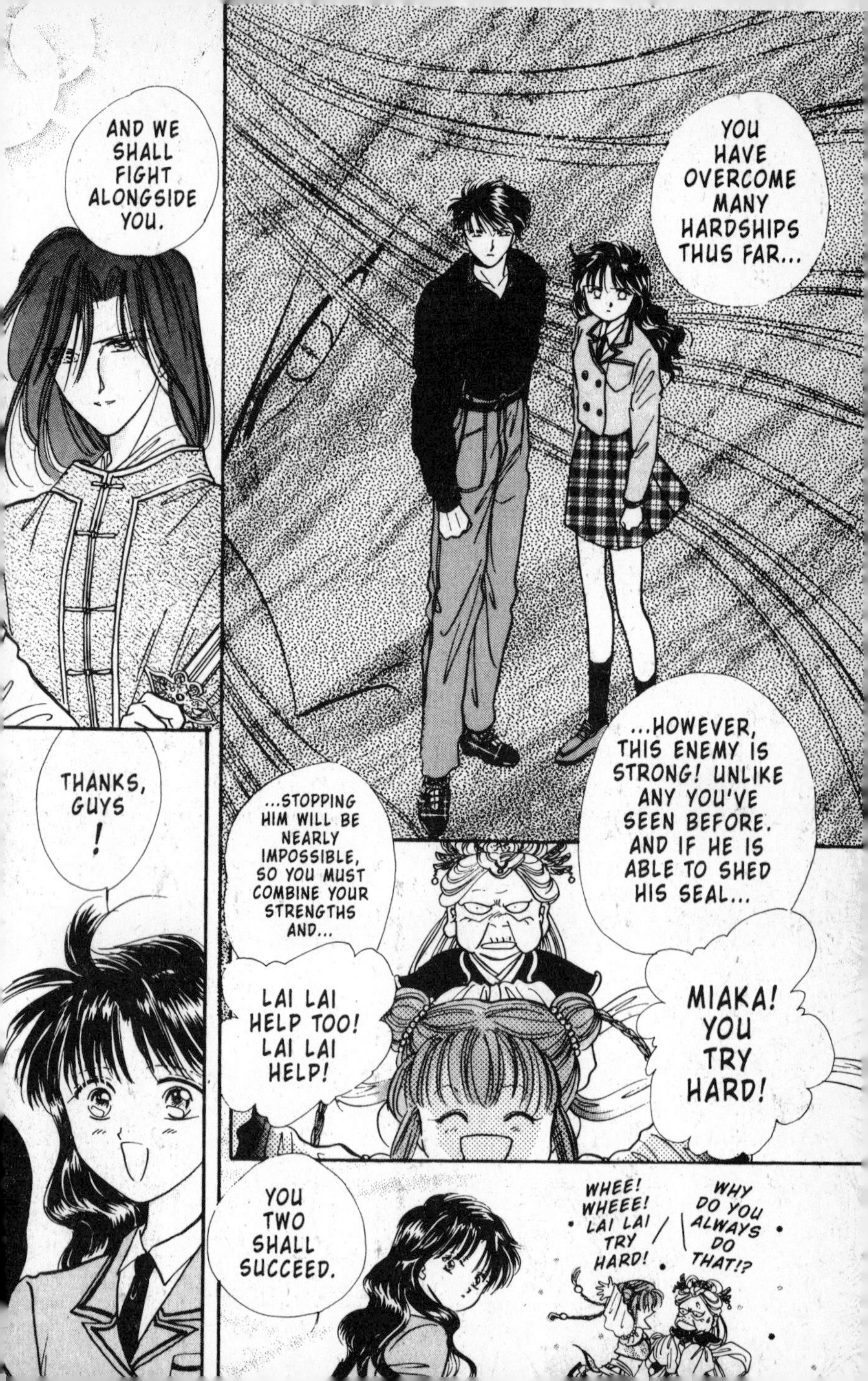
YOU HAVE OVERCOME MANY HARDSHIPS THUS FAR...
...HOWEVER, THIS ENEMY IS STRONG! UNLIKE ANY YOU'VE SEEN BEFORE. AND IF HE IS ABLE TO SHED HIS SEAL...
...STOPPING HIM WILL BE NEARLY IMPOSSIBLE, SO YOU MUST COMBINE YOUR STRENGTHS AND...
MIAKA! YOU TRY HARD!
LAI LAI HELP TOO! LAI LAI HELP!
YOU TWO SHALL SUCCEED.
WHEE! WHEEE! LAI LAI TRY HARD!
WHY DO YOU ALWAYS DO THAT!?
AND WE SHALL FIGHT ALONGSIDE YOU.
THANKS, GUYS!

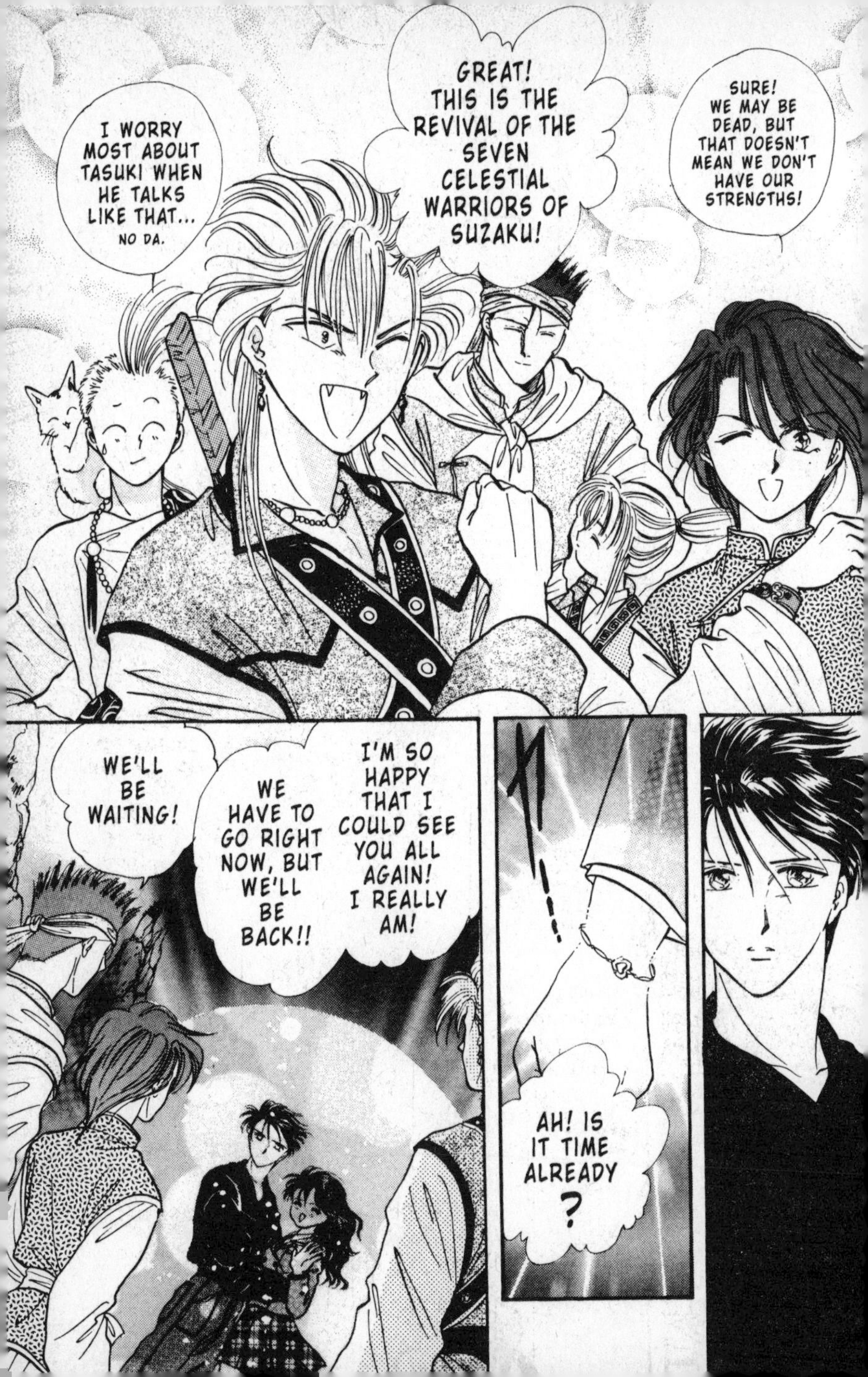
SURE! WE MAY BE DEAD, BUT THAT DOESN'T MEAN WE DON'T HAVE OUR STRENGTHS!
GREAT! THIS IS THE REVIVAL OF THE SEVEN CELESTIAL WARRIORS OF SUZAKU!
I WORRY MOST ABOUT TASUKI WHEN HE TALKS LIKE THAT... NO DA.
AH! IS IT TIME ALREADY ?
I'M SO HAPPY THAT I COULD SEE YOU ALL AGAIN! I REALLY AM!
WE HAVE TO GO RIGHT NOW, BUT WE'LL BE BACK!!
WE'LL BE WAITING!

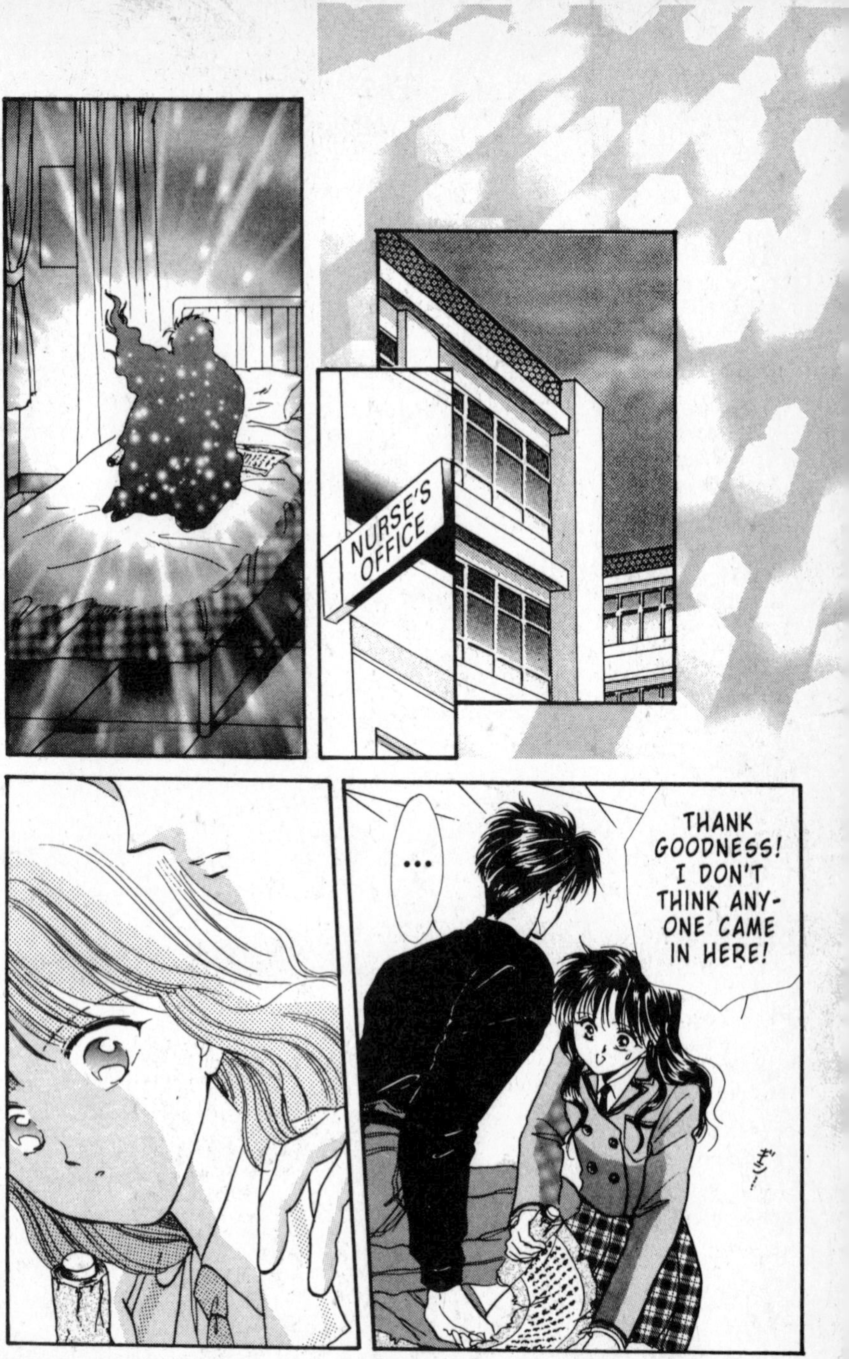
NURSE'S OFFICE
THANK GOODNESS! I DON'T THINK ANY-ONE CAME IN HERE!
...

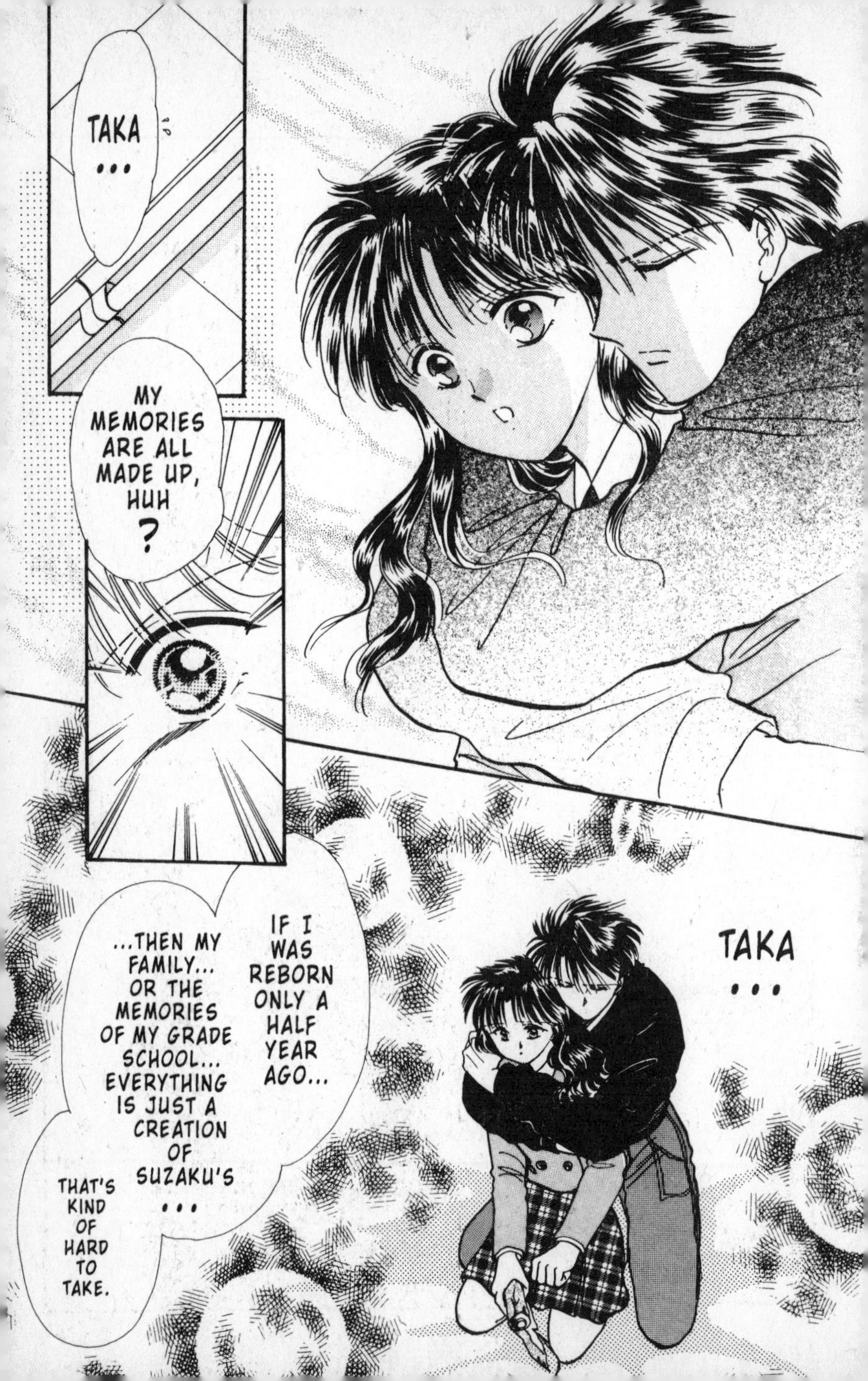
TAKA...
MY MEMORIES ARE ALL MADE UP, HUH?
TAKA...
IF I WAS REBORN ONLY A HALF YEAR AGO...
...THEN MY FAMILY... OR THE MEMORIES OF MY GRADE SCHOOL... EVERYTHING IS JUST A CREATION OF SUZAKU'S...
THAT'S KIND OF HARD TO TAKE.

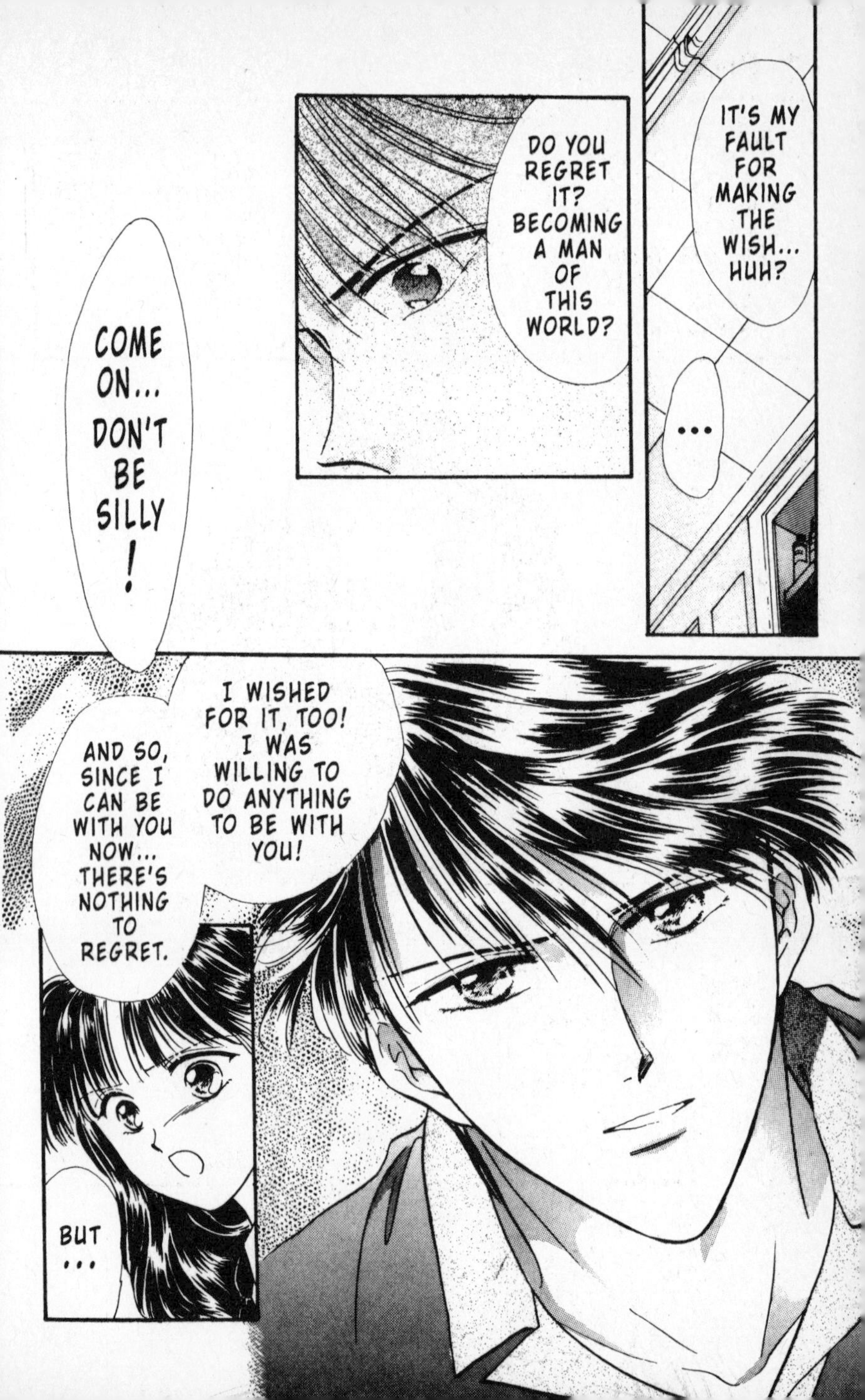
IT'S MY FAULT FOR MAKING THE WISH... HUH?
...
DO YOU REGRET IT? BECOMING A MAN OF THIS WORLD?
COME ON... DON'T BE SILLY!
I WISHED FOR IT, TOO! I WAS WILLING TO DO ANYTHING TO BE WITH YOU!
AND SO, SINCE I CAN BE WITH YOU NOW... THERE'S NOTHING TO REGRET.
BUT...

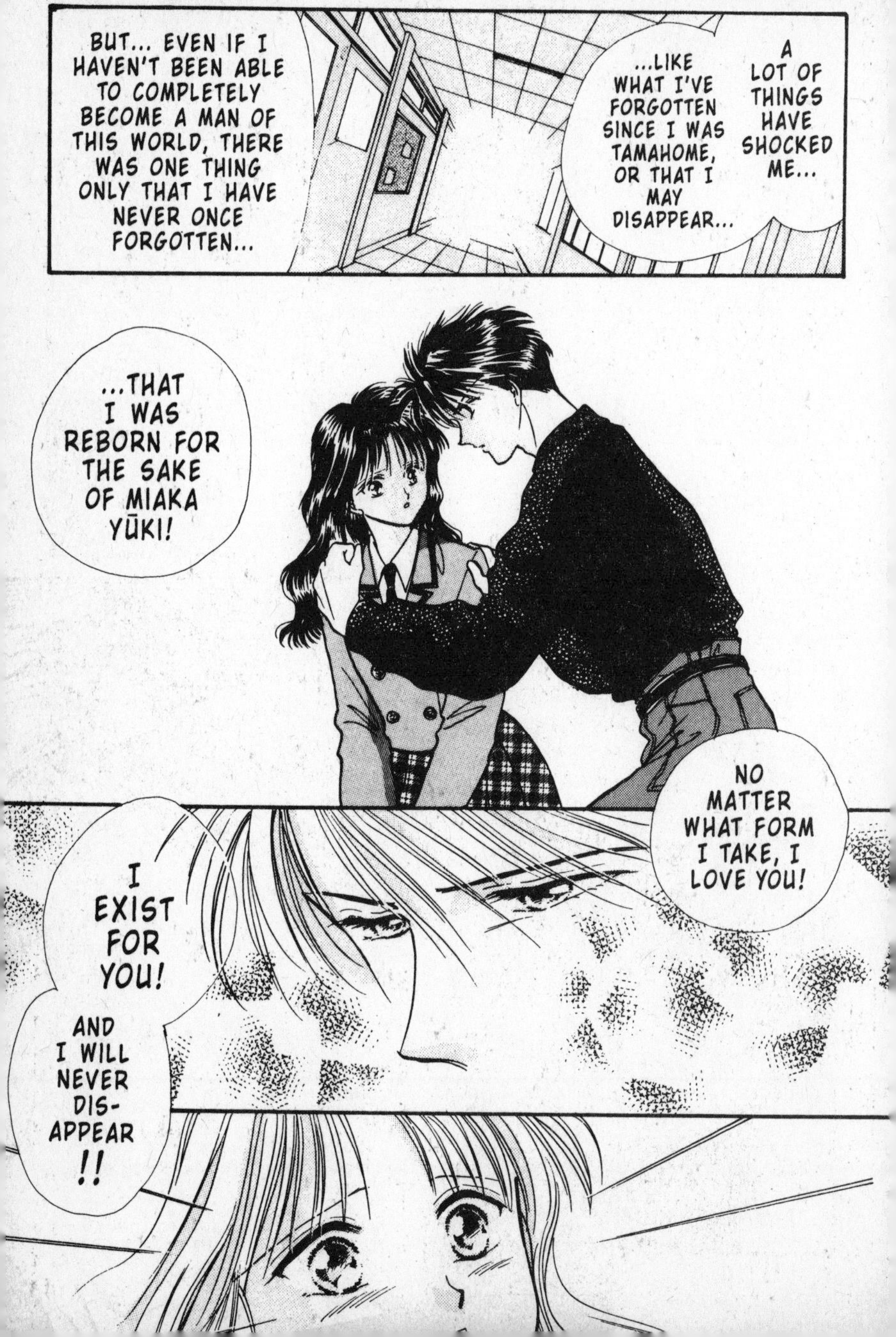
A LOT OF THINGS HAVE SHOCKED ME...
...LIKE WHAT I'VE FORGOTTEN SINCE I WAS TAMAHOME, OR THAT I MAY DISAPPEAR...
BUT... EVEN IF I HAVEN'T BEEN ABLE TO COMPLETELY BECOME A MAN OF THIS WORLD, THERE WAS ONE THING ONLY THAT I HAVE NEVER ONCE FORGOTTEN...
...THAT I WAS REBORN FOR THE SAKE OF MIAKA YŪKI!
NO MATTER WHAT FORM I TAKE, I LOVE YOU!
I EXIST FOR YOU!
AND I WILL NEVER DIS-APPEAR !!

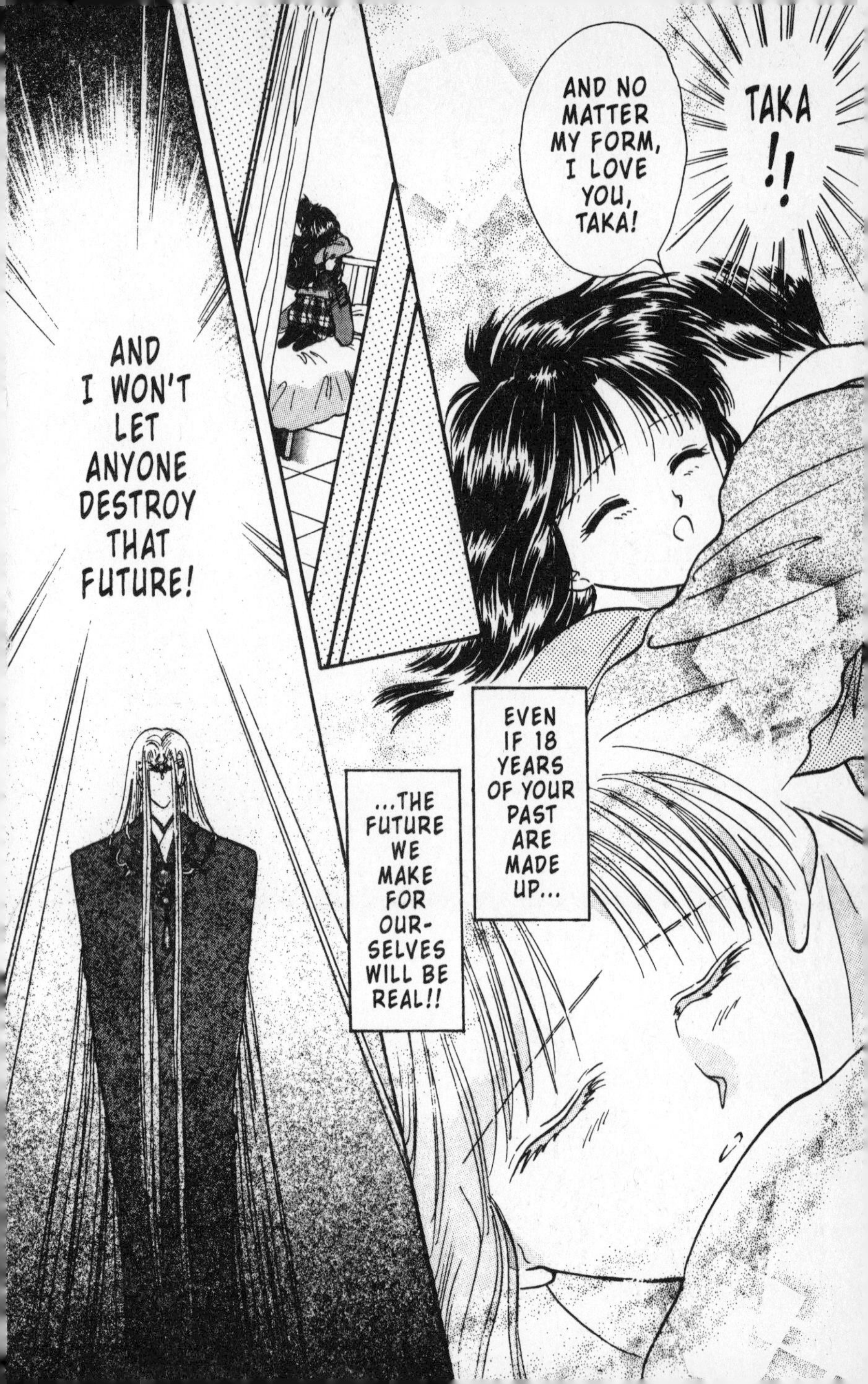
TAKA!!
AND NO MATTER MY FORM, I LOVE YOU, TAKA!
EVEN IF 18 YEARS OF YOUR PAST ARE MADE UP...
...THE FUTURE WE MAKE FOR OUR-SELVES WILL BE REAL!!
AND I WON'T LET ANYONE DESTROY THAT FUTURE!

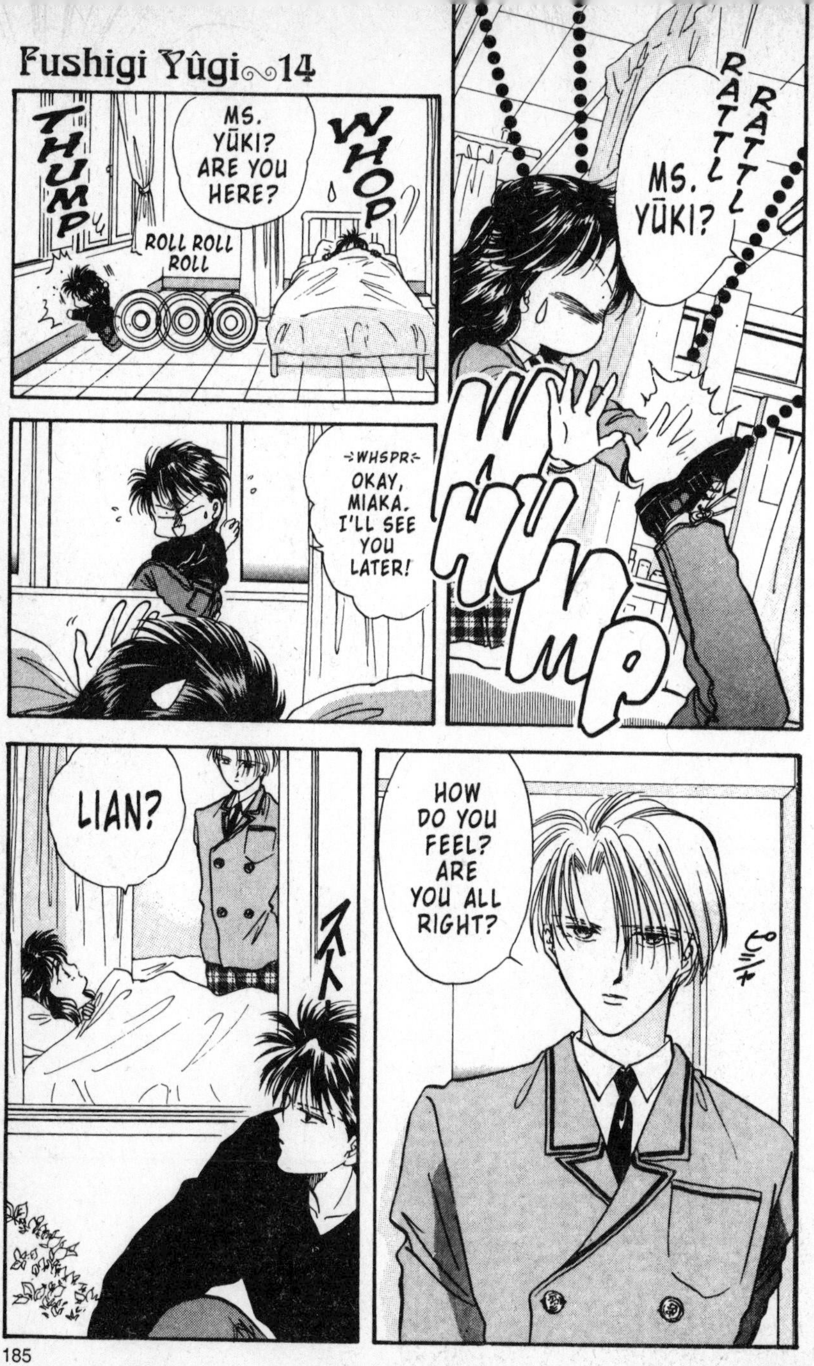
RATTL RATTL
MS. YŪKI?
WHUMP
WHOP
MS. YŪKI? ARE YOU HERE?
THUMP
ROLL ROLL ROLL
WHSPR
OKAY, MIAKA. I'LL SEE YOU LATER!
HOW DO YOU FEEL? ARE YOU ALL RIGHT?
LIAN?

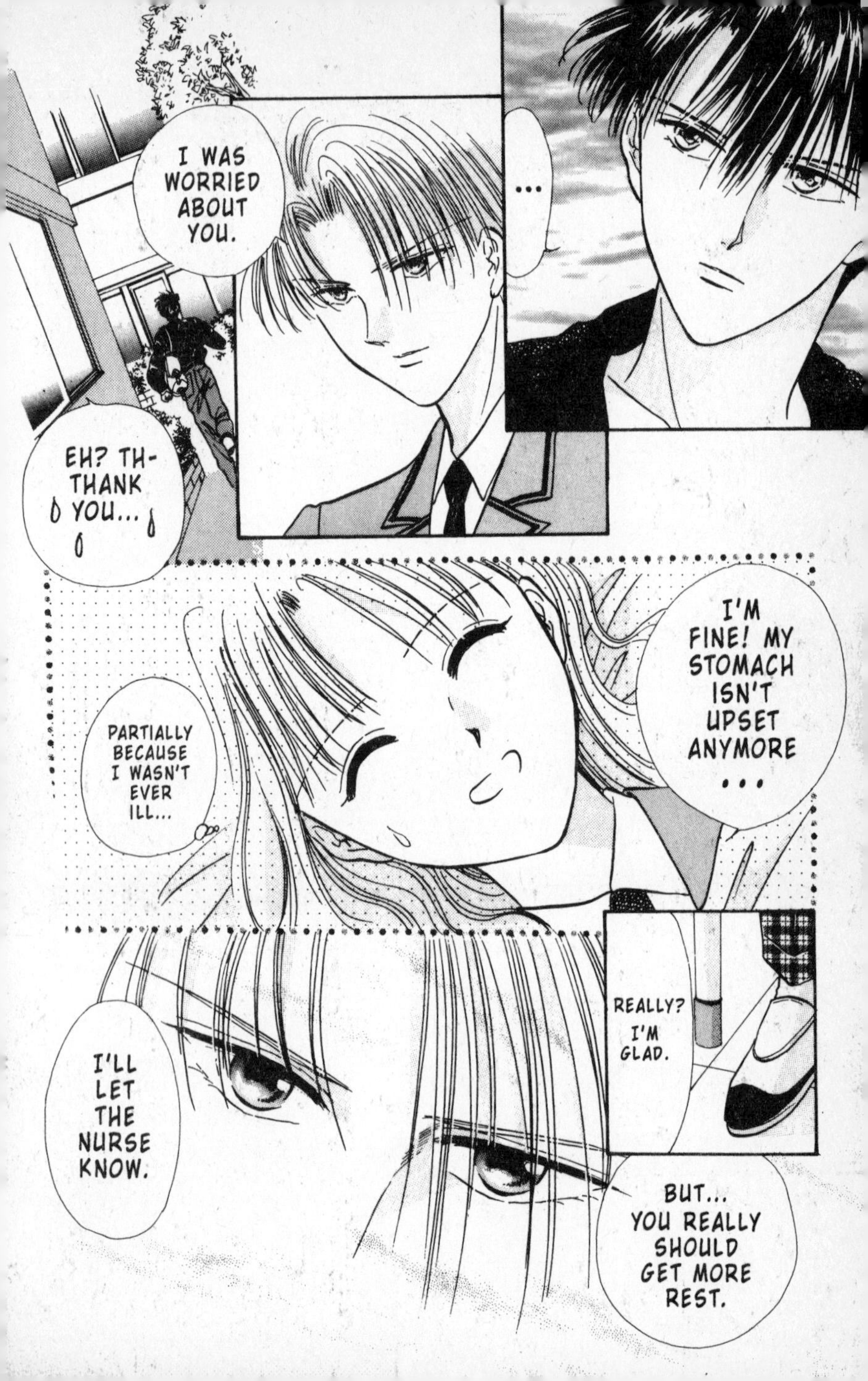
...
I WAS WORRIED ABOUT YOU.
EH? TH-THANK YOU...
I'M FINE! MY STOMACH ISN'T UPSET ANYMORE...
PARTIALLY BECAUSE I WASN'T EVER ILL...
REALLY? I'M GLAD.
BUT... YOU REALLY SHOULD GET MORE REST.
I'LL LET THE NURSE KNOW.

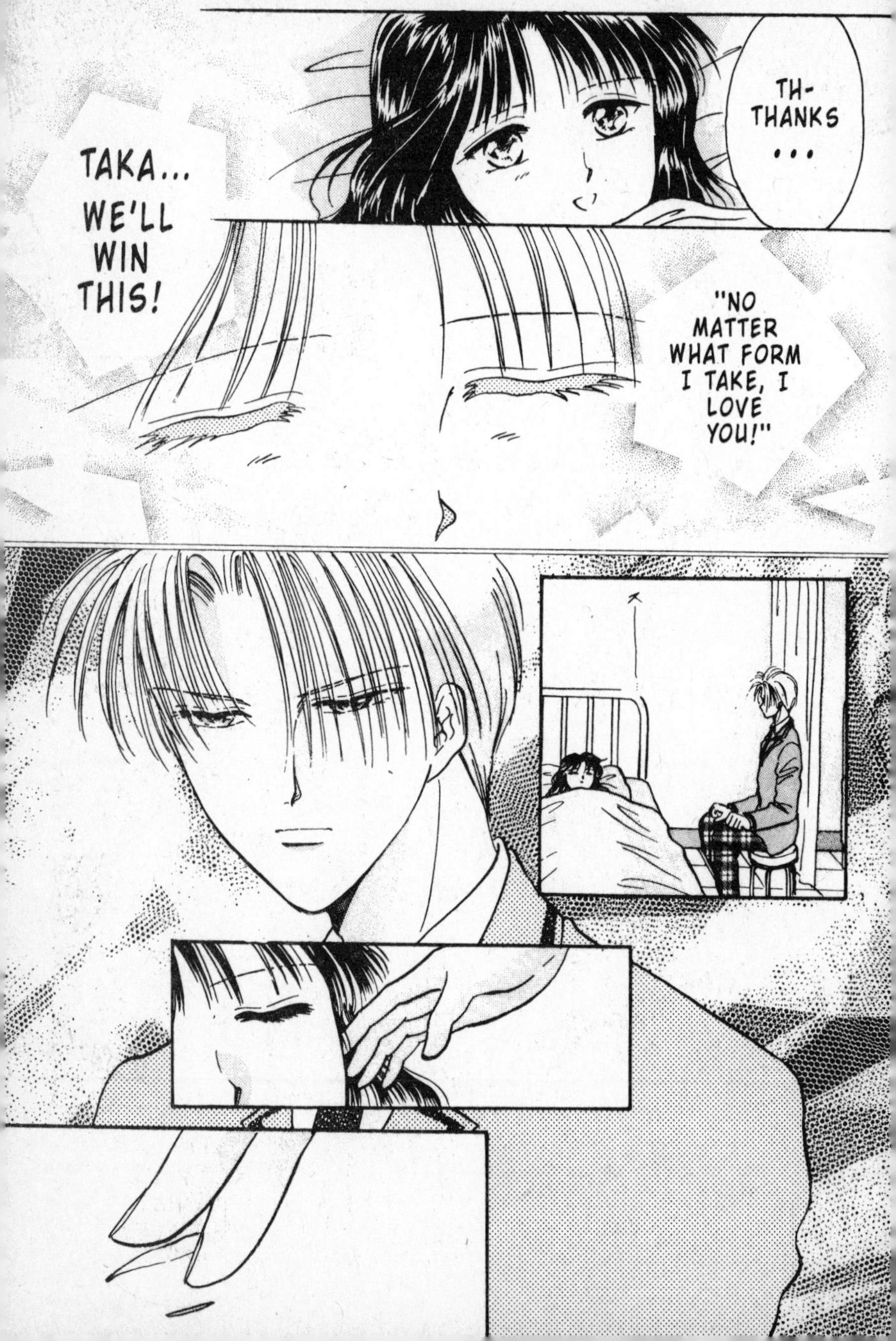
TH- THANKS ...
TAKA... WE'LL WIN THIS!
"NO MATTER WHAT FORM I TAKE, I LOVE YOU!"

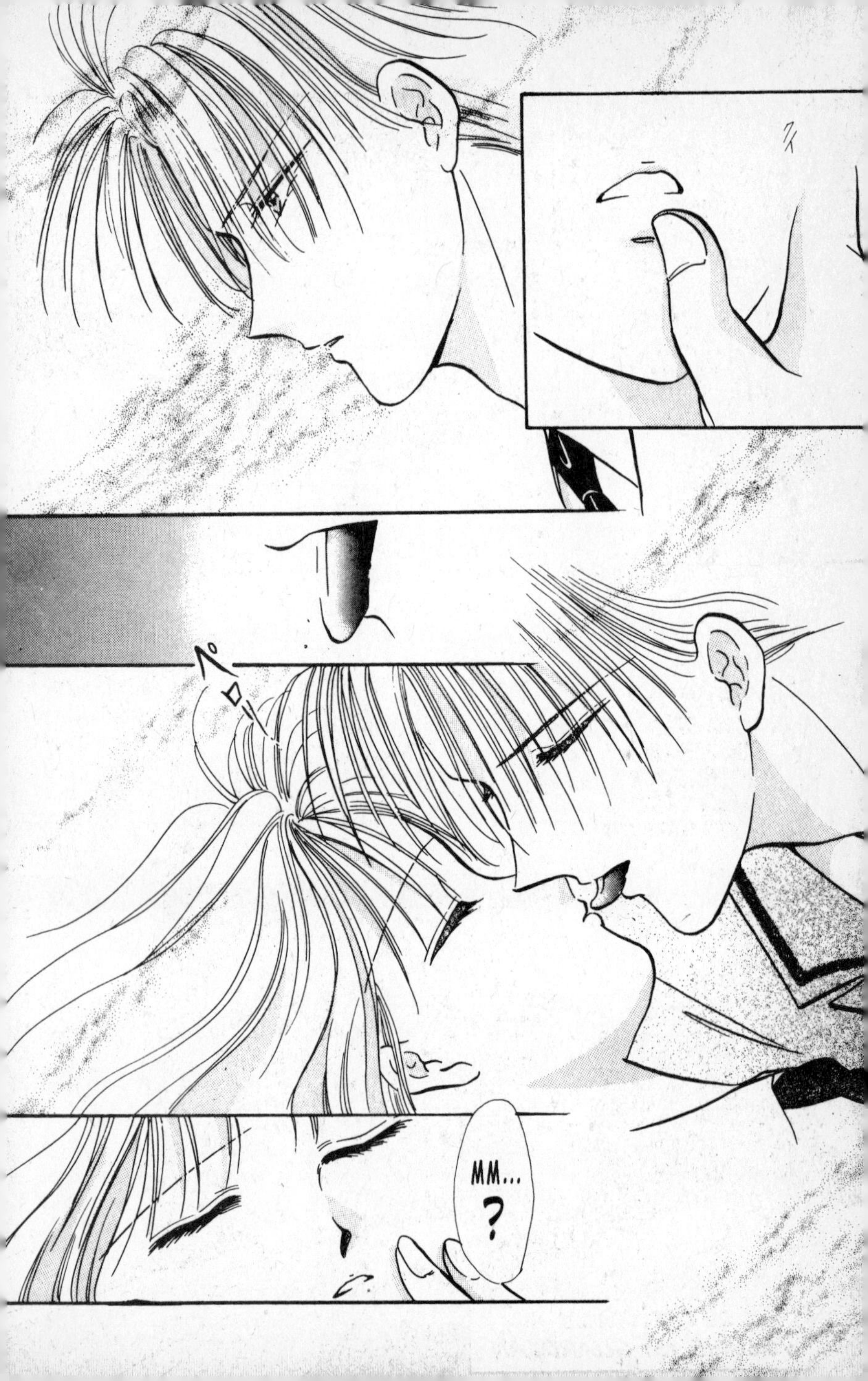
MM...
?

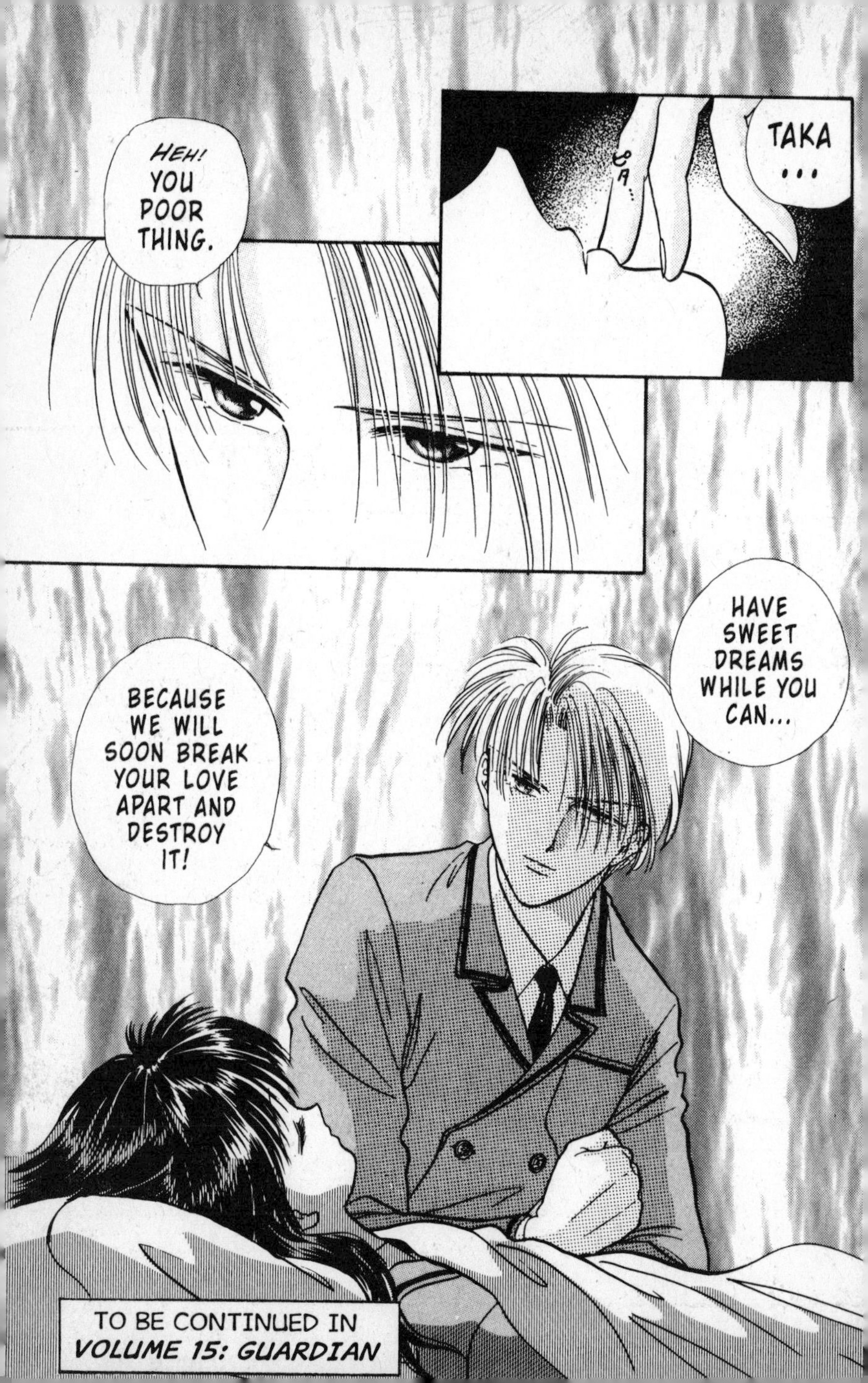
TAKA ...
HEH! YOU POOR THING.
HAVE SWEET DREAMS WHILE YOU CAN...
BECAUSE WE WILL SOON BREAK YOUR LOVE APART AND DESTROY IT!
TO BE CONTINUED IN
VOLUME 15: GUARDIAN

ABOUT THE AUTHOR

Yû Watase was born on March 5 in a town near Osaka, Japan, and she was raised there before moving to Tokyo to follow her dream of creating manga. In the decade since her debut short story, *PAJAMA DE OJAMA* ("An Intrusion in Pajamas"), she has produced more than 50 compiled volumes of short stories and continuing series. Her latest work, *ZETTAI KARESHI* ("Absolute Boyfriend"), has recently completed its run in Japan in the anthology magazine *SHÔJO COMIC*. Watase's other beloved series *CERES: CELESTIAL LEGEND*, *IMADOKI! (NOWADAYS)*, and *ALICE 19TH* are now available in North America in English editions published by VIZ.

The Fushigi Yûgi Guide to Sound Effects

Most of the sound effects in FUSHIGI YÛGI are the way Yû Watase created them, in their original Japanese.

We created this glossary for a page-by-page, panel-by-panel explanation of the action and background noises. By using this guide, you may even learn some Japanese.

The glossary lists page and panel number. For example, page 1, panel 3, would be listed as 1.3.

36.3 FX: KURU (twirl)
36.3 FX: BATA (shut)

38.4 FX: BATAN (door closing)

39.1 FX: DOKI DOKI (heart beating)
39.2 FX: ZAKU (rustling)
39.2-4 FX: KIIIIIIIII (screeching sound)

40.4 FX: GA (thump)

41.5 FX: SUU (appearing)

43.3 FX: ZAWA ZAWA (stepping)

47.1-4 FX: DOOOOOO (explosion)

55.6 FX: KA (flash)

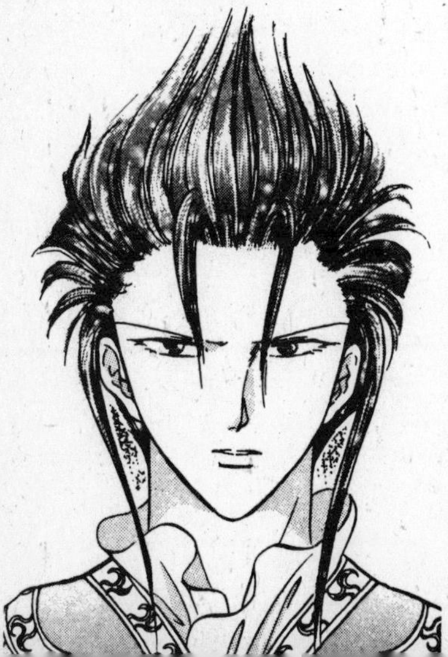

CHAPTER SEVENTY-EIGHT: THE CALL TO BEGIN

10.4 FX: SA (avoidance)
10.5 FX: SA (avoidance)

11.2 FX: SHIIIIN (silence)
11.2 FX: NIKO NIKO (smiles)

16.4 FX: KARA (empty)

17.3 FX: GASHI (grab)

18.1 FX: SHIRA (leaning on her fist)
18.3 FX: GUSHA (squish)

20.1 FX: KI (twirl)
20.3 FX: TOBO TOBO (quiet walking)
20.4 FX: NIKO (smile)
20.4 NOTE: ¥1000 is about US$10.

27.2 FX: CHI CHI CHI CHI (clock ticking)
27.3 FX: CHI CHI CHI CHI (clock ticking)

30.2 FX: DO TA TA TA TA (running)
30.2 FX: BAN (banging)
30.4 NOTE: In Japanese, Miaka said, "Su...Suika tabetai!" ("I'm hungry for watermelon!")
30.4 FX: GUSHA (stepping on)
30.5 FX: BATAN (door slamming shut)

32.1 FX: GAAAA (oh, no)

74.1 FX: SHAKA SHAKA (stirring)
74.2 FX: BOOOO (out of it)
74.4 FX: ZU ZUZU (movement)

77.1 FX: ZAKU (rustling)
77.1 FX: GAMI GAMI (scolding)
77.2 FX: VULULULULU (growling)
77.3 FX: ZA (disappearing)

78.4 FX: PON (slap on the back)

79.3 FX: GORO GORO GORO (thunder)
79.4 FX: PO PO (raindrops hitting)
79.5 FX: ZAAAA (heavy rain)

80.1 FX: BATAN (door shutting)

81.1 FX: SHAAAA (shower spray)

82.2 FX: GOSHI GOSHI (drying off)
82.2 FX: DOKI (heart beat)

83.2 FX: DOKIN (heavy heartbeat)

84.2 FX: SU (hand sliding through hair)

85.2 FX: ZAAAAA (pouring rain)
85.3 FX: DOKUN DOKUN (heavy heartbeats)
85.3 FX: DOKUN DOKUN (heavy heartbeats)
85.4 FX: DOKUN (heavy heartbeat)

86.1 FX: GORON (rolling over)
86.2 FX: DOKUN DOKUN DOKUN (heavy heartbeats)
86.3 FX: DOKUN (heavy heartbeat)
86.3 FX: DOKUN DOKUN (heavy heartbeats)

88.1 FX: VURURURU (growling)
88.3-4 FX: GAAAAAA (roaring)

89.2 FX: SHU (throwing)
89.4 FX: PARA (paper flapping)

CHAPTER SEVENTY-NINE: THE OPEN DOOR

59.1 FX: ZAWA (wind blowing through bamboo)

61.2 NOTE:Miaka made a rather poor pun in the original. "Demon God" is "Majin" in Japanese, and her response was, "maji?" which means, "Are you serious?"

63.3 FX: PORO (thump)
63.5 FX: SU (appearance)

65.6 FX: KA (flash)

66.3 FX: HA (sudden realization)

67.2 FX: GABA (hug)

68.1 FX: PON (tap)
68.4 FX: DAAA (running away)

71.3 FX: SHIKU SHIKU (crying)
71.5 FX: BURU BURU BURU (rattling)

72.1 FX: PAN (glass breaking)
72.1 FX: BIKU (shock or surprise)

73.5 FX: KACHAN (hanging up)

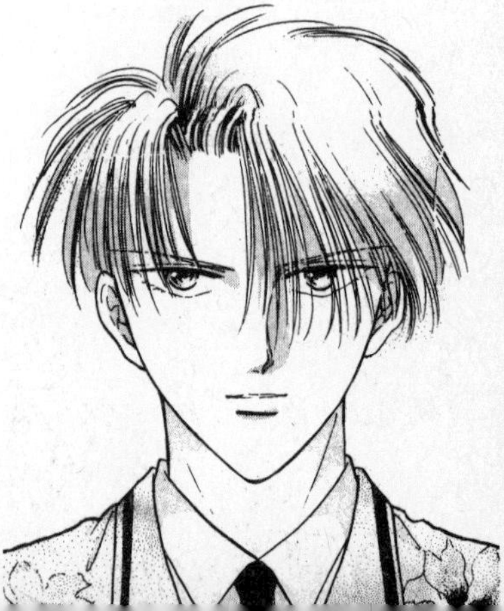

90.2 FX: KAAAAA (blinding light)

93.2-3 FX: GURURURU (growling)

94.1 FX: VUOOO (roaring)
94.2 FX: HA (sudden realization)

95.1 FX: SUTA (a step)
95.2 FX: FU (disappearing)
95.3 FX: DOKIN DOKIN (heartbeats)
95.3 FX: DOKIN DOKIN (heartbeats)
95.4 FX: ZA (rustling)

96.1 FX: DON (thump)

CHAPTER EIGHTY: THE LOST HEART

98.2 FX: ZAAAAAA (pouring rain)

104.3 FX: GATAAN (twirl)

105.2 FX: DOSU (thump)

106.2 FX: KATA (rattle)
106.2 FX: KATAKATAKATA (rattling)
106.3 FX: DOO (explosion)

107.3 FX: DOO (exploding)
107.4 FX: GOOOOO (flames)

108.1 FX: GUZUGUZUGUZU (sizzling)

111.2 FX: BURU (trembling)
111.4 FX: POH (glowing)

112.1 FX: BA (grabbing)
112.2 FX: PAN (burst)

113.1 FX: FU (appearing)

114.3 FX: KAAAAA (light)

115.1 FX: FU (vanishing)
115.3 FX: ZAAAAA (rain)

115.4 FX: BARI BARI (electricity)

117.1 FX: GISHI (bed movement)

118.1 FX: ZULU (sliding)
118.1 FX: DOKI (heartbeat)
118.4 FX: SAAAAAAA (rain sound)

123.1 FX: SAAAAA (rain falling)

125.1 FX: SAAAAA (rain falling)

CHAPTER EIGHTY-ONE: SEVEN DESTINATIONS

128.1 FX: CHICHICHI (birds chirping)
128.1 FX: CHICHI… (birds chirping)
128.3 FX: KOTO KOTO KOTO (pot lid rattling)

129.3 FX: PATA PATA (pitter-pat of feet)
129.5 FX: KURU (twirl)

134.3 FX: SU (appearing)
134.4 FX: GEHO GEHO (choking)

135.2 FX: KYAAAAA (excited shouts)
135.3 FX: GAKU GAKU (shaking)
135.4 FX: ZAKU ZAKU (steps)
135.5 FX: KATAN (rattle)

138.1 FX: ZAWA ZAWA (background conversation)
138.5 FX: SUTA SUTA SUTA (stomping off)

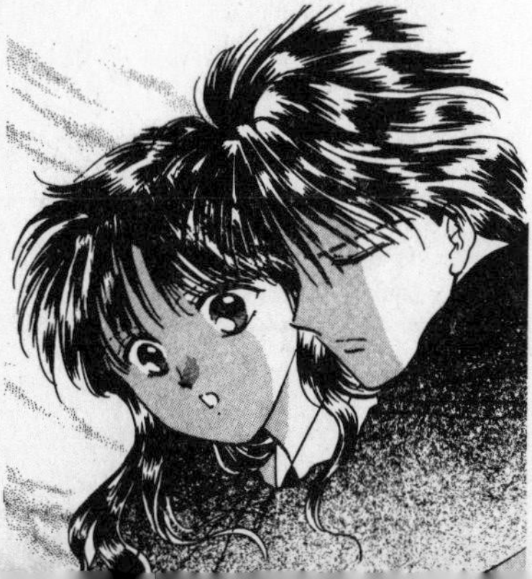

139.2 Note:¥10,000 is about US$100.

140.3 FX: DA (running)
140.4 FX: IRA IRA (worry)

141.5 FX: SA (rustling)

142.3 FX: BURU BURU (head shaking)
142.5 FX: SHURU (unscrolling)
142.6 FX: KA (flash)

143.3 FX: BA (sudden appearance)

144.3 FX: DOSA (landing)

145.2 FX: SUTA SUTA SUTA (stomping off)
145.3 FX: KURU (turning)

149.1 FX: SHAN (clanking)
149.4 FX: BA (throwing)

150.1 FX: FU (disappearing)
150.2 FX: PASHI (grab)

153.2 FX: POKAN (surprise)

155.4 FX: ZUZUZUZUZU (rumbling)

CHAPTER EIGHTY-TWO: THE QUICKENING OF EVIL

159.3 FX: PASHI (grab)

160.3 FX: DOSA (landing)
160.3 FX: ZUZU (slithering)
160.4 FX: ZU (slithering)

161.1 FX: GURU GURU (growling)

163.3 Note:Miaka called him "Tenkô" and "Senkô," which means incense.

167.1 FX: DA (rush)
167.3 FX: KA (flash)

168.1 FX: BASHII (a hard hit)
168.3-4 FX:ZUZUZUZUZU (rumbling)

169.3 FX: KA (barked words)
169.4 FX: HA (realization)
169.5 FX: GYU GYU (tugging)
169.6 FX: SUUU (appearing)

170.2 FX: DON (explosion)

171.4 FX: BAN (explosion)
171.5 FX: SUTA (stopping)

175.2 FX: POUU (glowing)
175.3 FX: FU (floating)
175.4 FX: DON (hitting)

179.3 FX: KA (flash)

180.5 FX: GISHI (bed sound)

185.4 FX: PISHA (closing)
185.5 FX: SUTO (stepping)

187.3 FX: SUUU (light snoring)

188.1 FX: KUI (pulling)
188.4 FX: PERON (licking)

189.1 FX: PITA (closing)

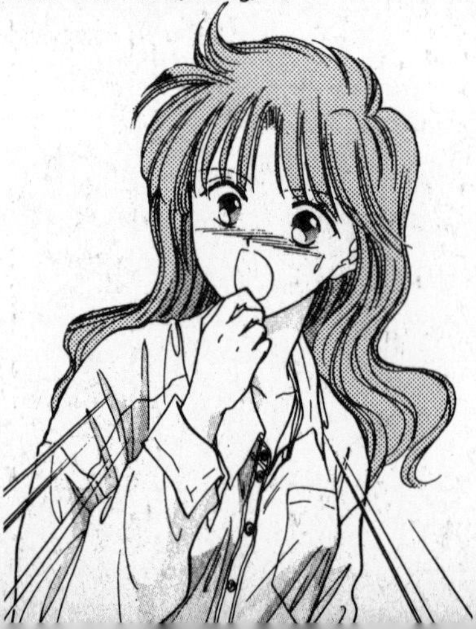

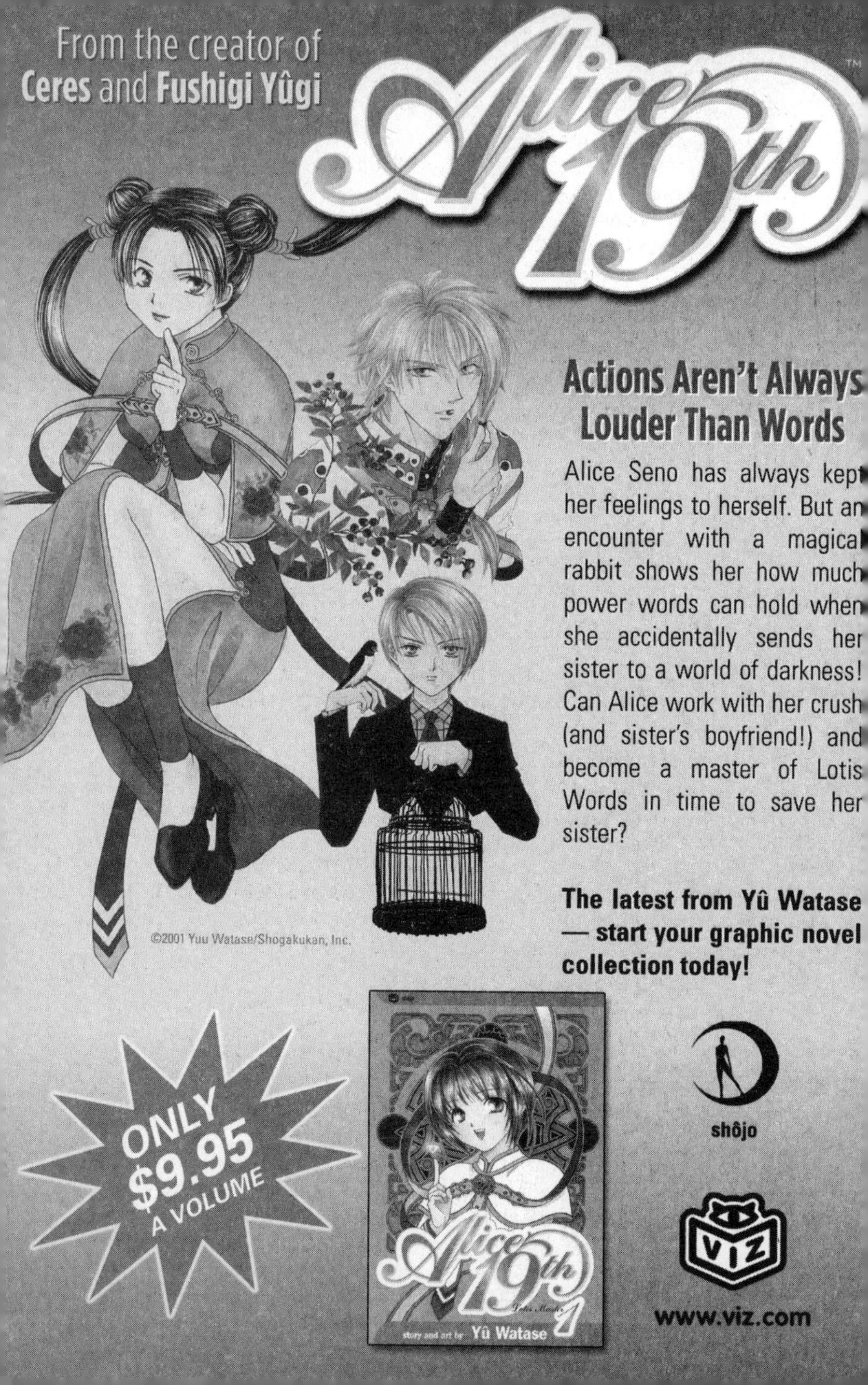
From the creator of
Ceres and Fushigi Yûgi
Alice 19th
Actions Aren't Always Louder Than Words
Alice Seno has always kept her feelings to herself. But an encounter with a magical rabbit shows her how much power words can hold when she accidentally sends her sister to a world of darkness! Can Alice work with her crush (and sister's boyfriend!) and become a master of Lotis Words in time to save her sister?
The latest from Yû Watase — start your graphic novel collection today!
©2001 Yuu Watase/Shogakukan, Inc.
ONLY $9.95 A VOLUME
story and art by Yû Watase
shôjo
VIZ
www.viz.com

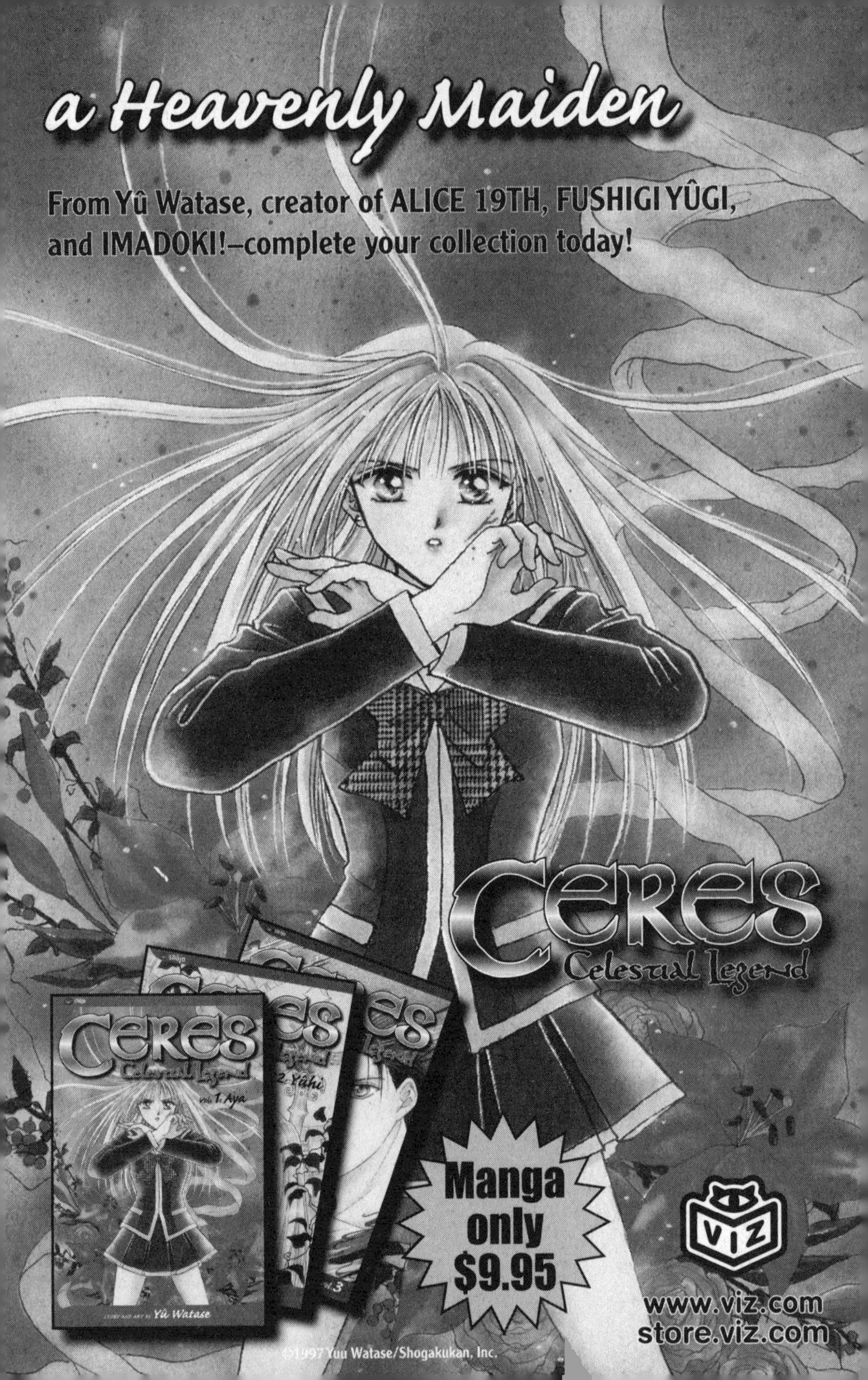

a Heavenly Maiden
From Yû Watase, creator of ALICE 19TH, FUSHIGI YÛGI, and IMADOKI!—complete your collection today!
Ceres
Celestial Legend
Manga only $9.95
VIZ
www.viz.com
store.viz.com
©1997 Yuu Watase/Shogakukan, Inc.

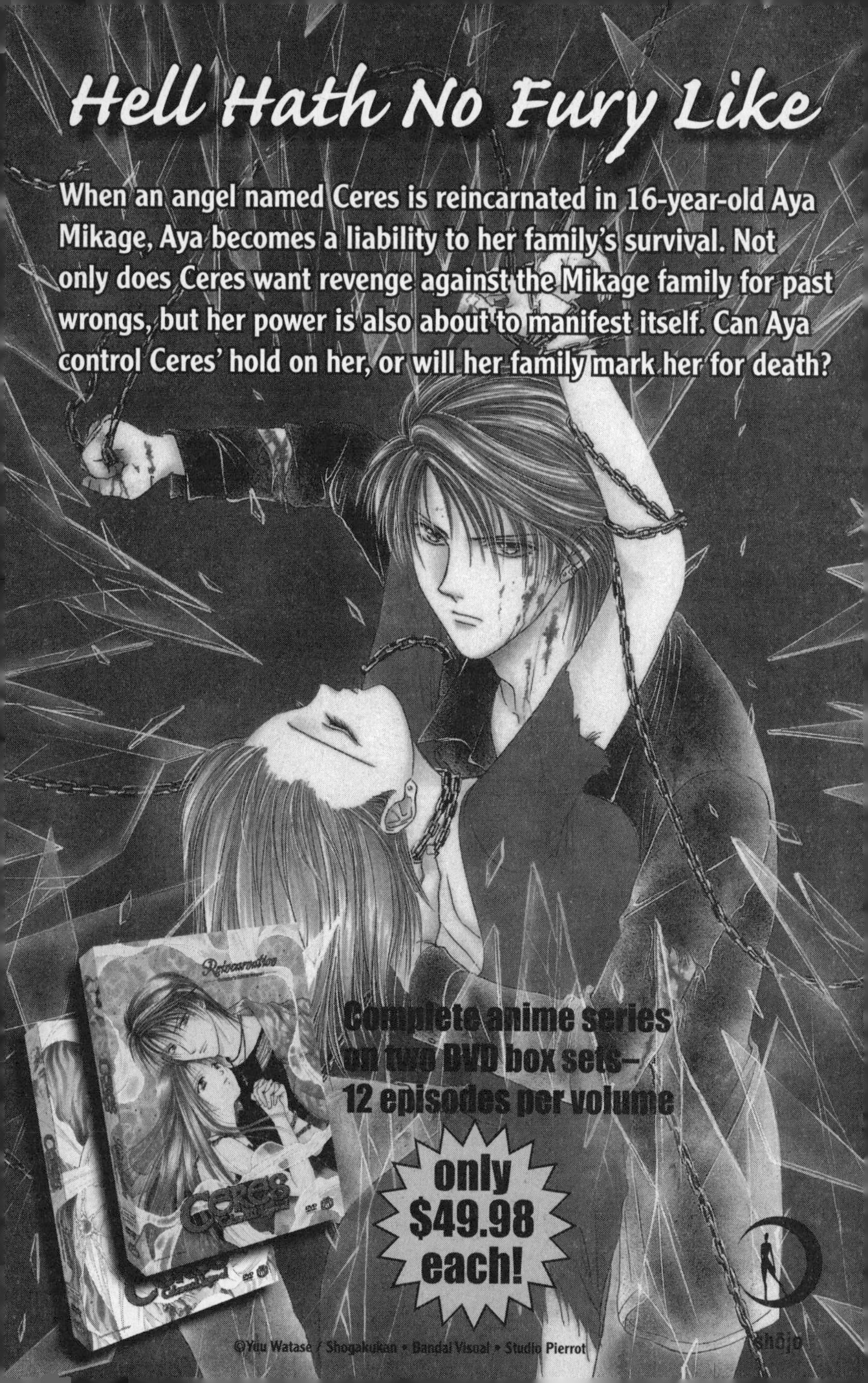
Hell Hath No Fury Like
When an angel named Ceres is reincarnated in 16-year-old Aya Mikage, Aya becomes a liability to her family's survival. Not only does Ceres want revenge against the Mikage family for past wrongs, but her power is also about to manifest itself. Can Aya control Ceres' hold on her, or will her family mark her for death?
Complete anime series on two DVD box sets–12 episodes per volume
only $49.98 each!
©Yuu Watase / Shogakukan • Bandai Visual • Studio Pierrot
shôjo

COMPLETE OUR SURVEY AND LET
US KNOW WHAT YOU THINK!

☐ Please do NOT send me information about VIZ products, news and events, special offers, or other information.

☐ Please do NOT send me information from VIZ's trusted business partners.

Name: _____

Address: _____

City: _____ **State:** _____ **Zip:** _____

E-mail: _____

☐ Male ☐ Female   Date of Birth (mm/dd/yyyy): ___ / ___ / ___   (Under 13? Parental consent required)

What race/ethnicity do you consider yourself? (please check one)

☐ Asian/Pacific Islander ☐ Black/African American ☐ Hispanic/Latino

☐ Native American/Alaskan Native ☐ White/Caucasian ☐ Other: _____

What VIZ product did you purchase? (check all that apply and indicate title purchased)

☐ DVD/VHS _____

☐ Graphic Novel _____

☐ Magazines _____

☐ Merchandise _____

Reason for purchase: (check all that apply)

☐ Special offer ☐ Favorite title ☐ Gift

☐ Recommendation ☐ Other _____

Where did you make your purchase? (please check one)

☐ Comic store ☐ Bookstore ☐ Mass/Grocery Store

☐ Newsstand ☐ Video/Video Game Store ☐ Other: _____

☐ Online (site: _____)

What other VIZ properties have you purchased/own? _____

_____

How many anime and/or manga titles have you purchased in the last year? How many were VIZ titles? **(please check one from each column)**

ANIME	MANGA	VIZ
☐ None	☐ None	☐ None
☐ 1-4	☐ 1-4	☐ 1-4
☐ 5-10	☐ 5-10	☐ 5-10
☐ 11+	☐ 11+	☐ 11+

I find the pricing of VIZ products to be: **(please check one)**

☐ Cheap ☐ Reasonable ☐ Expensive

What genre of manga and anime would you like to see from VIZ? **(please check two)**

☐ Adventure ☐ Comic Strip ☐ Science Fiction ☐ Fighting

☐ Horror ☐ Romance ☐ Fantasy ☐ Sports

What do you think of VIZ's new look?

☐ Love It ☐ It's OK ☐ Hate It ☐ Didn't Notice ☐ No Opinion

Which do you prefer? **(please check one)**

☐ Reading right-to-left

☐ Reading left-to-right

Which do you prefer? **(please check one)**

☐ Sound effects in English

☐ Sound effects in Japanese with English captions

☐ Sound effects in Japanese only with a glossary at the back

THANK YOU! Please send the completed form to:

NJW Research
42 Catharine St.
Poughkeepsie, NY 12601

All information provided will be used for internal purposes only. We promise not to sell or otherwise divulge your information.